HD 58.7 CLA

Organisations in Action

Combining strategy, international business and organisational theory, *Organisations in Action* represents a ground-breaking critique of prevailing mainstream modernist theories of organisation. This original and ambitious work provides a fascinating examination of organisations from both a postmodern and new organisational economics position, adopting a neomodern political economy perspective to strategic management at corporate, regional and policy-maker level.

Distinctive features include:

- a comprehensive analysis of social and organisational theory
- a discussion and exploration of knowledge capitalism
- a critique of core competencies and resource-based approaches to strategy, human resource management and organisational behaviour
- coverage of public sector and not-for-profit organisation
- a wide selection of core examples from the UK, USA, Japan and Europe.

Neither apocalyptic nor evangelical, this up-to-date and provocative text forcefully sets the agenda for debate on organisational behaviour and strategy for all advanced students and researchers.

Peter Clark is Professor of Organisational Management at the University of Birmingham Business School.

Organisational Behaviour/Strategy/International Business

Organisations in Action

Competition between contexts

Peter Clark

London and New York

First published 2000 by Routledge
2 Park Square, Milton Park, Abingdon, Oxon, OX14 4RN

Simultaneously published in the USA and Canada
by Routledge
270 Madison Ave, New York NY 10016

Routledge is an imprint of the Taylor & Francis Group

Transferred to Digital Printing 2005

© 2000 Peter Clark

Typeset in Baskerville by J&L Composition Ltd, Filey, North Yorkshire

British Library Cataloguing in Publication Data
A catalogue record for this book is available from the British Library

Library of Congress Cataloging in Publication Data
Clark, Peter A.
   Organisations in action: competition between contexts/Peter Clark.
      p.   cm.
   Includes bibliographical references and index.
   1. Industrial organization (Economic theory)   2. Corporations.
   3. Competition.   4. Knowledge management.   5. Organizational
   behavior.   6. Strategic planning.   7. International business enterprises.
   I. Title.
   HD2326.C498   1999
   338.7—dc21   99–17479
                          CIP

ISBN 0–415–18230–1 (hbk)
ISBN 0–415–18231–X (pbk)

Contents

Illustrations

Figures

Tables

Part I
New political economy

1   Two themes, three disciplines and five perspectives

INTRODUCTION

This chapter introduces two themes, three disciplines and five perspectives examined in the next fifteen chapters.

THEMES

- organisations in action
- competition between contexts

DISCIPLINES

- organisation and organisation economics
- strategy
- international business

PERSPECTIVES

- modern-positivist
- post-modern
- structuration and symbolic
- realist turn
- neo-modern political economy

The two themes are 'organisations in action' and 'competition between contexts'. These two themes connect the three core disciplines of organisation theory/organisation economics, resource based strategy and international business. The five perspectives being applied to the two themes cross-cut the three disciplines. The examination of the five perspectives commences with the limitations of the modern-positivistic. Then three perspectives offering critiques of the modern-positivist are examined: post-modern, structuration and the realist turn. These offer distinct solutions and open the way to the fifth perspective. The fifth perspective ingests key elements of the post-modern critique and selectively combines the neo-modern, realist turn and structuration with elements of political economy.

'Organisations in action' is the title of a seminal and influential account by James Thompson (1967) of the conditions for rationality in organisation theory and the title also suggests a rich mixture of dynamics and politics. As Clegg (1989: 197) observes: 'Organisational action is an indeterminate outcome of substantive struggles between . . . people who deploy different resources'. In important respects Thompson's prepositional theorising was part of the modern perspective. His analysis tended towards the buffering of the firm in a just-in-case format and curiously omitted the seminal analysis by Burns and Stalker (1961) of the management of innovation (Clark and Staunton 1989). In Thompson the modernist concept of power is implicated, but its implications are not resolved. Clegg's account of the everyday frameworks of power points towards forms of theorising that explain dynamics in the metaphor of the political arena. Clegg (1989), unlike Thompson, embraces the stratified reality of societal institutions and draws international comparisons into the conversation.

As a theme, 'competition between contexts' goes far beyond the conventional approach to international comparisons in organisational analysis and strategy. Competition between contexts means that if Henry Ford had attempted to finance, design and launch the Ford T in the automobile region of England he would have failed because the configuration of necessary institutional and market features was absent. Likewise, McDonald's was more probably successful by starting from the USA and California than from continental Europe. Contexts matter. Recently, the analysis of contexts has been the focus of much attention (e.g. complexity theory). In economics the debate over location involving Dunning (1993) and Porter (1990, 1997) provides a useful complement to the massive interest by evolutionary economists (e.g. Metcalfe) in national systems of innovation (e.g. Freeman, Rosenberg, Nelson). Equally, sociological perspectives have implicitly contributed through the new institutional perspectives (e.g. DiMaggio, Powell, Scott, Fligstein) and societal effects (e.g. Sorge). All these studies converge on the theme of competition between contexts.

Coupling the two themes implies that organisations and contexts are in co-evolution and that the sources of stasis or morphogenesis are interactive.

Three disciplines address these two themes. International business extends the previous tightly focused analysis of the immediate context of the firm into a rich analytic description of multiple contexts. If there is competition between contexts then this theme should drive presentations of organisation theory (see Hatch 1997; Thompson and McHugh 1995) and of strategy (see Grant 1990, 1998) because the firm cannot easily be buffered. In fact, the theme of competition between contexts is already taken very seriously by many multinational businesses. The theme of organisations in action deeply impacts upon organisation theory and strategy, yet each tends to approach dynamics and political arenas through 'time' rather than temporality.

Perspectives are theoretical-cum-ideological interpretations that transform methodologies into explanatory programmes (Alexander 1995; Archer 1995). Five perspectives are relevant to the two themes and three disciplines. Each of the three disciplines has been impacted by the positivist-modern tendency that dominated the 1950s and 1960s and holds a lingering grip with the intelligent positivists. Modern theories sought universal time-space free solutions to economic and social problems through frameworks that were often technocratic, individual, utopian, linear and rationalistic (Bennis 1966). The critique of positivistic and modern theories was initially led by the post-modern movement. Equally, structuration theory in sociology (e.g. Giddens) and to a lesser extent the action frame of reference in organisational analysis (e.g. Silverman) constructed significant alternatives to positivism and to modern theories. The 'realist turn' claims that hidden structures and mechanisms explain patterns of events (e.g. Harre, Bhaskar) and that critical analysis must provide emancipation and alternatives. Thompson and McHugh (1995) demonstrate just how demanding that realist manifesto is for its followers. Finally, I propose that the theoretical-cum-ideological movement currently unfolding combines a neo-Gramscian political economy with elements of neo-modern theorising.

The implication of the discussion of perspectives is that the neo-modern political economy theory-cum-ideological formation transforms the three disciplines and successfully explains the two themes of organisations in action and competition between contexts.

Two themes, three disciplines and five perspectives require some road maps to guide the conversation with the reader. Before coming to the one of these road maps it is worth amplifying the journey being taken from the modern-positivistic through the post-modern, structuration and realist turns into the neo-modern political economy. The next section sketches ten shifts that are taking place as organisation theory moves towards the neo-modern political economy. The section after that sets out the structure of the book as a whole. Meanwhile Figure 1.1 sets out the broad structure of the book. In Part I, Chapters 1 to 5 set out the five perspectives and the contention that neo-modern political economy best characterises the intellectual-cum-ideological configuration relevant to our task. In Part II, Chapters 6 to 10 explore the claim that there is competition between contexts and that the finite zones of manoeuvre in the home base of sectoral clusters often shapes their performance. In Part III, Chapters 11 to 14 explore and reformulate the claims of the resource-based theory of the firm in the light of the previous analysis and of the theme of 'organisations in action'. Part IV is a single, long chapter combining the finite capacities of the firm and its contexts with an exploration of how management can address the 'is', 'ought' and 'can' statements.

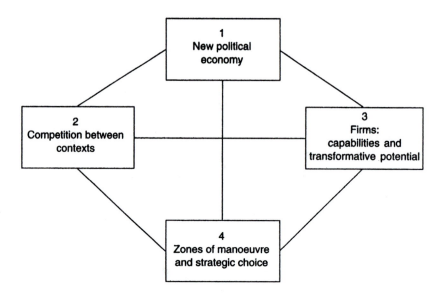

Figure 1.1 Structure of the book: the four areas

MOVING AWAY . . . TOWARDS?

In contemporary debates and conversations there is a powerful sense of moving away from certain ways of theorising and towards other ways of theorising, describing and explaining the organisation, its context, the experience of work and engaging in a critical search for alternatives (Thompson and McHugh 1995). Reed (1989) contends that the major shift taking place involves travelling away from the notion of organisation theory as a discipline examining order, permanence and techniques in a deterministic framework *towards* fragmented fields examining the politics of technology, control and change within a voluntaristic, historical pluralism and notions of structuration (Giddens 1984). Reed illustrates the multiple fields by scrutinising five contemporary research programmes: adaptation, order, control, organisation reality and organisational assembly. This chapter introduces ten of the shifts that are unfolding and that indicate the core issues of this book: knowledge and reality; intra-organisational and Americanised background; variables or configurations; pre-existing structuration and agency; realist, neo-contingency and crypto post-modern; time-free or temporality; national characteristics and markets; comparative studies between nations; creative destruction and time-space compression; multiple levels and layers of analysis.

Knowledge and reality

Organisation theory in the positivistic mode is typified by an ontology of reality and knowledge as:

- reality as determinate and knowledge as objective and scientific;
- theories that are universal and free from the specifics of time and place;
- the linearity of time and space theorised by the application of uniform scales;
- history is efficient because the market exits the inefficient firms in frictionless time;
- universities possess a monopoly of knowledge;
- certified experts are politically neutral;
- knowledge is useful and utilised;
- depthless ontologies (Reed 1997)

The movement away is towards a variety of competing and incommensurable points of view. Knowledge in the neo-contingency and realist turn is causal, indeterminate, situated, mediated and contested. The many frameworks, each doing local tasks, are held together by theory, bricolage and analytically structured narratives. The new production of knowledge incorporates structure and agency by asking: what are the mechanisms which create, constitute and sustain particular firms and contexts? How and in what sequence can policy alter these situations?

The new production of knowledge is also outside the university sector (Gibbons *et al.* 1994). In British science the citation rate for articles now favours corporations rather than the universities. Moreover, the growth in demand for systematic, rich analytic exposition is provided by the growth of specialist firms that intensively investigate particular sectors (e.g. retail) and areas (e.g. Eastern Europe) on a commercial basis. The major accounting consultancies are involved in the production of knowledge. In part this is because of the production of knowledge and feedback through auditing (Power 1994). In Great Britain the accounting firm of Coopers Lybrand was employed by the government during the beef crisis to supply analysis on aspects of bovine spongiform encephalitis and to evaluate the performance of the firms rendering the carcasses.

Intra-organisational focus and Americanised background

Organisation theory is moving away from the separate and narrow analysis of:

- the context of the firm;
- the intra-firm levels.

The majority of attention has been upon the intra-organisational level, even though the emergent design of an appropriate form of work organisation depends upon the characteristics of the context.

The context of the firm has been dealt with very narrowly by examining a few dimensions such as uncertainty, complexity and variability. International aspects were disconnected. Moreover, because so many of the contributors to organisation theory are located in the USA they tended to take it as the undiscussed background (Searle 1995). More recently, international differences have been increasingly acknowledged, but serious cross-national analysis of the contexts is muted by the tendency to impose an equivalence between nations. There is still widespread neglect of political economy and problems of the regimes of regulation for capital (Harvey 1989). The role of the state and of inter-state regulation (e.g. Bretton Woods) is virtually omitted or relegated to a footnote.

The previous split between the firm and the context is slowly being replaced by their joint analysis within an international perspective because the location and context that a firm starts from have strategic consequences.

Variables or configurations

The neo-contingency and new political economy approaches displace the previous preoccupation with the use of a small number of thin, sharply operationalised variables to describe states of affairs and to evaluate their consequences. This narrowness becomes regarded as seductive and dangerous, but variables are not dismissed. Rather, there is an acceptance of the relevance and centrality of rich analytic description and thick analysis (Porter 1991).

Pre-existing structuration and agency

The problem of organisational change and transformation, sometimes referred to as the morphogenesis debate, defines a major theoretical issue (Buckley 1967; Archer 1995). How do we theorise the relationship between pre-existing structuration and ongoing processes in order to explain the reproduction or transformation of the pre-existing? In orthodox organisation theory the theories of the firm presumed that top management and the analyst had a high competence and capacity to transform existing situations. Giddens (1979) refers to this as high discursive penetration. Pragmatic theory making relied on the need-to-know framework so carefully nurtured in the American academy (Clark 1987: 280). So, the focus was placed narrowly on controllable, intra-organisation elements such as motivation, leadership, job design and selection.

The problem of agency (voluntarism) and structure (constraining) was proclaimed. Giddens (1979, 1981, 1984) proposes the solution of structuration and this solution has had some impact in organisation studies, accounting, information technology and related areas, but not in strategy or marketing to any degree. As we shall observe, the issue of agency versus structure involves key assumptions about social reality. After the challenge to and eventual displacement of the orthodox position then the problem of aligning the different properties and characteristics of individual and systemic levels became central (see Layder 1997). Structuration as a solution is regarded as incomplete by the realist school of Harre, Bhaskar and Archer (see Chapter 4). The realist, neo-contingency approach treats the explanatory methodology programme as the necessary link between the social ontology and practical theory.

Realist, neo-contingency and crypto post-modern

The realist approach (see Chapter 4) draws attention to the hidden, underlying generative mechanisms and their coupling with chance and emergence. Consequently, the position of agency and voluntarism becomes problematic. It is argued that the thesis of strategic choice (see Child 1972, 1997) becomes problematic because of the influence of pre-existing structural conditions at all levels (Thompson and McHugh 1995). Unintended outcomes are brought to centre stage and redefine the possible role of any design school (Clark 1975a; cf. Mintzberg 1990).

Time-free or temporality

The orthodox approach has been and largely still is towards theories which are universalistic and therefore free from places, events and historical contingency. There has been a continuous invocation of the relevance of an historical dimension to deal with the past and of scenario writing to envisage possible futures. In organisation theory the burden of a temporal perspective has not been in the widespread use of the biological metaphor of the life cycle, especially the life cycle of firms (Daft 1997) rather than the 'exquisite sense of time' proposed by Weick (1969).

Since the 1980s there have been numerous, largely individual attempts to develop historical analyses of firms and occasionally of sectors. Perhaps this is most evident in the longitudinal analysis of the reconfiguration of Fordism by flexible accumulation by historical geographers like Harvey (1989). A variety of studies of particular firms and sectors aimed to demonstrate how pre-existing structures and groupings of vested interests shaped the ground upon which specific instances of agency aimed at transformation of the firm were attempted – and failed.

After the post-modern intervention it becomes very difficult to regard the linear dimension as unproblematic. Burrell's (1997) retro-organisation theory is a challenging presentation of the anti-linear sceptical on a playful stance. Moreover, a variety of new perspectives claims to offer solutions (e.g. complexity theory) and attention is increasingly focused upon how instrumental time is dislocated (Holmer Nadeesan 1997). Gradually the limitations of the extended present have been prised open at each end – the past and possible future. Suppressed themes (e.g. gender and power) are revealed. The new literature is a search for macro mechanisms bridging between capitalism, socialism and the social market (e.g. Germany). There is extensive exploration of new concepts (e.g. punctuated equilibrium; dissipative structures; capabilities; historical accidents). Theory routinely includes contradiction, paradox, irony and even comedic asides. One group emphasises disorder, the snake pit metaphor and de-institutionalisation.

Also, there is exploration and speculation about events which did not/might not have happened (Schama 1991) and the discussion of virtual history (Ferguson 1997). It is 'possibilities' which require explanation (Hawthorne 1991).

National characteristics and markets

To what extent are national contexts typified by unique characteristics that shape the indigenous firms? To what degree is the firms' formative learning from the national market (Penrose 1959; Clark 1987; Porter 1990) as well as from the national predispositions in forms of organising (Sorge 1991)? Attention to national differences does not drive organisation theory. Rather it is a feature which is introduced in a very broad brush with slight attention to intra-nation bands of typical variety. National specificities in the context of the global, geo-political context should enter the analysis from the start in conjunction with the analysis of the specificities of firms (Clark and Mueller 1996).

In organisation studies, national specificities are increasingly acknowledged. The general approach is to follow the analysis proposed by Hofstede (1980; cf. Sorge 1995). Hofstede demonstrated that national differences are present even in a large, transnational corporation with a reputation by building a corporate culture to overcome national differences. However, his account of social programming unwittingly suggests that there is a narrow form of behaviour rather than a significant typical variety. A similar problem arises in the plethora of studies proposing 'national systems' of innovation (e.g. Freeman, Nelson), of knowledge (Lundvall 1992); of business systems (Whitley 1992) and so on.

There is virtual neglect of the co-evolution of firms and their national markets. It is essential to explore the relationship between the peculiarities of national tastes and consumption patterns – the market – and the capabilities of firms to survive, grow and move abroad. There is the possibility that national contexts that might entrain firms, thereby posing them with considerable problems in moving abroad, are largely neglected, even though the early theorising on organisational learning (e.g. Dill 1962) outlined the key concepts and possible mechanisms. For example, British retailers like Marks & Spencer have an international reputation, yet their capacity to move their supply chain outside the high profit margins of the British market into Europe and North America has so far been less than seemed possible.

In the USA there is a capacity for high volume distribution and production as well as the emergence of firms in new sectors and of speciality goods such as aircraft. The competitive consequences of the US domestic market and of the USA as a market for goods and services needs much more exacting attention. For example, the US system of agricultural support and allowances to farmers in cattle production produces a different shape of cow to that found on the British farm within the British system. The significance of the national market was apparent in the mid-nineteenth century when British observers sought to understand American manufacturing of goods (Rosenberg 1969), but the implications of that kind of analysis have been largely ignored. Porter (1990) rightly makes the national market a major factor in his analysis. Sorge's (1991) useful application of an elective affinities framework to the entraining potentials of the firms/nations relationship provides a starting point which requires development. Within nations there is a typical variety which is considerably greater and more consequential than so far acknowledged (Clark 1987).

Comparative studies between nations

Comparative perspectives in organisation behaviour were greatly invigorated by Hofstede's (1980) cross-cultural analysis. Even so, there is a strong tendency to use abstracted cameos of a variety of nations rather than to develop systematic analytic skills and exemplars in area analysis (Porter 1990, 1991). The orthodox universal theories treated specific geographical location and features as almost irrelevant. Even socio-evolutionary theory glosses over national and regional contexts (e.g. Weick 1969). Likewise, the spatial dimensions of the firm were treated as unproblematic.

The neo-contingency perspective treats the nation as a/the major contingency dimension (Maurice 1979; Clark 1987; Sorge 1991) and draws attention to the actuality of competition between contexts (Clark 1987; Porter 1990). These approaches aim to operate in contingent time-space and give significant attention to the geo-physical context (Schama 1991; Gregory 1994; Harvey 1989, 1996). There is a groping search for an understanding of the respective influence of the region (e.g. Porter 1990) and the nation state. Greater attention is given to explaining the significance of local determinisms and of the implications of place over space (Gregory 1994). Notions such as fitness landscapes (Gell-Man 1994) draw attention to the detailed analyses of how specific sectors and firms handle contexts and thereby add a needed dimension to population ecology studies. Contexts contain emerging surprises and also vary in their capacities to enable/ hinder corporate success. Examining the implications of 'competition between contexts' is of considerable practical importance.

Creative destruction and time-space compression

The neglect of possible patterns in the wider long-term transitions in capitalism and socialism came to the fore in the 1980s and 1990s. Long wave theorists (e.g. Mandel 1978) and the French regulation school (e.g. Aglietta 1974) were among the earliest to observe that the conditions enabling mass production were unravelling. Their thinking and analysis renewed interest in the longer-term theories of capitalism and creative destruction. Mandel's analysis of long waves inspired the post-modern thinking of Jameson (Anderson 1998). The proposition is that for more than the past two decades there has been a qualitative jump in the ways in which time-space are commodified and therefore compressed. An everyday example for air travellers is in the packing of more flights into an airport. Chicago airport is reported to be significantly increasing its throughput by streaming flights and reducing the distances between them (*Sunday Times* 1998). The air traffic controllers contend that these compressions of time and space endanger flights. The commodification and compression of time-space is massively enabled when groups, strata and firms utilise the new information technologies.

Eliminating this porosity in value-adding processes is heightened by the ways in which information technology makes the firm potentially transparent as a network of flows. Analysts of the firm can look at the horizontal processes through data and iconic simulations to reveal areas of low performance. It is a short, yet politically significant step to eliminating such areas. This process of elimination and the redesign of the firm in terms of horizontal processes has been referred to as business process engineering. Certainly firms are introducing a new organisational discipline which is reshaping organisational identities (Sennett 1998).

Neo-contingency approaches locate the state as a central player enabling these transitions, even though some capacities which the state was presumed to have, for example, over the national economy and the price of national currencies, have been demonstrated to be illusory. In fact the welfare-oriented European states played an enormous role after 1945. In Germany the state expended more than 45 per cent of GDP, much higher in Sweden and somewhat lower in Great Britain. Post-1979 the Thatcherist influence in Britain has aimed at less than 40 per cent of GDP. Neo-contingency approaches need to explain the role of the state much more fully.

Are there new organisational forms and linkages between pivotal firms and their networks? Is there an N-form (new) organisation? In the millennium period there are co-existing forms of accumulation. McDonaldisation co-exists with agile, small firms. Most firms are competing on knowledge and expertise.

Multiple levels and layers of analysis

The issue here is the extent to which analysis implicates the global context and the layers of analysis which are applied. The approach taken is that there are at least four major levels of analysis which are implicated, even in the analysis of small firms:

- the global economy and the capacities of the hundred largest transnational corporations to shape their contexts and influence the small firms which occupy the interstices;
- nations and their relative power in the geo-political contests: which nations are able to gain extra-territoriality in the application of their domestic laws (e.g. intellectual property rights) in other nations;
- firms and sectors, especially the pivotal multinational businesses;
- intra-firm.

These four levels are illustrative rather than definitive.

The purpose of taking the global, geo-political context is – in conjunction with a longitudinal perspective – to examine how certain nations can set major rules of competition. The geo-politics of the Cold War has certainly influenced relations between the USA and Japan so that Japan occupied a particular position within US containment of the former USSR and China. Consequently Japan received access to US markets and US knowledge, both licensed knowledge and also knowledge of best practice in corporate America (Clark 1987: Chapter 13). Japan used this knowledge differently (Clark and Staunton 1993: 151–153). US firms are major players in Europe for certain sectors and in some the USA/Germany connection has been important for German firms.

There are several variants of the new political economy perspectives. It is therefore relevant to return to Marx's account of how knowledge is compressed to remove porosity and give value to capital. The role of knowledge making and ownership was a minor element mainly outside organisation theory until the 1980s. Since then knowledge and its ownership have replaced embodied knowledge in technology as the key residual. This means that we should think of innovation in technology and organisation (Clark and Staunton 1993).

STRUCTURE OF THE BOOK

Organisations in Action is concerned with understanding, describing, explaining, designing and critically viewing organisations. The argument is approached in four major and related parts as shown in Figure 1.1. The book commences by examining the five perspectives in Chapters 2 to 5. The examination leads through to the neo-modern and political economy perspective. Then, if the reader were able simultaneously to read two parallel parts, these refer to the two core themes. In each of these themes the previous discussion of perspectives is elaborated further. Competition between contexts is developed in Chapters 6 to 10. Organisations in action occupies Chapters 11 to 14. The short final part uses the notion of zones of manoeuvre in conjunction with the notion of strategic choice with both notions applied conjointly to the organisation and the context (Chapter 15).

The perspective of the neo-modern political economy is introduced in Chapters 2 to 5 through a review of the main theoretical issues. Chapter 2 seeks to position the five perspectives. Each perspective is a theoretical-cum-ideological point of view. The positivist-modern perspective contains many problematic features and these have influenced each of the three disciplines, but in different ways. Each of the disciplines is already shifting away from the positivistic-modern perspective, yet the original imprint still holds its influence. The post-modern and post-structural theories have vibrantly challenged organisation theory, though they have had minimal effects on strategy and international business. I have given particular stress to the hypothesis that there is a qualitative shift in commodification of time-space and their compression (Clark 1985; Harvey 1989). Exponents of organisation theory sometimes attempt to incorporate elements from the post-modern position. However, the more the protective belt within orthodox organisation theory is penetrated by equivocality which cannot be encoded, the more the problems. Equally, the structuration perspective and the realist turn challenge the architecture of organisation theory. Moreover, Alexander (1995) has identified a 'neo-modern' tendency to return to some of the issues of practical theory central to modernism with new theoretical requirements. The neo-modern tendency differs from earlier modernist theory in its intention to provide the theoretical and conceptual basis for handling the contingent specificities of history/time and place/space in a dynamic, non-teleological approach.

Chapter 3 scrutinises the architecture of organisation theory and shows how its protective belt is being prised off to leave a degenerating theoretical and research regime. Chapter 4 examines some of the requirements of a neo-modern approach. Structuration theory represents major and significant contributions whose 'omelette' of concepts and angles has been consumed by only a small number of exponents, and their usage tends to be cautious (Clark and Mueller 1995). The realist theories of Harre, Bhaskar and Sayer have re-asserted the place of causal analysis as the cutting edge. The realist agenda directs analysis and explanation to the underlying generative mechanisms and to the pre-existing structural conditions. These pre-existing structural conditions set the constraints upon future action. Consequently, useful and usable theory assumes a new role in organisation design as 'possibility' enters the new frame of analysis. Moreover, the realist perspective claims to situate modern symbolic and interpretivist approaches within its theorising, though not necessarily in ways that their exponents would prefer. A central part of the realist case concerns the debate over temporality and the claim that the structuration theorising developed by Giddens (1984) correctly includes the role of competition between nation states, but unfortunately conflates the temporal to an extended present. Unpacking these issues is one of the major pathways. There is a significant and exciting conflict between the mainstream and the critical perspectives. The critical perspectives can lend realist causal analysis and a searching scrutiny of the possible alternatives to contemporary forms of capitalism. It may be observed that the critical theorists and realists do share a number of themes, especially around the influence of pre-existing structural conditions.

Chapter 5 addresses the rise of organisational economics and its challenge over the definition of economic action by the new economic sociology.

Why give attention to competition between contexts? In the 1980s the performance of German, Japanese and Pacific Rim economies began to puzzle western analysts and revealed significant national differences within the west between USA, Germany and the rest of Europe. The nation as an explanatory configuration became important (e.g. Hofstede). There was the growth of attention to the national level. Within the European Union there is a quickly growing attention to problems of discovering new forms of organisation and to enabling certain types of innovation. Chapter 6 examines the shifting cores of the capitalist economy through a discussion of linearity, time and historical perspectives. The neo-Gramscian dynamic is explained and juxtaposed with the more orthodox narrative of western political economy over the past five centuries by Landes (1998). The extent to which time-space commodification is a focus of attention is evident in the attention given to knowledge about organising as a priority in the knowledge-based economies (Dunning 1997). The issue is how to design and control long chains and networks (Elias 1994; Hughes 1990). For example, in the typical automobile firm less than 10 per cent of expenditure is accounted for by final assembly. Ninety per cent of expenditure is accounted for by innovation-design and managing the entire flow from early suppliers to distributors. Large firms are instances of strategic system co-ordination through design and innovation. Contemporary design cycles tend to be short and extremely expensive. One of the major developments has been the implication that nations contained and constituted distinctive (regional) contexts so that there was competition between contexts (Clark 1987; Porter 1990; Harvey 1990; Sorge 1991).

Chapter 7 commences with a general framework for examining national systems of innovation-design. The role of sectoral clusters within national systems is explored through the locational approaches of Dunning (1993, 1997) and Porter (1990, 1998). Chapter 8 reviews the place of Hofstede's actor/system analysis within the innovation-design framework. That leaves the system-institutional aspects insufficiently developed. The new institutional school (e.g. DiMaggio, Powell, Scott) provides crucial contributions. The new institutionalism (Scott 1995) placed innovation centrally on the agenda. However, although analysis was extended to the symbolic, normative, coercive and regulative features, the comparisons have been more intra-societal than cross-national (e.g. Scott 1995). Also, the institutionalisation tendency has so far dominated over de-institutionalisation. Sorge's (1991) focused speculation shows the interaction between national predispositions and inter-sectoral strengths within nations, but the elective affinities hypothesis requires extension and revision. The pathways through Chapters 6 to 8 lead into a short account of American exceptionalism in Chapter 9. The aim is to highlight the potentials for adaptation at multiple levels and layers. Chapter 10 provides two cameos to illustrate how the constellation of features just examined impacts upon the capacity of a sector to survive and to break away from the entraining potentials of the domestic context and move abroad. Chapters 6 to 10 elaborate the theme of competition between contexts.

Organisations in Action is an indeterminate outcome of substantive struggles between people who deploy different resources (Clegg 1989). Chapter 11 contrasts this view with that of the resource-based strategic analysis. The resource-based theory is a major tributary in organisation economics and a leading edge in strategic theorising (Grant 1990, 1991). The resource-based view claims to embrace Penrosian learning, organisational routines and corporate knowledge when discovering the competitive advantage of firms (Grant 1998). The role of Penrosian learning is scrutinised. There are further problems with the lack of action in the resource-based strategic approach. Chapter 12 unpacks organisational dynamics with the theory of structural repertoires and structural activation. Chapter 13 examines knowledge, power and information technology. Chapter 14 examines the dynamics of stasis/morphogenesis and the innovation-design issue.

Zones of manoeuvre as a notion provides one way of expressing the interaction effects within and between organisations and the competitive capacities of their contexts. Chapter 15 relates the notion of zones of manoeuvre to the claim that managing is about assembling practices (Reed 1992: 189). The strategic choice perspective does not imply that the pre-existing capacities of the firm can be ignored and this point is implicated in the seminal account of strategic choice (Child 1972: Figure 1), but some users of the strategic choice argument have underplayed the zones of manoeuvre.[1] Chapter 15 summarises the journey taken so far.

NOTE

1 I am indebted to John Child's observations on zones of manœuvre at the Paris seminar, 1995, on structuration and related themes (see Whittington *et al.* 1995).

2 From modernism to neo-modern political economy

INTRODUCTION

There is no doubt that profound changes have been unfolding and are occurring in the institutional fabric and individual lives within contemporary capitalist societies. Are these changes, especially those crowded into the last three decades, a rupture introducing a new phase of capitalism as Harvey (1989, 1996) suggests, or simply a radicalising of what has occurred earlier in the century as Giddens (1990) proposes? The question of how contemporary changes might be characterised and interpreted has some parallels in the debates between Weber and Schumpeter to reinterpret the theories and visions proposed by Marx. The similarity is deceptive and important differences are more apparent.

Figure 2.1 is a simple map devised to introduce the debates that have characterised the period since the mid-twentieth century. The Cold War era coincided with a strong restatement of the positivist themes in the management and social sciences within the wide scientific and intellectual movement known as modernism and shown as (1). Positivist tendencies and modern vision blossomed and peaked in the late 1960s, yet lingered on and on. Three major rivals to positivism and modernism developed. The post-modern movement (PoMo) shown as (2) had and has considerable implications for the study of organisations, yet in Organisation Behaviour and Organisation Studies (OBOS) much of the analytic interest was in the social construction of reality, symbolic and structuration perspectives (3). The realist turn (4) rejects positivism, incorporates social construction and borrows some elements from PoMo as well reinterpreting the project of political economy (Bhaskar 1975, 1989). Since the end of the Cold War and the rise of attention to market mechanisms a fifth perspective (5) may be observed: neo-modern political economy (NMPE). This re-focalises the firm in the global economy, yet aims to constitute forms of knowledge which are distinctive in their implications for work organisation.

This chapter aims to unpack Figure 2.1. My approach has certainly been influenced by Alexander's (1995) notion that theories and intellectual movements intermingle. My map is slightly different, especially in the position of the realist turn and in my point of view on neo-modern political economy. The chapter starts

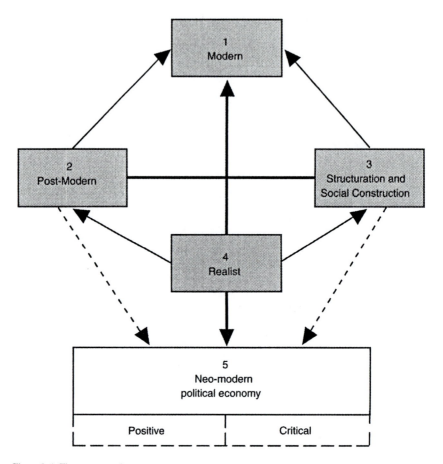

Figure 2.1 Five perspectives

by overviewing the challenge to modernism and then examining the alternative positions.

THE MODERNIST PROJECT CHALLENGED

Radical planning and experimentation

Modernity refers to a whole cluster of systems (social, economic and political) which surfaced in eighteenth-century North Western Europe and dominated the North Atlantic world. There were crucial differences between each side of the Atlantic, although to non-westerners it was the similarities which are striking and significant. The North Atlantic societies developed forms of science and the construction of a notion of reason as an arbitrating framework for judging all aspects of life, especially human behaviour and its control (e.g. Foucault). Modernity implied a vision of planning, especially radical utopian planning based on reason. The steering rule of reason was the search to establish reliable foundations for generalisable knowledge by undermining tradition, dogma and religion through the requirement for proof. The end of modernity would therefore be a high drama.

Modernism is a set of aesthetic and cultural styles opposed to classicism and located in the arts, literature, poetry and architecture. Modernism is therefore found in the realistic faction of the novels of Zola and Tolstoy. In architecture modernism was found in the notions of housing and homes as 'machines for living'. Le Corbusier's designs for urban apartments provides a utopian vision anchored in the plasticity of raw materials developed in the twentieth century. Modernism emphasised experimentation in the social arena. The modern vision of space and its domination of place was applied equally to warehousing, offices and to the design of skyscraper apartments as experiments in horizontal living. Modernism in architecture proved a convenient front for the construction industry and urban planners.

After modernism

The confrontation between modernism and post-modernism oversimplifies and obscures important differences among the critics of modernism about the emerging positions for the new millennium. There are alternative positions (see Figure 2.1). Therefore I will adapt the fourfold distinction proposed by Alexander (1995). I shall argue that the neo-modern political economy and post-modernism represent intriguing although stark alternatives to the criticisms of modernism (Alexander 1995; Gregory 1994; Harvey 1996). Alexander contends that for intellectuals like social scientists there are meta-languages containing symbolic systems that function to define, explain and interpret the world in a rational manner which provides meaning and motivation. Intellectuals seek to interpret the world through distinctions which seem meaningful and possibly also inspiring in particular moments of history. Historical periods can be characterised in terms of genres. The social scientific theory (e.g. modernisation) is a generalised discourse containing research programmes and situating these in terms of extra-scientific criteria. Following Alexander (1995) it is proposed to refer to four major theoretical-cum-ideological episodes since the end of World War II:

- modernisation theory and romantic liberalism;
- anti-modernisation and heroic radicalism;
- post-modern theory and comic detachment;
- neo-modern political economy and ironic detachment.

These do not sufficiently cover the development of the perspectives of social construction of reality or the realist turn, but they will be dealt with later.

Modernisation theory and romantic liberalism

Modernisation and romantic liberalism characterised the Cold War period for almost two decades when mainly US intellectuals in social science and development studies advanced an anti-Marxian theory of modernisation in which the seemingly politically neutral perspective of early systems thinking (cf. Von Bertalanfy 1968) was used to depict societies as:

- tightly connected systems;
- moving along an unfolding linear spectrum from traditional into modern societies;
- through incremental evolution rather than radical change.

The modern society being promoted was an ideal variant of the North Atlantic civilisation.

Modernisation theories were relatively sophisticated and did not exclude emergent possibilities (e.g. Eisenstadt) or contingency, yet they were flawed. The dichotomy between traditional and modern was embodied in a code and situated in a language of universalism (e.g. Parsons; Eisenstadt). Modernisation theory provided a vision which permitted intervention by the core nations by legitimating the intervention. Criticism of the new colonialism being practised by the west was suppressed (Wallerstein 1979).

Romanticism was the dominant narrative form implying the possibility of progress as in the notion of the active society (e.g. Etzioni 1968) giving individual opportunities. The psychological and aesthetic goal of modernity was the expansion of complexity coupled to tolerance of ambiguity with psychoanalysis combining introspection and moral control. Welfare capitalism was an ideal. In architecture and urban renewal, modernism implied spareness under the banner of functionality. In the USA there was massive transformation in urban life with increased prosperity and less labour–management conflict. However, poverty became increasingly apparent. Modernism probably peaked somewhere in the mid-1960s and thereafter succumbed.

Anti-modernism emerges

Second, anti-modernism and the heroic radical became the prevalent form eventually influencing the diverse movements of post-modernism and more recently the emergence of neo-modernism, social construction and critical theory. Modernisation theory continuously encountered disabling problems. For example, surveys revealed corrosive poverty on a world basis, wars, revolutions and dictatorships. The dualism of modern–traditional was unable to cope. So, the new theories emphasised the prevalence of conflict and its basis in real differences of interest and exploitation. The new explanations began to emphasise that modern was repressive (e.g. western religion) and bureaucratic (i.e. a cover for corporate control), thereby labelling modernism as backward. Humanistic socialism replaced welfare capitalism. For a decade the ethical and political positions were now strongly etched in the narrative rhetoric of emancipation and revolution.

The signs of rejection were evident in the critical writing of C. W. Mills (sociology), Arthur Miller (author) and Fromm (social analyst). In Britain the 'angry young men' were sceptical about utopianism and sought to expose their conceptions of hypocrisy.

Post-modernism

By the end of the 1970s the heroic revival was dissipated and right-wing movements came to the fore in the USA, to a degree in the UK, and were given credence in continental Europe. Moreover, the critique of Marx and the exposure of Soviet political practice was well under way, especially in France. Post-modernity is a condition in which the unrealistic aspirations and unrealisable objectives of modernity are recognised and critiqued. Emancipation requires the undermining of the modernist claim that reason provides the universal categories of experience and representation. Popper proposed that the foundations of knowledge cannot be supported because empirical assertions cannot be proved. Moreover, the taken for granted notion of there being a single centre was gradually replaced. Increasingly there are a multitude of forms of authority, of contexts and of actions. Pluralism is institutionalised along with contingency and ambivalence. Knowledge gains a fragmented visage (Burrel 1997).

In post-modernity the most powerful mechanism of integration is the consumer market so that order is achieved through the capacities for choice by individuals. The space of the market becomes one in which there is an indeterminacy. Post-modernism is not a reversion to the earlier classicism or tradition. There is a profusion of styles and Dylon may be considered alongside Keats. The profusion of styles are transient, fleeting, without any deeper meaning, yet autonomous. The absence of a deeper meaning undermines the relevance of copying. Consequently, after the post-modern turn even those still holding to the orthodox base-superstructure perspective of Marx highlight fragmentation and individualism as inevitable (e.g. Harvey 1989). Post-modern theories contain theoretical perplexity, alternative accounts of reality and manifestations of existential despair.

Post-modernism is used as a periodising label to signal the novel character of a newly emergent social order. This emergent social order was frequently analysed as a new phase of symbolic capitalism (e.g. Baudrillard) and as requiring a consideration of the aesthetic, civil and social dimensions (e.g. Walter Benjamin). For example, the privatised, the fragmented and the commercial are interwoven in the interpretations (e.g. Jameson). The question of meaning becomes central: the rise of the empty symbol or simulacrum (e.g. Baudrillard) coupled with the emphasis upon disconnected plurality and difference. These all deflate any lingering conceptions of progress and presage a revisionism within the discipline of history. There is a break with the universalist grand narrative and the insertion of the local. Space must meet place; time must confront contingent events. This rejects romanticism and heroism, replacing them by the fatalistic, critical, agnostic, relativist. There is a comic frame. Tongue in cheek and pastiche abound.

Neo-modern political economy

According to Alexander (1995) the current period has much in common with earlier debates over political economy between the versions which are pro-capitalism and the critical political economy. Alexander prefers to refer to neo-modernism. I will use the label of neo-modern political economy (NMPE).

Although the 1980s commenced with the Cold War seeming to be an enduring iron curtain, there were dislocating changes unfolding in the Soviet bloc. The visit by the Pope to Poland enabled non-communist groupings to break free and symbolically challenge Soviet hegemony. Within a decade the Berlin Wall was removed and by the early 1990s there was Soviet compliance in the containment of Iraq. Contrary to the overstretch thesis of Kennedy (1987), the USA and capitalism seemed reinvigorated, symbolically in terms of standards of living.

The capitalist market was being presented as the necessary step to democratic governance and to consumerism. There is a renewed interest in universal theories and models accompanied by the intellectual rehabilitation of Adam Smith (Boltanski and Thevenot 1988). New heroes of the rupture surface, even from unlikely locations (e.g. Gorbachev). All this has been accompanied by attention to the non-economic civil society. There are intriguing developments after half a millennium of western dominance including elements of de-Christianisation (Giddens 1984).

WESTERN MODERNISM (1500–1950s)

In this section the main elements of western modernism are reviewed. The following section examines the position of the anti-modernists. The category of anti-modernist is useful because it reveals areas of agreement in rejecting modernist predispositions among almost opposing groupings like the post-modernism position, the realist turn (Bhaskar 1979, 1989) and the NMPE approaches from the right (positive) and from the left (neo-Gramscian and critical).

Modernity may be defined in terms of the five centuries long social construction of knowledge around science and reason which commenced during the Renaissance in Europe and enveloped the North Atlantic nations. From the Renaissance and through the Enlightenment the constitution of knowledge, especially the form of knowledge known as science (e.g. astronomy) and the definitions of reason sought to establish a coherent system. There was a strong implication that real knowledge was obtained through direct observation: for example, in the use of the camera obscura to paint cities such as Amsterdam or in Newton's modification to the telescope and in the extensive mapping of territories by the French state.

There are three clusters of common features that underpin western modernist predispositions:

1 The emphasis upon a *secular science and humanist thought* which was different from religion and opposed to witchcraft: this led to a separation between the sacred and secular, permitting their co-existence (e.g. USA). There was a strong notion of rational thought based on individual responsibility.

2 From the fourteenth century onward the intention and practices of *measuring reality* and the rational calculation of means and ends developed in the towns and cities where this tendency was closely allied with the development of long-distance commerce (Thevenot and Boltanski 1988). In urban centres the newly rich invested in producing this new kind of knowledge both directly in their activities and indirectly in patronising artistic forms (e.g. music) which embodied the mentality (Crosby 1998). The orderliness developed in the Christian church's use of time was transferred and transformed in the cities into homogeneous units of time which could be used to measure and appraise activity. There was extensive recording of activities and this permitted their use in reflection and planning.

3 The position of modernity has been closely coupled to the putting of a price on all goods and activities. This process, later referred to as *commodification*, became extensive and involved the theorising of the price mechanism and the market relationship. Market mechanisms were theorised and justified in the seminal contributions of classical economists (e.g. Adam Smith) and applied to increasing areas of social life. For example, the early Europeans colonising North America in the seventeenth century viewed the landscape, animals and fish as commodities while the Indians did not (Cronon 1983). In the nineteenth century the Americans treated endowed factors – oil, wood, gold, coal – as commodities and developed special knowledge about them whereas the British Empire, which was comparable in size, did not attempt to create such knowledge. Modernism is most at home in North America.

In the North Atlantic nations these features led to the progressive rejection of the legitimacy of tradition, mysticism, religion, witchcraft and similar in validating knowledge; also to the confinement of God or the replacement by a form of Christian agnosticism.

The last five centuries can be characterised in four broad periods. First, throughout the sixteenth and seventeenth centuries a significant collection of European intellectuals promoted the idea and practice of science as a powerful analytic technique for studying nature (e.g. light, time, space, navigation). The leading exponents proposed that there is a real world separate from God's world and that this real world is known through direct representation as in Newton's telescope for looking at the stars. Their construction of knowledge, which emphasised how things are rather than how they should be, could be defined by constructing a law-like knowledge of how things are in nature: for example, through astronomy and then by mapping the Earth. Many intellectuals assumed that the eye catches raw experience (e.g. painting by camera obscura; attempts to capture light effects in painting in the Renaissance). Even so, it was presumed that there were law-like hidden processes such as gravity which explained the surface events (e.g. apples falling on heads). Toulmin (1992) concludes that these processes led to the dominance of the written word over the spoken word; of general laws over particular cases; of general explicit knowledge over local knowledge; of the timeless theory over events. Science interfaced with practice and technique claiming to be a reflective long-term investment which would provide its followers with general navigational skills and the capacity to adapt to the unchangeable. European science differed in its embedding and trajectory from Chinese science even though each shared some common interests (Landes 1983). In everyday life for the bourgeoisie the use of simple lists was an important innovation (Goodey 1963).

Second, in the eighteenth and nineteenth centuries the use of science was extended to the study of society and the individual, initially through observing human behaviour and constructing laws of human behaviour. This was the origin of the human sciences. Next, in a significant step came the development of reason and critique as the acceptable framework for social life. The notion of the utopian goal as an alternative to everyday existence was developed. It was claimed that reason was liberating and this claim became a centrepiece of the Enlightenment. Thus, the combining of science and reason by Adam Smith's economics in the 1760s illustrates one line of development. The subsequent critique of Adam Smith through the development of critical reason is exemplified in Marx's theorising and grand narrative of economy and society. The main tenets of modernity constructed by social scientists were based on their understanding of the processes of science. These assumptions colonised the arts and humanities. In literature it was assumed that there was an orderly reality revealed in the narrative so that fiction and fact were transformed into faction (e.g. Zola). This narrative might contain some surprising twists and turns as in Tolstoy's account of victories arising from the order to retreat. What was clear and accepted was that the author decided and it was down to the reader to discover the intended message. In history and politics there was an assumption of linearity and of direction (i.e. teleology). Marx provides one example and, according to Bauman, communism has been the most developed form of modernity because it was implicated in the anticipation that the world could be reshaped according to human agency – albeit a lengthy process. Communism was based on the notion of reason – the good society – which was supposed to overcome the irrationalities of the market and of capitalism.

Third, in the early twentieth century the notion of political and social sciences was extended to create the policy sciences and to establish the link to romantic liberalism (Alexander 1995). Many institutes (e.g. London School of Economics) and movements were founded (e.g. socialism).

The main elements were later clustered into the *doctrine of positivism* which can be characterised as possessing the following six elements:

1   An understanding of the natural sciences *as the production of deterministic, law-like generalisations providing predictions*; the claim that the activity of science provides *determinate laws* revealing otherwise hidden processes such as gravity or the impacts of the price mechanism. Therefore all claims to be scientific should be accompanied by the presentation of laws. The laws provide a reliable base from which the ends-means relationship can be calculated and consequences can be predicted. Scientific knowledge is presented as the outcome of *rigorous tests of proof* based on experiments, reasoning and public debates.

2   *Representational knowledge*: knowledge is based on the reality of raw experience apprehended through the senses. It is assumed that the theories mirror the real world. There is no knowledge independent of the senses or that can be apprehended by the perceiver. This results in the attempt to apply *experimental methods* and assumptions from natural science into the study of human and organisational 'behaviour'; for example, the application of laboratory experiments in social psychology (Harre and Secord 1972). Therefore human intentions cannot be considered.

3   Knowledge is presented to the public and to the scientific community as *objective, technical and neutral*. The knowledge is universal and homogeneous and can be applied anywhere. The objectivity and truth of knowledge could be defined according to a set of epistemological rules also covering the nature of reality (i.e. ontological status). The knowledge is presumed to be value free.

4   Knowledge is *constructed by scientists at particular centres*. The use of experiments provides a key means of controlling conditions so that predictions can be tested. Scientific knowledge was created by licensed practitioners who were detached experts. This knowledge was organised around a hierarchy of centres so that disputes could be settled by reference to the rules applied by the peer group and assessed through publication.

5   The use of *time-space trajectories* which are law-like and deterministic to describe scientific action such as the movements of the planets. These features can be transferred to the Earth and to its circumnavigation and indicate the importance of longitude (Sobal 1995). There is a single coherent framework of time and space. Time was defined as a regular process outside events. The units corresponded to those of the clock and the calendar so that units were homogeneous. Time was given a linear format (the time line). Knowledge was given a linear format (e.g. the organisation life cycle). Similar time-space trajectories can then be applied, with caveats and modification to social activities. In anthropology the time-space framework was applied to the movement of non-western societies and this provided both a means of understanding for the westerners and also rules of thumb for aligning these societies with western capitalism.

6   There is the notion that value judgements can have no empirical aspects which render them accessible to any tests of validity based on experience.

These six elements are then transposed to the development of the arts and the social sciences. In painting there is the attempt to combine perspective, configuration and lighting. In literature narratives are given an ordering decided by the author. In the social sciences the linear framework is freely imposed to examine the existing and the ideal situation. One of the intellectual movements applying these principles was logical positivism and their influence carried forward into the fourth period.

Fourth, the two decades after World War II were the peak of modernism and of the positivist approach to social sciences and economics. The modernist movement experienced a period of restatement, possibly influenced by the role of Big Science in the Cold War.

Positivism and modernism significantly shaped the search for a professional model of the social sciences and of the re-badged management sciences with its array of journals including *Management Science* and the *Administrative Science Quarterly* (b. 1956). Organisation behaviour exemplifies these claims in the proclamation of design rules as building blocks. Design rules included the contingency theory of design sketched by J. D. Thompson (1967) and Jay Galbraith (1977). Similar design rules undergirded motivation theories (e.g. Maslow hierarchy). The design rules could be used by experts to construct plans for the future as in the design of new workplaces in layouts, choice of control systems, technology and work organisation (Clark 1972, 1975a). It was assumed that the existing world could be redesigned. The metaphor, albeit unrealised (Kilduff 1990), was writing the computer program. So the existing could be transformed into green fields by knocking down the earlier world and rebuilding the new. Eighty per cent of US shops and malls were built in the last two decades. Child and Kieser (1981) discuss how these approaches adopted a *linear view of development* which imposed order as in the widely cited theory of the organisational life cycle models.

Within organisation theory and behaviour positivism was vigorously espoused: for example, the whole development of scales for measuring organisational characteristics (centralisation, specialisation, complexity, normalisation) as dependent variables in order to produce appropriate amounts of statistical variance which could then – through regression analysis – be allocated between independent variables (size, technology, dependence on external resources). The tenets of modernism were certainly dominant into the late 1960s and were a powerful normative framework well into the 1970s. In the 1980s and 1990s they were vigorously, thoughtfully and openly defended by Donaldson (1985, 1996) and Pugh and Hickson (1976). Moreover, the tenets were taken for granted – perhaps unknowingly – even by many who claimed to have developed radically different positions.

POST-MODERNISM

A sketch

Post-modernism shares some important criticisms of modernism and of positivist organisation behaviour with other movements including the symbolic interactionists, critical management and the realist turn (Cahoone 1996). Post-modernism may have its severe critics and the turn away from and beyond post-modernism is underway. However, there is much more of relevance from post-modernism than the simplistic substituting of 'post-modern' for 'organic' in texts on organisation theory. In particular the post-modern critique of linearity will increasingly affect any attempt to impose linear, multi-stage models and calendrical-historical explanations upon events. Retro-organisation theory has arrived (Burrel 1997). Dystopia abounds (Heatherington 1997). Now, because of the intention of avoiding teleological theories the contemporary world is not regarded as an end state (e.g. Giddens 1984). At the same moment there is an anxiety to describe and explain the transformation of the contemporary world. My contention is that post-modernism has drawn attention to the time-space experience embedded in the commodification of economic action.

Post-modernism refers to a movement which developed in France from the 1960s onward and entered organisation studies in the 1980s. The French context is held to be important by Best and Kellner (1991), yet Anderson (1998) contends that the American context has been the most influential. In the French post-1945 period of reconstruction and recovery, the most visible intellectual and academic movements opposing the status quo were Marxism, existentialism, phenomenology and psychoanalysis which were rationalistic and scientifically orientated. These movements depicted the individual as alienated, largely because capitalism estranged individuals from their authentic selves. Meanwhile in urban redevelopment the modern movement in architecture imposed its technocratic solutions of simplicity, completeness, certainty and grid-like complexes of apartments upon the urban poor who were uprooted from their neighbourhoods by the telos of state welfarism. French society was riven by numerous strains, including the loss of an empire and a rapprochement with Germany. There were the events of 1968. By the early 1970s the attractiveness of Leninist state planning was being rejected and Marx was increasingly criticised. It might seem that a new generation were ready to acknowledge that we were being orphaned (Cahoone 1996). In that sense post-modernism is a stepchild of Marxism. By the late 1960s a new grouping of young French academics were using the theories of structuralist analysis drawn from Saussure and Lévi-Strauss to reject the focus upon the self and its historical development. These new structuralists focused upon those superstructures of language, kinship and ritual which shape the individual: culture creates the selves. The key to analysis becomes the study of abstract relations and their 'codes' of cultural signs. Therefore the notions of being authentic, searching for origins and foundations are illusory. Soon, the new movement, increasingly known as post-structuralist and then post-modern, transformed structuralism and ejected its scientific claims.

The post-modernists in the North Atlantic societies drew on their societal-relational perspective to argue that perception is mediated through the cultural signs already acquired from societal and occupational languages and therefore there was no possibility of searching for the raw, immediate experience. Sense data cannot be the immediate channel for reality. Post-modernists insert the analysis of representations for the discussion of 'the thing' itself because, even if there is a real world, we encounter that world through the representations (signs). Therefore the surface and the depth are intermingled and it is useless to search for a deeper level. Moreover, since words, meanings and even selves can only be examined within relations to other elements there can be no single meaning to a word or text. Concepts have a plurality of meanings which are context related and within particular relational codes. Since the human self is also a product of those relationships the self is less a unified, hierarchically composed, self-contained single self than a plurality of selves. It also follows that transcendent values such as truth, beauty and goodness must be examined as elements in those relations and processes they seek to judge.

The methodological strategy of post-modernists is to show that what appear to be cultural units (e.g. meanings) require an active process of opposition, exclusion and hierarchisation to maintain their apparent unity. The methodological strategy, known as constitutive otherness, is to make opposition, exclusion and hierarchisation transparent by highlighting just those areas frequently left at the margins of analysis in the text and in social situations. Methodological post-modernism is opposed to realist analysis because knowledge is only made valid by reference to pragmatic and vested interests rather than by its relationship to the objects of inquiry.

Post-modernism rejects the notion of language as a mirror of reality and as a carrier of meaning, thereby rejecting the philosophy of presence and giving precedence to that which in language is not decidable. Textuality is central. Language contains constitutive powers for objects which are viewed as discursively produced and in the treatment of technology as text (Grint and Woolgar 1998). Elements from five examples of post-modernism – Harvey, Lyotard, Baudrillard, retro-organisation theory and architecture – are briefly examined in the following sections. The purpose is to show that there are elements in the rejection of modernism that are of considerable interest to a neo-modern political economy perspective.

Time-space compression and commodification: Harvey

David Harvey (1989) interprets the 'post-modern condition' as one of a small, series of climactic, lengthy historical transformations in the nexus of money-space-time. These transformations shift the innovative edge of capitalism from one competitive context to another as the process of capital accumulation migrates. The earliest came in the Renaissance. Another major rupture and transformation occurred immediately around and after 1848. More recently, since the early 1970s the capitalist world economy has been internally restructured by transnational corporations which have reconfigured the workplace and the urban setting to alter our experience of events and places (Thrift 1996).

Capitalism is analysed as a series of interdependent flows which on different levels and locations involve competition between firms and the accumulation processes centred in particular places (e.g. Chicago) that make up the full circuit of capitalism. The key elements are the commodification of time and space in particular. In nineteenth-century Chicago urban space was revalued dispossessing the least profitable activities (e.g. homes) by industrialised agriculture so that low value time was eliminated through the introduction of a vast array of organisational innovations and technological innovations (e.g. grain conveyors and silos). The organisational innovations included the establishment of standard categories for grain, thereby removing the need for small-scale market activities. The accumulation process in Chicago was enhanced by its central location at the end/start for the rail systems going east and westward. Chicago wealth was spent in the growing department stores and in the steel-framed buildings designed and built by engineers rather than architects. Skyscrapers represent an excellent illustration of space designed tightly for time activities at defined costs and with estimable benefits to investors. Harvey defines 1848 – also the publication date for the Communist Manifesto – as initiating a special era of intensification in the time-space-money nexus leading to extensive urban transformation illustrated by Hausman's rebuilding of Paris. According to Harvey, that era unfolded into the twentieth-century regime of political and economic accumulation known as Fordism. Then in the 1970s a new period of step change in the time-space-money nexus commenced.

Two guiding propositions are advanced. First, this experience of modernity after 1848 does not fit with the established discourse on modernism as an enlightenment project of reason, progress and the enhancement of the quality of life. Instead, the outcomes were the primacy of instrumental rational knowledge through expert planners inside corporations and urban areas where it was used to alter individual existence. Second, this altering of the objective nexus also caused established experiences of space and time to be disrupted and displaced. These transformations can be read off by examining the new forms of art which emerged (e.g. Impressionism, Picasso). The post-modern condition follows modernity or, as Harvey prefers, the myth of the modern.

The post-modern condition of knowledge performativity: Lyotard

Lyotard was commissioned in the late 1970s by the province of Quebec to reflect upon the future condition of knowledge (Lyotard 1984). In his account society is analysed as collections of language games played in particular communities, one of which is known broadly as science. Assuming that modernity is more a mode of thought, speech and sensibility, then the characteristic mode of the science language game has been largely one of the truthfulness of denotative statements: that is, statements about how relationships are rather than how they should be. Science in the modern mode since the early nineteenth century has legitimated its activities and their funding from national budgets largely in terms of truthfulness. That truth claim seemed secure when science provided an image of actions that were subject to deterministic, orderly and consensually validated statements based on defined methods such as experiments. Science became equated with knowable, stable systems that are predictable. However, in order to justify continuing funding and continuing autonomy science has increasingly sought out the instabilities and claimed that understanding these is now the central activity.

In modern science the language game of justification is the spirit of speculation. However, administrators and users of science are more concerned with efficiency than with truth and the pursuit of the speculative spirit. Legitimacy for them is therefore in terms of the useful and exploitable knowledge: *performativity*. Hence, as anticipated in Marx, science is a force of production. However, performativity is equated with the knowable and this is in tension with the tendency in science to search for instabilities and to question its own rules of inquiry in order to produce new, publishable statements.

Lyotard contends that since the 1960s there has been a framework of economic world contest in which advanced liberal capitalism has been used as a rhetoric to legitimate the organisation of society on competitive grounds. One of the major developments has been the technologies of information processing and communication. Information processing machines are continually miniaturised and commercialised so that circuits of information become transformed in a revolution which is analogous to the transport revolutions of earlier epochs. One consequence is that there are vast data banks of information in both crude categorical form and in highly organised forms. Lyotard suggests that 'Data banks are the Encyclopaedia of tomorrow. They transcend the capacity of their users. They are the nature for post-modern man' (1984: 51 and footnote 179).

In an important point Lyotard claims that the technological transformations based on computing alter research activity and the transmission of knowledge by introducing new ways in which knowledge can be classified, acquired, made available and exploited. Thus the understanding of knowledge is being altered (has already been altered) to fit into new channels. The explicit knowledge will (he contends) be commodified so that knowledge becomes an end itself. Given that much of this knowledge will be in data banks not controlled by the state in a direct way (e.g. data on purchasing activities of American males with respect to erotic video watching in chain hotels) then the state may face competition over the understanding of organisational processes. Moreover, learning might circulate on the same lines as money to introduce a greater separation between payment–knowledge exchanged on an everyday basis with the workforce and investment–knowledge dedicated to optimising the performance of projects.

There are some sharp contrasts between the modes of knowing before the 1960s and the future modes of knowing envisaged by Lyotard and he warns against a backward longing for a lost community which was warm and bonded. Like Baudrillard, he argues against grand narratives. Instead we should aim to understand the language of games, especially linguistic communities. Lyotard hypothesises that untranslatable knowledge will be rejected (Lyotard 1984). However, that contention sits uneasily with the massive growth of interest in non-explicit knowledge (see Chapter 13).

Commodifying culture and consuming signs: Baudrillard

Baudrillard broke from his earlier involvement in the Marxist tradition in the early 1970s with the 'Mirror of Production' (Baudrillard 1973) with the proposition that consumption is now the organising principle. In the new capitalist societies the focus shifts from the problems of production (i.e. Fordism) to the problems of promoting and enabling consumption by motivating the consumer to search for attributes whose attractive features are constantly being replaced. The foundation of capitalism becomes the circulation and production of signs (e.g. 501, Louis Vuitton, Gucci, Mercedes). The issue for the individual becomes signs value rather than use value. Consumption then provides the basis for the claim to status through the display of the brand name. Baudrillard (1983) maintains that the signs displayed in consumption are the pre-eminent indicators of status: 'there is no responsibility without a Rolex watch'. So, the code of social standing involves knowing the value of signs (e.g. MBA).

Baudrillard (1983) observes that the contemporary world depends upon a great deal of the simulation of the real and that the correspondence of the simulation to the real becomes loosened. The loosening can arise when a real airliner is shot down by weapons operators misreading the signs experienced in simulation. The loosening problematises what constitutes reality and how to differentiate which reality is more real. There can be an implosion of the real. The issue here is whether what is consumed possesses an original or not: the simulacrum. Is there an original for the themed 'traditional' Irish bar that draws on notions of fun, craic and community or are these a pastiche of Irish cultural artefacts as in engraving the image of a shamrock on the head of a pint of Guinness. The Irish themed bar has been marketed with the myth of its origin and authenticity: it is more real than the reality. Baudrillard refers to this situation as hyperreality.

Baudrillard's contribution is much more extensive than suggested in the previous paragraphs. He leads the rejection of grand narratives (e.g. Marxian theory). His recent reputation is for arousing controversy as in statements about the Gulf War. His impact on organisation theory is slight, but is greater in political economy and the interface between sociology and geography (Lash and Urry 1994). Baudrillard's theorising anticipates the intensification of the design activity in modern capitalism which I discuss in Chapter 7 and Chapter 14. The continuing production of sign value and its perishability increases the proportion of investment in design.

Retro-organisation theory: Burrel

Burrel (1997a) states that modernity has embraced the hegemony of vision and its unbending linearity. This mentality is grounded in the search by the British and French navies in the seventeenth century to solve the problem of longitude (Sobel 1996). The solution involved the creation of a complex actor network through the enforcement of linear conceptions of time and space. Various portable devices were developed involving the clock so that the British navy possibly embodied the leading edge of thinking about linearity in its everyday practices (e.g. grid reference). Without the multiple crossings of linear co-ordinates the British comparative advantage in world trading would collapse. In the navy the record of directions taken was kept by the master not be the crew.

Social scientists are like the navigators. They engage in the mapping of fields and establishing concepts which imprison thought. This was a Cartesian scopic regime in which the eye was the key sensory device. The emphasis is upon the optocentric so that sound and smell are downgraded. This aspect is found in the ways in which insurance firms reduce the real lives of their clients to the 'form', a genre developed in the mid-1850s (Hoskin and Macve 1988). The emphasis on the visual reflects the silencing of voice which began with the innovation of silent reading by Ambrose, a fifth-century cleric. The modernist world fetishises sight, thereby privileging grids, 2x2 matrices in management, the causal diagram and flat designs. Linearity gained impetus from the ways of ordering natural history by the French encyclopaediaists and by Napoleon's approach to warfare and control. Maps and lines were used to develop military strategy. Linearity and the timetable were conjoined in World War I when railway timetables brought soldiers to the front line. So, linearity kills and it is tempting to construct oppositions such as linear versus the labyrinth. Burrel does not wish to be beset with dualistic thinking posing false oppositions, but he does want to disrupt linearity. That is the task of retro-organisation theory and the book, pandemonium.

Organisation theory, according to Burrel (1997b), suppresses major aspects of organisational life and he intends to expose those massive limitations through retro-organisation theory. In organisation theory there is order and linearity, but 'linearity kills'. Therefore in retro-organisation theory it is necessary to reject concerns about chronology, anachronism, narrative and antecedent causality (Burrel 1997: 31). In the post-modern discourse of collage the layout of the book is a playful toying with ideas (Burrel 1997: 28) and hopping from 'story' to 'story'. So we as readers should be playful about the calendrical dates (e.g. 1580) which are given and about the attempt to trace modernity (e.g. the role of West Point). Partly following Harvey (1990: 427) Burrel (1997: 30) asks 'Who are we and to what space/place do we belong?' and continues: 'So, welcome to a world of time space compression.' Retro-organisation theory self-consciously pushes back the study of organisations to the pre-modern period some four hundred years ago when Christ and the Devil were everyday features of life in Western Europe. The aim is to surface the sights and sounds of four hundred years ago when pre-modern life was engrossed in gift relationships, affection and local markets. Life was shaped by the emotions of fear and hate. The book is a journey into pandemonium and a challenge to facile retro-organisation theory (see later in Chapter 14).

Modern and post-modern in the built environment

Modernism was anticipated in the later nineteenth century with the development of the skyscraper in Chicago and New York (Giedion 1967). Those buildings and the industrial development of that period in Chicago (Cronon 1991) represented the engineers' conception of how to design space as a commodified environment possessing a functional capacity to enable work processes: for example, the development of grain elevators in Chicago. Flexibility in the use of space became central as with the large warehouse. These provided templates that could be used as standard solutions (Giedion 1967). The twentieth-century buildings, certainly in the USA, used the new technologies to combine steel frames and glass curtains to face the world with sleek, machined faces that were uniformly aesthetic, striking and could be erected rapidly and cheaply. Although the modernist movement of architects claimed centre stage in providing a public language of their meaning, the most powerful shapers were a clustering of property developers, engineers and specialised professions such as caisson building for skyscrapers. The so-called modern approaches to built space were honed in the design of factories, hotels, department stores and similar vehicles of capitalist revenue flows and profit. The rationalist code was that space should be functional and profitable. Similar propositions were applied to the building of skyscraper apartments. The rationalist code later acquired modernist rhetoric such as 'a machine for living in'.

The attack on modern architecture was led by a collection of books which contrasted the claims of modernism with the actuality of everyday life in their homes. Post-modernism in architecture is mainly recognised as a stylistic phenomenon (e.g. multi-coloured buildings) arriving in the late 1960s and taking root in the USA yet, because of the marginalised role of the architect, not being quite as central as in Europe (Ghirardo 1996). Post-modernism denotes particular aesthetic approaches in the humanities and social sciences, but in the built environment the movement rejects 'less is more' and proposes 'less is a bore'. In many respects the architectural examples combine time-space compression with the use of signs to seduce consumers and to regulate who enters particular buildings (Ghirardo 1996). There is a strong theme of exclusion for those with small disposable incomes through the use of small doors leading into large atriums containing surveillance.

NEO-MODERN POLITICAL ECONOMY

The post-war era of modernisation theory was, according to Giddens (1981), an ideological defence of western domination. Since then two of the key dichotomies in modernisation theory have been transformed:

- the traditional versus modern distinction;
- modernising the Third World.

Equally, the deflated narrative of the post-modern and its comedic metre is being challenged by a new code of universalising in social theory. Alexander (1995) concludes that a new 'world historical frame' is being articulated which he terms neo-modern because of the combination of universal categories applied to nations (as modernism) with dramatic inflation (contra-modernism). There is an interest in and enthusiasm for the role of market processes in an 'emancipator narrative of the market' (Alexander 1995: 32). The market is not – for the moment – viewed as the vehicle for capitalist exploitation, but its weak ties (Granovetter 1973) are seen as enabling political and economic benefits (cf. Gray 1998). Consequently economic sociology is being redefined and restated (see Chapter 5). The development of néo-modern political economy (NMPE) as situated in Figure 2.1 will be linked to the theme of competition between contexts.

The rise of the American liberal right in the 1980s initiated key transitions in world politics. These included its technology boycott that so pressured Soviet economic decision-making in the context of globalisation. The final economic breakdown of the Soviet Union coincided with the computer-based military expansion of the USA and its allies during the early 1990s in the Middle East and even in the South China Seas. The liberal right gained a negative triumph over state socialism and reinvigorated capitalist notions of the positive role of the market – for the moment, anyway. History has not ended, but events challenged those who earlier proclaimed the immanent end of capitalism (e.g. Mandel 1978). Indeed, Harvey (1989) retained the base–superstructure reasoning and postulated similar kinds of social differentiation, fragmentation, individuation and privatisation as deployed by Durkheim (1915) in his analysis of the social division of labour. In the capitalist west the market is reinvigorated aesthetically, symbolically and objectively. These developments engender a different coding of the contemporary to that proposed by the post-modernists.

I shall argue that new schools of neo-modern political economy have emerged from the liberal right (e.g. positive political economy) and from the left (e.g. neo-Gramscian critical political economy) and that their themes jostle with a host of ongoing developments including the following:

1 The *neo-contingency perspective* on the influence of national contexts in shaping organisational identities and destinies (Clark 1987; Sorge 1991, 1995).
2 The *realist turn* contributes to the interest in political economy (e.g. Harvey 1996).
3 The emphasis upon *globalisation as an interpretative schema* (e.g. Albrow 1996) in the social sciences and, especially in the schools of business.
4 Much returning and *re-working to modernisation theory* (e.g. Eisenstadt 1985, 1986). So, earlier modernisation theory should be understood as a specifically western, North Atlantic phenomenon (Eisenstadt 1987).
5 Giddens *attempts to historicise the contemporary world.*
6 Invoking the key debates at the start of the twentieth century between Weber and Schumpeter (Powell 1996).
7 Western domination is more precarious and challenged.
8 Neo-modernisation theory incorporates significant shifts in *symbolic time and symbolic space* (Alexander 1995: 36).
9 There is a revival of the '*drama of democracy*' (e.g. Poland) and a new interest in the 'civil society' which suggests that any contemporary society should aspire

to creating an economic market within a distinct political zone and an institutional field.

10   The profane can no longer be equated with the traditional and also not the contemporary. The implicitly Christian elements of modernisation are displaced and relativised. Modernity is now regarded as a state of affairs rather than an end point. Likewise, neo-modern political economy.

The new geographies of Gregory (1994) and Dicken (1998) each illustrate different aspects of the claim that there is a neo-modern theorising political economy. They also illustrate the difficulties of establishing its point of view. I will take the example of Dicken's widely read text on global shifts. While omitting certain key features, Dicken (1998) addresses and exemplifies the renewed interest in developmental typologies and theories. His account also bridges that of Dunning (1993) examined in Chapter 7 and contains five major elements.

First, there is a rich analytic description of the significant shifts in the global division of labour which have unfolded in the past half-century and are still unfolding. These shifts mean that the relationships between nations have moved from shallow integration to deep integration with increasing interconnections and increasing interpenetration arising from various sources, especially foreign direct investment. The extent of shifts is usually acknowledged by referring to the immediate post-war period as one of internationalisation and the current era as one of globalisation. The rate of growth of world trade has increased from under 6 per cent to almost 9 per cent per annum. There are paradoxical elements. The USA's share of world automobile exports has declined from 51 per cent to around 20 per cent, yet the USA remains the leader among those continuingly dominant advanced economies. Within the advanced nations there are some shifts. The Japanese bubble has burst (Dicken 1998: 28, 131f) and the position of Britain within the European bloc looks increasingly precarious (Dicken 1998: 65). China illustrates some of new possibilities. The rise of the transnational corporation is central to the analysis of the shifts (see below).

Second, these shifts require new concepts and the revision of established theories. Dicken highlights certain 'forces' and these tend to gain a disembodied sense of action. For example, new technology is presented as a 'prime mover' with negligible attention to the milieu in which major advances in knowledge are occurring and being appropriated by firms in particular nation states which develop strong property rights allied to extra-territorial influences (e.g. USA). However, Dicken fruitfully explores modes of production by constructing simple models of world production chains and by illustrating the concept of production chains in four sectoral studies. These production chains arise from the actions of transnationals, particularly their capacity and tendency to fragment production stages between different national contexts. The concept of production chains introduces important revisions to established theories explaining international trade, even to the recent eclectic theory of Dunning (Dicken 1998: 78f). Dicken's attempt to theorise is replete with many linear, multi-stage typologies requiring analysts dramatically to increase their capacities for using multiple perspectives.

Dicken's re-theorising is incomplete and problematic. For example, the treatment of Porter's (1990) framework is idiosyncratic and clearly reveals the low position given to societal and corporate knowledge. Likewise, the endorsement of various systemic aspects of national systems of organising and of innovation remains undeveloped.

Third, re-theorising the firm leads into the examination of transnational corporations (TNCs) as the agencies which move economic activity about and shape national experiences. TNCs are the movers and shapers and it is their development of new technologies which is consequential. However, not only are they crossing national boundaries, but the new information technologies are implicated in the emergence of webs of firms in which TNCs occupy a pivotal role. Webs of TNCs constitute multi-nation contexts of alliance and competition for one another. So, at one level in the automobile industry there are implicit alliances within the USA (e.g. Ford, General Motors) and Europe (e.g. Renault, Peugeot) while the strong performance of German speciality automobile manufacturers has enabled them to envisage the Mercedes/Chrysler linkage. Dicken's account of the TNC underlines the significance of Alexander's suggestion regarding neo-modern theories and the new political economies.

Fourth, Dicken treats nation states as containers, as implicated in national and international regulation of the quasi-capitalist global economy, and as bases for competition between contexts (e.g. Japan). There are useful typologies of nations (Dicken 1998: 89, 115) and interesting descriptions of nations (e.g. China).

Fifth, the analytic description and the search for relevant explanatory theories hinges on resolving the relationship between nation states and TNCs (Dicken 1998: Chapter 8). We know that production chains are constituted in dissolvable, modularised, heterogeneous networks by TNCs and that corporate power involves building networks which limit the discretion of organisational members as well as the raw materials. However, because specific firms – the very agencies involved – are given a place mainly as puppets (e.g. Benetton) the state–TNC relationship is underdeveloped.

Dicken exemplifies the relevance of a geographical and spatial dimension. However, unlike Gregory (1994), the historical imagination of Dicken tends to prioritise time over events and space over place. In various ways these analytic concerns also bring 'competition between contexts' to the foreground. Competition between contexts is the heartland of whole series of recent analyses from varying sources in history, sociology, strategy and organisation studies. The neo-modern political economy challenges the architecture of organisation behaviour (Chapter 3) and requires further attention to theories of structuration and the contribution of the realist turn (Chapter 4). Also, the position of economic action requires examination (Chapter 5) before coming to Part II: Competition between contexts.

3 Organisation theory
Design rules

INTRODUCTION

Neo-modern political economy, post-modern theory and the structuration approach are critical of organisation theory and strategic analysis. To explain their criticisms it is analytically convenient to view organisation theory and related areas of strategy as a clusters of research programmes held together by the discourse of specific communities of theorists with overlapping interests. Some clusters of research programmes will be rising to future eminence while other clusters may be degenerating. The notions of ascending and degenerating should not be taken to imply a teleology of progress and perception of ups and downs is relative to the observer. Also, there are likely to be switches and surprises. The key journals and their editorial boards provide an important mechanism giving the sense of a brand to organisation theory.

The foundations of organisation theory and design possess strong, deep layers and elements of the modernist and positivist agenda (Silverman 1970; Clark 1975a). The visage of organisation theory was and is much more fragmented than presumed (Burrel 1997). Organisation theory was certainly shaped by the positivist tendency in empirical research (e.g. Aston Programme) and in the propositional approach to theory (e.g. J. D. Thompson), but even this seminal piece did not produce a unified collection of design rules. Also, although the espoused theory was of the practical goal of organisation design the theory in use left organisation theory largely in the ivory tower. There have been remarkably few documented evaluations studies of organisation theory being used to design specific organisations (Clark 1972, 1975a). Organisation theory offered an intellectual-ideological discourse to members of the technostructure in large firms. The discourse provided a set of categories for cognitising the structuring of work activity through time and space.

Design rules have a double meaning when applied to organisation theory. Design rules as a metaphor declares a tendency towards an architectural view of the role of organisation theorists. Design rules also refers to the desire to construct clusters of rules to control organisations. There is a strong implication that the design rules do provide organisational blueprints. However, there is considerable scepticism about the capacity of organisation design to succeed in its modernist formation. We may review the cluster of research programmes contributing design rules to organisation theory and their relationship to strategy in three parts. The neglect of classical political economy (e.g. Marx) and the emergence of neo-modern political economy is dealt with later. My purpose is to review the main research programmes in organisation theory through indicative, stylised summaries.

First, the architecture of organisation theory can be understood in terms of the often tortuous attempt to align a dozen or more research programmes:

- simple systems models (Boulding taxonomy);
- codified, explicit knowledge for organisation design as blueprints;
- the definition of the firm;
- uncertainty and rationality;
- prioritising structure over process;
- prioritising strategy before organisation design;
- contingency: mechanistic and organic systems;
- technology and social technology framework;
- organisation life cycle models;
- structuration and actors' frame of reference;
- managed evolutionary change;
- political coalitions and strategic choice.

Second, my purpose is to illustrate the gap between ascending and declining research programmes. The existing heuristic rules are challenged. The challenge within organisation theory can be observed by comparing the papers given at the annual meetings of the American Academy of Management over the past two decades and noting the growth of new sections (e.g. critical theory). Another indicator is the increasing attention to the theorising of Karl Weick (1979, 1995), who although never marginalised was until the 1990s more honoured in the footnotes than followed in the core of the discourse (Czarniawska, 1998). In strategy the heuristic rules were initially defined through the conferences and publications convened by Hofer and Schendel (1978). Revising those rules was signalled in the late 1980s with major reviews later published in various forms by Rumelt *et al.* (1991).

Third, existing approaches to organisation design do not provide adequately for the execution of strategy and do not possess an adequate theory of knowledge utilisation (Clark 1972, 1975a). There are problems of transforming existing forms of organising and of establishing the desired forms. Despite heavy citation of Burns and Stalker (1961) there has been a gross simplification of the processes of innovation and of exnovation and although the issues of organisational inertia and environmental selection are well known their incorporation is problematic. Consequently there is too little attention to how the actions of senior executives are constrained by the degrees of freedom inherent in pre-existing processes and emergence. The guiding principles that dominated organisation theory and organisation design are being displaced and replaced, but are still evident.

THEORISING ORTHODOX ORGANISATION DESIGN

Boulding's simple/complex taxonomy of systems

All research programmes in organisation theory claim to adopt an open system approach, yet few programmes deliver on the fulsome account of open systems as event cycles proposed by Katz and Kahn (1966). The early research programmes adopted system models of tightly connected elements coupled into specific time-space trajectories and tracks. The tendency of organisation theory towards simple system analogies during its formative positivistic-modern period can be illustrated from Boulding's (1956: 89–94) taxonomy with a nine-level hierarchy of system in which the simplest system is a list or a framework and the most complex systems are human and social systems. The Boulding taxonomy can be recast in three levels.

The basic third included the use of lists, frameworks and typologies as the simplest level with clockwork and the thermostat because they control low complexity in the feedback process. Even so, the analogy of clockwork and the thermostat still provides a powerful framework to part of the orthodox approach in the discipline of organisation behaviour. The clock is a simple moving system and the thermostat differs in degree because it provides the user with the capacity to reset a complex pattern. An analogy which is unlike the firm, but is frequently implied to provide an image of corporate control is the swimming pool robot cleaner. Swimmers prefer pools to be free from infectious elements and from detritus such as dead insects and leaves. The former is handled through injections of chemicals into the waterflow and the latter by the robot cleaner. The robot cleaner is programmed to operate in defined parameters by the servomechanism embodied in the equipment. The user defines the parameters so that the robot ·operates when the pool is not being used. The robot travels across the surface in a defined zigzag pattern slowly covering the whole pool. It possesses various appendages operating like the tentacles of an octopus and sweeping the debris along the carefully concaved bottom of the pool to a central area from which the rubbish is drawn out and sent away. The robot can be used with swimmers in the water and will persist in its pattern unless that pattern is altered from the central control panel. Under most conditions the robot cleans the pool very effectively. It does so with a minimum of costly human labour. The cost is in the design. The models of control in organisation theory and in strategy have unintentionally drawn from the analogy with the swimming pool robot and thereby implied that management has key capacities to manipulate situations.

The middle third introduces systems that are increasingly open, yet close to servomechanisms. Richardson (1991) suggests that two streams of system thinking – servomechanisms and cybernetics – have been influential in positioning the loop concept as one of most fundamental in strategy and organisation design. The servomechanism analogy fits neatly into this level of the framework while cybernetics provides an introduction into the upper third.

The upper third strongly rejects closed system analogies and espouses open system models, especially cybernetics, complexity theory and autopoeisis. Among the more cybernetic models, the theory of requisite theory and its replacement of feedback by anticipation provides a significant shift towards models more analogous with social processes (Richardson 1991). In the cybernetic models the guidance and steering process is by management, albeit with the romantic assumption that strategic choice can be equated with total degrees of freedom. The third segment is the agenda for theorists of the open system taking up the challenge given by Buckley (1967).

Boulding's typology suggests that few of the system models used in organisation theory and strategy are analogous with complex organisational and contextual interactions and processes that we all agree surround us. Therefore there is a serious gap between the heritage of systems models in organisation theory and the requirements for a neo-modern political economy. Early systems models were very simplistic and assumed the tight, non-interactive coupling of the sub-systems (Burns 1966; Buckley 1967) and implied too much control for the designer (Boguslaw 1966). Subtle research programmes had been formulated (Lockwood 1964; Buckley 1967; Weick 1979), but these were honoured more in the covering footnotes than in the images and metaphors of organising. Later systems models sought to move away from the analogy of the servomechanism and towards the concern of cybernetic theory with the anticipation of future states (Richardson 1991). Managerial cybernetics produced models that were claimed to be capable of providing actionable understanding of social entities ranging from the firm to the reorganisation of a nation's economy (e.g. Beer).

Codified, explicit knowledge rules

The design of organisational systems was an explicit objective for research and for the development of normative theories in the late 1950s and 1960s leading to seminal books (e.g. March and Simon 1958; Thompson 1967) and symposia, especially the Pittsburgh conferences, proclaiming the possibility of organisation design and gradually providing examples of application. Normative theories set out the ideal design given the measurement of key features of a situation. The situation to be designed might refer to an actual firm or to an intended firm at a time in the future or to both. Early organisation theory possessed attributes which are currently being revised and rejected, yet are still influential (e.g. Donaldson 1996). Many of the original themes persist and influence contemporary thinking. The four key attributes are as follows.

First, the aim is to be able to produce organisation designs around those variables that combine access to intervention with high significance. The reasoning through which this is undertaken has been based upon an eclectic admixture of empirical regularities (e.g. Aston Programme) and abstracted models (e.g. Thompson 1967). It was presumed that research had identified *causal laws*. Knowledge, is made explicit in the form of *codified frameworks*. The law-like knowledge implies that firms whose organisation deviates from the most satisfactory design will experience excessive costs of operating and will therefore be selected out in an evolutionary process (Galbraith 1977; Aldrich 1979). This evolutionary dimension challenges the dominant elites within firms to anticipate future dangers and develop collective action through new organisation designs. The causal propositions suggest that there should be and is a deterministic kind of knowledge which they can use to design the firm. Although these propositions are intended to be an open system approach, it is similar to those posited in closed system thinking (Harre 1979; Sayer 1992). So, the role of the organisation designer is analogous to that of the designer of domestic swimming pools in warm climates. The pool can have certain attributes according to the capacity of the householder to pay. One attribute is keeping the pool fresh and free from debris. This can be achieved by having a programmed power source which creates a water flow and periodically sends the robot cleaner on a predetermined time-space pattern which criss-crosses the pool. The robot cleaner has tentacles which swish debris (leaves, dead insects) down the concave slopes into a central collecting area hidden beneath a cover. The programme is set to cope with local conditions and the owner's preferences. The pool and the robot are co-designed so that the robot does not get stuck behind obstacles such as entry/exit ladders. In an analogous way it assumed that the chosen organisation designs will work in practice.

Second, the scope of the analytic frameworks is tightly focused inside the firm and on the firm's position in a narrowly circumscribed environment. The intra-organisation focus is reflected in the attention to how managers control non-managers through analysing the external environment, through leadership, motivation, job design, selection and claims about strategic human resource management (Purcell and Arhlstrand 1994; Townley 1994; Legge 1995). The external environment is very significant, yet can be defined by measuring the degree of uncertainty, complexity and dependence upon external sources of resources (e.g. Daft 1997). Variations in the environment necessitate adaptive change of the organisation design. The aim of the designer should be to co-align the organisation design with the environment in which the firm should be situated. Because the normative theory focuses on those variables which are manipulable and important there are many dimensions which are not controllable and therefore tend to be neglected. Hence the attention paid to the nearby task environment rather than analysing the contexts in which rivals are developing.

Third, time is dealt with in a idealist linear form and spatial aspects of activities are generally omitted. The history of firms and their pre-existing capacities have been conflated to an over-stylised, token history indicated by locating key moments on a calendrical scale. Firms seem to be able frictionlessly to change their forms as they progress in the theory of the organisation life cycle. There is only a very slight analysis of time-space configurations and of activity patterns (Stinchcombe 1968: Chapter 6).

Fourth, organisation design is treated as matter of evaluating the existing organisation and recommending a blueprint of the ideal solution. Galbraith (1977), perhaps the most thoughtful contributor to designing, suggests that many alternatives designs should be generated and assessed. Frequently only one design is suggested. These attributes intermingle with the way in which the firm is defined.

Definitions of the firm

One of the clearest definitions of the firm in organisation theory is by Daft (1997: 22) in the neo-rational contingency approach to organisation design which presumes that the capitalist system of property rights and ownership provides the background assumptions. The six defining features are:

1   Firms are *legally recognised entities subject to national regulations about governability and the auditing of performance.* The position of the public and private firm is well known. The not-for-profit firm is normally expected to avoid losses and may be required to produce defined rates of return on its assets. For example, the British state introduced trust status for the publicly owned hospital system in which each trust was required to earn a return on its assets and to develop prices for its services. It was required to provide those services at average cost, thereby creating a potential market. Firms possess legal definitions of the domain of activities which have been registered. There are sets of regulations derived from the role of the state.
2   *External stakeholders* are implicated in the firm in varying activities and functions.
3   The directors of the firm and top management are expected to translate the legal definition of the domain of activities of the firm into *strategic and organisational goals* which are carried out within and across the boundaries of the firm.
4   The directors and senior management are expected deliberately *to structure activities within the firm* in order to achieve the strategic and operational goals. This will include the organisational and human aspects. The structuring of activities by specialists in the technostructure is a major feature (e.g. Thompson 1967). There will be systems of authority including hierarchy, definition of roles, reporting relationships and governance. Also, structuring will normally give massive attention to the time-space flows and processes. These structuring activities were once considered to be the sole province of engineers. Their varied roles (e.g. chemical engineers, industrial engineers) are still extensive, yet have been extended to include a plurality of specialists within firms and from external agencies (e.g. consultants).
5   The *boundary of the firm* is a key area of managerial concern along many dimensions. The boundary is defined as permeable in open system theory and is obviously open, yet monitored and there are attempts to control action at the boundaries. Thompson's (1967) theorising is directed at the problem of controlling the boundary and the interface with the external context.
6   The firm is usually differentiated in ways which require analysis, but three levels of qualitative difference in managerial action have to be acknowledged: *institutional, managerial, technical* (Parsons 1956; Scott 1995). The institutional level of the firm's board and the vice presidents is typically involved in

handling the issues of legitimacy, of political lobbying to protect the interests of the firm and of providing the governance structure. At this level strategy is about directions (Grant 1995). The managerial level relates the firm to its immediate task environment and the dependencies upon suppliers and customers (Thompson 1967). The technical level refers to offices, shops, hospital theatres, schools and similar.

These features view the firm from a unitarist, managerial perspective with respect to the structuring of activities and the firms' boundary while seeing the goals of the firm as deriving from the exigencies of the capitalist system of ownership. The definition may be compared with that of economic sociologist in Chapter 5. Daft's definition of the firm in strategy and organisation design interprets management's role as a global agent of capital. Therefore management and the dominant groupings establish the goals and shape the activities. Hence, the reference to goals has to be understood in these terms (cf. Silverman 1970). This kind of definition is not a politically neutral perspective because there is not a social contract between the different strata and the various stakeholders (Thompson and McHugh 1995: 15, 125). Also the definition does not highlight the dynamics and complexities of managerial action (Reed 1992: 182f).

Uncertainty and rationality

Organisations in action: J. D. Thompson (1967)

J. D. Thompson's short book (1967) has been highly influential upon the rational approach (e.g. J. R. Galbraith 1977). The question being asked is: what determines how and when organisations should act rationally? Thompson (1967) provided a conceptual inventory and some potentially significant propositions derived from a variety of sources: theoretical (e.g. Parsons, March and Simon, Barnard) and conceptual (e.g. Perrow) case studies. The conceptual inventory was designed to locate patterns in organisational phenomena. Thompson's approach departed from the empiricism of that time and also from inventories of propositions.

Prior theorising and research had established the distinction between open and closed systems and suggested that the capacity of management to plan and control was dependent upon its expectations of uncertainty. Was it possible to link the concept of rational action with variations in uncertainty, or was rationality tied to closed system thinking? The problem is that so far there are no concepts which permit thinking simultaneously about rationality and indeterminateness (1967: 16). Thompson sought to show that the closed/open system dilemma might be resolved by examining organisations as problem facing and problem solving. This is suggested in the approach of Simon, March and Cyert that distinguishes between deciding (routine situations) from searching and learning (novel situations).

A first step is to recognise organisations that exhibit three distinct levels of responsibility and control: institutional, managerial and technical (Parsons 1960). There are two points of articulation between them and each level is different so that there are qualitative breaks. The institutional level embraces all three levels and locates the organisation in the institutional webs and external agencies which raise issues of legitimacy. The managerial level administers and services the technical sub-organisation by procuring resources necessary to the functioning of the technical level and by mediating between the technical level and the users of its outputs. The technical level – the technical core – is focused around the exigencies imposed by the task and materials being processed. The technical level in the school is that occupied by the teachers and the kinds of co-operation they require to meet the demands placed upon the organisation. Complex organisations possess these three distinct levels with dynamic properties.

How do we conceptualise complex organisations characterised by dynamic properties and with three distinct levels as an open system subject to the criteria of rationality? Thompson introduces a simple, complex solution: the criteria of rationality can be approached by removing as much uncertainty as possible from the technical core. Management can handle resource acquisition and output disposal for the technical core, but cannot protect the institutional level which is most like an open system facing uncertainty. The managerial level can however mediate to reduce external uncertainties while pressuring the technical core to modify its actions when external conditions are shifting. In this way it is feasible to conceptualise the organisation as an open system faced with uncertainty and subject to the criteria of rationality and therefore needing to establish certainty.

Thompson now turns to conceptualising variations in technology by identifying three main patterns of interdependence in between the sub-units of the technical core. First, the units may be linked together through serial, sequential linkages: the long-linked technology. Second, there are technologies which provide extensive standardised ways of linking actors and activities (e.g. borrowers and lenders in a bank). Standardisation ensures each segment operates in compatible ways, possibly through systems of categories and impersonal rules. This is the mediating technology. Third is the situation where there is high interactive feedback of a somewhat customised way: the intensive technology.

Organisation rationality will involve the protection of core technologies from external disturbances, possibly by inserting buffers at the input and output areas. This can include the use of specialists to anticipate and smooth work flows and/or by various forms of quota and rationing. Otherwise the institutional and managerial levels will seek to anticipate altering innovations and devise actions to ease their introduction.

Rationality can be enhanced by the approach to the external context. This includes establishing the external domain which is serviced. Health agencies define the diseases covered, the population served and the services provided. The firm should define its task environment to be tightly focused upon those immediate parts relevant to goal setting and formation (Dill 1958). The domain surrounds the focal organisation as a set analogous to the role set (Merton 1957; Blau and Scott 1961). Organisations should aim to create consensus within their domain as part of handling uncertainty. The external task environment shapes the power of the organisation and hence the extent to which the focal organisation is politically dependent upon other organisations. The pursuit of rationality involves the focal organisation reducing dependence by developing alternatives and by seeking prestige from the context. Acquiring power involves a variety of co-operative strategies (e.g. co-opting). Rational norms require the firm that is constrained to attempt to exercise power in those areas not constrained.

Under norms of rationality organisations seek to bound activities in the task environment which are crucial contingencies. In the case of long linked technologies this protection will lead to vertical integration.

The structuring of activities is a major managerial activity. A contrast may be drawn between the temporary (synthetic) organisation which arises to handle exceptional events such as disasters and the norms of rationality for handling co-ordination and interdependence in the permanent organisation. Thompson incorporates the established distinction between co-ordination by predesigned plan (routine situations) and co-ordination by mutual feedback (non-routine) developed by March and Simon (1958). Under norms of rationality organisations aim to minimise co-ordination costs.[1] Structural sub-divisions are established to reduce the complexity of co-ordination.

Norms of rationality set out the role of structures which span the boundary of the organisation thereby interfacing the external and internal environments. Their roles vary according to the characteristics of the task environment along three variables: homogeneous/heterogeneous, stable/rapidly shifting, unified/segmented. Some environments will be highly complex scoring high on heterogeneous, rapidly shifting and segmentedness. There are many constraints and norms of rationality which indicate that internal organisation should sacrifice sub-unit specialisation to the greater self-containment of separate programmes (as March and Simon 1958: 159).

Figure 3.1 makes the design rules explicit. There are two routes downward towards organisational performance. The left-hand route commences with the degree of environmental certainty (5) based on the state of the four variables (1–4). In this case there is high certainty in the environment, therefore there is formality of structure (6) and problems are resolved by monitoring rather than reacting (7). Workers can be of lowish skill (8). The degree of reciprocal interdependence (9) will be low and reinforce the formality of structure (6) and co-ordination by rules (10) thereby increasing the emphasis upon communication (11). The intensity of interdependence (12) reinforces the formality of structure (6), permits firm priorities between departments to be established (13) and requires particular forms of grouping (14). The route leads into good organisational performance (15). The right-hand route also leads into good organisational performance, but commences with the protective role of boundary units at the inbound and outbound areas of the boundary (16). Their strong protective role derived from the left-hand route gives those boundary units formality of structure (17) and high efficiency (18), thus supporting high organisational performance (15). Also, the boundary units create certainty for the technical core (19) and sustain the formality of its structure (20).

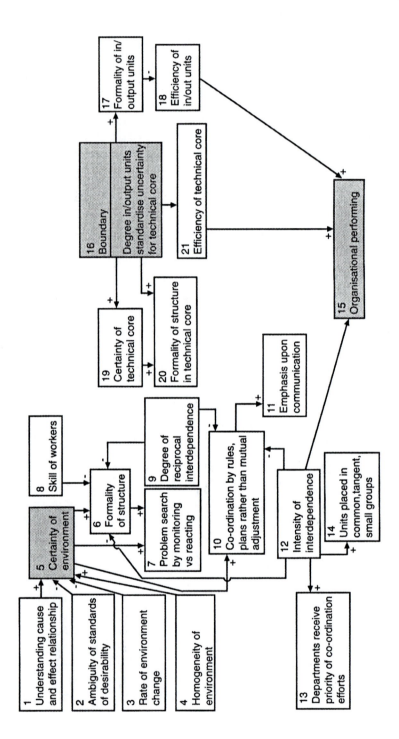

Figure 3.1 Design rules
Source: Derived from the Cape Cod Conference, 1967, attributed to G. D. Bell.

The role of the boundary units ensures the rational efficiency of the core (21) and good organisational performance.

This is one view of organisations in action.

Prioritising structure over process

The distinction between the structure and its processes was widely accepted from the 1950s onward (e.g. Blau and Scott 1961) and sat easily in the first decade of publications from the *Administrative Science Quarterly* (*ASQ*). Then, during the 1960s, the prioritising of structure over process was established. From then on the *ASQ* became one of many key journals which questioned the scientific status of studying events through time in small samples by single case studies. The position of the process school was vigorously promoted by the network of practitioner-theorists in enabling change programmes through organisation development, most notably Bennis (1966). Also, the forum of scholars defined as being in organisation studies was much more processual and gave leadership to key issues, especially in the study of symbolism (e.g. Czarnawskia). However, and despite Weick's (1979) implicit critique of size as a confounded variable, the process perspective was talked to the edge of the stage. Hall (1972) elegantly constructed the new script by explaining that the unfolding of processes constituted enduring forms which possessed stable structural features. Therefore, the study of processes should be left until the study of structure had been completed (Pugh and Hickson 1976: 1).

The structure priority favours studies which are synchronous, cross-sectional, extensive research designs with large populations versus longitudinal case studies (Sayer 1992). It was the members of the Aston School (Hage 1998) who gave impetus to the prioritising of structure. Pugh and Hickson (1976) expressed the argument very clearly when they observed that the temporal dimension is flux (cf. Clark 1985). They argued that their positivist operationalisation of the dimensions of structure through scales with known reliabilities and applicabilty in any context provided stable, replicable accounts of action in relation to independent, contextual variables within the firm (e.g. size) and in its relationship to external resource linkages (e.g. suppliers and customers). The scales of organisational variables created by the Aston School also demonstrated that the structure of the firm could be measured without aggregating the individual scores based on questionnaires promoted by the Institute for Social Research, Ann Arbor, Michigan. In practice the major consumers of the Aston Programme were not their European colleagues, but more their American cousins. The influence of their approach can be readily observed as underpinning the top selling textbook on organisation theory and design by Daft (1997).

It is convenient briefly to note the main features of approach by the Aston Programme and later Donaldson (1996). They argued that insufficient attention had been given to testing the generalisations being made about how various organisational characteristics cohered and covaried. Consequently, they observed, these generalisations could be utilised to design organisations. Their targets were both the many single case studies, yet also large-scale studies without statistical analysis, yet making law-like generalisations about which dimensions shaped structure (e.g. Woodward 1958). Their aim became to develop universal scales for examining the structure of the firm and the context of the structure within the firm and with respect to the input–output dependencies on resources. In order to construct the scales they drew a distinction between the stable, enduring features of organisation – the structure – and those features which were variable – the process (Pugh and Hickson 1976: 1). It has proved easier to describe certain stable, enduring features of organisations such as the degree to which decisions are centralised or decentralised.

In the 1960s Pugh, Hickson, Hinings and colleagues in Birmingham, England, were pioneers and central players in establishing an analytic principle which shaped approaches to organisational dynamics for a long period. The analytic principle introduced a distinction between structure and process and a parallel distinction between methods which were statistical variance from case study methods. Thus structure was equated with variance analysis and process with case studies. They argued, with skill and conviction, that most progress could be made by applying statistical analysis of variance to the study of structure and its context. By skilfully enrolling the early, slow and overly linear capabilities of early data processing in the computer they were able to mobilise their claim for an 'empirical theory' of structure (Pugh and Hickson 1976). Two largish samples (n = 52 and n = 92) were analysed to show that organisational units of vastly differing kinds could be described on the same scales and that many of the dimensions co-varied with increasing size of the unit. Size was measured in terms of employees, sales and similar features.

This was not a trivial discovery. The discovery and its seeming replication in an array of small-scale studies (e.g. n = 9, n = 23) undertaken around the world was impressive. It seemed that similar connections between the core features of structure could be found in the USA, Canada, Israel, China and so on. Hickson generalised these results and claimed that structures were very similar irrespective of the national context (Lammers and Hickson 1979). The impact of this definition of structure shaped the subject matter and fundamental questions regarded as worth pursuing, especially in North American accounts of organisation theory and how to design organisations. We should note that a major rhetoric was the promise of an 'empirical theory' of structure and this was given priority over exploring process, dynamics and 'in action'.

Studying process and dynamics tended to be equally concerned to examine intra-organisational dynamics (Dalton 1959; Pettigrew 1973). The study of managers might have been more dynamic, but most studies abstracted managerial work from even its immediate context (e.g. Mintzberg). The problems of planned organisational change were approached through multi-stage models of how to change the organisation. Theories of change tended to give the impression that organisations had largely unlimited capacities for re-adaptation to changing circumstances. One of the most respected studies was Crozier's (1964, 1973) description and explanation of the forms and inertial capacities of French public agencies such as the state-owned cigarette factories. The account of the relationships in public bureaucracies was in terms of how collective action was pursued through strategies which were so embracing that configurations of conflict and association surrounding zones of uncertainty remained in place for long periods: several decades. The specific features were attributed to tendencies in France. This approach differed sharply from the one advocated by Pugh, Hickson and Hinings. However, although the approach was frequently honoured, most notably by Silverman (1970), there were few attempts at development (Crozier and Frieberg 1980) or towards comparison (Clark 1979). Yet, more than any other analyst, Crozier explored the underlying generative mechanisms which shaped particular configurations and boldly sought to define their consequences for action.

Prioritising strategy before organisation design

The disciplines of strategy and organisation design have been connected through the proposition attributed to Chandler (1962) that 'strategy determines structure'. The broad relationships between strategy and organisation design are expressed schematically in the four linear steps as displayed in Figure 3.2. The four linear steps are:

- analysis of the environment;
- strategy formulation (see Schendel and Hofer 1978);
- organisation design is the execution of the strategic plan through choice of structure;
- the desired performance is expected to occur.

The top line shows how strategy and organisation might be combined while the second and third lines illustrate some differences of emphasis within the overall priorities according to whether economic organisation or sociology perspectives predominate. Strategy and organisation design possess a strong linear ordering and also tended (less so now) to start from the outside with environmental analysis and then move inside. Their approaches to environmental analysis are different and complementary. The construction of corporate level strategies is more strongly developed in strategy, but that approach tends to leave the next stage to organisation design. Each approach presumes that a favourable performance is likely outcome.

Figure 3.2 does reveal the underlying tendencies, yet oversimplifies. For example, in strategy the seminal contribution of Hofer and Schendel (1978) included negative feedback loops and in an important footnote mentioned the iterative, convoluted nature of decision-making and the impact of political factors. Also, there is widespread acceptance that the intended strategy may be transformed into an emergent strategy which also includes chance impacts and unintended directions. Mintzberg (1990) suggests how the emergent aspects of strategic action might be noticed, recorded and incorporated. Representing strategy by a single author is complex, especially since the theoretical review by Rumelt *et al.* (1991).

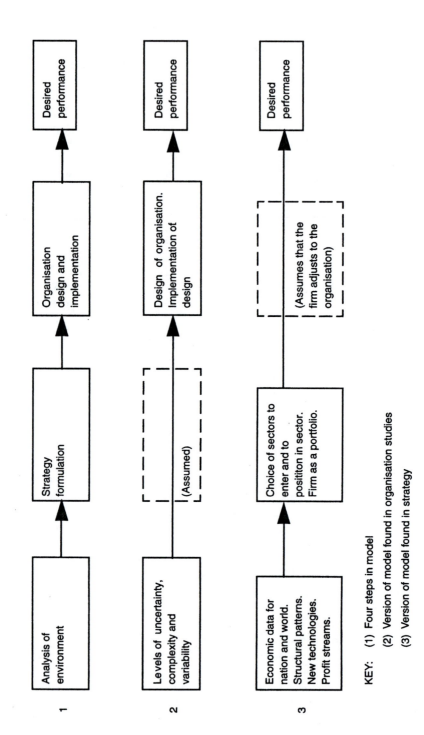

1

| Analysis of environment | → | Strategy formulation | → | Organisation design and implementation | → | Desired performance |

2

| Levels of uncertainty, complexity and variability | → | (Assumed) | → | Design of organisation. Implementation of design | → | Desired performance |

3

| Economic data for nation and world. Structural patterns. New technologies. Profit streams. | → | Choice of sectors to enter and to position in sector. Firm as a portfolio. | → | (Assumes that the firm adjusts to the organisation) | → | Desired performance |

KEY: (1) Four steps in model

(2) Version of model found in organisation studies

(3) Version of model found in strategy

Figure 3.2 Neo-rational, linear model of performance

There are many similar statements setting out the normative theory of organisation design (e.g. Daft 1997), yet few match Jay Galbraith's (1977) awareness that the theory and practice of design ought to include the generation of multiple alternative designs for the same situation.

The problems of using the design theories have been addressed in three quite different ways. First, some design texts concentrate solely upon the thinking necessary to develop ideal, abstract models based on the theories. Second, many texts provide the basis for developing ideal models and observe that there is likely to be a gap between actual design and the required design. It is then assumed that the gap can be tackled through some form of organisational change and this is usually referred to as implementation. Third, there are those who contend that design theory does not provide sufficient basis for application and that both organisation change theory and implementation approaches lack a practical account of what can be achieved (Clark 1972, 1975a). An essential requirement of any approach to designing future organisational systems would always assume that the dynamics of the pre-existing context–firm relationships had to be investigated and then consideration given to the degree to which alteration was likely and the means to be employed (Clark 1972).

Contingency: mechanistic and organic systems

The contribution of Burns and Stalker's (1961) seminal analysis of management organisation under varying conditions, *The Management of Innovation,* provides a key exemplar of how the contingency perspective has been used to promote an image of organisation design. Their analyses reveal the dilemma between efficiency and innovation (Abernathy 1978). It is vital to observe that forty years ago they sought to answer a very specific, practical question and one central to the neo-modern political economy. The question was: could the Scottish electronics industry move from government protection in the defence industry into the competitive market for computers and consumer durables? This section concentrates upon showing how in organisation theory the institutional analysis of Burns and Stalker, which occupies the majority of the text, has been eliminated from the retention systems (as Weick 1969) of the knowledge community known as organisation behaviour. What has been extracted, compacted and retained is a very narrow point of view. Organisation theorists and design rulers only focused upon the very well known continuum of mechanistic management system and organic management system (Burns and Stalker 1961: 119–125).

In his early research Burns questioned the classic theories of organisation that recommend universal solutions (e.g. Fayol). He also rejected the general checklists (e.g. Urwick Orr) that ignored the institutional and national context and content of managerial work. Burns rejected the applicability of universal generalisations to all situations for two reasons.

First, they were well aware of the new theories of the firm by Herbert Simon and the cybernetic school of Ashby's (1956) Law of Requisite Variety within the overall development of systems theories. They became sceptical of general system theories which depicted the position of management as analogous to a system whose own systems should and could vary according to the complexity of information to be ingested and transformed into action (Burns 1966). They recognised that management systems did vary from field studies of different firms where they observed widespread variations in managerial work, especially its systematic features, yet varied forms seemed to possess their own situational logics. Also, in their neo-rational modality they speculated that managements operating in market contexts with low rates of novelty could be successful by being centralised, formalised and hierarchical, while those managing in contexts of invention and innovation could be successful when they adopted forms which were network, conversational and with horizontally hierarchised relations were also successful. Their theorising paralleled and complemented the distinction between routine and non-routine decision-making advanced by March and Simon (1958).

Second, Burns and Stalker certainly contributed to the making of the contingency perspective as one form of normative theory. However, they sought to demonstrate that the utopian application of design rules was extremely problematic. Thereby they anticipated the issue of strategic choice by showing how preexisting zones of manoeuvre and corporate politics constrained the notion of design choice. Their analysis also introduced elements of the realist turn. Their reasoning asked whether the ideal solution could be introduced in practice. Their analysis of the Scottish question (see earlier) is instructive. It suggested that there were many, virtually impenetrable barriers. The evidence of the last four decades apparently confirms their assessment. It may be noted that there was little sense of history being otherwise (see Ferguson 1997). Burns and Stalker answered their question by scoping the history of institutions concerned with science in Britain, especially the ways in which status and career systems promoted a form of possessive individualism: the search for well-paid autonomy. They concluded that this search was characteristic of the British and that this feature of Britishness penetrated the British firm where its tendencies challenged the capacity of the firm to co-ordinate and control the discretion of its knowledge workers. They did not preclude the positive outcome because their case study of a textile firm was within the scientific sector and its shopfloor work organisation was a major site for work study (Clark 1987, 1991). However, in their detailed reflections they considered that the requirement for a consumer-oriented electronic industry to possess features of the organic and be profitable in a world market were certainly challenging. The forms of organisation actually found in England and Scotland represented very British solutions – so much so that the likelihood of transformation was questioned.

We simply need to note that their interpretation of contingency design rules requires that they are matched to the dynamic, contingent specificities (Clark and Staunton 1989) and not presumed to be a grand narrative.

In addition to their theory they revealed that firms face a dilemma between being oriented to efficiency or to innovation. This dilemma became central to Abernathy's (1978) analysis of the long-term adaptations of Ford to changing market variability. Also, the dilemma, although never mentioned, is central to Thompson's (1967) theory of uncertainty and rationality.

Technology and social technology framework

The distinction between routine and non-routine task activities was central to the Carnegie School's cognitive, knowledge-based and behavioural theory of organisation. Routines, and their variations in complexity, were introduced in March and Simon (1958), absorbed into the behavioural theory of the firm (Cyert and March 1963) and into the evolutionary theory of the firm (Nelson and Winter 1982). The implication was that some departments and hence firms might be characterised by routine tasks (e.g. canmaking) while others would have many non-routine tasks. This distinction was used powerfully by Perrow (1967). His theory of social technology reasoned that the strategic goals of the organisation articulated both the firms intentions and also expressed its remit as defined by external stakeholders. Therefore, in the effective organisation there should be a causal connection between the tasks undertaken at the departmental level and the strategic goals. Perrow's theorising anticipates later claims that embodied technologies are the social made durable (Clark 1987; Bijker *et al.* 1987; Grint and Woolgar 1998).

Organisation life cycle models

The aim of organisation life theory is to invoke the analogy of the life cycle starting with birth, leading into the stages of growth (e.g. mature) and ending in death, while making generous, utopian offers for remission, transplants and escape. Past research on the founding of new organisations shows that, so far, only a small proportion reach their tenth year and only a small proportion of these expand from the location of origin in a particular region to being multi-site over many regions and nations. The well-known large organisations are not only the survivors, but have the exceptional feature of having expanded in products, employment, revenue and so on. These experiences of corporate failure and growth are the everyday material for financial journalism and for best-selling books.

Lievegoede (1973), who was working in an institute specialising in growth problems for children, foresaw the opportunities of applying similar categories of problem to organisations. The best known typology is that of Griener (1972). Child and Kieser (1981) provide a neatly theorised account, but the major aim of the organisation life cycle is to provide a performative account that stylises problems and solutions. The depiction of the typology has been an exemplar of modern semiology while also being modified to incorporate recent experiences such as downsizing (e.g. Daft 1997: 182–183). I shall avoid presenting this piece of iconography in the hope that it will induce critical insight. There are pretty strong connections between the organisation life cycle model and the role of advising consultants.

The basic model takes the form of a left-right linear time line from founding to maturity and beyond. Situated along the time line are a series of snapshots of stylised blueprint organisation designs each appropriate to different conditions. The snapshot blueprints are informed by extensive research, including the research on size as a variable (Child and Kieser 1981). The Aston Programme shows that as size increases, so does formalisation and decentralisation (Pugh and Hickson 1976). The number of blueprints of ideal organisations varies. A typical profile depicts five or more possible blueprints. In the spaces along the line and between the blueprints are gaps filled with design rules for action. These action points are usually drawn from change theories (see Hatch 1997: Chapter 12).

In the organisation life cycle the external context of the firm is minimally dealt with and there is barely a mention of the problem of competition between contexts. In most respects the organisation life cycle embodies the modernist values of linearity, order, control, expert knowledge and utopian solutions. Hatch (1997) contends that the organisation life cycle is a clear example of introducing the dynamic into a previously static organisation theory. Equally, it may be observed that these dynamics are deceptive (Clark 1975a; Clark and Staunton 1989: Figure 2.1; Wilson 1992). The organisation life cycle mainly suggests success and there are few failures.

Structuration and actors' frame of reference

This section addresses the position of Giddens's (1979, 1981, 1984) theory of structuration and Silverman's (1970) theory of the actors' frame of reference in organisation theory. There are two issues:

- the choice of analytic unit – individual or system?
- a sociological relational theory embracing actors' definitions and structures.

Organisation theory was originally constructed by March and Simon (1958) around the notion of individuals being located within positions, relations and role sets inside organisations. The individuals acquire subjectively rational organisational cognitions from the organisations which they inhabit in the everyday work. The subjective cognitions differ markedly from the objective imperatives of neo-classical economics. Organisations are theorised as having structures and that those structures are, as it were, a mosaic of performance programmes waiting to be activated. The individuals in the organisation theory of March and Simon seem to be close to developing their own actors' frame of reference (Bannister and Franscella 1971) and seem to be enacting their environment (as Weick 1969). The point of view of March and Simon has evolved in organisation economics while retaining its essential features. Theirs is the dominant view in organisation theory and is embodied in Galbraith's (1977) theory of design.

An alternative view comes from the sociological perspectives and starts from the rejection of the individual/structure dichotomy of the positivist era (Giddens

1974) and the introduction of the notion of the actors' frame of reference (Silverman 1970).

Minimal analysis of the international political economy

Organisation theory was constructed to be free from the ties of place and specific locations were transformed into sites for application of the design rules. Although the design rules gave a heavy weight to the contingent matching of the states of various sectors in the environment of the firm to the internal design, there was only slight attention to national features. The modern influence on the sedimented collection of design rules meant that the implicit role model was the USA and there was an assumption that world best practice emerged in that 'advanced laboratory' and was then diffused through consultants around the globe. Hence, the historical studies of Chandler (1962, 1977, 1990), provided accounts of a stream of US organisational innovations commencing with the multi-divisional form. This viewpoint dominated theorising until the rise of serious international competition from Japan and Germany. From a US perspective the issue was to design organisations for the domestic scene and then introduce adaptations for operating abroad. The problems that this form of knowledge construction introduced for non-American organisations was in the margins of the discourse of organisation theory. Hence there was minimal analysis of British, German, Japanese, Italian, French (and so on) national characteristics. The exceptions were Crozier's (1964) claim that French cultural and structural features led to distinctly French forms of organising.

Although Hofstede's (1980) seminal study demonstrated the presence of national differences within IBM, it was not until Porter's (1990) contention that there is 'competition between contexts' that the issue of the international political economy began to enter the script of organisation theory. Even then, the theme of competition between contexts was added in at the end of the discourse rather than situated in the opening scenes. My contention is that organisation theory should deal with the firm and context as co-evolution and this will be addressed in Part II.

Strategic choice and evolutionary principles

Some theorists have argued that organisation theory has been and still is a varied collection of design rules with the semblance of a single canon of truth, reality and progress (Reed 1992; Clegg *et al.* 1996). Child (1972) contended that organisation theory was a coherent, positivist and deterministic knowledge system that gave very small zones of choice to the senior managements involved in formulating strategy. Yet, he observed widespread deviations from the recommended design rules. Galbraith (1977) targets the gap between the actual and theoretical ideal as the contribution of the organisation theorist. According to Galbraith, any top management can choose to ignore the gap, but to do so persistently might lead the offending firm to be so inefficient in its processing of information that it will be forced to exit from the population. That belief informed my own design research and consultancy (e.g. Clark 1972). This evolutionary perspective, derived from D. T. Campbell (1965) underpins Weick (1969), Galbraith (1977) and Aldrich (1979). So, is there a special problem about strategic choice as Child suggests? Child's trenchant critique of determinism and tight system models of organisational variables can be viewed as part of the anti-modern turn noted in the previous chapter. Equally, his attention to open system models, including his review of Buckley (1967), can be read as an invitation in that direction and into the actors' frame of reference. That direction did not, however, prise open the possibility that there are firms and contexts which do not possess infinite zones of manoeuvre (Clark 1996).

KEY PROBLEMS FOR DESIGN RULES

Clark (1975) observes that key problems in organisation design arise from the theory of reality (ontology) and epistemology in the architecture of organisation theory. The normative theory exaggerates the practicality of existing designs and does not sufficiently analyse the possibilities of the existing situations to be transformed in the desired direction. Clegg *et al.* (1996) show in their *Handbook of Organisation Studies* that the orthodox approach in organisation theory through design rules embraces an extensive array of problems. Their contributors reveal the extensive critique from post-modern, realist, structuration and political economy perspectives. However, orthodox organisation theory has a strong modern-positivist heritage that is difficult to transform (Hatch 1997). Thirteen problems may be used to illustrate why a cluster of generative research programmes is required:

1   The analysis of the context ignores the theme of competition between contexts.
2   Organisation theory is ahistorical, linear with utopian future.
3   The definition of the firm relies on strong culture and controlled knowledge.
4   Pre-existing capacities and situations are often neglected.
5   Suppression of the innovation-efficiency dilemma.
6   Functionalism.
7   Static structure replaced by resource-based capabilities and knowledge.
8   Exclusion of dislocation, unplanned order and emergent features.
9   Too much voluntarism/agency.
10 Weak theory for the utilisation of knowledge.
11 The selection role of the context is highly significant.
12 Too little attention to self-referential autopoetic processes.
13 Time-space commodification, compression and embodiment.

These problems are briefly discussed and then developed in the following chapters.

First, in orthodox organisation theory the context of the firm is dealt with in a very narrow way relative to the analytic scope implied by the post-modern critique and the political economy perspective. Organisation theory has focused excessively inside the firm and taken a very thin slice from the external context. The narrow analytic scope has been largely informed by the perspective of structure, resource dependency, technology and task characteristics. There has been minimal examination of the meso levels. Although the national and global levels are mentioned, they are treated as being 'out there'. The consequences of global competitors inside a nation are considerable, yet rarely discussed (Porter 1990; Dunning 1993). Also, although increasing attention is given to structuration, symbolic and cognitive elements (see Hatch 1997), this tends to be within a modern perspective (e.g. strong cultures) and concentrated within the firm and its immediate context. The institutional social fields within a nation are treated as a distant feature rather than as an actor that penetrates the fabric and texture of the firm. The concern of the neo-modern political economy is almost totally neglected.

Second, organisation theory is often abstractly linear and largely ahistorical in its conception of time (Clark 1985; Clark and Staunton 1989: Figure 2.1). The abstract linearity is a time line without a periodised past or present, yet with a sense of progress from a bad situation to a good situation: the new utopia. Consequently the time line gives the past a quick, helicopter overview. In the main the time line imagines a utopian future when the blueprints are implemented, as illustrated earlier in Figure 3.1. This linearity provides an image of dynamics as in Thompson's 'organisations in action' while suppressing processes. The life cycle model has always been problematic (Penrose 1959; Abernathy 1978; Child and Kieser 1981), yet those models are deployed to provide the image of practical knowledge as in the organisation life cycle.

Third, the rational definition of the firm successfully presents the viewpoint of management though less so of the principals owning capital or of the non-owning stakeholders including non-managerial employees. We need to return to definitions of the firm similar to that proposed by Burns and Stalker and discussed in the penultimate section of the chapter.

Fourth, successful strategy depends in large part on how far the pre-existing capabilities of the firm can be stretched and leveraged into those forms required in the future (Clark 1975a). However, the design rules fail to reconstruct the pre-existing capacities and dynamics of the firm and even tend to presume a clean slate. The neglect of the pre-existing invalidates much of organisation design (Clark 1972, 1975a).

Fifth, there is suppression of the innovation-efficiency dilemma (Abernathy 1978) and so innovation is handled in a idealised manner (Clark and Staunton 1989). For example, in Thompson (1967) information uncertainty and norms of rationality remain a problem. The theoretically elegant solution of protecting the core from uncertainty has been overtaken by events such as just-in-time practices and the increasing elements of mass customisation. One of the reasons why 'risk' has become so significant is that the firm cannot buffer its core elements, except through the ownership of intellectual property rights. Frequently, readers and users are invited to imagine that organisation designs have unlimited capacities for being ambidextrous. A design rule is invented whereby the organisation control-lers can switch between a mechanistic management system for efficiency and an organic management system for innovation (e.g. Duncan 1972). If firms were ontologically similar to computer program there would be no problem. However, the capacity to be ambidextrous assumes a realist repertoire of different capacities that can be generatively activated and improvised (Clark 1975b). Therefore, purely logical or software-based rule systems do not provide an appropriate analogy for real organisations in action. It follows that attempts to combine design rules for managing the uncertainties of innovation created by the J. D. Thompson theory are overdetermined (cf. Spender and Kessler 1995).

Sixth, there is a strong tendency towards functionalist reasoning through the widely used notions of system needs. Functionalism tends to attribute an intelli-gence to systems. It is meaningless to separate capitalism and attribute needs to capitalism separate from the actions of groups of capitalists. Giddens (1981, 1984) criticises all varieties of functionalism because there cannot be a theoretically satisfactory explanation by attributing needs to a system. Contrary to discussions of the organisation mind, organisations do not think or have minds.

Seventh, the analytic priority of structure has been swept away by attention to the underlying mechanisms and processes from which the structure is eventually crystallised. Consequently, a large segment of the already constructed knowledge about structure has a limited use. Now, the analysis of the activities of the firm as processes is the major requirement. This includes developing an intellectual toolkit for analysing resources and capabilities (Grant 1995) and elements in the firm-specific knowledge (Clark and Staunton 1989; Spender 1996; Grant 1996; Nonaka and Takeuchi 1995).

Eighth, design rules give an impression of planned order and controlled devel-opment through feedback (e.g. Hofer and Schendel 1978). Consequently, the very great possibilities for dislocation are ignored (Holmer Nadeesan 1997). There is increasing awareness of unplanned order (Elias 1994). Porter (1990) introduces chance and indeterminacy as a central element in his theorising of competition between contexts, though this feature is more muted in the competitive advantage of the firm (Porter 1998). There is now considerable recognition, especially in strategic theory, that new situations can be emergent. Mintzberg (1994) observes that good strategic practice should actually discover and reflectively reveal emer-gent strategies to members of the firm because they may be unaware of their unfolding. Even so, the notions of dislocation, unplanned order and emergence jostle with a more rule-bound view of organising.

Ninth, the case against determinism made on behalf of strategic choice by Child (1972) was a powerful corrective, but as the later reflection clearly shows (Child 1997) the problem is that users of strategic choice ignored Child's caveats and underplayed the existence of zones of manoeuvre (Clark and Mueller 1995, 1996; Clark 1996).

Tenth, the previous paragraphs lead into the conclusion that the design rules form a rather problematic knowledge base for reinventing and re-cognitising the firm (Clark 1975a). There is a wide gap between these rules and the contents of programmatic change devised to improve organisational performance (Wilson 1992: Chapter 7). Research on knowledge utilisation highlights the interface between the explicit knowledge contained in design rules and situated, tacit knowing and expertise of knowledge communities in the organisation (Clark 1972; Nonaka and Takeuchi 1995; Boisot 1995, 1998).

Eleventh, organisation theory and also strategy tend to mention population ecologist models and their assumptions about environmental selection, yet fall far short of their analytic discussion by Whittington (1992a, b). We expect most product launches and many organisations to fail. The political economy approach gives competition between firms a central place. Competition between contexts is a development from within the theories of international business and these theories also emphasise environmental selection.

Twelfth, contemporary theorising replaces the dichotomy between stability/ change with theories of process that include inertia, recursiveness and autopoetic systems (see later).

Thirteenth, the embodiment of social relationships into time-space artefacts is ubiquitous in work organisation, widely understood in the political economy of neo-Marxian theories and yet totally ignored in organisation theory. It is as though the heritage of industrial engineering, the management sciences and operations research had been swept away. Organisation theory has a mindscape, but no landscape of actual buildings, clocks, transport systems, nations and similar. Hatch (1997) is an exception in her attention to space, yet even her analysis omits time and is sometimes awkward with temporality. The research programmes from the political economy perspective show how competition through markets has massive effects on the landscape and the urban setting (Harvey 1996). These effects are discussed in Chapter 6.

The critique of the (declining) cluster of research programmes within orthodox organisation theory and design is being displaced and replaced. There is now an array of alternative clusterings to research programmes. From that array it may be noted that there is a well-established cluster under the umbrella of radical organisation theory, critical management, critical theory. Also, though necessarily separately, the research programmes clustered around gender now occupy a salient position. The array also includes considerable variety (Clegg *et al.* 1996). However, the research programmes addressing and connecting the two themes of 'competition between contexts' and 'organisations in action' still require enrolment.

COMPLEXITY, REQUISITE VARIETY AND AUTOPOETIC SYSTEMS

Systems theories are the heartland of orthodox and much current organisation theory. Transforming the tight system models of the modern-positivist era has occupied the past three decades: for example, with Buckley's (1967) prising open of system connectivity and the distinction between tight and loose coupling. Boulding (1956) observed that moving beyond and above the lower third and mid-third of the taxonomy of systems analogies has been the objective of organisational analysis, but developing useful analytic frameworks is difficult. Within organisation theory several research programmes offer solutions to this problem. Cybernetic organisational management does not interface with the themes of either organisations in action or competition between contexts. However, Richardson's (1991) careful examination of system feedback models indicates the relevance and limits in organisational cybernetics. Therefore this final section in Chapter 3 notes three research programmes that certainly influence systems thinking within organisation theory:

- complexity theory;
- Ashby's law of requisite variety;
- autopoetic systems.

These research programmes provide a lexicon and language of categories and exemplars for theorising and managing complex organisational systems. Their scope embraces some of the positivist-modern research programmes (e.g. design rules; soft-system modelling). Complexity theory and cybernetic control models have and do influence upon the imagery of corporate control in organisational management. Analogies are dangerous, especially the attempt to describe social and organisational reality through non-social analogies. Yet that is partly what has happened with the interdiction of systems and control models into organisation theory and design (Buckley 1967). Cybernetic thinking occupies an important and complex position because there are significant differences between the early open systems approaches and the more recent theorising and uses of complexity theory.

First, complexity theory involves subtle revisions to orthodox notions of control over activities. Control may be defined as purposive influence towards an already determined goal (Beniger 1986: 39f). All controls are programmed through encoded information. The programming can be embedded in the social technologies (as Perrow 1967) of particular social groups as in the case of health professionals involved in the control of infectious diseases (see Chapter 14). Programming of coded information can also be embedded into raw materials through their design, into equipment and into the aesthetics of the material environment (Clark and Staunton 1989: Figure 3.1). Action is towards the constitution of a certain pattern of events as in the notion of recurrent action patterns, but with the insertion of instrumental rationality. The programme is coded with pre-arranged information steering actions towards the configuration. This programming does not require either the positivist notion of objective facts or the idealist notion of practical reason. The maintenance of control over the long-term depends upon the replication of recurrent action programmes in new organisational situations.

Programming requires fidelity of communication and the differential selection of messages (Beniger 1986: 65f). Understanding of programming has been disrupted by the preoccupation of cybernetics with feedback rather than programming decisions. After all it is the human user who controls the swimming pool robot and the robot is a simple example of what social constructionists mean by the social made durable (Bijker *et al.* 1987). In organisations we have examined the situation of those actors who maintain the mechanisms on which control depends and of those persons through whom the control mechanism is revised and retained (Weick 1969). There are therefore three levels of control and each possesses distinct temporal dimensions:

- the maintenance of the organisation in relation to the same contextual dynamics;
- adapting the programming to cope with variations in the contextual dynamics;
- observing actions and experimenting with actions that lead to alterations in the programming

Complexity theory claims to provide a significant elaboration of these dimensions.

The complexity perspective draws attention to the importance of past events in shaping the context and performance of an organisation. The organisation tends to take a particular journey and so the past and future trajectories need to be understood. This requirement might be inserted into the various approaches to knowledge management discussed in Chapter 14. Management can influence these trajectories, but can only rarely control them in a detailed way, yet we need to study the trajectories and notice when chance events enter. These situate pre-existing cycles in the capabilities of the context and the organisation and constitute the initial conditions for any new cycle. Both the organisation and the context possess high non-linearity and so there is an intricate admixture of order and disorder and of regularity and irregularity. In these situations small events might and can have importance because the dependence on initial conditions is sensitive. There is sensitive dependence in the new cycle on initial powers and liabilities. Moreover, for actors the understanding of the context and of events inside the organisation is impacted by imperfect information and by 'misjudgements' about consequences.

Complexity theory suggests two lines of thinking for organisational management. First, we need to note that pre-existing configurations of events, including those that embrace the organisation and its context, are held in place by the system attractors. The attractor leads patterns of repeated yet irregular performance and binds the system to a pattern of behaviour. There are difficulties in altering the role binding and role of attractors. Strange attractors entering the configuration can introduce multiple points of attraction that unbind the existing system. For example, the introduction of quasi-market into the British health system altered the configuration of relationships between those doctors who were situated in the hospitals from those who controlled the supply of patients. Alteration is possible, though interactive emergent effects may ensue and surprise those altering the programming.

Second, each organisation is a distinct system whose future emerges from a complex interplay of actions and reactions. Complex systems can be understood much more than controlled and their future tends to have a high degree of unknowability. So, although management perceives itself as having strategic choice of actions, there are consequences. Also, it is often difficult to anticipate the outcomes. Complexity theory claims to provide better mapping of processes and therefore to provide an actionable understanding through the finer calibration of situations, especially the role of attractors in binding and unbinding the existing configuration.

Ashby's (1956) theory and law of requisite variety is another way in which different levels of complexity can be considered. The law states that for a system to survive it must possess internal capacities and mechanisms to ingest and process information that match the level of complexity in the external context. This same principle is found in the contingent theorising about management systems in Burns and Stalker (1961). If systems are open and if, as proposed by the Law of Requisite Variety, the degree of variety in the external context should be matched by internal capacities to process variety in order for the firm to survive then there is the basis for a normative design theory. Developing the theory was led by the socio-technical school (Emery 1959; Rice 1963; Emery and Trist 1965) based at the Tavistock Institute of Human Relations (Trist and Murray 1990) and by the social psychologists, Katz and Kahn (1966, 1978) at the Institute for Social Research, Ann Arbor, University of Michigan. The law of requisite variety strongly influenced the normative theory of organisation design and provided the platform upon which Galbraith (1977) constructed an information costs theory.

Third, the systems approach of autopoetic systems[2] is advocated by Luhman (1995). Autopoetic systems analysis starts from the notion that social systems are co-ordinated social relationships, albeit relationships whose co-ordination may be a complex web of tight-loose couplings and the whole configuration might have 'one foot in the grave'. There are important parallels and differences between Luhman and the notion of enactment and organising proposed by Weick (1969, 1979). Autopoetic social systems generate and realise the networks that produce the systems because they are self-reproducing. The self-reproduction arises from the communication codes actioned within the system. Codes are abstract and general, providing abstract rules for the selection of possibilities. The selection of possibilities based on the rules in the code gives action, interpretation and enactment. The communication codes organise uncertainty into categories with associated standardising operations thereby providing for continuity and self-reproduction. The communication codes interface with conventional definitions of routines in organisation economics (see Chapters 5 and 12).

In autopoetic systems the codes give two pieces of steering to the organisation. First, the codes enact the environment because they are about the external context, but the codes do not communicate directly with the external context. The codes are the shared temporal framework of the firm (Clark 1985, 1990, 1997a, b). In social systems temporality is the general communication implicated in editing the past and planning the future. In autopoetic systems there is a strong element of de-futurisation because the temporal codes distinguish and identify the iterative, temporal modalities of the past/present/future. The codes are temporal planning and organisation. Second, in modern western organisations there has been and still is a tendency for modern time to be instrumental and to involve a complex mixing of reflexiveness with reification. Information technology modalises the social system by holding the identity of the social system constant and situated in the present. That imprisonment of self-referentiality is projected into the future and is open to disappointment.

Autopoetic systems are an example of managerial cybernetics, but Luhman's viewpoint differs dramatically from that of those offering to transform existing social systems through discursive penetration. Richardson (1991) discusses the work of Beer as an illustration of discursive penetration.

REVISITING BURNS AND STALKER (1961)

Based on their earlier studies of managerial action and on the main study Burns and Stalker (1961) separated the normative theory of 'what ought to be' from the examination of 'what is' and 'what might be'. Their normative theory presumes that firms have low control over the competitive contexts in which they operate. Therefore, in the theory of 'what ought to be' they suggest that the system of management is regarded as a dependent variable which ought to conform to the variable of rates of technical or market change (1961: 103–106). However, in terms of 'what might be' they observe that there are two variables internal to the firm that affect the capacity of management systems to match 'what ought to be'. These are: first, the relative strength and direction of individual commitments to political and status gaining ends and the relative strengths of self-interest; second, the relative capacity of the directors of a firm to interpret the external situation and to shape the personal commitments of managers to the purposes of the firm. In other words to transform 'what is' into 'what ought to be'. These distinctions have been misleadingly neglected. In particular, the issue of 'what can be' and 'what might be' were suppressed and many contingency theorists failed to examine the context of application for their theoretical analysis (Clark 1972, 1975a).

There are five features of the original work by Burns and Stalker (1961) that are relevant to the two themes of 'organisations in action' and 'competition between contexts' which have been ignored in the gutting of the 'management of innovation'.

First, Burns and Stalker rejected equilibrium models (1961: 110) in order to draw upon the event-structure theory of F. H. Allport (1962) thereby anticipating its later centrality to the open systems framework of Katz and Kahn (1966: 22). Burns and Stalker define the firm as both an economic enterprise faced by exit in a market context and also as a working community suffused with individual and collective politics. The economic dimension is expressed through the theories of expectations and uncertainty with extensive attention to the theorising of G. L. S. Shackle and H. A. Simon as well as key 1950s thinkers on the economics of innovation. Burns and Stalker's notion of the firm-and-context as working communities is grounded in the classics of sociology from Toennies, Simmel, Marx, Weber to Durkheim. The firm is analysed as a relational network and the aim is that of describing a firm in action as an interpretative process possessing a large variety of technical and specialist 'languages' ranging from cost accountants and fitters to scientists. Language is analysed as a facet of organisational action in order to reveal the variety of special meanings for people experiencing a period of change (1961: 155) and also to examine the structural changes.

Second, the members of firms possess latent social identities with private purposes that involve personal autonomy which are separate to the 'rational needs' of the firm (see Layder 1997). These predispositions energise the intra-organisational politics. In the research-based firms, scientists and technicians in research and development laboratories tend to define themselves as professionals possessing autonomy from employing firms and being affiliated to a social movement located in the universities and professions (1961: 175). These scientists claim elite status relative to other industrial employees including line management. Their claims lead to many zones of conflict between them with production and sales. Also, the language of the administrator is full of notions of scientists as inventors and as being similar to the consultants advisory role (1961: 199) rather than being an integral element of the large, science-based firm.

Third, the foregoing points lead into an extensive examination of the wider national-societal context. Very significantly and yet hardly noticed they provided extensive, detailed analysis of why Scottish and English firms might be shaped by national predispositions to adopt particular ways of working. Their analysis of societal features posits the existence of hardly noticed cumulative tendencies in ways of organising which persist over decades and alter at irregular moments. Their insightful analysis of British institutional features and their implication for re-adaptation of the Scottish electronics industry reaffirms the entraining features of national contexts and resonates with Crozier's explanation of how French cultural predispositions shape French public organisations.

Fourth, Burns and Stalker linked the intra-organisational politics and the wider national-societal context.

Fifth, they carefully analysed the conditions under which the introduction and installation of the rationally chosen design were likely to fail or succeed (1961: 103f). They explored the restrictions to transformation of the existing situation and were very cautious of the future of the Scottish electronics sectoral cluster. Burns and Stalker noted that the Scottish electronics industry had moved from its protected position within the state defence procurement (e.g. radar) into a more commercial situation, yet the firms had not been able to move from the more mechanistic management systems towards the more organic. Their policy-oriented interpretation is crucial and represents the neglected aspect of their proposals for contingency theory.

Far too many analysts have assumed that there is a frictionless switch between mechanistic and organic tendencies (Clark 1975a, b; Clark and Staunton 1989: Chapter 2). Even where the requirement for switching rules has been acknowledged, analysts have been silent on how those capacities are situated in the repertoire of the firm (Clark 1975b). Burns and Stalker are so clear about the problems that they provide a lengthy essay (Chapters 8 and 9) exploring the historical, societal and institutional features of industrial Britain which enable and constrain changes in management systems.

The 'management of innovation' bridges from our examination of the design rules approach to organisation theory into the examination of sociological and economic perspectives in the next two chapters.

NOTES

1 Note the linkages to transaction costs economics.
2 I am indebted to Majia Holmer Nadeesan (1997) for her discussion of autopoetic systems and temporality in her article and through her e-mail conversations.

4 Structuration, domain theory and the realist turn

INTRODUCTION

In social theory the notion of open systems as organised complexity requires an explication of the nature of recursiveness in all areas of social life. Theorising recursiveness is problematic, especially with respect to the notion of a theory of structural activation (Clark 1975a; 1985; 1987). This chapter briefly examines the contributions to recursiveness in open systems and morphogenesis (Buckley 1967) and structuration theory (Giddens 1984) before moving into Layder's (1997) revisions, known as domain theory. Then consideration is given to how the realist turn in social science handles recursiveness and morphogenesis.

The realist turn occupies a significant position in the map introduced in Figure 2.1 because of the claim that interpretivist perspectives require location in their structural and cultural contexts (Archer 1995). The realist turn gained impetus and focus when Bhaskar (1975, 1989) developed Harre's[1] relational theory of process (e.g. Harre 1979) and initially incorporated structuration theory. Archer (1989) argued that structuration theory conflated the time dimension by allowing the analyst to elide from the past into the present without attention to the separate ontologies of the pre-existing from the next cycle of activity. Then she argued that her theorising of structural transformation and Bhaskar's realist turn provided the most incisive and concise treatment of processual dynamics by distinguishing the reproduction of social structures from their possible transformation (Archer 1995). Their theory of morphogenesis corrects some of the problems inherent in the much earlier theory of morphogenesis proposed by Buckley (1967) and largely ignored. Archer joined the realist turn. Thus, structuration theory, the domain theory of Layder and the realist turn provide a useful introduction to the scope of issues now relevant to examining organisations in action and competition between contexts. The realist turn is seductive yet, as Layder (1997) implies, social constructionists can also read the realist text and author developments not requiring the realist solution.

This chapter draws upon sociological perspectives relevant to the debate over structuration and the realist turn in three steps:

- recursiveness, morphogenesis and structuration;

- social fields (Boudieu); the configurational perspective (Elias); four domains theory (Layder);
- the realist turn (Harre 1979; Archer 1995) and the issue of transformation/morphogenesis (Archer 1995).

RECURSIVENESS, MORPHOGENESIS AND STRUCTURATION

Recursiveness

The problem with open systems analysis has been the struggle between espousers of system theorising (e.g. Katz and Kahn 1966) and the critics of system thinking in organisation theory (e.g. Silverman 1970). The critics have rightly argued that many system analogies that do not approximate towards the very top of Boulding's (1955) nine-point scale are inappropriate for socio-cultural systems. The espousers have elegantly referred us all back to notions such as 'cycles of events' (e.g. Allport 1962) while providing few bold exemplars. Why? And why do Burns and Stalker (1961) present a revised Preface (1966) reporting that their earlier work was overly static?

One of the missing elements is the development of the concept of recursiveness (March and Simon 1958; Weick 1969; Clark 1975a, b, 1985; Giddens 1979: 75–79; Harre 1979).

Recursiveness means the socially accomplished reproduction of sequences of activity and action because the actors involved possess a negotiated sense that one template from their repertoire will address a new situation. The sequences are activated and unfold in accordance with the socially constructed durational time based on events within processes (Clark 1975a, b, 1985). Recursiveness is always improvised, even when the new cycle seems to replicate the old cycle and even when those seeking to impose reproduction are in agreement (Clark 1975a, b). Recursiveness in social systems tends towards the autopoetic and is a form of self-organising complexity subject to dislocation (Luhman 1995; Holmer Nadeesan 1997). Equally, there can be a durability about recursiveness that constrains attempts to transform the sequences. There is, as Giddens (1984) aptly states, chronic recursiveness in all social situations. Without timetabling and lists and recursiveness, organisation would not exist (Clark 1975a, b). Giddens's original attention to recursiveness becomes obscured and disappears from the index to later texts. I will deal with this more fully in Chapter 12.

Socio-cultural systems and morphogenesis: Buckley

The application of systems thinking to socio-cultural entities like organisations requires the avoidance of inappropriate system analogies and using Boulding's levels framework at levels eight and nine. Buckley (1967: 8–17) argues that there has been a long history of using mechanical, biological and more recently computer programming as analogies (e.g. March and Simon 1958). Buckley (1967: 18) proposes a process model in which organising is viewed as multi-faceted, temporary, containing varying degrees and intensities of association and dissociation and with forms that are dormant as well as active. These are achieved by studying actual social processes in full and not abridging their key features as in game theory. A process perspective of action treats structure as an event structure (Nadel 1957: 128; Katz and Kahn 1966: 20–22) containing cleavages, enclaves and conflicts. Buckley rejects the approach to systems of Parsons (1951) and although more sympathetic to Homans (1951) is critical of the tendency to determinate reciprocal interrelationships of all the parts and the mechanically derived notion of equilibrium (Buckley 1967: 31–34).

Buckley prefers the notion of organised complexity as a collection of entities interconnected by a complex set of institutionalised and enduring relationships (Buckley 1967: 38). Thus the emphasis is not upon entities (e.g. swimming pool robots) but upon relations between elements and their likelihood of being durable or transformed. Relationships exist separately from the people who might occupy positions and roles (Nadel 1957). Those interchanges which become repetitive constitute configurations and process patterns. Therefore, we should examine open systems to assess their connectedness or entivity. High connectedness should not be presumed and there is likely to be considerable loose coupling of elements.

Nadel (1957) sought to construct a dynamic theory of social structure in the singular. Buckley (1967) realised that a dynamic theory requires attention to multiple social structures, including those that are dormant (Clark 1975a, b).

Structuration

There is widespread acceptance that the structuration approach developed over more than two decades by Giddens (1979, 1981, 1984) represents a serious, widely acknowledged definition of the new rules for sociological enquiry. Giddens (1974, 1979) provided a powerful rejection of positivistic approaches to social phenomena (Giddens 1974) and a proposed a revision to the dichotomous relationship between the two key analytic units favoured in positivist approaches:

- the voluntarism of individuals (agency);
- holistic constraining structures and systems (e.g. groups, organisations, cities).

Giddens located the structure and agency debate and proposed the theory of structuration as a working solution (1984).

Structuration theory presented action in the context of pre-existing structures whereby agency was partially enabled and partially constrained. Giddens sought to replace the process oriented account of the evolution of capitalism with a non-teleological longitudinal perspective in which history was redefined as structuration unfolding. Giddens (1984) 'accords a fundamental role to language and to cognitive faculties in the explication of social life' (1984: xvi) and to the routine, habitual aspects of everyday life (1984: xxiii) and to the time-space dimensions of social structure. Giddens is well known for his claims about the knowledgeability of actors and for their postulated capacities to interpret and undertake action against pre-existing, hidden forms of structuring sedimented in the distant past.

Structuration theory did seem to deal with the relationship between pre-existing social structures and their shaping of the unfolding present. However, Archer's (1988, 1995) critical assessment emphasises temporal conflation and the eliding of the pre-existing into the ongoing. Structuration theory seemed absorbed by social interaction in the extended present.

Giddens's critique of positivism and proposal of structuration had an indirect, mediated influence on organisation studies (cf. Whittington 1992b):

- accounting (e.g. *Journal of Accounting, Organisations, Society*);
- theories of how to introduce information technology (DeSanctis and Poole 1994; Orlikowski 1992; Barley 1986, 1990);

The perspective of structuration is more frequently truncated in organisation studies than fully deployed. Barley (1986, 1990) in one of the few full-blown attempts to apply structuration theory to organisation change reveals some of the potentials and requirements for further development (see Grint and Woolgar 1998).

DOMAIN THEORY AND IMPROVISATION

Relational theories using social analogies give attention to chronic recursiveness (Harre 1979). The problem is how to theorise recurrent action patterns. This section reviews five basic concepts of recursiveness in relational social theory: social fields, habitus, long-term configurations, unplanned order and improvisation. These five concepts can be located in the four-domain theory proposed by Layder (1997) as a general framework that also draws upon the realist turn and from structuration theory. Each of these theories considers the possibilities for improvisation within social structures.

Social fields and habitus: Bourdieu

The approach of Bourdieu is just beginning to influence organisation theory through its broadening and deepening of the New Institutional School (DiMaggio and Powell 1991). Alexander (1995) is an interesting critic of Bourdieu and maintains that the New Institutional School – to be examined in Chapter 7 – does not fully appreciate the Marxian heritage in Bourdieu's intellectual tool kit.

Bourdieu addresses the problem of how to develop concepts which handle recurrent action patterns. Concepts are used pragmatically as tool kits to solve particular problems because the theoretical construction of the object of study is intimately bound up with methods of data collection. The intention is to provide tools for distinguishing zones of necessity and freedom: the spaces open to moral action. Bourdieu is concerned to analyse long-term trends and to avoid masking the fundamental ruptures which occur. Krieken (1998) contrasts the attention to fundamental ruptures with Elias's tendency to over-emphasise the continuities. Bourdieu seeks to enable the emergence of something like a rational subject through a reflexive application of social science knowledge (cf. orthodox design theory). Reflexivity is central and involves the analysts situating themselves in the field of their community and of their subjects of study in order to understand how the sociological gaze becomes blurred.

The task of sociology is to uncover the double life of social structures by crafting a set of double-focus analytic lenses (Bourdieu and Wacquant 1992). The double analytic lens provides a relational conception and the opportunity to grasp the interweaving of the social structure and the social experience.

One lens needs to reconstruct the distribution of social and material resources and values: the species of capital. These are the determinate relations within which men and women enter to produce their social existence. So, the external observer aims to use a variety of thinking tools (e.g. ethnography, statistics, modelling) to decode the unwritten musical score. This hidden score is more like a riff in jazz. The social actors (agents) use the unwritten social score and they believe that they are improvising their social melody. The social score constructs the regularities that actors follow. Yet these regularities cannot be reified and treated as autonomous entities able to act by themselves. That is the reductionist trap.

The second lens embraces the pride of place given to agency (e.g. Schutz 1967) with attention to the contingent nature of ongoing practices of everyday life. The second lens is required to examine the subjectivist or constructionist point of view. The construction of the configuration of social relationships observed by the first lens arises because the experience of meanings is part and parcel of the total meaning of experience. The first lens examines the systems of classification, the symbolic templates constituted by the mental and bodily schemata which shape the practical activities of social agents, their conduct, thoughts and social judgements. The immediate lived experience of agents is introduced to unravel the shared dispositions that structure action from inside.

So we have to recapture the double reality while giving epistemological priority to the objectivist rupture over subjective understandings. The analysis of the objective structures carries over into the analysis of subjective dispositions. Social structures and mental structures are in correspondence because they are genetically linked. The correspondence reveals that symbolic systems are instruments of domination. Social knowledge is not neutral. The symbolic system contains the operators of cognitive integration that, by their practical logic, establish the social integration on an arbitrary order. It is the orchestration of categories which while being adjusted to the interests of those who dominate, are imposed, yet appear neutral and objective. The symbolic systems constitute the social relations. The social taxonomies (e.g. salary scale in the sugar beet factory) that organise the representation of groups are implicated in the power relations within the firm and between societal strata. In this approach the formation, selection and imposition of systems of classifications are recursively and structurally connected.

Three analytic categories are essential to Bourdieu's tool kit. First, Bourdieu replaces the notion of society with those of social fields. Examples of social fields include the academic world, the economic production of art or political power. The social field is an ensemble containing many relatively autonomous spheres of play and because society is differentiated these cannot be collapsed into an overall societal logic. Each field possesses its own regulative principles and particular values. The relations in the field exist apart from the consciousness of the people located in the field and the field influences their intersubjective worlds even though this is unrecognised. For example, Zerubavel contends that nurses in the field of the American private hospital are largely unaware of how their time-space trajectories are influenced by the central administration's awareness of the revenues deriving from insurance funds. Fields of activity are defined around the struggle for control over economic resources and cultural capital. So fields are organised, probably in various hierarchies, around these struggles. Fields intersect with one another and vary in their capacity to impact on other fields. Among the most powerful fields are those of class and cultural relationships. Fields therefore act as relays (Clegg 1989) which activate contextual resources.

Second, orthodox approaches tend to dichotomise the apparent realism of structures and the presence of individuals, but the organisation is a particular environment in which the activities and actions are collectively orchestrated without being the product of the orchestrating action of a conductor (Bourdieu 1977: 72). The orchestration of action unfolds without being the product of either obedience to rules (cf. Giddens 1984) or being the outcome of the conscious pursuit of interests and rational goals. Recurrent action patterns involve habits and habitual actions. These features are already acknowledged though not central in organisation theory. Collective action suggests systems of durable, recurring, transposable dispositions to act in particular ways which are regulated in some way. Bourdieu defines the habitus as:

> The durably installed generative principle of regulated improvisation produces practices which tend to reproduce the regularities immanent in the objective conditions of the production of their generative principle, while adjusting to the demands inscribed as objective potentialities in the situation, as defined by the cognitive and motivating structures making up the habitus.
> (Bourdieu 1977: 78)

This is one of the most compacted and complex definitions encountered in organisational analysis. What does habitus mean?

It means that we cannot deduce recurrent action patterns from the objective conditions which the analyst might apprehend when looking at a factory or the environment of the Inuit. Regulated improvisation means generative rules which are internalised by actors on the basis of previous experience.

The habitus contains the past, present and future and assumes that within the human body there is deposited a range of situations derived from the past and providing the basis for activation. The habitus generates lines of action based on practical logic rather than the neat logic of a normative principle in organisation theory. Consequently Bourdieu has great scepticism about the neo-rational approaches of the utilitarians and the intentionalists. The approach is opposed to notions of purposive pursuit of calculated goals. Instead his approach would be to discover *in situ* for particular organisations what are the lines of action which form intelligent patterns in the relation between the collective habitus and the context. The concept of interest therefore is to be disregarded because each field of action 'fills the empty bottle of interest with a different wine'.

The habitus, assigns orientations which produce the structure through which the habitus governs practice as a socially produced recurrent action pattern. The habitus engenders and aligns thoughts and actions to the particular conditions in which it was and is constituted. Thus the objects of this form of knowing are constructed through practical activities. Practice does imply a cognitive operation through systems of classification which organise perceptions and structure practice. The calendar is one of the most codified facets of social experience as is illustrated by the example of sugar beet operation. These symbolic systems possess regularities and contradictions and have a practical rather than logical coherence. Thus, understanding ritual practice is a matter of restoring and connecting it to the real conditions of its genesis rather than discovering some internal logic (cf. Daft 1997; Archer 1995). It becomes possible to understand the economic rationality of conduct only by drawing up a comprehensive balance sheet of symbolic profits even though economic thought might label these as absurd.

Habitus emphasises the taken for granted elements of action such as social classifications, knowledge without concepts and the situated, embodied reproduction of structuring. Habitus explains how and why strategically located actors reproduce action which is not in their interests. There is a grammar of strategic action which is anchored though not determined by past situations.

Third, the social agent is characterised as having knowledge without cognitive intent (cf. Giddens 1984). The social agents acquire a pre-reflective mastery from their continuous immersion as, for example, in sports. The social agent is involved in mutual possession between the habitus and the context which determines the habitus. Social agents use a practical sense which constitutes meanings and seeks to anticipate immanent tendencies within processes as, for example, soccer players in the Italian series A who use their field of vision to size up the next move. That involves anticipating – perhaps wrongly – the actions of the opposition. For the soccer player the field is not objectively given but is understood as configurations of players and as twisting trajectories according to the offensive or defensive posture. Every configuration introduces new possibilities and alters the field. The practical sense of the players recognises by reading the present state in terms of the possible future states contained within the field. Obviously players and teams differ in their capacities.

Long-term configurations and unplanned order: Elias

Elias (1897–1990) embedded his theorising of process and his major concepts in empirical studies. Only in his later years did he write extensively on time, process and temporality (Krieken 1998). There are four major contributions:

1   theorising of the long-term as a minimum of three generations;
2   the relational theory of process as (con)figuration and unplanned order;
3   the theory of habitus and personality controls over emotion;
4   the analysis of states, in particular twentieth century Germany.

I will only examine the first two because there are some overlaps with Bourdieu.

First, to examine the long-term Elias selectively combined and introduced revisions to the perspectives of Marx on the development of capitalism, of Weber on the role the state and Freud on personality and the role of the superego. These revisions commenced with an analysis of manners in the medieval period (Elias 1982) and led into a theory-laden narrative on the French court in the seventeenth century (Elias 1994). These studies were not translated from German until Elias was in his eighties and were rarely cited until after the 1960s. From then on Elias's theorising enrolled a constituency and this may be examined at the web site (Krieken 1998).

Second, Elias was an early user of the relational approach to social analysis proposed by Cassirer (1923–4 circa) and also used by Lewin (1946) and others (e.g. Bourdieu, Harre). Elias seemed to consider his variant the most fruitful and was passionately critical of the approach of Lewin's field theory. The reasons will become apparent. Elias's approach to processes uses notions of social configuration to explain people in networks. Elias's theorising operates simultaneously at several levels and within a political economy frame of reference. Central to his theorising is the claim that it is unplanned order and the unintended consequences of intended action which predominate. Elias passionately criticised the reification of the social and the misleading influence of everyday language as a source of relevant concepts (e.g. individuals, society). His earliest writing incorporated elements from Freud. Elias's use of Freud's concept of the superego and his account of a dramatic shift in forms of self-control since the Middle Ages has met considerable criticism.

Elias (1994) sought to demonstrate that in the seventeenth century a configuration of power relationships between and within European states created strategic arenas in which new forms of social relationship were developed and new forms of self-control surfaced among certain elite strata. His narrative emphasises how people found themselves in networks which imposed considerable constraint on their actions. In the strategic arena of courtly society the nobility constructed and developed habits based on high sensitivity to the gaze of others. Elias contends that the nobility acquired extensive control mechanisms over their short-term actions and emotions. The habitus of the nobility centred upon self-control. In contrast, the subsequent development of bourgeois habits pivoted around economic gain. These power fields constrained people while at the same time providing zones which were less controlled in which people could search for excitement. Elias sought to avoid the notions of structure being used in sociology and preferred to develop social analogies which contained a powerful image of ordered dynamics. One analogy was the ordered dance with its known template and opportunity for rehearsals. The dance could be viewed as a configuration being reproduced by the dancers.

I was a student of Elias and the experience of his exciting, analytical thinking was an early influence upon the puzzles I formulated in my initial pieces of research on structural activation in Europe's largest knitwear firm.[2] My research on time-and-process was theoretically driven by and anchored in the explanatory role of the recursive, sequential features of organisations (Clark 1975a, b) and their location in a variety of contexts. My explanation of processes in organisations as a theory of structural activation (Clark 1975a, b, 1985) has, from the early 1960s, sought to rescue process from what Elias rightly termed its suppression within inappropriate metaphors drawn uncritically from the natural and biological sciences. Hence I have used the analogy of American Football to explain both features of the US service strata as a modernising elite and also to illustrate a particular form of organising for the future (Clark 1987). I preferred the specifics of that form of sport to the abstract notion of games. My analysis of Anglo-American differences was partly influenced by Elias's sense of the long-term and of inter-state relationships. Central to my analysis developed here is the contention that there is extensive recursiveness and that the explanation of the mechanisms and causes of its formation is essential to the analysis of whether change/. transformation/morphogenesis has occurred and is likely to occur (Clark 1975a, b, 1978, 1985). So, it is necessary to distinguish between this sociological approach to the longitudinal and those approaches typical to organisation behaviour in which the pre-existing structural capacities are minimised because of the preoccupation with strategic agency.

Four domains theory: Layder

Layder (1997) seeks to reconcile some of the criticisms of structuration theory with elements from other theorists including Habermas, Bourdieu and Elias by constructing a theory of four domains. The central objective is to weld together aspects of the lifeworld and the subjective with the objectified, institutionalised social life. Each aspect contains two domains. The four domains are completely interdependent and are connected through political and social relations so no domain is the prime mover. Moreover, the domains overlap. Layder (1997: 245) deliberately concentrates upon 'the pockets of routinised continuity that exist in the spaces between periodic structural or systemic changes and that ride on the back of the recurrent everyday activities of people in relatively entrenched and established institutional circumstances' and therefore social change has been bracketed. Layder's account of everyday life emphasises many of the features found in Bourdieu with the added attempt to define a generally portable framework as

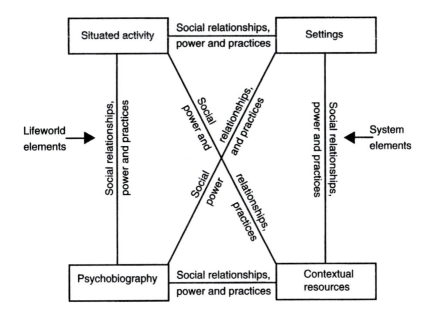

Figure 4.1 The social domains
Source: Layder (1997: 82)

shown in Figure 4.1. The framework domains refer to the local level while the lines connecting the four domains refer to the macro level institutional features. This macro level might be displaced by attention to the four domains.

The subjective and lifeworld on the left-hand side contains:

1 The *psychobiography* of the 'self as a historical emergent' (Layder 1997: 47–51) with a subjective career; these careers are 'a linked series of evolutionary transitions' (1997: 47). Individuals are initially located in particular settings and, although unique in their experiences and the interpretation of those experiences, pass through common stages. Layder distinguishes between the subjective construction of careers and the notion of a time-space trajectory for individuals. For the individual there are varying levels of anxiety in the emotional work of face-to-face encounters where self-identity is constantly implicated. The objective trajectories are the focus of French research on cohorts passing through the educational system into work (e.g. Maurice *et al.* 1986). Contemporary society provides a habitus to psychobiography which emphasises individuation, though this must not be confused with the bourgeois myth of autonomy. Attention to this domain means addressing identity, especially the extent to which in modern work settings there are human resource experts who specialise in the production of identities (see Thompson and McHugh 1995: Chapters 8–11; Sennett 1998).

2 In their everyday lives at work and in other settings individuals are situated in

activities which possess particular orders of interaction. These immediate contexts contain other people with whom there are sometimes face-to-face encounters and there are many encounters in which people are passing one another: for example, the rules of behaviour in a shopping centre or at a Disney theme park (Bryman 1995). Goffman underscores the extent to which there is civil inattention, for example, when travelling on the London underground railways. Central to the analysis of the subjective is accounting for explaining the features of emotion and trust (1959: 62–72) and the self's experience of security.

On the right-hand side there are the system, contextual elements:

3   The *contextual resources* are drawn from by social agents/people to construct their social behaviour. Resources are of three main types:

- material resources (e.g. ownership of property, money, goods which can be exchanged);
- dominative resources enabling agents to secure power, authority, control;
- cultural/discursive resources used in gaining membership and the opportunity to interact in particular situated activities.

The *contextual resources* exist as part of the distributive profile of particular societies at the macro level and there are also local aggregations which lubricate social activity (Layder 1997: 81). Contextual resources are implicated with the other four domains.

4   *Settings* 'serve as the local holding points for aggregations of reproduced social relations and practices' (1997: 80). Settings are key areas for studying the reproduction of the wider society.

Layder acknowledges the realist turn (see next) and Archer's critique of temporal conflation in Giddens, but warns against confusing epistemological and ontological issues.

THE REALIST TURN

Voluntarism is rife in everyday causal accounts.

(Sayer 1992: 121)

Rejecting positivism

The realist school rejects positivism and post-modernism. The leading contributors to the realist position include Harre (1972, 1979), his colleague Bhaskar (1978, 1989), Sayer (1992) and Archer (1995). Harre is known for his critique of the positivist orientation in psychology, which slowly gained a constituency (e.g.

Miles and Huberman 1994). The recently formed Centre for Critical Realism has proclaimed that the realist turn is occurring and that this is the way forward.[3]

The realist position is that there is a real world which is independent, pre-existing and possesses multiple, different domains each with distinctive ontologies. By ontology we mean the nature, constitution and structure of the objects which are the focus of inquiry. This includes a theory of their existence or being. The realist claims that there is a variety of necessarily different ontologies for the natural, biological and social sciences. Realist approaches distinguish between the natural, biological and social sciences. Any difference in ontology between disciplines has to be accommodated and dealt with by specific approaches for the chosen domain. Consequently the transfer of analogies and principles from the study of astronomy or the mechanical sciences to the study of society is fraught with so many flaws, pitfalls and dangers that a different form of analysis should be chosen for economics.

According to the realists the problem of how and through which mechanisms future actions are enabled or constrained has been only partially unpacked by Giddens and Bourdieu. Archer's (1988, 1995) critique of structuration emphasises a degree of eliding from the past into the present which led to temporal conflation. Archer concludes that although the pre-existing social structure is a powerful shaper of the future, its analytic properties and the analytic properties of the unfolding action were ontologically distinct and could neither be elided nor conflated. There is an analytic duality of structure and agency. Archer aligned her approach with the realist position and is applying the 'realist turn' to transform the structure-and-agency approach. This section examines the claim that there is a realist turn. Later, in Chapter 14, we examine Archer's (1995) theorising of the realist turn with an application of transformation/morphogenesis to organisations.

Establishing the realist approach

The realist approach asks how do we conceptualise, abstract and generalise. A major problem is examining and attributing causation. Realist approaches claim to offer a causal analysis of events in terms of the interplay between pre-existing structures, their generative causal mechanisms and relatively autonomous actors and agents. Pre-existing structures and causal mechanisms carry the weight of the past into the present, yet the question of whether they are reproduced or transformed depends on their interplay with agents and actors. The realist analyst must be an analytical dualist giving equal attention to the pre-existing and the actors/agents through their interplay. The realist also has to examine how the interplay of the pre-existing and the emergent leads to reproduction or transformation. There are therefore hidden sources of socio-genesis and transformation (see Archer 1988, 1995).

Realist approaches are a critique of immediate experience. Therefore the debate shifts from the theory of knowledge (epistemology) to what the world is like for science to be possible (ontological assumptions). Science is a historical accident (Sayer 1992). Science operates at different levels of reality by taking seriously the existence of things, structures and mechanisms – fundamental structures. Things exist independently of our descriptions. We only know these objects through theory laden description. This might be a locational and interaction theory which interprets phenomena and events through the metaphors of mechanisms and structures (Harre 1972). Therefore the realm of the concept of science is theory dependent. Causal mechanisms are real.

The realist approach starts with the initial definition of the field of study and the conceptualisation of the key objects because these shape much of what follows. Those starting assumptions ontologically define a field of study and are theory laden. The realist definition of theory would be 'an examined conceptualisation of some object' (Sayer 1992: 51). Realist theorising consists of grasping the differentiations of the world by abstracting through individuating (social) objects and then characterising their attributes and relationships. Abstractions should distinguish the core characteristics from the incidental characteristics. For example, in the study of Taylorism orthodox analysis has failed to account for its different major features and to notice that the original bundle of characteristics was so loosely bundled that they were unbundled and recombined differently in the USA, UK and Germany (Clark 1987).

The realist approach starts out with the assumption that the real world is differentiated and stratified into distinct domains each with their own distinctive properties with reference to the causal process and mechanisms. For example:

- natural world;
- biological world;
- psycho-biological world;
- social and various subsets.

The objects in the real world, both natural and social, necessarily possess particular causal powers (i.e. ways of acting). The realist position is similar in the natural, biological and social sciences. However, there are overpowering differences between them in the constitution of their objects of analysis: the ontologies. Earlier in the chapter we noted that the social theorist, Layder (1997: 78), proposes a fourfold taxonomy of distinct domains: psycho-biography; situated activity; settings and contextual resources (in Figure 4.1). They are however connected through social relations, power and practices. Each of the domains possesses distinct properties and one domain therefore cannot be reduced to another. So, simple aggregations of psycho-biographies are not equivalent to the domain of situated activity because that domain has distinct properties of its own. The realist position has considerable implications for certain orthodox approaches at the frontier between organisational psychology and the social psychology of work.

The real world contains open systems of varying complexity in which events are to some degree the outcome of deep, pre-existing structures and ways of acting (mechanisms). Causal mechanisms are real. The pre-existing structures set the conditions of social action and are not adequately analysed by the 'here and now', localism and temporal conflation which besets micro-level organisation analysis (cf. Boden 1994).

Open and closed systems

The ontological assumptions required to examine closed systems need to be different from those required for open systems in order to develop practical theory in the social and economic sciences (Sayer 1992). The realists contend that most analytic work in the natural/biological sciences and all analytic work in the social sciences cannot be undertaken within the closed system model.

In closed systems there are regularities that can be satisfactorily described and understood through instrumental laws which describe them. Closed system theory does not require the extensive consideration of mechanisms, because mechanisms create closure of the system. Consequently there are no new emergent processes. The instrumental laws expressing the regularities which are central in the positivist position are in the form 'whenever event x then event y'. The aim of the positivist approach is to elaborate instrumental laws and these then form the basis of prescriptive approaches. The event regularities and their accompanying instrumental laws can then be assessed to be corroborated or falsified. Prediction of event regularities is a core element. The aim of the closed system is to control the conditions of the experiment so that regularities can be identified in the form of 'whenever event x then event y'. The exponents of these approaches considered that they were transferring epistemologies from the natural sciences – according to their definition of the natural sciences. In the closed system and positivist position based on empirical regularities there is an assumption that the empirical activity penetrates the actual world. The empirical activity of positivist science proceeds through experience, perception and impression – being mediated by the sense. The actual world for the positivist only consists of events and 'states of affairs'.

According to the realist agenda the positivists are making an unacceptable assumption about reality when they transfer their intellectual tool kit from closed to open systems. The positivist ontology assumes that the real is known through our senses. In positivism these assumptions are applied to social systems so there is a danger of turning action, social processes and relationships into things (e.g. archetypes), that is, of reifying the world. Some social scientists, originally defined as positivists and as empiricist, have applied closed systems thinking to organisation behaviour and action. The critique of empiricism and positivism is a critique of experience through the senses and therefore requires reformulating the problem.

The realist contends that our perceptions of the real world are mediated, filtered and directed through our membership of particular language communities – sense and reference are interdependent rather than separated. The realists claim that visual fields are conceptually saturated. There is no perception without concepts. So, the languages of social science are theory laden and this theory constitutes the knowledge and much of the knowing of a particular community. In the realist approach the language communities will often include both occupational communities (e.g. organisation analyst) and also wider communities based on national, stratificational and biographical features (e.g. age and gender).

The exponents of positivist approaches consider that they were transferring epistemologies from the natural sciences – according to their definition of the natural sciences. Harre (1979) contended that the use of closed system models to create behavioural regularities and instrumental laws can only provide a useful understanding for highly deterministic, simple systems. Harre and Secord (1972) reasoned, based on the relational philosophy of the natural sciences (Harre, 1972), that the laboratory methods were also defective in that they operated in synchronous time and were therefore unable to explore the pre-existing influences (Harre, 1979, 1985).

Retroduction: events, mechanisms and structures

Social systems are not usefully examined by applying the closed system analogy because the social world is a structured mess. Open systems can and do possess regularities, but these are approximate and transitory. If there are regularities then we must enquire about the system and how the constituent parts must hold together for regularities to occur. Events are causally explained by retroducing and confirming the existence of mechanisms. Mechanisms are explained by reference to the structures and the constitution of objects which possess the mechanisms. There are emergent powers in open systems and therefore the realist conception qualifies the notion of laws. Consequently the position of prediction requires reformulation. Theorising needs to ensure that any use of prediction does not reify social action or assume an instrumental, regulative theory of laws.

The common element across the different ontologies found in the varying domains of the natural, biological and social sciences emphasises two elements. First, in open system approaches the event regularities are difficult to construct and cannot be explained by instrumental laws stating co-variations. Explanation requires the detection of the mechanisms whose tendencies drive states of affairs and those event regularities which do occur. Moreover, 'hidden' behind the mechanisms are complex structures and powers. The explanatory flow requires an alignment between events, mechanisms and structures. Second, the causal tendencies of structures transmitted through mechanisms are most unlikely to be in the same synchronous time frame. Therefore, explaining states of affairs and events, including any regularities, is likely to involve the detection of structures whose powers have been unfolding at some distant period in the past. It is necessary to distinguish between events, experience and the deep mechanisms and structures which are operating.

In the realist approach there are three separate domains as shown in Figure 4.2:

	Domain of Real	Domain of Actual	Domain of Empirical
Mechanisms	✓		
Events	✓	✓	
Experiences	✓	✓	✓

Figure 4.2 Domains of real, actual and empirical
Source: Tsoukas (1994: 291), based on Bhaskar (1978: 13).

1   The real domain contains natural and social objects and mechanisms. Mechanisms are defined as tendencies to behave in particular ways. There are real structures which endure independently of our experience and of our knowledge (Sayer 1992: 33).

Effects ← mechanism ← existence of mechanisms ← structure.

2   The actual domain is made up of events that can occur without being experienced.

3   The empirical domain is made up of experiences.

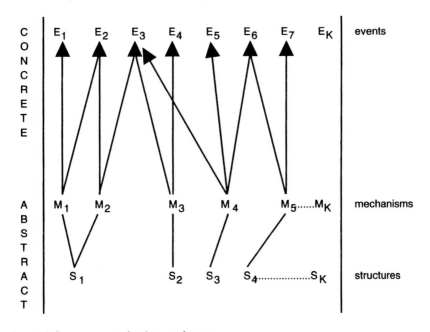

Figure 4.3 Structures, mechanisms and events
Source: Sayer (1992: 117).

The realist analysis should locate the empirical domain within the real domain.

The aim of the realist approach is to discover whether events are shaped by mechanisms which are situated within structures as illustrated in Figure 4.3. Causality is not a relationship between discrete events as in 'cause and effect'. Causal explanation involves grasping the mechanisms. One of the central issues is the degree to which structures – although hidden – constrain and shape everyday patterns of action and events. From this perspective far too many of the case studies in strategy are from the perspective of the storyteller (e.g. the chief executive and the academic) therefore overplaying the capacities and freedom of movement available to most persons (or firms). Such case studies underplay the shaping influence of pre-existing conditions and causal relations.

Four basic issues

Four issues are highlighted:

1   How do we constrain abstraction? Sayer (1992: 140–152) suggests that we must always keep in mind what we are abstracting from and that theorising involves adjusting our abstraction of objects and things. We need to grasp differentiation as a way of individuating (social) objects through characterising their attributes and relationships. The key relations are shown in Figure 4.3 and illustrated in Figure 4.4.

2   The distinction between external and internal relations should be applied (Sayer 1992). External relations are contingent, outside context, while internal relations are necessary as in the master–slave and landlord–tenant–rent connections. Many internal relationships involve differences in power and are therefore asymmetrical. Structures are sets of internally related objects and practices and are largely invisible. Structures can be big social objects (e.g. international division of labour) and small. Social structures co-exist and endure, thereby locking occupants into situations which they cannot unilaterally change.

3   Structure, agency and reproduction must acknowledge that structures are historically and contextually specific. The reproduction of social structures involves situated practices which have to be assembled.

4   Analysis must examine the temporal ordering of causality. We need to be aware that in organisation behaviour abstraction and generalisations tend to be synchronous rather than diachronic. So the analysis of process and change requires a causal analysis. Causality concerns the causal powers (and liabilities) of objects and relations and the mechanisms (i.e. ways of acting). The relationships between causal powers are contingent. The analysis of events requires the identification of immediate causes as well as reference to the necessary conditions for existence of mechanisms.

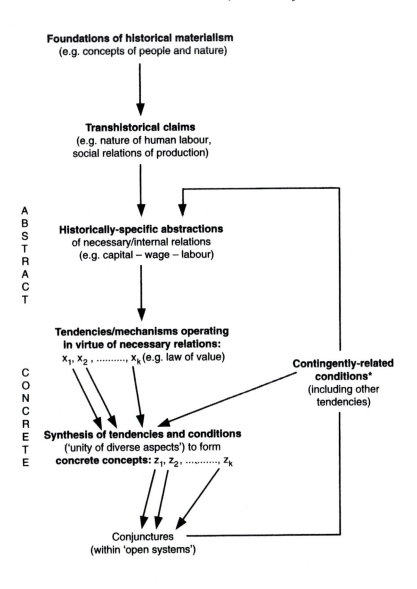

* The theorisation of these, and their explanation by means of abstraction, is often not the sole prerogative of Marxism.

Figure 4.4 Relating the abstract and concrete
Source: Sayer (1992)

Structures and events

A structure is a set of relationships and positions which has a more than temporary durability and persists over years, decades and sometimes generations. One illustration concerns the position of students as tenants in the open market (Sayer 1992: Figure 5). The structure might be constructed by starting with the societal level, the role of private property in general and the investment of private property rights in land and buildings. In western capitalist nations, especially in North America, ongoing property rights are delineated and articulated through the role of the state and the legal profession. Owners and non-owners are distinguished in triangle relationships at the macro level. A second triangle embraces a specific landlord (owner), the rent to be paid and the tenant (non-owner). These three are also connected and the relationships are necessary to the structure and internal. The student as tenant is within a structure that articulates out from the concrete immediate set of events in everyday life into the long-term history of property relations. This structure illustrates necessary relationships which limit individual agency. The occupants of the structure can be very diverse in terms of gender, ethnicity and whether an individual or an association or firm. The structure is always being interpreted by its occupants. Later we shall note that in critical realism the aim is to make the opacity of the structure transparent and therefore open to radical alteration. For the moment we may note that structures – while having persisted – may be dislocated (Holmer Nadeesan 1997). However, the pre-existing structures may be dislocated and permit zones of manoeuvre which individual and collective actors (e.g. firms) explore and occupy.

Events have already been implicated in our discussion. In a realist approach it is assumed that events in everyday life which seem disconnected, random and voluntaristic are shaped by pre-existing structures which enable some zones of manoeuvre while inhibiting others. The nurses in private US hospitals may have been unaware of the structure of private property relationships, yet a realist analysis would claim that understanding required a form of theorising which re-situated what the nurses told the interviewer.

So far reference has been made to events and to structures. As shown in Figure 4.4 there are causal, generative mechanisms which produce the effects and sustain (for the moment) the structures. The analysis of process and change requires causal analysis. In the realist approach the objects or relations possess ways of acting (mechanisms) which are powers or liabilities. The powers and liabilities can exist irrespective of their usage. These ways of acting exist necessarily because of the constitution of the objects. A plane can fly because of its engines, its shape and so on. If the constitution of the object changes (e.g. the engines do not work) then its causal powers will change. The object will no longer be able to perform. The requirement is to understand the occurrence of events by postulating and exploring some mechanisms which are capable of producing the events. The relationship between causal powers and their effects is contingent because they have to be activated. The realist turn combines different types of research as shown in Figure 4.5.

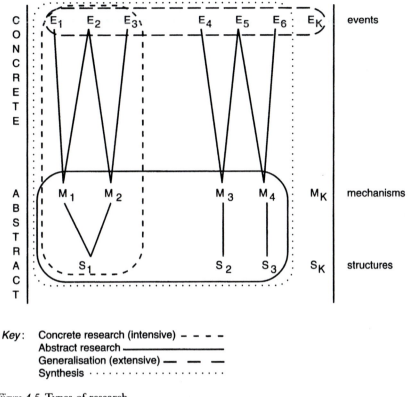

Key: Concrete research (intensive) – – – –
Abstract research ──────────
Generalisation (extensive) — — —
Synthesis · · · · · · · · · · · · · · · · · ·

Figure 4.5 Types of research
Source: Sayer (1992)

To summarise

In the realist approach the analysis should start with the object including social objects (e.g. bureaucracy) and should commence by analysing its features to locate the multiple dimensions. The idea is to distinguish the properties which are necessary from those which are accidental. It is possible that for explanatory reasons the accidental properties may be more important. Complex objects (e.g. Englishness) will have complex features and objects will vary in their durability.

There are important tensions between structuration and the realist turn which Layder (1997) seeks to align, yet like Giddens one outcome is that the economic dimension becomes truncated and represented at a distance. Giddens acknowledges the role of the economy as a mechanism and the role of money, yet minimises the contemporary claims of Mandel regarding economic pulsations and crises in capitalism in an effort to avoid teleological tendencies. This feature is explored in the next chapter and the economic dimension is located as in Figures 5.1 and 7.1. In Chapter 5 we examine the market as an actor and the sociology of economic action.

NOTES

1 Rom Harre's contribution to the critique of positivism and to developing of the realist perspective deserves its own, separate, full treatment. Here I simply draw upon some fragments from that œuvre.
2 My field studies of recursiveness in sugar beet, supermarkets and can-making was funded by the Department of Scientific and Industrial Research (1964–6).
3 This section draws upon Andrew Sayer (1992) *Method in Social Science* and the First International Conference on Critical Realism, Warwick University, England, 1997 and the special conversation between Harre and Bhaskar held at the School of Oriental and African Studies, University of London, England, 1997.

5 Organisation economics and economic sociology

INTRODUCTION

Becker (1965, 1976, 1981); Stiglitz (1991) and Stigler (1984), leaders in the new economics, have labelled the growth of organisation economics and related areas as economic imperialism. Mainstream organisation behaviour has acknowledged some of the very considerable developments in organisation economics, yet has underestimated the weight of those developments, failed to notice the outflanking and has underplayed the significance of the new economic sociology.

Economic imperialism is addressed by the new economic sociology which has recognised the autonomy of the economic system (Swedberg *et al.* 1990: 66). The new economic sociology also combines the historical-social approach to economic action with the new institutional school of DiMaggio, Powell, Scott and Fligstein.

There are sharp differences between economists and sociologists. These differences centre on the definition of economic action and the analysis of markets as embedded institutions. Economists define economic action as the application of rational choice models to choosing under conditions where resources and techniques have alternative opportunity costs. Sociologists maintain that economic action is socially constructed. The chapter selectively explores the interface between organisational economics and the sociological approach to economic action at the levels of the firm and the nation. There are three sections:

1   Differences in approach between economics and sociology.
2   Organisation economics:

- agency theories and transaction costs;
- routines and quasi-genetic traits in evolutionary models;
- resource based analysis (RBA);
- national systems of innovation (see Chapter 7);
- revived interest in Penrosian learning (see Chapter 11).

3   New economic sociology.

This chapter utilises the neo-structuration, long-term perspective on economic action as depicted in Figure 5.1 (Clark 1987: Figure 7.2). The chapter aims

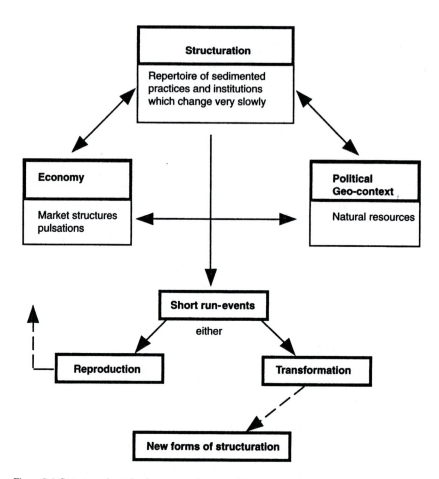

Figure 5.1 Structuration: the long-term framework
Source: Clark (1987).

to develop those pathways sustaining the neo-modern political economy perspective.

DIFFERENCES: ECONOMICS AND SOCIOLOGY

The economist Adam Smith (1776) blended abstract-deductive analysis with historical materials, but by the nineteenth century the Anglo-American academy had firmly separated them. In continental Europe the gap between models and historical materials was less and the connections were more fiercely debated: methodenstreit (1880–1920). That debate provided the opportunity for Weber and Schumpeter to address the interface between economic action and sociology

(Powell 1996). Durkheim (1964) constructed the new rules of sociological method to define the differences and promote sociology as a separate discipline. Today the separation is contested by the imperialist tendencies in organisation economics and in the new economic sociology (Hirsch *et al.* 1990; Swedberg *et al.* 1990). The contrasts, separation and contest can be expressed in respect of three areas:

- basic assumptions about reality and knowledge;
- approach to theory and research;
- policy implications. .

First, differences in basic assumptions are extensive. Economists construct models based on individual behaviour as self-interested, instrumental and dominated by hierarchical preferences leading to the maximising of rational choice. Society is largely treated as an aggregate of atomistic individuals, households and firms making social contracts. Actions are exclusively rational, that is formal rationality. The aim is that economic models can be applied to any situation where there is choice and scarcity of resources as defined by the economist irrespective of local definitions. Economists view the market as a major, ideal, autonomous mechanism for distributing resources. The starting point and result of economic actions is the tendency to equilibrium.

Sociology assumes that human nature is complex, situated in national predispositions, possesses fluid, dynamic, inconsistent preferences which are subject to social influences. Society pre-exists, is real and its structure of relationships has consequences. Actions include both forms of economic action and relational actions because the economic system is part of society. There are markets and social organisation (Braudel 1985). The starting point is tensioned filled struggles between vested interest groups and their pre-existing, institutionalised structure may or may not be reproduced through action.

Second, in theory and research the economist is depicted as a producer of objective scientific results from the perspective of the detached, neutral observer. The results combine predictions and explanations. Economics uses models that are highly abstract with few variables tightly drawn in deductive, axiomatic theorising. There are three main types: theoretical-analytical modelling, quantitative mathematical modelling and/or the use of secondary data sources. Time is treated as stylised and quasi-stationary. The criteria of validity is testing predictions within the models.

Sociologists are both 'objective insiders' and members of an occupational community which produces concepts, data and interpretations for consumption (Bourdieu 1977; Archer 1995; Luhman 1995). The method is to produce descriptions and explanations based on empirical abstractions. Research is model and data driven through inductive, grounded theory building. The models are often messy with numerous variables. There is an awareness of blending qualitative and quantitative methods; also, of combining secondary and primary data including ethnography and interpretavist materials. Temporality is a problem (Clark 1990). In economic sociology there is an extended time concept beyond the action which is being investigated, yet there is much to be done in developing temporality (Clark 1997a).

Third, in policy making economics is generally solution oriented through normative theories which define the appropriate treatments. Economics possesses a strong orientation to market solutions and prioritises the market over the firm. So, the policy solution to the allocation of resources in the health care services can be the introduction of market forces as in the market experiments in the UK during the 1990s.

Sociology claims to be uncovering problems through a largely value neutral stance which is diagnostic. Their solutions would be more neutral to the market and may well favour the firm over the market. Critical perspectives will seek to debunk existing arrangements and alter the status quo towards some proclaimed objective (e.g. emancipation).

According to Backhouse (1998) mainstream economists contend that the recent proliferation of criticism about economics as a discipline from within the profession (e.g. McClosky 1990) as well as the numerous special interest groups claiming to be providing a more realistic framework is a very small proportion of the total profession. The code of mainstream economics is to develop a general purpose theory which is of such wide scope that it can be applied to a variety of situations from the economy to marriage and crime. The exemplar for this code is in emulating physics. The wide scope, general theory does not usually lead economists to 'visit with' other disciplines. Economists do not feel the need for history. In part the formal mathematisation of economics arises from American style of professionalism and from their tendency to formalise for high rates of publication. Economists encounter an abundance of public data which capture and reveal economic action. The models are the instruments (as physics). So applied work establishes the facts and reveals the mechanisms. Moreover, relative to the criticisms, in economics it is argued that the domain of application has been expanded; that game theory successfully models strategic interaction; that the information-and-uncertainty perspective resolves earlier difficulties; that time series handles the longitudinal; that models as are instruments.

The economics perspective treats economic action by the firm and industry as being in equilibrium in a market of perfect competition. The market consists of a large number of small firms from which none are able to exert an exceptional influence upon the prevailing market price. Firms are unitary (like super-individuals) and possess the homogeneous, single goal of profit. All firms have no history, are stylised, anonymous and lack variations. Any industry produces a homogeneous output. Buyers and sellers possess similar, perfect knowledge and have access to new knowledge at no cost and are in equality with other firms in absorbing productive knowledge.

We can conclude that economics and sociology do differ substantially (Zukin and DiMaggio 1990). The next section samples from organisational economics.

ORGANISATIONAL ECONOMICS

The main research programmes

The purpose of this section is to sample the strands within organisation economics in order to illustrate their main themes (Douma and Schreuder 1991; Milgrom and Roberts 1992), their position in related disciplines such as accounting (Macintosh, 1994) and their role in the debate over organisations and institutions (North 1990; Scott 1995; Rowlinson 1997) at the interface with sociology and organisation behaviour. It has been argued that agency theories throw a poor light on salaried managers (e.g. Ghoshall 1996; Donaldson 1995).

Throughout much of the twentieth century economists treated the firm within the context of industrial structures, the national economy and international issues. The firm was not analysed. An exception was Penrose (1959), whose contribution is discussed in Chapter 11. Penrose contended that economists misapplied biological metaphors and made dubious assumptions about the firm. Her interpretation of business history suggested a different line of attack. In one of the earliest uses of tacit knowledge Penrose reasoned that managerial teams created firm-specific languages and practices which were largely tacit and virtually impossible to trade. Therefore the conventional instruments of economic analysis were inappropriate for understanding the firm. Her analysis was ignored until the 1990s and her theorising was at the remotest margin of organisation behaviour and rarely mentioned in organisation theory.

Organisation economics is being developed through a small set of research programmes. First, Coase's (1937) analysis of markets and hierarchies as alternative mechanisms for resource application did not come into centre field until the development of transaction costs economics (TCE) in the mid-1970s (e.g. O. E. Williamson 1975). Since the 1970s rational choice economics and TCE have developed vigorously. Second, and taking a quite different line, the Carnegie School (e.g. March, Cyert, Simon) located routines at the centre of their analysis and this was powerfully developed by Nelson and Winter into an evolutionary approach to dynamic capabilities. Third, within strategy and industrial organisation, the approach of resource-and-capability analysis has become central.

Agency theory

Agency theory is an exemplar in the development of organisation economics. Its portrayal of economic action is intended to provide an ideal model against which 'reality' can be described, understood and redesigned. The agency theorist claims to be an architect of the firm's organisation and its motivational dynamics. Agency theory in organisation economics should never be confused with the use of agency in sociology.

The origins of agency theory are to some degree in the sixteenth-century Hobbesian assumptions about social life and the proposed solution of a social contract designating a sovereign power which everyone agrees should be the ruler.

There is a powerful influence from the neo-classical economics of Adam Smith and the role of the market mechanism in co-ordinating an atomistic society of individuals. The market is depicted as a mechanism anchored in choice and therefore consent. Given the strong US origins to agency theory there is a recognisably Spencerian influence of rational, utilitarianism and willing competition between individuals who receive differential rewards depending upon their willingness to self-invest (Hofstadter 1955; Clark 1987).

Agency theory defines the firm as a nexus of two-person contracts which may be explicit or implicit. One person is known as the principal and is the equivalent of an owner. The other person is the agent acting on behalf of the principal. Everyone enters into such contracts (e.g. marriage). It is assumed that all persons are motivated by rational economic self-interest. The agency relationship is a contract in which the principal delegates to the agent who performs on behalf of the principal. Agents will tend – because they are rational and pursuing their self-interest – to undertake actions which are not intended or required by the principals yet incur costs and reduce profits. This assumption provides a neat contrast with motivational theories in organisation behaviour.

There are two main streams in agency theory. First, one stream commences with the well-established theme of the separation between ownership and control (Berle and Means 1932) and explores the implications for the varied existing forms of the firm from entrepreneurial to publicly owned. It is assumed that existing forms only exist because they are efficient. Given that there is widespread separation of ownership from control the key question is the relationship between the owners (principals) and management (agents). The separation between ownership and control is reflected in the fact that the salaried management of medium and large firms typically owns a very small fraction of the firm's stock, yet makes all the strategic decisions and is not easily controlled by external shareholders on a day-to-day basis. The interests of owners and managers differ (Berle and Means 1967). The owners will seek to maximise their financial returns. The managers may seek to enhance their own prestige, style of life and retirement through company cars, splendid offices and large bonuses. It is probable that owner-managed firms are more profitable, which suggests that owners (principals) ought to consider how they can control their management.

The principals face a number of common problems before and after hiring agents (e.g. managers). Potentially the owner faces costs of monitoring and of finding a solution which is optimal for both parties. Before hiring agents the principals have not directly observed earlier performances. This is known as adverse selection. After hiring agents the problem of moral hazard arises because there is likely to be hidden information and information which has been massaged according to the interests of the agents. The agents may shirk by taking less care of assets than can be achieved. Through the concept of teamwork (Alchian and Demsetz 1986), the problem of shirking within the team is handled through having someone specialise in monitoring, that is, playing the role of principal.

Precision is given to the analysis of managerial behaviour and ownership structures of control by modelling the relationship in a framework of certainty and symmetrical information. The aim is to place the costs of monitoring and the consequences of any social bonding among managers against the interests of owners onto the managers. There are five mechanisms through which principals can obtain some control:

1   There is a market for corporate control and parenting because owners can sell off parts of larger firms on the open market.
2   The development of performance measures and corporate models arising from advances in information software provides the 'signal information' which shareholders can use to exercise some influence and ultimately to transfer their investments.
3   There is competition between managers – a market for managerial labour – to obtain the top jobs.
4   If there is intense competition for the company's products and services this may contain the capacity of managers to pursue their own interests.
5   The owners can devise reward packages.

Second, incentive schemes play a strong role in agency theory. The question is: how should principals design a reward structure for agents? The attention to incentive schemes provides a strong contrast with their total omission in texts on organisation behaviour and their replacement by motivation theories. The principal-agent theory requires the specification of a reward structure in order to incentivise the agent (i.e. the manager).

Transaction costs economics

By the mid-twentieth century the large corporation was prevalent and innovation was undertaken within the firm (Freeman 1974) so the economists' reliance upon the external market mechanism required a re-analysis of the firm's internal hierarchy against a new perfect model. Agency theory provides a key and illustrates that the 'transaction' and its costs is the key analytic event requiring specification.

The existence of modern societies depends upon divisions of labour that create opportunities for specialisation and which require co-ordination mechanisms using information to articulate either markets or hierarchies (Douma and Schreuder 1991: Figure 1.1). Organisation economists contend that whenever an exchange takes place this can be analysed as an economic transaction. Since Coase (1937) there has been a strong case for considering that the two most prevalent mechanisms for allocation and co-ordination are the market and hierarchy of the firm. These are alternatives and according to Coase each has certain costs arising for the making of the contracts and for their delivery. The costs of the market mechanisms can be considerable and therefore efficiency can be achieved by locating alternative mechanisms which reduce market costs. The alternative is the firm which can reduce the need to bargain with every individual over wage rates by using broad categories and benchmarking their wage rates against national and local surveys. These activities by the firm also generate costs, yet under certain circumstances the market mechanisms may fail because the firm can substitute lower transaction costs.

Transaction costs economics (TCE) pivots around the role of information. If the market were considered to be the only relevant mechanisms then price would be the single, overwhelming source of information. Price is regarded as a highly efficient mechanism. However, price information can be supplemented and substituted by co-ordination mechanisms inside the firm because firms are more suited to deal with certain information problems than markets. Information other than prices may contain a degree of uncertainty.

According to Williamson (1975, 1985) existing organisational forms can be explained by assuming that firms and the economic institutions of capitalism evolve towards those forms which reduce transaction costs to their minimum. TCE is based on elements from the behavioural theory of the firm on the assumption that 'human nature as we know it' is boundedly rational (e.g. Simon) and includes lying, cheating and rampant opportunism when situations permit. Given these tendencies then transaction costs will be affected by three dimensions:

1   Whether an investment is for a specific or general purpose: specific assets face the problem of risk and the firm may prefer to locate them internally.
2   Uncertainty is an estimate of what parties to a contract will do in the future and high uncertainty presents the parties with particular problems.
3   The greater the frequency of contracting, then the more likely there will be vertical integration.

For example, in the semi-fashion clothing sector a firm like Marks and Spencer faces uncertainty about future sales and prefers to locate that uncertainty with the supplier while enabling their investment in specific assets through advice and avoiding vertical integration even though there are stable, long-term relationships (e.g. with Dewhirsts).

Routines: still a foundational concept?

This section examines the foundational concept of routine and later introduces the notion of recurrent action patterns (Cohen *et al.* 1996). The chapter is linked to the discussion of the resource-based approach in Chapter 11. It is proposed that recurrent action patterns as a foundational concept provides additional analytic power because of the potentials for linking with foundational concepts in economic sociology such as habitus. The reader's attention is drawn to elements of similarity and difference from the notion of habitus proposed by Bourdieu and discussed in Chapter 4.

Routines, introduced and initially defined by March and Simon (1958), are regarded as a foundational concept in the behavioural theory of the firm (Cyert and March 1963) and in the evolutionary theory of Nelson and Winter (1982) routines are treated as equivalent to DNA and genes. The concept of routines is central to developments in strategy and organisation where Grant (1990, 1998) uses organisational routines as the link between intangible resources and organisation capabilities. The analytic use of routines has increased because of the limitations in a simply cognitive view of organisations. A recent symposium scrutinised the concept of routines as an alternative foundational concept (Cohen *et al.* 1996) and explicitly raised the possibility of the 'recurrent action pattern' as a replacement.

Cognitive realism

Cognitive realism views organisational actors as possessing 'short-term memory limits, reasoning powers, differentiated long-term memory and learning' (Cohen *et al.* 1996: 654) and being situated within the political and social forces found in firms and their contexts. Cognitive realism has used routines as a fundamental concept and so usage of the concept has become very broad and the concept is ripe for some reappraisal. For example, in Nelson and Winter the routine is equated with being the organisational replicator. Given that the cultural phenomena explored in evolutionary perspectives include many replicators then there are problems. By contrast, the tightest definition is that by computer scientists: 'the definition and formalisation of routines'. Unfortunately this neither conveys the original usage by March and Simon (1958) nor addresses the richness in recent usages.

Cognitive realism is a stream of theorising which defines organisations as 'systems of co-ordinated actions among individuals and groups whose preferences, informations, interests and knowledge differ' (March and Simon 1958: 2). This refers to the interlocked behaviours central to Weick (1969) and gives much more attention to the delicate 'conversion of conflict into co-operation' (March 1958: 2). The approach has never been simply cognitive, but has always been multi-person and aware of the conflicts within the firm. Cognitive realism has not extended the political to embrace political economy although some users of the routine concept have done so. How does cognitive realism represent action? Not through raw representational templates as in positivism. The approach of March and Simon has already warned against that tendency even where it is ignored as in large parts of organisation economics. In cognitive realism we assume that within the firm a symbolic construction produces a template (Harre 1979) of small chunks of sequential actions that are constructed symbolically through local languages, the consensually grounded grammar of Weick (1969), and are also embedded in oral codes which are replete with political contest at firm and inter-firm levels. Routines incorporate material and spatial dimensions though these are often at the margins of theorising. Also, in ways yet to be explicated, the routines articulate with the notions in strategy of architectural knowledge (e.g. Henderson 1990). The problem is to explicate the storing processes and yet take account of the possibility for new variations since variations are central to economic and technical change.

March and Simon (1958)

Routines, initially introduced by March and Simon (1958) through an analogy to computer programming, is one of the key analytic units that connects and separates the economic and the sociological. Routines have come to include elements of tacit knowledge, yet the concept has been so stretched that it requires re-specification. The examination of routines provides a bridge into outlining the agenda of economic sociology and showing how its analysis of the market as a social and economic institution (Braudel 1983) can be taken as the direction for selective collaboration with institutional, historical perspectives from economics (e.g. North 1990). The starting point is the approach of March and Simon (1958: 157–177) who developed the behavioural theory of the cognitive limits to rationality as a direct alternative to the neglect of organisations by economists (March and Simon 1958: 1). March and Simon's theorising of routines in the perspective of cognitive realism has provided a foundational concept in organisation theory. Subsequent users have introduced a range of additional features and conditions. In March and Simon (1958):

1   Actors are conceptualised as cognitively constructing their situation in a problem-solving modality. Defining the situation in a particular way arises from a complex interweaving of affective and cognitive processes (p. 172). Choice is present and is potential, yet the actor engages in problem recognition rather than problem solving.
2   Most of organisational activity is a tightly coupled evoking of responses to pre-selected stimuli within and outside the firm. The stimuli include 'situations' cognitively defined and directives/instructions/communications (written and oral). Actors require the ability to recognise and respond. Much organisational action is handled through routine responses.
3   A distinction is drawn between the routine and the non-routine activity. Routine activity is when the selected stimulus is based on a well-structured definition of the situation and evokes a response programme from the repertoire with the minimum of problem solving;
4   Performance programmes are complex sets of responses based on routines (March and Simon 1958: 162–163) which they claim can be identified from observation, interviewing and examining standard operating procedures. The structure of the firm is a mosaic of performance programmes. The content of performance programmes will vary in the degree to which activities and product specifications are detailed as well as in inbuilt rules for pacing activities. Performance programmes function as control systems and 'serve as co-ordination devices' by synchronising activities. The programmes have two steps: the evoking and the execution. Evoking can arise in numerous ways including scanning the organisation and scanning the context. Execution is contingent upon the situation.

These four attributes indicate the extent to which March and Simon considered that the firm was typified by inertial qualities. By contrast the same concept of routine was invoked within organisation economics in an evolutionary perspective where the major influence has been from Nelson and Winter's (1982) theory of routines as an organisational DNA.

Nelson and Winter: quasi-genetic traits

Within the imperialism of the new economics, evolutionary economics has promoted a dynamic perspective on capabilities and innovation (e.g. Metcalfe 1998) in which the roster of key concepts includes – in addition to routines – the following list of starting points, cumulative path dependency models, historical accidents, 'stickiness of institutions', inefficient history, innovation and trajectories. Since the publication of Nelson and Winter's (1982) evolutionary theory, 'the routine' has been a foundational concept in evolutionary theory and has influenced organisation economics (e.g. Douma and Schreuder 1991) and strategy (e.g. Grant 1990, 1998). Many users have been puzzled by the metaphor depicting routines as the DNA of firms because they have ignored the detail of Nelson and Winter and have overridden the caveats. Also, there have been important developments in theory and research which develop the cognitive theory of organising (see Cohen *et al.* 1996: 667–671). Given these developments and the wide, varying senses in which routine is now being used the foundational concept is ripe for reappraisal (Winter 1994, 1996) and restatement of quasi-genetic traits (see Cohen *et al.* 1996: 663–666). The issue is whether the definition of routine by Nelson and Winter requires revision and perhaps replacement. There are numerous problems, especially with respect to whether routines are replicators as suggested in an evolutionary theory. We shall argue against that interpretation and prefer to relocate routine relative to other 'recurring action patterns' in organisations (Clark and Staunton 1989).

The evolutionary theory of economic change by Nelson and Winter (1982: Chapter 5) locates routines at the core of the analysis because organisational routines 'play the role that genes play in evolutionary theory. . . persistent feature . . . determine its possible behaviour . . . are heritable . . . selectable and their relative importance is augmented over time' (1982: 14). The term routine is used very broadly to refer to 'most of what is regular and predictable about business behaviour' including 'the relatively constant dispositions and strategic heuristics that shape the approach of a firm to the non-routine problems it faces' (1982: 15). At the level of department a routine is 'a web of co-ordinating relationships connecting specific resources' (1994: 149) and would not exist without those resources. Those resources are therefore not available through the market in this firm because their combining is specific to one firm.

Nelson and Winter build upon, contribute to, extend and formalise cognitive realism through the notion of routines. Through their influence routines has become a foundational concept in organisation economics and in evolutionary economics. Since the early 1990s routines are now used in a wide variety of ways and within organisation economics only a part of cognitive realism is involved (e.g. Douma and Schreuder 1991).

How should routines be defined? The definition of routine used in computer science is an 'executable program' and this is much too restrictive. After considerable and careful recent debate, Cohen and colleagues (1996: 683) propose that a routine 'is an executable *capability* for repeated performance in some *context* that has been *learned* by an organisation in response to *selective pressures*'. Capability refers to the capacity to generate action (e.g. an unfolding action sequence) which is in the 'memory' of that part of the organisation. Context is interpreted as a powerful feature of remembering and consists of routinised interpretations and actions which are both firm and situation specific. Learned routines are habits characterised by high tacit knowledge and by invariant reproduction vis-à-vis fine-grained informational change. Selective pressures is meant broadly to denote a wide variety of forces that could make particular sequences of action more or less likely to be unfolded. It should be noted that the notion of selective pressures still requires further scrutiny because context dependence is so difficult to account for and there is a strong tendency to neglect or to obfuscate context dependency (p. 662). The problem is similar to that arising in respect of Penrose's (1959) much cited analysis of learned experience (e.g. Grant 1990).

This leads back into how in their own formulation Nelson and Winter invoked the metaphor of the routine as DNA. That is clearly problematic because routines are neither replicated or replicators. Cohen and colleagues (1996) seek to rescue and refine the original thinking by the notion of quasi-genetic traits (Cohen *et al.* 1996: 663–666). These traits cover three parts: routines, heuristics and paradigms.

1   There are *routines and simple decision rules.* Routines can be evoked and are complex, repetitive behaviours functioning as a unit possessing capacities for information processing. Decision rules simplify and are part of the bounded rationality.

2   *Strategic heuristics are categories and dispositions* which orient and structure a continuum of problem-solving actions directed at situations which some categories define as similar. Within universities, for example, there are strategic heuristics reducing the overall space of buildings and campus to broad scope formulae which are invoked in competitive struggles over resources within the university.

3   There are *cognitive frameworks, models and paradigms* arising from long periods of experience which are used to shape corporate actions.

The definition of quasi-genetic traits (QGTs) refines the earlier definition of routines by Nelson and Winter, but at a price. The biological analogy of DNA and genes is grossly overdrawn. There are many examples of pre-existing firms that open branch plants which lack key genes. Thus, Clark and Starkey (1988) describe the failure of Europe's largest knitwear firm to provide its major new branch factory with the architectural knowledge necessary to its survival. Therefore, it is prudent to abandon the genetic analogy and to interpret the notion of QGTs as an attempt to incorporate some aspects of the sociological analysis of recursiveness (Giddens 1984; Clark 1977). In considering QGTs it is useful to note the growing literature on corporate conversations (e.g. Boden 1994), on sensemaking (Weick 1995), on sequences and durations (Clark 1985) and on managerial realism (Reed 1992).

Are all recurrent action patterns in organisations covered by this definition of routines? Marengo (in Cohen *et al.* 1996) illustrates the problem by describing the case of the kanban in an assembly system and asking: is the routine an adequate language and do we have the analytic language for analysing this action? Kanban systems are carefully designed artificial environments in which workers have been taught and learned co-ordinated behaviours of the kind which March and Simon considered to be central. The workers follow explicitly stated rules and instructions as well as possessing tacit knowledge and non-deliberate behaviours. These are examples of the ingredients of a definition of routines which keep recurring, are selectable from the repertoire and are located in an organisational context. However, the ingredients differ in their cognitive character and in the ways in which they are reproduced. The unexplained aspect is the relations between the ingredients, how they reciprocate within their clustering and in relation to other clusterings which make a kanban system possible. These other elements include parallel actions such as the reduction in set-up times and in working capital. These relational ingredients possess their own architecture. This relational architecture is recurring, selectable and may be transferable.

Resource based analysis introduced

The resource based analysis (RBA) of the firm develops from the proposal of Wernerfelt (1984, 1995) and, within strategic management, represents a major development. This section introduces RBA and primes the ground for the discussion of resources in Chapter 10. Wernerfelt's definition of resources is pretty broad and includes the knowledge underpinning the productive capabilities of the firm. Resources are anything which can be a strength or weakness that is tied to the firm on a semi-permanent basis. There are tangible resources (e.g. physical plant and buildings) that are relatively easily measured and can be traded in the open market. The intangibles are idiosyncratic and firm specific. In a recent assessment it was concluded that intangibles account for approximately half the market value of the 6,000 leading firms in the USA. It is therefore the intangible resources (e.g. corporate reputation) which are occupying attention, especially in the distinction between resources and capabilities (Grant 1995). The effective deployment of the firm's resources requires the development of a diverse array of managerial tasks. Exponents of RBA frequently invoke Penrose's analysis of managerial teams to explain the mechanism linking resources to capabilities and performance. Amit and Shoemaker (1993) suggest that resources should only refer to those factors owned and controlled by the firm which are tradable in the market, while capabilities refers to the capacity to use those resources.

NEW ECONOMIC SOCIOLOGY

Romancing the market

The debate over the economy in a social perspective resurfaced in the 1980s after having been quiescent since the debates joined by Weber, Durkheim and Schumpeter in the first quarter of the twentieth century (Swedberg and Granovetter 1992; Powell *et al.* 1996). The stimulus for this debate arose from the attention given to the market mechanism in the positive political economy and from an urgency in describing, explaining and responding to the very successful performance of Japanese firms in penetrating the European and North American markets. By the 1990s a vigorous, robust response to organisational economics had proclaimed the new economic sociology. The new economic sociology responded to the claims of organisational economics with objections, revisions and rejections while situating economic action in a social perspective. The tensions within organisation economics, for example, between the resource based theory and evolutionary economics, are not usefully suppressed in road maps displaying their respective positions in dealing with context and dynamics (e.g. Douma and Schreuder 1991: Figure 10.3). The tensions highlight the importance of analytic power in a realist perspective.

Economy as a social perspective stipulates that economic action is a form of social action. The basic building block is economic action, but sociological concepts (e.g. Weber) differ from those in economic theory. In the earlier debates Weber proposed that all action is oriented towards other peoples and takes into account the behaviour of others through socially constructed meanings. The economy as a peaceful mechanism constitutes a major source of power only through its legal sanctioning. Exchange relationships and economic action represent substantive regulation. Polyani (1957) revived the debate by examining the role of markets, but confused theorising by polarising the degree to which markets are embedded between traditional societies (totally embedded) and modern societies (lightly embedded). Braudel (1985) stated that Polyani was wrong and that all types of exchange are economic and social as illustrated in Figure 5.1.

In the 1967 version of the *Encyclopaedia of the Social Sciences* edited by Shils there was a section on competition but not a section on the market. By the 1980s the 'market' had become a key word in political discourse everywhere and represents one of the most important economic institutions for understanding economic performance of the firm and the nation (Hobsbawm 1998). According to Swedberg, the market is a specific type of social structure with recurrent and patterned interactions between agents that are maintained through power relations, normative frameworks, habitus-like action and socially constructed forms of explicit expertise. Sociologists note that the father of transaction costs opines that the market is a social institution which facilitates exchange.

Swedberg observes that the definition of markets and their analytic treatment by economists and political economists has passed through a complex journey in the last millennium. In the twelfth century the market meant a physical place to trade at designated times and a legal licensing of a form of gathering for that special purpose. By the sixteenth century the meaning of the market had extended from place and event into space and referred to the general exchange process involving buying and selling rather than gifts of exchange. Adam Smith (1776) heightened the abstraction in his seminal proposition that the depth and extent of the division of labour was connected to how the market influences prices and he was convinced that larger markets led to greater overall wealth. For Adam Smith the market was still quite concrete (e.g. the potential of the USA as an agricultural market) and the analytic role of the market price was undermined by the apparent influence of chance events (e.g. weather). By the close of the nineteenth century the market had become an abstract concept with a theoretically central role in price making and as mechanism for co-ordinating the allocation of resources.

In the twentieth century the analysis of markets in neo-classical economics is dealt with in abstract space and time (e.g. Marshall 1919) with decreasing attention to regulation (formal and informal) between buyers and sellers. The time dimension was very abstract and confined to analytical fictions like the 'short run' and the 'long run'. By contrast the market in neo-Austrian economics is the decentralised outcome of human action based on local knowledge of opportunities. These approaches shared the view that markets contain clearing mechanisms which ensure high levels of productivity and of general well-being.

Keynsian economics after 1936 is sceptical about market clearing, especially in the labour markets associated with levels of employment. Intervention is required by the state to regulate the market. The strategy-conduct-performance paradigm also deviates from the neo-classical lines in the critique of perfect competition by neglecting the differentiation of products arising from social factors, patents, trademarks and advertising. The contemporary version of the strategy-conduct-performance paradigm replaced the single market of many sellers with a network of related markets each with a single seller and boundaries between markets. Therefore the study of corporate pricing policies (the conduct) becomes important and can be derived from the market structure. Generally the market was equated with the industry; market structure was equated with barriers to entry and areas of concentration; market conduct referred to price setting and policies about rivals; market performance referred to employment and social consequences. The strategy-conduct-performance paradigm is influenced by industrial economics and also approaches to strategy, especially the earlier work of Porter.

A critical account of the clearing mechanisms of the market suggests that markets only clear when a variety of different mechanisms actually exists and that some of these mechanisms may be too expensive (e.g. auction markets). We are now close to the market as a social institution, but leaders of the new institutional economics do not quite reach that conclusion. Yet Coase *et al.* (1990) provide concepts which enable the analysis of markets anchored in property rights and transaction costs (e.g. for search, enforcement and measurement of transactions). North does not presume that markets are efficient or that history is efficient and emphasises that some economic institutions may increase costs. He does, however, draw an analytic distinction between institutional contexts which favoured economic growth (e.g. North West Europe in the long sixteenth century) and those which inhibit. The logic of North's analysis highlights the resource allocation mechanism potentials of historically efficient markets. We are now close – yet need to leap – to Braudel's claim that markets are both economic and social and to argue that the US market was a 'key base' from the 1870s until the 1960s (Clark 1987: Ch. 10).

Sociological attention to the market preoccupied Weber (1922) in *Economy and Society*. The level of analysis was usually the state and the region (e.g. Eastern Prussia). Weber saw markets as taking different forms depending on the degree to which they were regulated. Markets are the outcome of long historical struggles embracing the social and the economic within which shifts in power and struggle might lead national competition to enter exchange rather than warfare. From Weber until the rebirth of the sociology of markets only Polyani (1944, 1957) and Parsons with Smelser (1956) gave the market high attention even from a sociological perspective. Polyani concluded that the local market and long-distance market co-existed in the very distant past and were heavily embedded in social regulations. According to Polyani this political and social embedding was severely disrupted by the creation of the European mercantilist state with its internal, nationally regulated markets after the seventeenth century. Then, in mid-nineteenth century England, all regulations were removed in an attempt to create a massive market for products and labour. This event was taken by Polyani to have created a template and a utopian ideal which in paradoxical, unintended ways triggered the major European wars of the twentieth century.

The rebirth of a sociology of the market and of interest in economic action arose from several lines of analysis including the theorising of Giddens and Bourdieu as well as interest in historians such as Braudel. The aim of showing that the market is less of a featureless plane and more of lumpy terrain has used network analysis (Nohria and Eccles 1992) to depict the various ties between a clustering of firms in the same production market with its own revenue features. White (1987) observes that the markets revealed by networks are cliques of firms watching one another. Networks vary in their density of connections. Burt (1982) compares the structural autonomy of networks in respect of the relative proportion of competitors, suppliers and customers. It is assumed that autonomy is high when there are few competitors and many small suppliers/customers. These industrial markets are constituted from the interaction between firms in their sector leading to sectoral institutions.

The sociological definition of firms is important. Sociologists tend to define the firm in a capitalist world economy in the following way:

1   The firm is a working community containing mutually antagonistic and common interests that are connected to the struggle over the control of property rights inherent in capitalism.
2   The worker provides a good or service to a defined, yet varied population

ranging from customers and students to prisoners. The work may be consumed by the customer as a pleasure as in professionalised sport.

3   The working community is embedded in a national system and a national culture. Each of these contain mechanisms affecting their reproduction or transformation. It is likely that the national market is a major actor in shaping the expertise and learning of the firm's top management.

4   The working community is increasingly organised by abstract principles and templates of best practice contained in discourse from consultants who claim to provide the best analysis of value-adding activity.

5   The firm is often in competition with alternatives and also in co-operation with firms in its network and chain.

6   Unless the working community can construct a constitution for resolving conflicts of interest then the firm is likely to be selected out from its competitive domain.

7   Firms are located in networks and chains along supply lines. Some firms may be pivotal in shaping parts of the chain and even the chain as an overall structure. Ikea shapes the actions of a variety of suppliers across Europe.

8   Firms are often multi-site with sites in different nations. This extended network requires capacities to enrol and control the discretion of distant units while also adapting to local contexts and accumulating learning.

Sociological definitions of the firm are complemented by their theorising of markets (Fligstein 1990). Markets require political forces to operate and the institutionalised system of rules includes:

- social relations that determine who has claims upon the profits of the firm – that is property rights;
- general rules of competition and market specific definitions of the governance structures of firms;
- economic actors with a shared 'recipe knowledge' about interpreting situations in order to inhibit actions that might undermine the market they have defined;
- rules of exchange that specify who can transact with whom and the conditions under which transactions should be carried out.

These four elements are necessary for markets to operate. Sociologists argue that markets have to be socially constructed and politically maintained. Therefore the state plays a central role in its territorial domain even when that depends upon the rules of exchange shared by a number of states. The market is a cluster of regulated institutions.

Callon (1997) defines the market network as a co-ordination device in which:

- agents pursue their own interests, being guided by economic calculations;
- the agents as buyers and sellers have divergent interests;
- transactions between them resolve the conflict by defining a price.

The agents therefore engage in economic calculations from which the output is the price and:

- decision-making is decentralised;
- there is a process of translation (equivalence) between conflicting interests;
- there must be agents capable of calculation;
- contingent contracts represent one way of ordering the processes of conflict;
- there must be an *homo clausus*.

Callon (1997) provides an insightful analysis of ways in which the notion of an economic transaction depends upon breaking away from embeddedness.

Addressing economic imperialism

Economic imperialism through organisation economics, resource based analysis and evolutionary economics has drawn attention to issues and facets of the firm which mainstream organisation behaviour had minimised, but which the new sociology of economic action and the new institutionalism wish to address.

Organisation economics and its imperialism does highlight neglected elements. First, juxtaposing the market mechanism of price and the internal co-ordination mechanisms of the firm as alternatives provides an impetus away from a narrow focus upon structure inserted by the founding of the *Administrative Science Quarterly* in 1956 to a deeper consideration of the performance of internal processes. Second, agency theory provides a sharp contrast to the bland, optimistic theories of motivation, leadership, job design and structure which are still so central in organisation behaviour. Third, agency theory also highlights the question of what managers contribute as distinct from their activities (cf. Mintzberg 1970). The separation between ownership and management represents different vested interests. Fourth, developments in information technology provide new opportunities to disaggregate the firm and increase the transparency of activities (Clark 1996). The firm as a nexus of contracts has some substance in the services sector, perhaps in supermarket operations. Fifth, organisation economics uses concepts such as teamwork, corporate governance and incentivising in ways which challenge their bland treatment in organisation behaviour. Sixth, in the resource-based approaches the whole issue of intangible resources and capabilities has been developed in ways which expose the basic equilibrium assumptions and expose some of the claims of the evolutionary economists. Seventh, organisational economics has given serious and significant attention to the feature of incentivising for all strata. Indeed, incentivising is both a feature of the knowledge professional and also a tactic used to enrol them.

Economic imperialism has been taken by its proponents to mean that the forthcoming revolution in organisation theory, and hence organisation behaviour, will be driven by economic models. There is no doubting that mainstream economists can apply their basic theoretical frameworks to show that markets and equilibrium models as they define them provide an analytic tool kit and set of instruments which can embrace the market for crime and marriage almost as readily as more conventional applications. The issue is the analytic value which is deployed and the usefulness of the policy implications which follow. Therefore it is more likely that the revising and replacing of the existing analytic limits will be a hybrid and that organisation economics will continue as a parallel disciplinary community (Barney 1990; Buckley and Casson 1993; Hesterly *et al.* 1990). Figure 5.1 remains the framework within which the conversation between organisation economics and economic sociology is pursued.

SUMMARY

The imperialism by economists with respect to the analysis of the firm and its surrounding institutions represents a major, significant development with considerable implications for the analysis of the firm 'in action' by social scientists. This chapter has compared the approach of the organisation economists and the organisation theorists. The conversation between them provides an important background for the examination in Part II of the theme of competition between contexts.

Part II

Competition between contexts

6 Long-term political economy

Hegemony, dependence and markets

INTRODUCTION

This chapter examines the long-term shifts in the location of major regions of accumulation within the capitalist system and the major shifts in the role of knowledge and innovation design. The perspective applied draws from the notion of multiple world systems of Braudel (1972) rather than the notion of a singular world system. Braudellian world systems cluster around centres of accumulation and their capacity to establish inter-nation political economies governed by rules which benefit the core. In a neo-Gramscian perspective the world systems appear to be economies rather than empires because the justifying ideology typically emphasises a solution to the problem of regulating markets. Key concepts to be defined, explained and illustrated include hegemony and dependence. Cores are distinguished from dependent areas because of a combination of mode of production with forms of military power (Arrighi 1994; Kennedy 1987).

One puzzle is to explain the rise of the North West European and the North Atlantic economies, relative to Asia. The rise is remarkable because at the close of the first millennium Europe was the weakest and most ravaged major civilisation and well behind Islam and China in its science and technology (Landes 1998). However, by the sixteenth century North West Europe occupied a powerful position and was about to expand through commerce and hegemony rather than simple conquest and military control. From the sixteenth century onward the key zone of expansion was North America. This five-hundred-year period since the sixteenth century was one in which the seaboard towns and nations from North West Europe 'flowed up, down and then out of the Atlantic' taking their military and trading prowess into the Indian and Pacific Oceans. The Portuguese and Spanish were early pioneers, then the Dutch followed by the English (even the British) and French until the emergence of the USA at the start of the nineteenth century. The English were geographically well placed in this trading, seaboard world. In the twentieth century the USA was a major source of new production techniques and a key player in the regimes of accumulation. The USA was the home context for the notion of design, even design of the wilderness. It was also the home base to high volume production and distribution. Germany emerged as the major European player. Its form of technique has certainly been effective, though its analysis has been overshadowed by attention to the rise after 1870 of the Japanese who avoided colonisation and entered a period of appropriation of western technique and practices. In the last quarter of the twentieth century attention has focused upon the emergence of forms of market relationship and of work organisation which differ from those preceding.

The problem is to theorise and to describe the emergent forms and their relationship to the earlier 'quasi-Fordist' techniques and regimes of accumulation (Best 1990). Piore and Sabel (1984) initially proposed that the new major techniques were a return to earlier features such as the industrial district. In contrast Pine (1993) claims that there is a major shift to mass customisation. The latter proposition has been heavily promoted by one cluster of major new 'masters of meaning': the corporate consultancies and the gurus. The debate centres on the extent to which tendencies towards mass production and distribution have and are being displaced by mass customisation. This shift might have begun in the early 1970s and gained pace thereafter. The idea of mass customisation provides a framework within which the degree of shift and its possible development can be assessed.

The chapter contains four sections:

- hegemony, dependence and markets;
- the long term as an analytically structured narrative with slowly changing social fields and institutional ensembles;
- the case of the North Atlantic nations;
- design knowledge intensity and compression.

Chapters 7 and 8 develop the basic framework which is then illustrated by American exceptionalism (Chapter 9) and selected features from the British case (Chapter 10). These five chapters explain and illustrate the theme of competition between contexts.

HEGEMONY, DEPENDENCE AND MARKETS

In Europe the disciplinary fields of economic and social geography are in transition (Dicken 1998; Leyshon and Thrift 1997; Gregory 1994; Harvey 1996). The new geography[1] seeks to break from dominant discourse of neo-classical and neo-Marxist perspectives that made the economy the central motor of change towards an analysis of discourse and a more reflexive political economy. The new geography follows the realist and post-modern turns and takes a distinctive position on what the neo-modern might contribute to the exploration of competition between contexts. Leyshon and Thrift (1997: Chapter 8) argue that the new geography is deeply involved in the re-description of metaphors because these frequently shape thinking about political interventions and that requires a reflexive analysis of the discourse of economic geography to situate the dynamic within contingency and specificity (Clark and Staunton 1989: Chapter 3).

The problem with the dominant discourse in the economic geography of the economy and of money is the common underpinning inserted by neo-classical economics and Marxism. They both placed the economy as the master concept and the major driver of social change by invoking the laws of motion by using metaphors constructed from nineteenth-century physics. Consequently, their different discourse conspired to share a common notion of political intervention. The concepts of capital circulation and the reproduction of capitalism are too reified and suppress the capacity of actors to modify present action by imagining its consequences based on previous experiences: reflexivity. These concepts also underplay the singularities of time-space and the ever presence of contingency.

The dominant economic discourse in geography needs to be historicised and its own concepts need to be recognised as cultural tools deployed to impose order (Leyshon and Thrift 1997). The proposed line of analysis overlaps with the new economic sociology in rejecting mechanistic, multi-stage models. Two lines of analysis are proposed and playfully deployed: regulation theory and the neo-Gramscian political economy. First, regulation theory (Aglietta 1987: Boyer 1990; Coriat 1976, 1990; Lipietz 1992) replaces the Marxist between the economic base and social superstructure. The account of history is less teleological and more nuanced so that the crises of capitalism are contingent and uneven (cf. Althusser). Also, the key relationship is between:

- the accumulation system as a production-consumption nexus whereby the possibility for the supply side decisions of capitalist owners is articulated (by the state and intermediaries) with the demand to be realised in the market;
- the mode of social regulation is a collection of regulatory markets which ensure that capital accumulation becomes a reality. The mode of social regulation is totally implicated in capitalist accumulation, yet is socio-political.

There are variants of regulation theory, but the general tendency is to give these two elements equal analytic weighting, though there are also tendencies to underline reproduction (e.g. reproduction of a post-Fordist system). Regulation theory permits attention to ideology and cultural processes, yet the analytic weighting is light relative to neo-Gramscian political economy.

Neo-Gramscian political economy possesses important connections to and differences from the new economic sociology discussed in Chapter 4 (e.g. Swedberg, Fligstein, DiMaggio, Powell). More metaphorical re-description is involved, this time with respect to structural spaces and the reliance on equilibrium. Structural spaces now refer to inter-state relations somewhat in the manner of Arrighi's (1994) stimulating analysis of shifting hegemonies of historical capitalism expressing the world influence of the North Atlantic. Arrighi seeks to develop the lines of analysis on world hegemony (e.g. Britain in the nineteenth century) proposed by Braudel (1983) and Tilly's (1984, 1992) examination of European state power by distinguishing simple dominance based on military power from hegemony as the capacity of a dominant grouping to offer an apparently ethical, seemingly non-military relationship through which many states can undertake economic exchange. The rules of world hegemony favour particularly powerful clusters such as the USA for much of the middle twentieth century. Neo-Gramscian political economy possesses three elements:

- an economic structure;
- political society (formal and informal political institutions);
- civil society.

The civil society is where ideological, intellectual struggles take place and identities are constituted. Gramsci's concept of the civil society introduces indeterminacy and contingency as well as the notion of an ensemble containing ideas, institutions and material capacities. In effect this is a heterogeneous actor network.[2] The role of organic intellectuals is constituted by those propertyless elites working on intellectual production, including social explanation (e.g. media). These are the symbolic analysts so prized by Reich (1991). Intellectual work usually involves claims for justification and about the ordering of socio-political life. Some of this intellectual work consists of general principles which, although favouring the already powerful, can be presented as seemingly neutral guiding principles. The intellectuals write the scripts of hegemony order and these become the operating discourses of power-knowledge. Hegemonic principles enrol less powerful, potentially opposing groupings in a common network providing consent, albeit sceptical and critical consent. This is hegemonic control from the civil domain within societies and therefore can also be expressed as relationships between societies. Hegemonic scripts possess exciting metaphors, plots and narratives. Particular narratives dominate, provide interpretative flexibility yet constantly face challenges from alternative elites. Hegemonic scripts are a silent element in the new institutional perspectives (e.g. DiMaggio and Powell 1991) requiring more development.

Political economy contains examples of hegemonic principles dominating inter-state relationships. For example, the role of the Bretton Woods agreement in shaping co-operation in the North Atlantic from 1945 to 1970. The prime beneficiary was the USA and the new rules of the game publicly demonstrated the total passage of influence from earlier period of British hegemony. This theme is carried further in Chapter 9.

Hegemonic power is a form of inter-state competition that differs in key particulars from dominance by explicit military force and coercion (Arrighi 1994). Dominance of one nation by another through military force and coercion leading to the conquest, coercion and elimination of rivals is expensive to apply and rarely generates long-run revenue. This form of dominance can lead to inflation. By comparison hegemonic power and leadership between nations is the capacity to relocate some of the issues around which national conflict unfolds on another level by providing governing rules between nations to cover economic activities. The core nations can author and then edit the 'rules of the game' by claiming that these represent the general interest. The core nation obscures its distinctive benefits. These governing rules are often generative and open to improvisation when encountering new conditions. Once established, the governing rules can persist for generations. In the case of western capitalism the hegemonic rules reduce conflict and structure chaos by settling the conditions of trade between nations. In the late twentieth century these rules have been amplified to incorporate intellectual property rights through institutions with authority in particular nations (e.g. USA) and between nations. There are likely to be issues of contest as with the claims of Microsoft in China during the 1990s, yet the rules can gain centrality and eventually enrol more parties.

ANALYTICALLY STRUCTURED NARRATIVES SANS GRANDEUR

Temporality: conversations and issues

This section briefly explores and reviews the position of the claims of many exponents in each of the five perspectives (Figure 2.1) to be one or more of the following: historical, longitudinal, to take the long term and to do real time studies. There is a strong heritage of the positivist notion of time and modern concern with progressive time. The post-modern, the realist turn and the structuration perspectives each contribute to the critique of the positivist-modern position. My approach to the neo-modern political economy is to advocate the analytically structured narrative sans grandeur (Clark 1987; Archer 1995). Consequently this book contains numerous case-like cameos in which temporality of events and placeness of spatiality are implicated (Gregory 1994: 412). My contention is that these are analytically structured narratives without grandeur (Archer 1995). Moreover, this position does not preclude the continuity of structures over time, but it does preclude the assumption that the future can be extrapolated from the past. The analytically structured narrative assumes that the previous cycles of recursive structuring are dynamically contingent.

The dimension of history is frequently invoked in explanations offered in organisation studies and strategy. What do these statements mean? Typically, history is regarded as narrative and the telling of a story (Hexter 1972; Callinicos 1995). Often, though to a decreasing extent, the implication of narrative is that the readers can relax their critical, sceptical faculties. Also, there is the use of history to produce macro-patterns for informing ongoing policy making found in the old modernisation school (Eisenstadt 1967). Given that contingent linearity is a feature of the neo-modernisation perspective there are issues requiring attention.

In organisation studies there are many references to dynamic processual approaches, especially the variants of evolutionary dynamics and the 'in time' school of analysts. Linearity and homogeneous time are implicated in all these. The problematic of temporality and some of the problems of structuration are central to the analysis of time and structure in organisational sociology (Clark 1975b, 1978, 1985, 1997a, b). The position of linearity has been challenged by the post-modern critiques and they have set historians a full agenda of challenging problems (e.g. Evans 1997). The safe, previously unchallenged notion of history as a common-sense empirical account of what actually happened has been widely challenged and not only by the post-modern turn. In addition those following the realist turn also question the treatment of linearity in the modern perspective, yet promote the view of temporality that aims to make the enduring elements of structures and causal mechanisms contingent. Realists espouse a contingent time coupled with the contingent significance of pre-existing structures. Realists critique the claim of the structuration school to handle time and space. Archer argues that Giddens's version of structure and agency elides time (Archer 1988, 1995). These debates and conversations suggest four broad issues and questions:

1   Why is linearity problematic in history and in the longitudinal perspectives? What is the difference between time and temporality?
2   How quickly do clusters of social fields and institutional ensembles transform their core techniques? How long is the long-term and how are processes periodised? What is meant by the long-term? Is the long-term centuries (e.g. Braudel, Landes, Kieser), generations (e.g. Elias), fifteen years (e.g. Porter 1990), or three years as in many concurrent 'real time' studies of the long-itudinal in organisation studies. This section reviews the typical usages of the long-term in organisation theory/OS and some features of the conventional historians' approach. The problem is how to theorise linearity.
3   With respect to the future, how are possibilities, dislocations, scenarios and virtual history to be understood?
4   What is meant by the analytically structured narrative and how does it differ from the everyday case study?

We start the examination of these issues by returning to the positivist-modern heritage.

Positivist-modern tendencies

In organisation theory and strategy there is a strong positivist-modern heritage in dealing with processes, linearity and history. Therefore time is treated as a homogeneous variable. Consequently, the position of temporality and the plurality heterogeneous event-time reckoning is not thoroughly grasped (Clark 1985, 1997a, b).

1   Much of organisation theory and research is ahistorical and examines events within an extended present (Nowotony 1994).
2   Even when historical accounts are offered as in business histories there is a strong tendency to ignore the post-modern challenge and its claim that history is theoretical rather than empiricist, documentarist and simply factual (Jenkins 1997). The business histories may be presented in a common-sense, quasi-pluralist form whose lack of rhetoric and reflexivity leaves ideological assumptions unexplored (Eagleton 1996).

3 Frequently the time frame is only in calendar time and presumes a simple account of history (cf. Gurvitch 1964). Even studies which claim to be long-itudinal cover only two to three years – the time of a doctoral thesis. The references to 'real time' are less impressive than is suggested because these also tend to be short periods of time. Within these very short time frames the temporal sequencing of action is obscured within an extended present which neither addresses the possible influence of the pre-existing nor dislocations which might unfold in the future.

4 Often case studies found in business schools do not include an attenuated time scale in which the founding of the firm is mentioned and located on a simple calendar listing events. There is a leap from the founding period across time to the present so that there is grossly simplified periodisation into founding and the foreshortened extended present. It is rare to find an analytically sound periodisation of episodes.

5 Hagiography is the producing of histories to demonstrate the central and favourable role of key persons. This is sometimes found in the 'turnaround type' of analysis. It is rare for the analysis of the turnaround to adopt the wide analytic scope used by Reich and Donaghue (1986) in their insightful recon-struction of how Chrysler was rescued from bankruptcy. Hagiography is mainly about males and rarely about females.

6 Even when a narrative is presented it may be detached from the underlying mechanisms and the influence of the context – a surface narrative.

7 One widespread usage of the longitudinal dimension is life-cycle theories of organisation. These multi-stage type theories are widespread in organisation theory and redolent of the development theories from the modernist period (see Alexander 1995). Life-cycle theories contain several well known examples. Child and Kieser (1981) provide one of the most thoughtful and carefully nuanced accounts of the organisational life cycle. However, it is important to note just how far Kieser's (1998) recent approach has developed. Another useful example is from the sector life cycle of Abernathy (1978) because his work exemplified the need for care and a more sophisticated understanding of temporality (Clark and Starkey 1988).

8 The imposition of grand narratives upon 'historical materials', as in Marx's analysis of the dynamics of capital and the civil society, is a target for both the post-modern critique and the realist turn.

9 Although the Foucauldian discourse analysis has been widely invoked, this is frequently impressed into a vague extended present with only slight attention to struggles. Hoskin and Macve's (1988) analysis of particular configurations of power and knowledge at the West Point Academy tends to privilege the discourse and not to unpack the unplanned configuration of groups and interests involved, for example, the political economy of American conflict with Britain. Imagine how Elias would have analysed West Point.

10 Even when the positivist-modern perspective refers to the pre-existing situa-tion (e.g. Lewin's stage model) there is too much attention to the notion that future events can be ordered.

There needs to be analytic dualism between the previous event cycles and the unfolding cycles (Clark 1972). The requirement is for an analytic dualism that gives 'equal' attention to the pre-existing causal processes, mechanism and socio-structural conditions as well as the agentic unfolding of the new round of events. The implication is that some social fields (as Bourdieu) retain their core configurations for decades and generations, possibly longer.

Confining and replacing the positivist-modern tendencies may be informed by the issues discussed in the next sections and the proposal for narratives that are analytically structured and frequently, though not always, without grandeur.

Periodising and scoping the past, present, future

One issue for temporality is the scope of past, present and future required in specific pieces of analysis. Temporality requires attention to forms of periodisation embedded in the events and therefore indicative of the processes being analysed (Clark 1985). Roth (1963) and Dubinskas (1988) illustrate temporality from the medical and scientific fields revealing the problematic use of temporality in some studies of innovation in organisation and technology (Barley 1986, 1990; cf. Clark and Staunton 1989). The examples of studies attempting to periodise the past, present and future from a reflexively articulated analytic position by Lazonick (1991) and Schoenberger (1996) clarify some of the points in discussion. They each analyse the decline of the British cotton industry in the face of international competition, especially from the US industry. The British cotton industry is a useful example of a social field (as Bourdieu) persisting as an ensemble. The different explanations of Lazonick (1991) and Schoenberger (1996) illustrate the significance of the context and challenge conventional views of industrial competitiveness:

1   Lazonick (1991) notes that at the crucial moment after the 1830s when the self-acting mule was introduced into spinning the pre-existing division of labour remained intact because employers lacked the ability to insert new forms of co-ordination similar to their American rivals. In Lancashire the employers lacked the capacity to author and appropriate a supervisory role into management. In New England there was top-down control over time and space in production work organisation.

2   Schoenberger seeks to show the connection between the employers' competitive strategy in the face of strong craft control that disrupted the employers' control of time-space commodification in the organisation production and the employers' strategic choices. Schoenberger explains that in Lancashire (England), despite high wages and craft control, the industry remained internationally competitive through:

  • applying piecework systems to increase the productivity of the existing technology;
  • the use of cheaper cotton;

- altering the turnover time of capital by entering and dominating the Indian market for cheap goods to which they had privileged access.

Lancashire retained preferential market access until World War I (1914–18) after which the basis of the strategy was undermined. We shall briefly return to the British textile industry when examining the sectoral cluster surrounding Marks & Spencer in Chapter 10.

The analytically structured narrative of Lancashire cotton exemplifies the claim that there can be institutional durability and therefore the past has a powerful influence (Chandler 1977). The narrative also illustrates the attempt to establish periodisation of the past and to detect turning points. Lazonick and Schoenberger attempt to apply some analytic notion of causality to selected and theorised events while being aware of the ways in which enduring structures can be de-institutionalised (Oliver 1991).

The potential for periodising and scoping temporality involves the dimensions found in the spectrum of social times proposed by Gurvitch (1964) and organised as in Table 6.1 (Clark 1985: 44).[3] The three dimensions are: relation between the past, present and future; the degree of continuity, contingency and surprise; the durational experience, including the sense of pace. There is an eightfold taxonomy. The intention is that the temporality of institutions and structuration should be scoped by using these dimensions and types as an analytic tool (cf. Giddens 1979 on Gurvitch).

The temporality proposed by Gurvitch provides a strong challenge to the claim by evolutionary historians to have satisfactorily applied an institutional perspective to narratives through the models of cumulative path dependency, lock-in and trajectory. The evolutionary economists are primarily acknowledging that history is not necessarily efficient – at least, only in the very long run (North 1990). The applications of cumulative path dependency models by David and Arthur contain elements that are of interest. A favourite example is that of the inefficiency of the QWERTY keyboard. Evolutionary economists explain this by reference to an accidental conjunction of events. However, the applications frequently appear more like imprisoned time than the spectrum of temporality. There is restricted attention to irony and emergence. The critical search for alternatives is suppressed and even contingency and the unexpected are slotted into quasi-equilibrium thinking. Cumulative path dependency tends to neglect recursiveness, ignore failures and produce a single variety. In the case of the analysis of QWERTY it is not clear that their analytic narrative possesses additional strengths by imposing the focusing device of cumulative path dependency. The possibilities for discontinuity, dislocation and revolution require attention. More use should be made of notions such as ensembles (Gille 1978) and attention should be given to the context of exnovation.

Alternative pasts and uncertain possible futures

More recently some historians have questioned the degree of certainty presumed by historians (Schama 1994), proposed many possible futures (Hawthorne 1995)

Table 6.1 Gurvitch's spectrum of social time

Type	Relation of past, present and future	Continuity, contingency and surprise	Duration, incorporate pace
Enduring	Past is projected in the present and future. Remote past is dominant.	Most continuous.	Slowed down, long duration. Present can be quantitatively expressed.
Deceptive	Rupture between past and present	Discontinuity. Surprise time.	Seems like enduring, but sudden crisis. Paradox. Simultaneously slow and agitated.
Erratic	Present appears to prevail over the past and future.	Uncertainty and accentuated contingency. Discontinuity becomes prominent.	Irregular pulsation between appearance and disappearance of rhythms.
Cyclical	Each is mutually projected into the other.	Continuity accentuated. Contingency weakened.	'A dance on one spot'. Qualitative element strong.
Retarded	Future actualised in present.	No equilibrium between continuity and discontinuity. Contingent elements are reinforced.	Delayed, waiting for unfolding.
Alternating	Past and future compete in the present.	Discontinuity stronger than continuity. Contingency not exaggerated.	Alternating between delay and advance. Qualitative not accentuated.
Pushing forward	Future becomes present.	Discontinuity. Contingency.	Time in advance of itself (e.g. communions in revolt). Qualitative.
Explosive	Present and past dissolved. Creation of the immediately transcended future.	Discontinuity high. Contingency high.	Fast movements. Efferverscent. Qualitative high.

and introduced different, earlier outcomes as in Ferguson's (1997) virtual history. Could the past have emerged differently? The question may be illustrated with reference to the emergence of American Football in the USA and not elsewhere (Clark 1987). There are two initial issues. First, was it inevitable that American college boys would not adopt the English templates for similar sports of association football and rugby union. Second, even if association football and rugby union are rejected was it inevitable that the social groups promoting the rules of play that became American Football would dominate and enrol other colleges?

We shall return to these questions in Chapter 9 when the case of American Football is examined. My analytic narrative then will suggest that a structurally powerful and prestigious configuration of male-dominated universities (as Elias) were especially influential in rejecting the English games for their absence of 'strategic manhood'. In that episode (as Giddens) of the rejection of some directions, the same configuration of universities struggled among themselves and with other clusters of universities across the USA to impose and enrol everyone in Football.

The issue of alternative pasts and therefore uncertain futures directly challenges the claims of the realist turn to be able to estimate the degrees of freedom and hence the zones of manoeuvre available in specific unfolding situations. The framework of Gurvitch permits careful attention to the various possibilities. Critical perspectives within political economy require narratives that reveal the possibilities of struggle. Zeldin (1984) contends that history can provide a detachment to analysis of the present so that a wider range of choices about the future can be imagined.

Analytically structured narrative

This section proposes that the approach of the analytically structured narrative without grandeur can be applied at the societal level (Clark 1987, 1997a, b; Archer 1995) and the level of the firm and its sector. The study by Whipp and Clark (1986) of major events in the British automobile industry within a perspective derived from Ladurie and known as structure-event-structure is an example of the analytically structured narrative.

Serious attention to the analysis of the pre-existing situation requires a time perspective which searches backward, probably over decades and generations. The genealogical element should be based on a series of hypotheses about which traces are carried forward and the likelihood that tendency will continue. Three examples may be noted.

First, one interesting example worth examination is Harvey's (1989) historical-geography of capitalism (see Chapter 3) because of its focus upon a particular causal nexus located in the material base. In Harvey's perspective the political regimes of accumulation (e.g. Boyer) shape state roles and provide the pressures triggering new forms of work organisation possessing time-space commodification, compacting and stretching.

Another example of analytically structured narrative is by Whipp and Clark (1986) in their account of events on the saloon car side of the old Rover company by devoting equal amounts of space to the period 1986–1967 and 1967–1982 in order to identify the trajectory of events leading to the closure of major investment to create a European executive car. This study periodises the evolution of an internal strategic innovation-design capability (cf. Chandler 1990).

Third, Kieser (1998)[4] constructs an analytically structured narrative of the connection between organising and discipline in Germany. His analysis of structures and mechanisms on the issue of organisational discipline and self-discipline occupies a central position, yet how the core groups in different nations (e.g. Germany) acquired self-discipline and organisational knowledge has not been analysed sufficiently. Elias analysed the emergence of discipline and self-discipline in the competing nation states of Europe from the Middle Ages into the fifteenth century, showing the increasing role of normative, rule-governed frameworks rather than coercive discipline based on corporal punishment and death. Domination became depersonalised away from the specifics of royal personages. Protestant sects constructed norms that both contradicted tradition and established institutional strategies for maintaining collective discipline. The mechanisms utilised included devotional reading, moral logbooks and attendance at collective meetings for prayer as well as private prayers. Later, in the seventeenth century, the public rejected the theatrical performances of hanging and discipline as these forms were not able to guarantee the intimidation of criminals (Foucault 1977). Discipline resided in the relational framework and its regulative, normative and cognitive frameworks. The new disciplinary power was not experienced as oppressive.

In Germany the freemasons offered their members – drawn from the ascending societal elites – opportunities to prepare a new civic society through the mechanism of the lodge. Freemasonry enabled their members to develop skills and knowledge about organising for a variety of civic and economic activities that emerged from the pre-existing, traditional society. The new forms of organising included hierarchies that were quite separate from those associated with the Church and the military. Therefore, hierarchies were no longer regarded as a manifestation of God. The everyday morality of the freemasons made new additions to the societal stock of knowledge. The freemasons created a secret, inner space that was isolated from society where initiation rituals were introduced, including tests of moral courage. The lodge system cultivated new forms of sociability and edged towards the civil inattention (Giddens 1984) and experience of partial inclusion (Weick 1969) that are familiar today. Also in Germany discipline was learnt in the reading societies focused upon useful knowledge and the improvement of trade and industry. Then the merging patriotic societies devised elaborate statutes and notions of the decent person. They strongly propagated industry schools characterised by diligence in time keeping, obedience to authority and being truthful. These associations were the early examples of modern, complex, rationally effective organisations noted by Weber. The disciplinary techniques of the associations were not available 'off the shelf' in a Foucauldian discourse operating independently of the actors involved. Contrary to Foucault's theory there was a lengthy, specific and local process of accumulating the collective and self-discipline by using organisation knowledge about the design of mechanisms. In all probability members could belong to several associations.

These three examples provide an indication of the direction taken by the analytically structured narrative. They also illustrate the potentials for careful usage of the spectrum of temporality for the past, present and future proposed by Gurvitch. In the analytically structured narrative the role of a longitudinal perspective leads from the future into the present and looks backwards with temporality to analyse the selected problem focus. For example, the interesting temporal frame for the sectoral cluster of firms in the British pharmaceutical industry is how the previously favourable context that underpinned their global performance rested upon domestic features now being transformed. In Britain the role of the health service is altering and thereby impacting upon the relative balance between drug-based and other therapies.

The next sections examine the shifting political economy of nations and the emergence of knowledge-based capitalism within which the innovation-design is the critical element in the performance of nations.

EXPLAINING THE NORTH ATLANTIC DIMENSION: LANDES (1969, 1983, 1998)

Introduction

The economic historian David Landes (1969, 1983, 1998) has analysed the North Atlantic nations, especially the USA, Britain and Germany, with reference to their development of techniques, institutions, technologies and time mastery that provided them with the potentials to dominate one another and other parts of the world. This oeuvre is summarised in two facets of the recent explanation of the wealth of nations (Landes 1998). One facet is the template of ideal features that seem – with the advantage of the historian's hindsight – to be a configuration explaining success. The other facet is the narrative of the North Atlantic nations in the second millennium, particularly in the second half. Landes's account of the genesis of modernity involves locating the mechanisms and conjunctures through which reproduction and/or transformation occurred. Landes makes considerable use of notions of hegemony between nations and can therefore embrace dependency relationships between nations (e.g. Landes 1969). His account of modernity adopts a political economy perspective from what is known as a positive perspective (PPE) rather than the critical position represented by David Harvey discussed later in the chapter.

Landes: template for national success

Landes (1998: 217–218) follows a well-worn path in seeking to construct a template containing the elements which a society should possess in order to achieve material progress (e.g. Weber, Tawney, Merton, Chirot). The contents of the ideal template are somewhat towards positive political economy and this may be usefully compared with the explanation of Harvey (1989) which is examined later in this chapter. There are five clusters of interacting factors:

- geographical conditions;
- cultural features;
- political and social institutions;

- the political hegemony of the nation and the influence of market factors;
- capacities for problem solving and knowledge making.

Landes uses these ideal lists to explain the rise of Europe in general and the North Western nations (e.g. England, Netherlands, Germany, France) in particular. The degree of matching with the USA is implicit for Landes and I will examine this later in Chapter 9 on American Exceptionalism.

Geographical conditions

Geographical elements are important because nature provides potentials which in conjunction with cultural values and institutions give impetus in certain directions. Landes contends that geography favoured Europe more than China. He starts with the physical geography and the inherited material conditions of major civilisations and nations (1998: 1), but emphasises that it is how the indigenous population developed their techniques which was important. The reasoning rejects geographical determinism. European exceptionalism, especially North West Europe, includes the following.

1   In its geo-political and oceanic position it was far away from the Chinese. The Japanese were too near to the Chinese.
2   The surrounding seas provided fish and a formidable challenge to the techniques of sailing and navigation. The Mediterranean and North Sea provide different opportunities and contrasting environments for learning about navigation.
3   Its climate provides winters which are cold enough to kill germs and growing seasons which are exceptionally favourable to the growing of cereals and timber, together with rainfall which was sufficiently abundant and evenly spread through the year.
4   The plurality of river systems enabled transport and the geographical barriers (e.g. mountain ranges) enabled a plurality of political entities and new centres. Waterways provided channels of movement between terrains with different agricultural and material capacities. Independent towns and cities were able to develop and contain the power of the monarchies.
5   These conditions left Europeans with space and sustenance for feeding many large bulky animals such as sheep, cattle and horses. These animals had multiple uses: sources of clothing, food and the power to pull heavy weights.

Cultural features

Cultural features of importance include the following.

1   The separation between religious and secular domains means that theologians cannot impose their canons of proof in the secular areas of science and technique. The containment of the religious influence on economic

action as, for example, in the notions of the just wage and of controlling usury.

2 The existence of many independent states allows individuals and groups of an independent and sceptical thought to move between them.

3 There exists a sense of equal opportunity between individuals without discrimination, for example, with respect to gender.

4 There has been a development of secular time management and an obsession with time in relation to accountability for the organisation of work and its financial performance. Landes deals with space in an indirect way, but it is clear that his notion of being organised-in-time possesses a spatial dimension both in the workplace and in military campaigns.

5 There has been a development of extensive literacy and of capacities for dissent expressed through literary and other forms of non-overt violence.

Political and social institutions

The ideal society is one in which the political and societal institutions enable the following features:

- secure rights of private property to encourage saving and investment;
- secure property rights to protect the individual against private disorder and tyranny of abuse;
- capacities to enforce rights of contract, both explicit and implicit;
- providing stable government by publicly known rules; not necessarily democratic; if there are periodic elections then neither side violates the rights of the other;
- provide government which is responsive to complaints and will make redress;
- honest government with no rents to favour and position;
- government should be moderate, efficient, reduce claims on the social surplus;
- geographical and social mobility.

Political hegemony and influence of market factors

In external political relations with other nations the benefits come from political hegemony and the influence of market factors rather than simple domination, power and exploitation. This is Gramscian political economy by the back door (Arrighi 1994). It requires capacities to dominate through innovations which enrol both the non-human and the human in networks with political strength for nations as expressed in particular ensembles (as Gille 1978). For example, two essentials for success in the period up to the sixteenth century were:

- the development of armaments which fired straighter, further and could be directed at targets so that at sea enemies could be outgunned from a safe

distance: such capacities would enable a nation to bombard future trading partners in their home ports (e.g. Goa) and to be safe from piracy (Law 1987);
- to develop capacities in sailing, navigation and cargo carrying: the Portuguese spent a whole century learning how to circumnavigate Africa initially by travelling slowly against the currents and winds along the African coast and then by enrolling the currents and winds to travel westward to the Pacific via the southern tip of South America.

Knowledge making

Within the ideal society the essential elements for growth and development centre around knowledge making in its various forms. The ideal elements are:

- the capacity to search for instruments of production and new techniques at the technological frontier and to develop the know-how to operate and manage these: for example, the investment by the Portuguese and Dutch in systems of navigation and development of the sailing vessel, or the development of the American system of manufacture;
- to be able to impart this knowledge to each generation through forms of apprenticeship and education;
- to select/fire and promote/demote on the basis of competence and performance;
- to encourage initiative, competition and emulation;
- to allow people to enjoy the fruits of their labour and enterprise.

Landes's reasoning is that during the second millennium the five clusters of ideal factors were approximated to more often by the European nations and in North America than other nations.

The reasoning is applied to the nations bordering the North Atlantic in a sequence of steps which, although cumulative, are not deterministic and cannot be reproduced as in the linear economic development models:

- European development from 1000 to 1500 on a distinctive pathway;
- consolidation in the sixteenth and seventeenth centuries;
- the pivotal industrial revolution spanning the eighteenth and nineteenth century in Britain, then Germany and the USA;
- the twentieth-century technological revolutions.

Landes is silent on the situation for the twenty-first century (cf. Kennedy 1987).

Europe: a distinctive pathway (1000–1500)

Landes charts European exceptionalism and the distinctive path of its cumulating predispositions: the European habitus. The geography of Europe enabled though did not determine a high degree of fragmentation between nations compared to the water-based society of China. Intense European cultivation produced surpluses which could be traded and conveyed in specialist boats along the coastal and internal waterways. The surplus might have gone to the rulers, but the merchants and those in towns and cities, such as the Renaissance Italian city states, successfully contested their ownership.

Several fissures and the contests around their control became significant to the distinctive European pathway. First, the contest between rulers and their wealthy subjects was serious. Private property was rediscovered and reasserted after the fall of Rome (Landes 1998: 33) in the contest for power within the European states. The state rulers abandoned certain powers in return for revenue which in turn brought new powers. This solution, an unintended outcome of intended struggles, is a central difference from China. Second, there was the split between the secular and religious. Third, the cultures of North West Europe were typified by particular value systems in which the household as a unit was coupled with the principle of undivided inheritance and interfamilial alliances (Landes 1998: 22).

Existing techniques and problem solving in Europe were subject to extensive development and innovation:

- the waterwheel which supplied energy;
- the eyeglass doubled the working life of its user and set the template for the invention of robust, delicate instruments;
- the mechanical clock provided a template of homogeneous units, a coordinator of everyday work and a metaphor for organisation;
- printing accelerated the diffusion of written material (e.g. newspapers);
- gunpowder was applied to the trajectories of guns.

Europeans were not discursively aware of how intention and chance were constituting a distinctive pathway of development.

North West European consolidation: sixteenth and seventeenth century

Why did the North West European nations and North America prosper from sixteenth century onward rather than Spain and Portugal or any of the following: China, India, or nations from Africa, Arabia and South America? Landes contends that the prospering nations moved close to the ideal profile. Whether this was the outcome of deliberateness is a more awkward question. From the sixteenth century onward the Portuguese, like the Spanish, occupied the islands in the mid-Atlantic, but unlike the Spanish they sought trading relationships (e.g. Goa in India; Macaw in China) rather than conquests. Although the trading relationships were forced by naval and military action the Portuguese concentrated upon transporting pepper and spices from the Far East for sale in European entrepôts. Like the Dutch and the English, they also became involved in the costly though profitable sugar trade. Europeans played a key role in transferring crops around the world and in developing forms of work organisation for their commercial exploitation (e.g. tobacco plantations). By the seventeenth century sugar growth was integral to the triangular trade from the North Sea region to North West Africa from where slaves were transported to the West Indies and the American colonies to work on the plantations. The commodities (e.g. cotton) were sold in England and continental Europe where they altered diets, dress and life styles. Landes contends that this trade 'watered the garden of nascent capitalism' (1998: 119) and by increasing the volume of trade enlarged the market, thereby giving England opportunities for deepening the division of labour in the eighteenth century. By this period the centre of gravity in Europe had shifted from Italy and the Mediterranean to the North Sea towns and nations (e.g. London and Amsterdam).

Landes (1998: 63) observes that by the sixteenth century Europeans held a marked advantage in the control and deployment of firepower in naval and military projects and within Europe there were disparities between the nations in their military capacities. Also, the nature of political institutions provided access to the instruments of power. Europeans learned to enrol the winds and oceanic currents in their quest for the trade in valuable commodities with the Far East. From the mid-Atlantic isles the journey to the New World was explored, mapped and then became a routine journey for shipping. South America became the site of military conquests and annexation by Spain and Portugal. The North European traders preferred the highly profitable sugar trade established in the West Indies and infamously worked by slave labour.

European knowledge and technique

Three considerations favoured the growth of western science and its role in the economic growth of Europe and gave the base for the breakthrough relative to other regions (Landes 1998: 201f). First, there was growing autonomy given to intellectual inquiry whereby new ideas were not necessarily the cause of insult to the sacred or the dominant, but could find favourable forums in the towns and sprinkling of universities. Second, over many generations and centuries there was the gradual linking together of observation, description, experiment and the speculation about hidden systematic causes whose influence could be reconstructed by similar patterns across many settings. Perception, measurement, tests of verification and mathematics as a deductive framework were combined. The new method sought to measure reality (Crosby 1998). A new kind of knowledge was constructed: explicit, deductively arranged, seemingly open to refutation. There was a pursuit of precision and the linear conception of time. Specialist equipment was built and reproduced in small batch production. Third, discovery was routinised through a common language and set of practices.

First industrial revolution

It was a long time before all this kickstarted the growing pace of economic growth loosely referred to as the industrial revolution. That could not have occurred in Florence:

[The] streams of progress had to come together . . . in a conjuncture, in the relations of supply and demand, in prices and elasticities. Technology was not enough. What was needed was a technological change . . . the kind that would resonate through the market and change the distribution of resources. . . . One could not get an industrial revolution out of silk. Wool and cotton were something else.

(Landes 1998: 206–207)

England was the setting in which that revolution unfolded, enabling new techniques, technologies and internal labour markets less feasible in the woollen industry (Gregory 1982). England had already been the milieu in which the agricultural revolution and the transport revolution (e.g. canals) had been established. Agriculture was not conservative. (Crafts 1985). These developments broke the constraints arising from the medieval legacy with its guilds, the restraints on trade and the peasantry (Landes 1998: 242).

The process can be viewed as an ensemble or package with its pivot point in the new gains of productivity arising from the substitution of technology (capital) for human strength and gradually to embody human skills. These skills tended to be specific to a particular milieu such as the British steel firms and proved exceptionally difficult to emulate even after state-sponsored espionage, as with French attempts to emulating the English steel making. Likewise Jeremy (1981) illustrates the problems of transferring an ensemble of capacities developed in the English technology firms to the American entrepreneurs even when the latter had purchased the key artefacts (e.g. Samual Slater).

Second industrial revolution: USA and Germany

In the twentieth century further major epochal innovations were developed by the North Atlantic nations (e.g. USA and Germany):

- new sources of energy (e.g. oil and gas) and new systems of their distribution (e.g. electricity) and for their use in transportation (e.g. internal combustion engine);
- science-based organic chemicals (e.g. plastics);
- science-based pharmaceuticals (e.g. drugs);
- information and communication technologies.

These were principally developed within the western alliance. It is important to relate the above template to the USA since there are differences from Europe (see Chapter 9).

DESIGN KNOWLEDGE: INTENSITY AND COMPRESSION

Knowledge-based capitalism

There are many versions of how the contemporary world is differing from the previous century. Here we shall follow Dunning's (1997) account of knowledge-based capitalism in combination with alliances rather than competitive capitalism. The three major shifts of market-based western capitalism can be examined in terms of three dimensions:

- the primary source of wealth and form of activity;
- the spatial and location dimension;
- principal form of organisation.

From the seventeenth century into the early nineteenth century land was the primary source of wealth, with the principal activities being agriculture (e.g. crops and animals), forestry and related activities (e.g. textiles). The spatial dimension was dominated by local and regional features. The main forms of work organisation were a mixture of feudal and entrepreneurial. There was increasing decentralisation of economic ownership, legitimacy and authority.

From the nineteenth into the later twentieth century the primary sources of wealth were finance capital and machinery through the activity of manufacturing. The spatial dimension tended towards regional and national with increasing international incursions. Organisational forms were strongly hierarchical with vertically integrated firms containing extensive managerial strata. Firms were often in adversarial economic relationships even with their suppliers and customers.

Since the late twentieth century and onward the primary source of wealth has become finance and knowledge with bases in producer and consumer services. Dunning agrees with Pine's attention to the tendency of routinised mass customisation. The spatial dimension has become regional and global with clusters that are national and sub-national. Organisational forms are still somewhat hierarchical but with more extensive alliances within networks and with economic relations in which co-operation is more evident and highlighted.

Although these broad shifts have occurred there has been a tendency for earlier theoretical constructs to suppress the requirements of contemporary theorising. Earlier constructs tended towards the resource-based view and more recently attention is upon knowledge-based competitive advantages. The firm now needs to gain access to knowledge-intensive assets that are intangible and to supranational markets for learning and for exploitation of the knowledge-intensive assets. Firms therefore go abroad and foreign direct investment is now rising at approximately twice the rate of world trade. There is a massive growth in alliances with an increased emphasis upon co-operation among the network of firms along the value chain. Thus some of the firms' specific assets are becoming more mobile and slippery, while other assets are seen to be very locationally embedded and sticky. Markusan (1994) refers to 'sticky places in slippery spaces'. This is the case where there is a spatially linked network of activities as in Swedish engineering firms and universities (Hakansson 1987). Firms continually have to upgrade their knowing – the organisational expertise and the ways in which technology and other networks are co-ordinated.

There are implications and requirements of governments in the knowledge-based economy. The government should provide the context for corporations to be enabled and rewarded for knowledge-intensive assets (North 1990; Nelson, 1991, 1993) and if possible to supply a unique set of immobile (sticky) supports to assets in corporations. Kogut (1997) speculates on the advantages given by the US government to firms of certain technologies. Within the nation this will require a balance between the central and the regional state apparatus with particular attention to understanding how beneficial spatial clustering might be mobilised. Governments should aim at encouraging friendly alliances in coalitions in certain sector clusters while discouraging the distortion of the market. Dunning (1997) observes that governments should gain access to preserve and augment those resources and capabilities which are economically relevant and unique so that other governments cannot imitate. To some degree this strategy is pursued by the French state in its approach to tourism related investment, both in people and in the aesthetic fabric of France.

Design cycles: products, services and processes

The design cycle as a collection of activities is temporarily conflated in most accounts of strategy formulation and in theories of organisation. Miles and Snow (1986) illustrate how the key functions might be initially unpacked as in Figure 6.1 on flexible specialisation. In the early 1980s there was evidence of existing organisations being subjected to increased commodification and time-space compression through forms of creative destruction. Simultaneously, there were examples of different, difficult to describe new forms and these were initially referred to as N-Form to signify newness. Figure 6.1 draws attention to the vertically integrated firm that might be unpacked and re-connected through social brokers perhaps in the model of firm production. Miles and Snow prised open the firm to reveal the role that design might play. Developing that perspective was greatly accelerated by Pine (1993).

Pine shows how the role of design is altered when the shift is from mass production to mass customisation. Figure 6.2 illustrates some of the important differences between the dynamic reinforcing factors underpinning mass production and the emergent systems that are sometimes referred to as mass customisation (Pine 1993). Mass production requires markets in which taste is relatively homogenised and demand patterns are stable. These enable long life cycles for products which themselves depend upon long periods of development. The new products and services are produced through mass, standardised production processes so that output to the customer is of low cost and consistent quality. The new products and processes are standardised, thereby creating a homogeneous market which

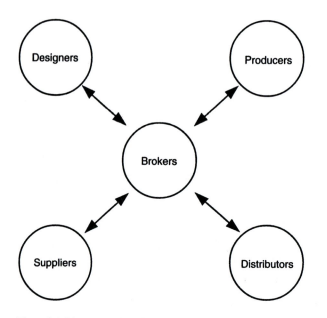

Figure 6.1 Disaggregating the firm
Source: Miles and Snow (1986).

completes the cycle. Suppose, however, that homogeneous markets are under-mined and that heterogeneous markets emerge and become prevalent. Then, as shown in Figure 6.3 the low cost goods are of higher quality and more customised, yet their life cycle is short and there is the constant need for replacement. Consequently developmental cycles are shortened and there is fragmentation of demand. These are key processes of mass customisation and in the short development cycles.

These points can now be expressed in terms of stylised comparison of the role of design in Japanese and US firms in the 1970s and 1980s. By the mid-1990s US firms had absorbed those of the new requirements relating to their market position. Japanese car firms have been widely cited as the key exemplar of firms which successfully developed a basis for using the design cycle effectively relative to North American and European firms (Clark and Fujimoto 1991). How might the differences between the Japanese and American approaches to design be highlighted in a stylised comparison? Figure 6.4 suggests that the American firms tended to use design – at which they possessed a distinctive world class capability in mass production – to control the customer and the supplier in a slowly changing market choreographed by advertising. The Japanese (Figure 6.5) developed a much stronger linkage between design and the customer while also involving their suppliers in the design process. In terms of the information theory perspective (Galbraith 1977) the Japanese faced increased equivocality from the customers by

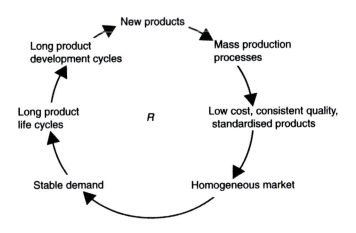

Figure 6.2 Innovation-design in mass customisation
Source: Pine (1993).

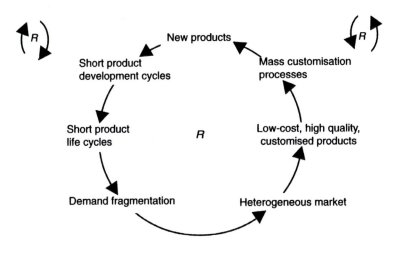

Figure 6.3 Innovation-design in mass customisation
Source: Pine (1993).

buffering (see Thompson 1967) the core with systems for absorbing requisite variety onto their suppliers who were closer to the everyday problems of innovation. In the Japanese framework of production institutions the political vulnerability of these tightly compressed time-space systems was not subjected to serious disturbance by labour bargaining (cf. Turner *et al.* 1967).

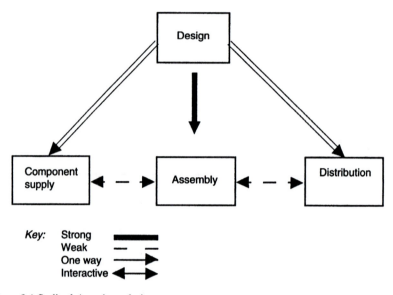

Figure 6.4 Stylised American design

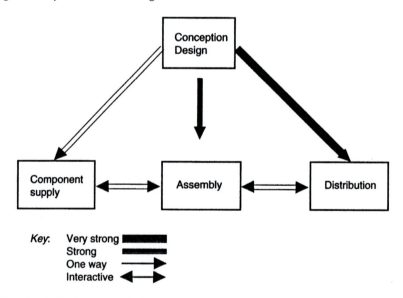

Figure 6.5 Stylised Japanese design

NOTES

1 See particularly Leyshon and Thrift (1997) *Money Space. Geographies of Monetary Transformation*, London: Routledge, Chapter 8.
2 See the references to Callon and Latour listed at the end of the book.
3 From Clark (1985) and cited in Hassard (1996). Similar to the depiction by Harvey (1989: 223–224).
4 See Alfred Kieser (1998) 'From Freemasons to industrial patriots. Organising and disciplining in 18th century Germany', *Organisation Studies* 19(1): 47–91.

7 National innovation-design systems

INTRODUCTION

The neo-modern and new political economy points of view are evidenced in the proliferation of a variety of labels involving national systems of industry (McMillan 1985), organising (Clark 1987; Kogut 1993), innovation (Lundvall 1992; Nelson 1993) and business (Whitley 1994). These national systems contain many common and some unique elements. This chapter explores the possibility for synthesis as national innovation-design systems (NIDS). Three lines of analyses are considered:

- networks of design knowledge (Clark 1987, 1998);
- sectoral clusters and the role of location (Porter 1990, 1998; Dunning 1997);
- business systems (Whitley 1993).

This exploration leads into Chapter 8 where the dimension of societal culture and institutions are more fully developed and then illustrated in Chapters 9 and 10.

NATIONAL NETWORKS OF DESIGN KNOWLEDGE

A road map

The previous chapter located the nation containing competitive contexts within the international political economy and used the theory of hegemonic domination and dependence through markets and latent power to characterise the difference between powerful nations and dependent nations within a capitalist system. That international political economy is one of the major contexts for firms. The clustering of nations around power centres involves differential access to markets. The aim now is to focus upon the question of whether nations can be characterised as possessing distinctive constellations of techniques of problem solving. The notion of competition between contexts implicates national configurations as contexts. How should the national configuration be characterised?

At this moment we require a general road map to confirm the broad configuration of elements necessary to understand the theme of competition between contexts and to build upon the contingently temporal dimension previously discussed. The road map needs to distinguish and separate levels of analysis in order to identify the causal processes and mechanisms operating in a stratified situation. The purpose of this road map is to suggest how the concept of a design knowledge template might be used to address the societal-institutional levels of analysis and also be applicable as a framework to corporate level innovations. Figure 7.1 sets out the key elements and some of the linkages forward and backward and implies the presence of a structure and mechanisms through which particular strata are involved.[1]

In Figure 7.1 there are three main clusters of elements that constitute the configuration and each of these possess their characteristic ontologies. First, we enter this road map along the middle line. The pre-existing situation combines the structural-institutional and cultural levels. The social structures and cultures of nations possess many features which persist through time, yet their reproduction is always problematic. There is an analytic dualism between pre-existing structural-institutional formations and ongoing agency (Archer 1995; Layder 1997). With respect to the societal level of structure and culture the framework seeks to cope with both reproduction and transformation of the pre-existing configuration. From within that formation attention is focused upon the possibility that there is a typical variety of institutional predispositions with distinctive enactments of problems and choices of problem-solving techniques (Chapter 8). Whether these institutional techniques and institutional innovations are beneficial to any nation and its indigenous firms is secondary to the causal influences in operation.

Nations vary in the types of design knowledge, problem solving and technique which are located in a configuration of interacting dimensions unfolding in a longitudinal time frame containing indeterminacy. The problematic of the longitudinal dimension in the new political economy was addressed in Chapter 6 and with reference to the analytic dualism between pre-existing structure and each new unfolding of episodes. There are significant unintended as well as emergent outcomes. Ekelund and Tollison (1981) explain the English parliamentary system as the unintended outcome of structural conflicts implicating the monarchy, various strata in the City of London, the landed aristocracy and the gentry. The notion of unintended outcomes and the perspective of indeterminacy caution against their omission from the formulation of industrial strategies.

When the pre-existing structure and culture is contingently reproduced the societal techniques and network of design continue to shape agency. The best researched example of a national network of design knowledge, problem solving and techniques is the American system of manufactures. Hounshell (1984) contends that the American system emerged in the early nineteenth century, became fully blown in the early twentieth century and reached its limits (as Gille 1978) by the mid-twentieth century. Box 7.1 sets out eight of the main practices in the discourse of the American system of manufacture, but it should be noted that these features did not become crystallised as a societal project until the 1850s and were not fully accomplished with the development of cigarette manufacture in the 1880s (Chandler 1977). There was considerable opposition (Hounshell 1984).

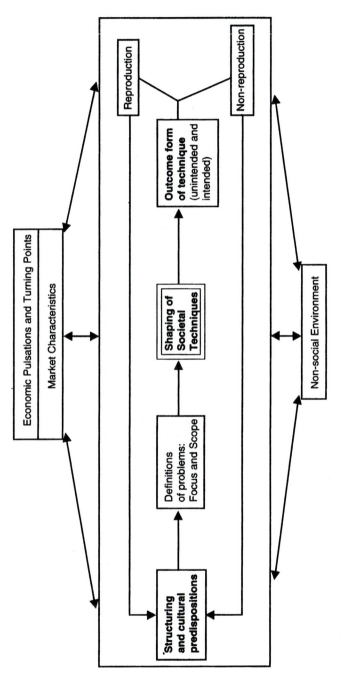

Figure 7.1 Factors influencing the formation of social technique
Source. Clark (1997).

BOX 7.1 AMERICAN TECHNIQUE AND DESIGN KNOWLEDGE

The American network of design knowledge possessed the following features:

1   There was *extensive standardisation* of economic activity and this was evident in standardised components which were interchangeable, thereby facilitating the ease of repair. The components were sometimes to a 'coarser' performance than was the case in Europe (Rosenberg 1969). The engines for the Ford T were more basic than European equivalents (Abernathy 1978).
2   There was *extensive measurement* of actual shapes and performance against pre-defined templates. Systematic rules were embodied in contracts so that imperfect items could be rejected by the purchaser. There was extensive development of tools (e.g. gauges) for assessing components (e.g. guns).
3   The approach to the design stage – an absolutely crucial element – was highly *functional to the purpose* and routinely implicated the problems of repair and replacement (Clark 1987: 215–222).
4   Equipment became increasingly specialised to *specific task*. Blanchard (1820) used the jacquard system to create a machine which only machined the stock of a rifle. Fifty years later Bonsack used the same principles to design and create the world's earliest cigarette-making machine. British firms tended to use more generalised equipment.
5   Production equipment was often *arranged in a sequence* to facilitate transfers between the cumulative stages, thereby reducing the costs of internal transportation and of inventory.
6   Occupational tasks gradually became more specialised, thereby increasing the ease and speed of training. This was a slow process and most new sectors (e.g. sewing machines) began with generalised tasks – the European model – and then after the initial period of fluid innovation moved to *specialised tasks*.
7   There was the *continuous creation of recorded, explicit knowledge in words, diagrams and metaphors which were owned by the employer*. A specialist stratum developed who made their living by undertaking this activity: the American service class of knowledge professionals and symbolic analysts.
8   *Cost assessment* was extensively introduced (e.g. retail) and became the basis of rationalisation as in the cigarette industry (Chandler 1977).

The American system of design embraced both manufacture and distribution (Chandler 1977). The unfolding process occurred over decades, generations and even centuries (Rosenberg 1969, 1982). The American system was part of a significant configuration of American societal capabilities in design and standard-isation (Clark 1987: 215–222). Its core feature was the capacity to standardise economic and production transactions. For example, the development of standardised categories for cereals in Chicago enabled the treatment of cereal production as an abstract flow which could actually be conveyed in bulk (Cronon 1991). The same principles of organisation underpinned the highly successful development of service industries in the USA (e.g. McDonald's). The Ford Motor Company persisted with many of the central elements of the American system until well into the 1980s (Abernathy 1978).

Awareness of the American system of manufactures arose after the 1851 exhibition at Crystal Palace, London (Rosenberg 1969). The American exhibits, including pistols and guns, were designed to be cheap and to provide fast repair close to the arena of warfare. Rosenberg (1969) highlights the significance of the American marketplace as a context for selecting in products which were func-tional, cheap and easy to repair/replace. In 1853–4 the British government sent a team of investigators to discover and describe how the Americans manufactured standardised products. Contemporary historians have reconstructed the con-figuration of causes and mechanisms creating and sustaining this specific national template for organising economic activity and simultaneously reflexively monitor-ing the effectiveness of the system relative to its own principles. It is clear that many of the basic practices and principles were developed along the whole length of the Connecticut Valley in New England. It is also clear that a significant stratum of those involved in manufacturing sought, constituted and sold explicit and tacit knowledge about the problems and solutions.

The American system of manufactures may therefore be regarded as a body of knowledge (cognitions) and cluster of practices (normative and regulative frame-works) to constitute a generic template defining problems and solutions for manufacturers and distributors. Historians have concluded that the American template was more explicitly and extensively understood than was the case for any British templates (Clark 1987, 1998). The American template was a widely accepted habitus of best practice. Organisation theory, especially the contributions of Herbert Simon, have contributed to its explication and constitution. In the European case there were competing templates mainly located in particular industrial complexes.

Since the 1970s US firms and their analysts have sought to replace the sedimented practices and taken for granted principles of the American system by new systems that deliver products and services which are individuated to the life-style needs of the consumer (Schoenberger 1996; Clark 1997b). The American historical setting is discussed more fully in Chapter 9.

Second, there are socially constructed markets and economic pulsations such as business cycles. There are several levels of analysis and theoretical positions which have to be invoked. Markets are socio-political constructions and actors, but are socially constituted (see Chapter 5). At the level of explaining the historical success of western nations, Landes (1998: 59) comments that in 'the last analysis . . . I would stress the market'. However, the market should be regarded as an actor possessing its own script and ontological level. Within the North Atlantic nations there are significant differences between national markets: for example, between the role of the state in France and in the USA. At the level of the nation the role of the market as a selection environment varies between nations (Clark 1987: Chapter 10). The early American market was significantly free from distinctions of preference based on status or region (Landes 1998). Consequently, there was widespread acceptance of standardised products and services by the consumer. The predispositions of the American consumer and their marketplace was one of the contributing mechanisms in enabling the distinctive type of enterprise and the role of all facets of marketing (Brown *et al.* 1998). The role of the market in shaping the learning experience of domestic firms is central to this chapter.

Third, nations are situated in non-social environments. These possess their own ontologies as argued in the realist turn. For some purposes they can be theorised as members of heterogeneous actor networks (see Callon 1997). The non-social environment contains the endowed elements and the socially constructed transport systems and buildings. One of the endowed factors is climate and geography. The other is the socially constructed features (e.g. irrigation systems, transport systems, towns and factories). Those natural spaces are typically reconstructed, very obviously in the case of the USA where the semi-desert areas of California have been transformed. Consequently the USA is the world's leading exporter of rice. Also, there are the technological artefacts of buildings and transportation. The endowed factors including the type of spaces mentioned by Landes in his ideal template (e.g. climate conditions).

The geo-political dimension refers to both endowed factors and to the spatial situation of nations vis-à-vis power blocks. For example, ever since the prising open of the Japanese economy by western forces in the mid-nineteenth century American foreign policy has been attentive to the balance of power in the Pacific Ocean. In the mid-twentieth century the emergence of China as a communist-dominated nation opposed to the USA situated Japan within the political economy of the USA. The defeat of the pro-western Chinese forces was followed by key changes in American dispositions towards Japan and these persisted throughout the Cold War.

Endowed factors refer to those national features of rivers, lakes, seas, land forms and the climate. The position taken here is that these are not deterministic, but that they provide zones of manoeuvre which are actualised/realised by the capacities of the people occupying the territory. Climate has some obvious impacts. Braudel (1983) summarises the research of the Annales School which used dendrochronology (tree dating) on European climate to show that variations in the climate affected the length of the growing season for a variety of crops (e.g. grapes, cereals) in specific regions differently and hence impacted on famines and commerce. Landes (1998) contends that Europe possessed highly favourable endowed factors, likewise North America. However, as Cronon (1983) brilliantly demonstrates, those potentials in North America were realised quite differently by the indigenous Indian populations and the incoming Europeans. Cronon's analysis of both the endowed terrain of New England and these two competing populations reveals key differences. The Indian populations migrated with the seasons to where the food supplies (e.g. fish) were most plentiful. The Europeans enacted the New England terrain, the flora and the fauna, from the perspective of its commodification and they were very excited. The supplies of fish could be sold in Europe as could the skins of animals. Also, the terrain possessed deep sheltered harbours (e.g. Boston and Cambridge), a climate favourable to agriculture and potentials for using water as both a source of power and for the transportation of goods. Cronon, in this analysis and also the analysis of the rise of Chicago in the mid-nineteenth century, demonstrates how different cultural values and capabilities transform space into different kinds of place (see also Harvey 1996). The interpretation here differs from that of Porter (1990) examined in the next chapter.

Knowledge professionals

Figure 7.1 raises the question of who are/were the principal agents defining the problems of work organisation and to what degree did they come to own particular problem-solving territories; also, whether those territories were contested by agents at a similar level – as in contests between professional groups (Larson 1977; Abbott 1988). The notion of a service class proposed by Lash and Urry (1987) partly overlaps with that of symbolic analysts (Reich 1991) and knowledge architects (Nonaka and Takeuchi 1995). Knowledge professionals may be defined as follows:

1   They do not own the means of production, but they work there and sell their expertise to representatives of the owners of capital. They are salaried.
2   They claim to possess expertise in certain problem domains which affect the performance of the firm. These domains can be isolated and exchanged for payment.
3   They seek to transform their expertise into knowledge requiring the attainment of credentials (e.g. university degrees, professional membership) so that entry can be restricted.
4   They develop the capacity to conceptualise problems through investing in certain categories and specific languages (Thevenot 1984). The problem domains which are cognitised will vary in the degree to which they are oriented towards the transformation of the social structure.
5   They develop the capacity to enforce their cognitive frameworks. This capacity will be contested. One line of contest will be jurisdictional conflicts between professional associations (Abbott 1988) and the other line of conflict will be with non-managerial groups.
6   They may successfully construct a collective mobility project. These collective projects vary in success from high (e.g. USA, France and Germany) to low (e.g. Britain).

The service class of knowledge professionals will, in effect, define frontiers of control for capitalism (Goodrich 1975) in specific nations. In the USA the frontier control penetrates the situation of organised labour in many sectors while in the British context there are variations from high penetration in retail services and the complex of food, drink and tobacco sectors to lower penetration in areas of engineering. The roles and capacities of the knowledge professionals arise from a distinct configuration as in the contrast between the case of the German engineer (Lane 1996) and the Japanese engineer (McMillan 1985).

In the Anglo-American nations there has been a distinct shift in the professional groups that constitute the discourse of the knowledge professionals from various engineering groups such as the civil and industrial engineers (Clark 1987) to the accounting and finance professionals (Clark 1997a, b). The extensiveness of the transformation (Perkin 1996) is reflected in the contention that Britain has become an audited society (Power 1994) with league tables covering massive areas of public and corporate activity. Organisation performance among the plurality of sub-units is now transparent (Clark 1996) and notions of performativity abound. In the audited society there are accounting and managerial practices that constitute and reconstitute the economic domain – rendering visible the processes and flow of valuation. Economic calculation is translated into the calculative practices and rationales of the accounting professionals, especially the members of the larger international accounting firms (Miller 1994). Accounting is depicted as a key element in the 'mythical structure' of rationalised societies (Meyer and Rowan 1977). Accounting as a genre becomes one of the major ways in which firms incorporate rational concepts of organisation and the set of techniques for monitoring specific activities. Fligstein (1990) contends that the accounting and finance professionals now occupy a pivotal position and firms are pressured to adopt their practices. The firm is increasingly defined as financial rather than as, for example, educational or health.

LOCATIONS AND INTER-FIRM CLUSTERS: COMPETITION BETWEEN CONTEXTS

Defining the problem

The issue of location has been largely absent in organisation theory and strategy, but location has occupied a central place in the theory of international business developed since the 1980s by Dunning (1993). His eclectic paradigm applied to international production lists four sets of variables (Dunning 1993: 98–101):

- ownership-specific features covering property rights and common governance;
- internalisation incentives to protect against market failure, including the avoidance of ownership and negotiating costs;
- location specific variables and how these affect a host nation;
- dynamic add-on of ten variables including the influence of strategic choices, product characteristics, sourcing, etc.

Dunning developed and applied the framework to the dynamic interplay between multinational businesses and the competitive advantages of specific nations. The aim was to discover the origin and composition of the resources and capabilities which enable a firm to do well nationally and then to move abroad. In Dunning's analysis the multinational businesses, once established, significantly mediate the position of the national location as a competitive context. Even so, Dunning amply supports the contention that there is competition between contexts. So the neglect of both location in general and unravelling the possible role of competition between contexts should be brought into centre stage. Location is at centre stage.

In part the attention to location arises from micro-economic theorising about the international firm, especially the perspective of Dunning and the studies by geographers of regional networks and clusters that are declining (e.g. American rust belt) and developing. Key studies involve Storper, Walker and Markusen.[2] Equally, the rampant performance of certain Japanese sectors relative to their American counterparts aroused the western schools of business. Initially much of their effort concentrated upon identifying Japanese best practice at the firm level and envisaging the transfer of Japanese practices *in toto* to western firms (Clark and Staunton 1989). Now the aim is to analyse the innovation-in-context and selectively to disembed best practice to enable appropriation of those features contingently relevant to the new context (Clark and Swan 2000). The stimulus of attention to Japanese practices provoked intense interest and included the creation of many 'round tables' to analyse the causal forces and mechanisms. Michael Porter became involved in one such round table and developed an approach to the competitive advantage of nations (Porter 1990) which has been developed and refined (Porter 1998). There are some interesting and relevant dynamics between the frameworks proposed by Porter and Dunning (Dunning 1993: 102–127; Das 1997). This section will selectively introduce Porter's approach and then propose an alignment with Dunning suited to exploring the weight that should be attached to location and to the issue of competition between contexts.

Porter: sectors and clusters in nations

As already indicated, the role of the nation as an explanatory and policy variable has become both more interesting and more intriguing. Porter (1990) offered a bold statement of how the nation as a formative context shapes the competitive advantage of the firm, the sector and location specific clusters (Nelson 1991). Moreover, in typical style, Porter has presented an analytic road map with interacting factors in the form of a diamond. This section introduces and then revises the diamond.

Although Porter regards events within the nation as of central importance, this does not imply that the nation is in control of its destiny, merely that understanding the forces at play provides the interpreter with some means of navigation and steering. The recent work of Porter edges into the neo-modernist. Also, there is now a strong emphasis on the indeterminacy of events (Porter 1991) and there are elements of a realist perspective combined with micro-economic theory (Das 1997). However, there is serious under-utilisation of the sociological perspective.

Porter (1990: 19) claims that the proximate context of the sector – the 'home base' – shapes its competitive success in the medium and longer term. Proximate refers to other firms within the same sector and the same nation with the likelihood that firms are agglomerated into regions. Porter argues that firms typically stay in a domestic context for a period before moving abroad and this early experience shapes the key learning experiences of top management, thereby influencing strategy, organisation and identity. The home base is the location where the resources and capabilities of the firm are shaped:

- the core technologies;
- the advanced skills;
- the leading edge activities.

Context and domestic base refers to the nation and region as specific, concrete locations rather than analytic spaces. Clusters are multiple inter-organisational networks in which firms become enmeshed. Therefore there is competition between clusteral contexts in their dis/enabling impacts on the firms with the role set.

Although not explicitly a theory of organisational learning, the theory unambiguously makes two key suggestions. First, the repertoire of capabilities developed by firms is encoded with action potentials which are distinctive to that home base location. So, firms in similar sectors but emerging from Birmingham, England, rather than Detroit, USA, are likely to have significant differences in capabilities (see later in Chapter 10). Second, the home base possesses a configuration of features which either enables or disables its competitive performance in the wider arena. So, entrepreneurs in genetic agriculture may be more likely to succeed domestically and internationally starting out from Denmark than from the Holderness region of England. There is competition between contexts.

How is the theory constructed and what are its key features? How can the location of the firm be analysed in a manner which can inform policy making at the corporate, regional and national levels?

Porter: league tables and case studies

Economists specialising in the analysis of the economic performance of nations had already produced a strong case for explaining national performance in terms of the presence/absence and performance of specific sectors. Pavitt (1980, 1984) analysed the complex migration of innovations between sectors to show that within one nation there were sharp differences in the international viability of sectors. The implication was that the sector was a key unit of analysis in explaining national performance. Analysing the nation in terms of its sectors is a direction which begins to qualify the grandiose explanations of national performance

(McKinsey 1998). Sectors are sometimes agglomerated in regions, as with the large internationally successful Italian tile designing and manufacturing sector (Porter 1998).

Porter takes the sector and its clustering as one of the basic units of analysis. The sector is a much smaller unit of analysis than the industry and corresponds to the three-digit level of a standard industrial classification. So the focus is shifted from the heterogeneous textile industry to, for example, the carpet sector as the unit of analysis (Clark and Probert 1989). Porter therefore identified and listed the fifty most successful exporting sectors in eight nations at three points in time (1971, 1978, 1985). The sectoral cluster combines many sectors into larger, heterogeneous analytic units.

A listing is produced of the fifty non-service sectors in each nation that have the highest share of world trade for that sector irrespective of the value. In the case of the USA the listing covers almost 50 per cent of trade value, while for Italy the listing only accounts for about 10 per cent. Scrutiny of the lists from nations at three points spread over seventeen years suggests that only the USA and to some degree Germany host a wide spread of sectors. Most nations are only represented in some sectors. The range might be quite narrow. The conclusion to be drawn is that most nations cannot expect to be strong exporters in a wide range of sectors. Most nations can expect to be competitive in a small range of sectors. Therefore, within globalisation and internalisation there is increased local specialisation (Das 1997).

The lists are also used to explore the extent to which sectors might be connected in an agglomeration of networks and channels including production chains which might be referred to as a cluster (Porter 1998). The issue here is the notion that sectors within nations may support or hinder one another. For example, between 1950–75 Britain possessed a domestically owned motor industry located in a production chain that embraced key design relationships to firms in the electrical components sector (e.g. Lucas). That local cluster came under intense pressure from multinationals already in the British marketplace (e.g. Ford and General Motors) and then from a host of new entrants (e.g. Peugeot, BMW, Honda). The British firms in the cluster were gradually undermined (Clark and Whipp 1984; Church 1994). Hence, by 1995 the remaining British firms came under overseas ownership (e.g. BMW and Rover).

The lists compiled by Porter are intriguing and should be treated with care. In the USA ten of the top twenty-five leading export sectors are concerned with endowed factors, including rice exports which account for 40 per cent of world trade. The British listing is headed by whisky and biscuits; even garden tools are mentioned.

Porter also draws upon more than a hundred case studies spread across the nations. Each case study describes the recent history of a sector. Cameo-1 (see shortly) summarises the case study of American patient monitoring technologies. Among the most interesting cases are those from Italy (e.g. ceramics, footwear). Only a small proportion of the cases are reported in the text. However, Porter clearly manages to carry a similar analytic narrative across many cases (see Abbott 1992).

Porter weaves his analytic narrative through the accumulated data compressed into the lists and cases. He concludes that six interacting factors explain the variance. There are four inner factors plus two outer factors whose interactions within a national sector explain why that sector is on the list of successful exporters. The inner factors are:

- market demand;
- firm structure and firm rivalry;
- supporting and related industries;
- endowed and created factors.

Impinging on the four interacting factors are the role of chance and of government.

Each factor might be thought of as containing sets of variables, yet Porter is less concerned with variables and regression analysis and more with what is known as rich analytic description (Dunning 1993: Chapter 5). Porter constructs his road map – the analytic diamond – with close attention to his data and with equal attention to the development of an interpretative approach to policy making. Almost every commentator notes that Porter's factors are loosely defined and those such as knowledge tend to overlap every factor in the diamond. Porter (1998) has refined the original argument constructively to embrace some of the criticisms. My usage of Porter (1990) will slightly reformulate the factors as shown in Figure 7.2. This does not avoid all criticisms (Grant 1991; Clark and Mueller 1996; Rugman 1995).

Porter-1: interacting factors and indeterminacy

As shown in Figure 7.2 there are six interacting factors for analysing the national base of the sector. Later, in Figure 7.3 the role of multinational firms within and between nations is acknowledged. Also, attention is given to the requirement for analysing both the home context and the overseas contexts of actual and potential rivals. There is strong evidence from the public presentations of large corporate strategy and marketing departments (e.g. Unilever) that the rich analytic description of various contexts is examined on a regular basis somewhat along the suggestions of Porter and Dunning.

Analysis needs to look at several levels: the national, regional, sector-firm clusters of related businesses. The elements in Figure 7.2 may be explained as follows.

Factor conditions

Factor conditions include the endowed factors which were the main focus of traditional competitiveness theory such as climate, minerals, soils, flora and fauna,

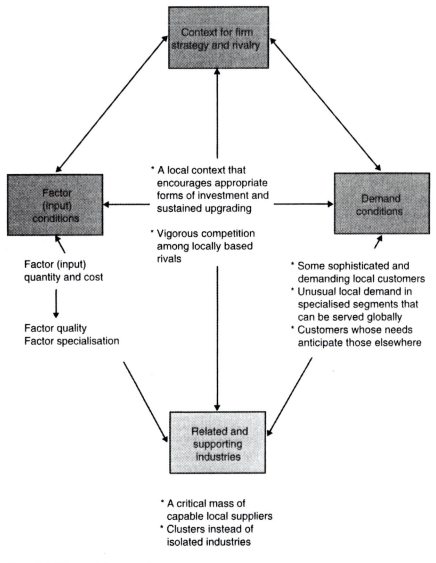

Factor (input)
quantity and cost

Factor quality
Factor specialisation

* A local context that
  encourages appropriate
  forms of investment and
  sustained upgrading

* Vigorous competition
  among locally based
  rivals

* Some sophisticated and
  demanding local customers
* Unusual local demand in
  specialised segments that
  can be served globally
* Customers whose needs
  anticipate those elsewhere

* A critical mass of
  capable local suppliers
* Clusters instead of
  isolated industries

Figure 7.2 Diamond framework
Source: Porter (1997).

demographics, but exclude geo-political location (cf. Clark 1987). Porter tends to conclude that endowed factors are no longer important relative to the created factors.

The created factors include basic conditions such as general education, transport infrastructure and information infrastructure plus advanced factors such as concentrated knowledge making. Basic factors are generalised. There are wide international variations in educational performance at the pre-university level (e.g. mathematics in Japan compared with the USA) and in transport infrastructure (e.g. French railways compared with US railways). The advanced created factors provide the enduring basis for competitive advantage and tend to be specialised in sectoral clusters and firms. Of particular significance is the existence, influence and usage of locations where advanced knowledge is developed, articulated and made accessible, yet benefits the domestic sectors rather than the world as a whole. For example, the development of tufted carpeting in the 1950s and its initial commercialisation was strongly assisted by the Georgia Tech University, USA. Likewise, US universities played a major role in the development of medical technology (e.g. Johns Hopkins) and in computer networks (e.g. Stanford). Anglo-German comparisons strongly indicate that advanced knowledge was more successfully organised in Germany in the automobile and foundry sectors than in Britain. In Japan many of the advanced locations have been within the conglomerates rather than in the universities.

Porter suggests that the absence of factors may induce actions to insert substitutes. The obvious example seems to be the development of chemicals in nineteenth-century Germany. Of course this happens, but Porter's invocation of the law of disadvantages requires revision because the created factors (e.g. knowledge about chemistry) are the translation of national predispositions into nation specific problem solving and design knowledge (Clark 1987: Figure 1.4).

Market and demand conditions

Market and demand conditions are extremely important. Porter misleadingly suggests that the size of the domestic market is unimportant when clearly in a small nation like Sweden its domestic automobile sector could not have survived without building sufficient overseas distribution volume to offset investment costs. It is worth noting that in the 1920s the history of Volvo documents how its founders were advised to enter multiple markets including the USA. In terms of size the huge, varied US market provides a key base within and for its neighbours (e.g. Canada, Mexico) and for the UK and South America. The North American Free Trade Area (NAFTA) is already impacting the Canadian situation. The size of the US retail market poses considerable problems for European designer-retail firms as they seek to gain market penetration more quickly than domestic entrants can occupy the emerging niches (e.g. Benetton, Laura Ashley, Marks & Spencer).

National demand and its influence have been insufficiently analysed. Rosenberg (1969) concludes that in the mid-nineteenth century the differences between the USA and Britain explained differences in the form of products and services. The American market was a homogeneous market for standardised basic goods while the British market was a heterogeneous, urban market for differentiated goods. This difference rests upon enormous institutional features (Hounshell 1984; Clark 1987: Chapter 10) and has immense consequences. Domestic demand provides the opportunity and impetus to firms and is a crucial shaping of the development of the firm's capabilities. Porter contends that Japanese success in consumer electronics rests upon the market in the Tokyo region with its 30 million customers. British success at exporting cream biscuits reflects a unique role of biscuit eating. Domestic demand varies in its relationship to world demand and in the speed with which the domestic market is saturated. Sophisticated and demanding customers within the nation are good for the firm's long success. Equally, customers who are at the leading edge of trends are invaluable.

The role of home demand is clearly given salience and rightly so. However, it is necessary to recognise that for many small nations (e.g. Swedish) firms effectively opt for elected learning markets.

Firm rivalry, strategy and structure

Porter states that the greater the number of domestic rivals in the same sector, the more domestic firms are pressured to 'upgrade' all their facets. This rule-like conclusion is drawn from a simple comparison of the higher number of rivals in Japan than in the USA for a diverse collection of international sectors. Rivalry is so good for the firm's long-term performance that it should be sought. Porter also speculates on how the structure of the firm might benefit or hinder high performance, but that discussion can better be understood in the frame of reference for my analysis as a whole.

Related and supporting industries

The internal quality and relevance found in clusters includes the infrastructure of services such as design and advertising. For example, the German textile industry is the world leader in exports (Dicken 1998) and this arises from a clustering of sectors which embraces varied textile machinery, dyeing firms, synthetic fibres, quality fabrics and apparel firms as well as firms in industrial textiles. Also, consultants are essential, but the nature of corporate dependence upon them is an area for caution.

Central government

The central government can support or undermine by its actions. Government has some degree of influence upon the regulative context within which firms operate, especially the product market and such aspects as land use (McKinsey 1998). The regulative environment shapes the extent to which competitive behaviour is constrained and constrained competitive behaviour inhibits the adoption of best practice. From this perspective low capital investment, low skills and problems of economic scale are secondary consequences rather than root causes. McKinsey (1998) contends that in Britain the competitiveness of key sectors is inhibited.

Three cameos from Porter

American patient monitoring technology

The American sector for patient monitoring provides an illustration of the diamond. The sector blossomed after 1960s when the medical profession engaged in aggressive data gathering about patients and about the ecology of illness.

First, demand and market factors include the existence of large populations of wealthy, health-conscious patients who sought to anticipate and understand their illnesses (e.g. heart decease) and created a sophisticated demand. The patients were often advised by a litigatious conscious legal sector and this heightened the hospitals' concern with medical liability. The wealthy patients provided the source of the private and autonomous hospitals that competed for patients.

Second, created advanced factor conditions include the growth of medical research in the 1950s and the establishment of world-class centres of research, development and design. A cadre of science-oriented medical personnel emerged with a culture of technical success.

Third, there was intense rivalry accompanied by public claims for success in both the medical journals and the more reflective popular journalism. There were many start-up enterprises which found a supply of entrants (i.e. factor conditions) in their search for new niches.

Fourth, the support came from a world-class electrical industry with developments in electronics (e.g. MIT, West Coast). Also there were spin-offs from the Cold War through the development of monitoring equipment originally devised to handle the military surveillance of the Soviet bloc. Software developments were considerable. Overall the USA was a very favourable home base which was able to export into the additional markets of Europe. Health expenditure in the USA is the highest proportion of the advanced nations and twice that of Britain. In Britain expenditure was less on equipment and more on pharmaceutical solutions to patient care.

German national profile

Porter's account of Germany was published before the effects of the Cold War and the contemporary international position. Given that Porter's analysis was mainly focused upon Japan it is curious and intriguing to note that the German economic performance was not given equal attention. In many respects the American business school has been much less interested in rich analytic description of German performance. Germany is the example of the late nineteenth century world leader that has constantly upgraded its performance. Germany is exceptional because the analysis of its sectors shows extensive breadth with concentration in several capital goods sectors specialising in machine goods and great depth in certain industries. There were no great strengths in services, although since the original survey software suppliers like SAP have been global players. There were 345 sectors of manufacturing in which Germany held world export shares exceeding 10 per cent (in 1985) of which the top fifty only accounted for about two-fifths of exports. There is extensive clustering with a vast array in chemicals and related products as well as in specialised equipment for the refining industries. There are strong clusters in metalworking and equipment, transport equipment, printing equipment, food and related industries and even in high value textile output and textile machinery.

1   Germany possesses the third largest market value after the USA in 1985 and this has risen since unification. The market tends to be quick in saturation and firms have frequently moved from this leading-edge demand in international supply. Demand is sophisticated and critical, probably more so than in the USA, especially in consumer goods and medical/health products. German firms are also very demanding with one another in terms of industrial goods.

2   The factor conditions that sustain the German position reveal very slight natural resources, yet created factor conditions are the best in the world. The general quality of education is high. There is an exceptional quality in the sorts of occupational training that integrate required knowledge, particular industries and the locality. So local needs are supplied, often through forms of apprenticeship systems. There is a significant combination of explicit theoretical skills with the tacit knowledge from leading edge firms. The general training is supplemented by specialised centres. Also, there are some outstanding centres for industry specific research.

3   With regard to the related, supporting industries there is extensive clustering with a strong technical orientation and a focus on industrial more than consumer marketing.

4   There is a mixture of small, medium and large firms. The small and medium-sized firms are internationally competitive with their strategy being differentiation rather than cost competition. The output (e.g. goods, equipment) is continuously upgraded at international standards. Domestic rivalry is strong in general and in key areas like performance and after sales servicing. Firms differ in their structure from American firms. There are excellent labour relations.

This characterisation illustrates the above four elements of the Porter framework while leaving the role of the German state and Länder underdeveloped. This limitation is partly corrected in the framework of Whitley examined later in the chapter.

Japanese national profile

The Japanese case is central to Porter's (1990) diagnostic approach and is also awkward, principally because his neo-modern tendency does not extend into a considered use of political economy. For example, Japan was largely excluded from key North American and European markets in the 1930s and then absorbed into the US market after the onset of the Korean War and the signing of the San Francisco Treaty (1951). Porter treats these events as an example of chance. However, standard texts on American foreign policy in the Pacific region since the incidents in Tokyo Bay (1853–4) might suggest otherwise.

Factor conditions in Japan provide a striking contrast to the USA

The endowed factors are much more exacting, less benign and beneficial. Japan consists of 2,000 islands in the China Sea with excellent access to fish supplies and very little flat land or climate suited to cereal production. There are extensive mountains and only a small number of rivers suited to navigation and/or to supplying sources of power. Moreover, the prevalence of earth tremors and quakes disturbs agricultural activity, transport and buildings. There are few resources such as wood, coal or minerals. Land is expensive and all space is cognitised as scarce. At work and home spaces are multi-activity with shifting daily rhythms quite unlike the American experience.

Japanese culture and problem solving provides an exceptional capacity to acquire certain forms of knowledge and teamworking. Since the 1870s there has been the development of excellent school education, especially in the sciences, and at the university level in a basic degree structure. Japan has a large, varied resource pool of engineers. There are few research-led universities of the American type because the knowledge for design and development is located within the corporate sector. Among the created factors Porter includes the propensity to save and this has been high in Japan in the period covered in the analysis (1971–84).

Government roles

The central state has been actively involved in the transformation of Japan. The restructuring of the educational system is top down. Since 1945 the central state has strategised the requirements for growth in the economy (McMillan 1985) through a sequence of steps commencing with the acquisition of overseas resources (e.g. coal and iron from Australia) to develop basic industries such as standardised shipbuilding (e.g. oil tankers). The sectors with potential for overseas earning have been highly encouraged (e.g. consumer electricals and electronics). There has been a remorseless shift away from expensive physical labour to knowledge intensive sectors. Government has supported the demand side factors through the civilian context. In schools there has been the support for purchase of pianos and Japan accounts for 40 per cent of world exports. Government strategy is credited with providing an extraordinary supply of corporate and sectoral intelligence to industry. Famously, the state strategies were wrong in seeking to inhibit the nascent automobile sector (Cusumano 1985). Porter's analysis of the government role over the past decade runs counter to American policy advice with respect to problems of indebtedness.

Demand conditions

Porter considers the demand conditions in certain Japanese sectors to be the single most important determinant. A unique stimulus comes from domestic markets into world sales (e.g. cameras, office equipment, automobiles). The market is the second largest and wealthiest with 130 million of whom nearly one-fourth are in the Tokyo area. The market is relatively homogeneous with concentrated purchasing power. The Japanese buyer is demanding and distinctive. They like goods which are compact, portable, quiet, aesthetically delightful, multi-functional and packaged with similar attention to that found among the French. There is conspicuous consumption of consumer products and of corporate equipment in an aesthetic as well as functional performance. There is a strong interest in recording and documentation which ranges from cameras in personal life to faxes in business life. The small spaces of the home, hotel and office have been tightly analysed and designed. The culture of design is well established with strong interfaces between design knowledge and production. Porter contends that these features are inscribed on key products which enter and saturate the homogeneous Japanese market at an early stage and that these products are also frequently at the leading edge of global preferences. So, Japanese firms have the potential for economies of scale and of scope in developing clusters of products.

Firm rivalry and structure

Porter concentrates upon the successful sectors (e.g. earthmoving equipment) and contends that because there are multiple suppliers of equipment therefore there is extensive rivalry. He concludes from the comparison of selected sectors between the USA and Japan that rivalry is a source of high performance and reasons that competition leads the firm's management constantly to upgrade performance.

Inside the successful firms there are key differences from the American firm and these have been analysed by Aoki (1988). Porter stresses the absence of possessive individualism and the presence of co-operation across boundaries in both the sequence from design-into-operating and horizontally across the firm. Japanese engineers have an enviable stereotype of virtue in their capacity to modularise best practice and to clone key activities. The Japanese employee seems to be more actively committed to everyday problem solving than some American employees.

Related sectors

There is a strong tendency to acknowledge the role of design in key sectors. Also, the boundaries between different kinds of knowledge are more open so that potentials for synthesis (e.g. mechatronics) across the boundaries do occur and emerge at an early stage (e.g. cameras into copiers).

Review

Porter's theory and analytic framework launched a debate onto the agenda of organisation, innovations and strategic studies and comparative international business systems. The framework bonds together the firm, sectoral and national levels in a dynamic innovation perspective replacing the stationary equilibrium framework. The framework reconfigures the basic approaches to strategy by showing that the national context of the firm is both highly differentiated and highly consequential. The required analysis cannot be compiled by simply using frameworks like PEST (politics, economic, social, technology). Moreover, the accessibility of the diamond to potential users corresponds to the iconic features of the five forces and value chain, but there the correspondence ends.

Unlike the earlier approach in the five forces and the value chain the new approach of Porter (1991) introduces novel requirements in analysis. These newer requirements affect the relationships between organisation theory, strategy and international perspectives:

1   The application of the diamond requires a rich analytic description which intermingles the explicit and the situated/tacit knowledge. Moreover, there are no simple rules of interpretation. The formative context theory is only weakly predictive and loosely normative. Rather, constructing rich analysis provides an input to strategic agendas.

2   Using the diamond approach requires multi-nation studies because the advantage of understanding the position of domestic firms needs the analysis of where and how the opposition arises. So, the British woven carpet firm of Brinton's which supplies major US firms and cities should be scrutinised in terms of at least two diamonds: the British and the American.

3   The diamond reveals the role of resources and capabilities and the heritage of the firm in its accumulated capacities (see Chapter 12) must be examined in relation to how the context and conditions of resource supply and creation shape the firm. Therefore, the role of inter-firm networks within and between nations becomes quite central for successful innovation.

The definition of the factors does provide an initial road map, yet there is need for considerable caution and considerable revision to give clarity and direction.

ECLECTIC DIAMONDS: COMBINING DUNNING AND PORTER

There are problems in creating a road map to express the analytic terrain occupied by Porter and Dunning. Figure 7.3 provides an integration of some of the possibilities and includes Rugman's comment about the need to analyse the domestic and other multiple diamonds. The integrating road map contains chance (1) and the original five interacting elements (2–6), but the elements are

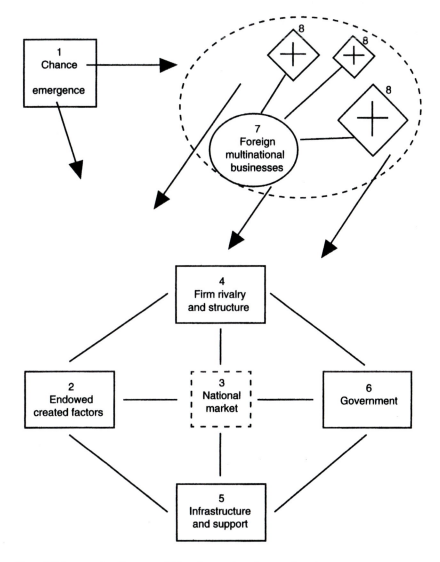

Figure 7.3 Integrating Porter and Dunning on locations and nations

arranged around the national market in the middle. The national market (3) is shown as a key domain. In the top right-hand corner the presence of foreign multinational businesses (7) is highlighted to acknowledge Dunning's analysis of their impact in many domestic settings. The position of foreign multinationals within specific nations is highly consequential for national events. One survey in Britain concluded that the Chairman of GEC (USA), Jack Welch, was one of the most powerful people in Britain. Equally relevant is the detailed position of overseas diamonds (8). This integrated road map[3] should be used in conjunction with societal-institutional analyses from Part II.

The role of MNBs within particular national contexts picks up Dunning's (1993) revision to Porter. The reasoning here is that foreign MNCs impact the national context to some degree (Bailey *et al.* 1994). In the British case, for example, American MNCs in its manufacturing industry are the leaders in productivity (McKinsey 1998) and their presence influences the role taken by suppliers of software for the co-ordination of activities within and between firms (Clark and Newell 1993).

The factors in the framework gain their influence interdependently and there are complex, sometimes unintended, interactions. Proximity and connections can accelerate the collective development of knowledge and the selective appropriation of innovations (Clark and Staunton 1993). For example, the role of British shoe firms may be unintentionally circumscribed by the actions of the major retailers (Cochrane 1988). The impacts are influenced by clustering of closely related sectors – and their unwinding – and possibly by regional concentration (e.g. Swiss pharmaceutical firms in Basle).

Using the road map in Figure 7.3 requires the analysis of firms, sectors and clusters for several nations. So, Swedish engineering firms require applications to themselves and to major rivals (e.g. Germany, USA, Japan) in order to construct useful scenarios of the future. There is clear evidence that leading firms are already undertaking this kind of analysis on a routine basis in support of strategic decision making. There is also evidence that the top executives of small firms have become aware of the implications even when their learning may be very painful. Stoves, a British firm in the kitchen equipment sector, actively located itself in the exacting German market in order to learn and develop design-led domestic equipment. It follows, logically, that notions such as Penrosian learning should acknowledge the contextual, national aspect of what might be learnt (see Chapters 10 and 11).

FIVE TYPES OF NATIONAL BUSINESS SYSTEM: WHITLEY

The national business systems (NBS) approach aims to compare firm–market relations in different national institutional contexts because the nature of technical demands for efficiency are institutionally shaped (Whitley 1994). The initial aim is to develop a framework of five types which can be used to compare broad similarities and differences between North America, Europe and East Asia.

Five major types of business system are constructed (see below). Each is relatively cohesive and stable in ordering market relationships and in articulating with the dominant social institutions. Each national business system has different consequences. First, the NBS provides a key context which conditions and guides the growth of those domestic firms which become multinational (1994: 177). Those NBSs which possess high institutional differentiation and separation combined with low legal regulation of labour relations (e.g. Britain) may find it easier to implement changes in labour practices than where these features are reversed (e.g. France). Second, the NBS of the leading economies (e.g. USA and Germany) will have spillover effects in other NBSs (e.g. Russia).

There are recognised differences between nations (e.g. USA and Japan) in the role of intermediary institutions and agents in articulating interfirm dynamics and in influencing the ways in which uncertainty is absorbed. Firms are usually constituted through their actions into discrete sectors that possess varying degrees of interdependence (Pavitt 1984). To address these problems Whitley raises three questions, each of which is used to define a set of elements which is included in the framework of national business systems:

1   How can we identify the roles of economic agents in the co-ordination of economies? How do their actions relate to national property rights and to the resources the agents may control?
2   How are the agents connected in networks?
3   At the inter-organisational level what are the degrees of national interdependence?

The aim is to characterise the broad features of the overall co-ordination and control of the economic systems by using thirteen elements drawn from previous research.

Within national business systems, firms as economic actors vary in four ways:

1   The degree varies to which the state decentralises economic power to private interests which can then occupy a dominating position. There is high though contested decentralisation in the USA in general terms (Fligstein) in areas like health relative to, say, the UK.
2   In some business systems there is a remoteness – a gap – between the property rights of owners and the actions of those who occupy managerial roles. The remoteness is high in the USA and is expressed in the attempt by agency theory to express how the principals (who own property rights) can control the agents (managers without property rights). In contrast, the Chinese family firms fuse ownership and management. Also, the extensive-ness of family businesses in Italy (e.g. Gucci, Fiat) contrasts with the American preference. The continental European situation possesses closer relationships (e.g. Germany).
3   Firms vary in the extent to which they are expected to be self-sufficient in risk taking (USA is high) or whether the firms are implicated in elaborate net-works of obligations and large business groups (e.g. Japan).
4   Firms vary in the degree to which they pursue a broad scope of unrelated activities (e.g. conglomerates) or are tightly focused or achieve some scope within highly articulated knowledge-power frameworks (e.g. Fujitsu).

These four features are combined in numerous ways across different national business systems.

Market relationships between firms vary:

5 In the degree to which there are mutual, reciprocal long term obligations between firms or whether relationships are adversarial, contractual and transitory: Japanese firms have been characterised as possessing much stronger obligations than their American counterparts (Cusumano 1985).
6 In the significance of intermediaries in enabling co-ordination between firms: markets vary in organisation from high (France, Germany) to low (USA).
7 Dependence of market relationships on personal ties: in Chinese family businesses personal ties are high while in Japan the obligations between collective entities are much less dependent upon personal ties.

The general logic governing the managerial integration of firms will vary:

8 The impersonality (or otherwise) of authority relationships.
9 The social and power distance between superiors and their subordinates including the degree to which subordinates tasks are specified.
10 The degree of de-centralisation of co-ordination and control examined in a multidimensional framework.
11 Integration and interdependence of activities.
12 Specialisation (tasks, roles, authority).
13 Commitment of employers and employees, as expressed in the internal and external labour markets.

In certain respects this third listing complements and differs in important respects from the structural items of the rational managerial approach (see Chapter 3) associated with organisation design (Daft 1997).

The thirteen characteristics are unlikely to be totally randomised. If each characteristic were dichotomised and randomised there would be (potentially) almost 10,000 combinations (Whitley 1994: 167), but some are unlikely and it becomes possible to reduce the immense variety to five main types of business system (1994: 174).

First is the *centrifugal* type dominated by largely self-reliant firms in low levels of institutionalised trust and weak mechanisms for economic disputes. Chinese family business illustrates this.

Second, *partitioned* business systems, exemplified in the Anglo-Saxon model, are differentiated, pluralistic with strong impersonal mechanisms whereby major players appear at arm's length.

Third, *collaborative economies* are co-ordinated through financial intermediaries (e.g. banks, chambers of commerce, regional institutions) and possess dense networks of collaboration.

Fourth, *state co-ordinated economies* possess autonomous firms and the state elites are active in sectoral development through central integration. There are likely to be horizontal networks.

Fifth, in the *state-dominated economies* the co-ordination of investment and resource strategies lies with the political executive and bureaucratic elites (e.g. Korea).

The NBS perspective shifts the level of analysis on to a comparative international level and underlines the consequences of certain long-term predispositions.

NOTES

1 Figure 7.1 is based on a comparative analysis of differences between the USA and Britain in their typical approaches to design and innovation (Clark 1987).
2 These were brought together in 1991 to examine national systems of innovation and the role of organisation networks. See the special issue of *Research Policy* edited by C. DeBresson and Amessi (1991).
3 In 1997 at the annual meeting of the American Management Academy in Boston one session brought Porter and Dunning together.

8 Nations

Structural and institutional variations

INTRODUCTION

The nation as a unit of analysis has now become of major interest with an array of different frameworks and collections of comparative studies as well as single nation studies (Clark and Mueller 1995, 1996). This chapter will review the development of institutional and structural perspectives and then compare three different current perspectives:

- the actor-culture theorising of Hofstede (1980);
- the new institutionalism (e.g. Scott 1995);
- the claim by Sorge (1991, 1995) that societal capacities are most significant when directed towards resolving tensions between sectors in respect of conflicting contingencies.

These three frameworks tend to minimise the role of national markets and the international political economy examined in the two previous chapters. Also, they tend to overstate the homogeneity within a nation. The final section of the chapter contends that nations probably contain a typical variety of institutional forms and considerable variation (Clark 1987).

Nations: unlike and alike

Attention to the nation as a significant dimension has unfolded in three major waves.

First, in the founding period for organisation behaviour cross-national comparisons were rare. The salient study by Crozier (1964) claimed that Franco-American differences in social structure did affect organisational processes, conflict, pace of organisational change, rationality and structure. In contrast to Crozier, most studies sought to discover universal features of the organisation found in all national settings (e.g. Pugh and Hickson 1976). There was only slight interest in how the differences between national contexts might shape the organisational action of firms within particular nations. That neglect was stimulated by the 'bold hypothesis' advanced by Hickson and colleagues (1974). They postulated that firms of similar size were remarkably alike even when they were located in unlike national contexts such as the USA and China. Hickson reasoned that firms were essentially similar in their structural unfolding and growth in size, irrespective of the differences in the context where they were located. The bold hypothesis challenged those who considered that the national context was a key feature to come into the open, yet did not preclude the possibility that the hypothesis might be refuted (e.g. Lammers and Hickson 1979).

Second, challenging the bold hypothesis was massively stimulated by three pieces of research:

- Hofstede (1980) demonstrated that within the same, large American-owned firm, IBM, there were significant national differences between its personnel across more than forty nations. Hofstede used questionnaires and factor analysis to demonstrate national differences in the values and attitudes of actors. Hofstede concluded that the members of each nation acquired nationally specific forms of mental programming which were likely to shape their interpretation of organisational action. Hofstede's data suggest quite small differences between the USA and UK with much larger differences between them from France (as Crozier 1964) and recognisable Franco-German differences. The focus of Hofstede on the actor and his theory of national mindsets has been highly visible.
- Stimulus to interest in the nation arose from attempts to explain the imbalances of trade between the USA and Japan. The Japanese gained massive advantages in certain sectors, for example, automobiles. Abernathy and colleagues (1980, 1981) produced seminal articles in the highly visible *Harvard Business Review* and then sought to rewrite American business history to decode and respond to rupture in the future dominance of established American paradigms of organising. They (1980, 1981) rightly invoke the influence of pre-existing American approaches in their variant of historical analysis which differs from the interpretation of Chandler (1962, 1977). Abernathy and Hofstede provide very different descriptions and explanations while agreeing that nations are significant.
- The structuralist approach by Maurice *et al.* (1986) used a series of Franco-German comparisons to argue that each nation possessed distinctive flows of personnel from education into work. They reasoned that these flows (*filières*) explained the differences in structure and human resource management between French and German firms in the same industry. This is the societal effects approach.

Third, recently there have been attempts to locate cross-cutting connections between different frameworks. Three examples illustrate the potentials and problems:

- The approach known as national systems of organising combines national characteristics, international political economy and strategic corporate innovation (Clark 1987). A major thrust of the national systems approach has been to locate innovation, knowledge and organisational networks at the centre of the analysis (e.g. Lundvall 1992). Geographers are making a distinctive and important contribution (e.g. Dicken 1998). Collaboration between geographers and sociologists highlights the central role played by the service class of salaried managers and technocrats (e.g. Lash and Urry 1987). Reich (1991) refers to them as the symbolic analysts who restructure the future and unravel the present. Their capacities are significantly shaped by national predispositions.

- The new institutional theory seeks to demonstrate that the zones of manoeuvre available to firms are deeply impacted by societal institutions including the pivotal role of professional associations (Scott 1995).
- Sorge (1989, 1991, 1995) tested the implicit claim of the societal effects approach by revealing gaps between the ideal profiles of French and German firms in the same sector and their actual forms of organisation. Initially, this discovery led Sorge to reason that nations vary in their capacities to tolerate contradictions between an ideal matching of societal predispositions at the inter-sectoral level. Then Sorge (1995) invokes the actor-structure framework attributed to Giddens (1984) in order to align Hofstede's actor-cultural approach with his own interpretation of the structural perspective (Sorge 1991).

NATIONAL CULTURE: ACTOR–SYSTEM INDEPENDENCE

This section examines the claim by Sorge (1995) that Hofstede's (1980) seminal study of national differences within IBM is at the actor level rather than the system level of national institutions and structures.

Hofstede's four dimensions analysis defines national culture as the collective mental programming with its roots in their common history and its potentials for reinforcement in everyday life and through the various culture-shaping institutions (e.g. media). The basis of the four dimensions lies in surveys administered in the early 1970s to employees in forty nations around the world with staff working for IBM. It might be anticipated that IBM had a strong and pervasive corporate culture. Therefore if significant national variations could be uncovered then the role of the national culture as a contingency variable is more powerful than variables preferred in the bold hypothesis (e.g. size) proposed by Hickson and colleagues. Hofstede's approach was not alone, but it did break the mould and has been both widely diffused and debated. Four dimensions arise from Hofstede's interpretation of the factor analysis:

1   *Power distance* is the extent to which power in society is experienced as unevenly distributed. Nations with large power distance will report that there should be inequality; that superordinates might consider subordinates to be

different kinds of persons; that few people should be independent and power is a basic fact.

2   *Uncertainty avoidance* indicates the extent to which the members of nations feel threatened when faced by situations which are uncertain and ambiguous so that they try to avoid them. Avoidance might arise through establishing protective formal rules and not tolerating deviant behaviours. Nations with low uncertainty avoidance would prefer few, flexible rules, would take risks, accept dissent and view the role of authority as serving everyone.

3   *Individualism–collectivism* are opposites. Individualism implies that everyone should take care of themselves and their family within a loose-knit social framework. Collectivism possesses a tight social framework with distinctions between in-groups and out-groups and strong emphasis upon loyalty.

4   *Masculinity* means that men should be assertive, be rather uncaring except for material goods, should dominate and be ambitious independents.

These four dimensions are then be used to distinguish between nations as illustrated in Figure 8.1 and Figure 8.2. The USA possesses small power distance, weak uncertainty avoidance, is individualist and masculine. Britain is very similar. Japan scores large power distance and strong uncertainty avoidance, is much more collectivist (cf. USA, GB) and rather more masculine. The Scandinavian countries combine weak uncertainty avoidance, small power distance with much lower masculinity scores than the USA, GB and Japan. Hofstede draws on this base to argue that the dominant management theories in the world's textbooks (e.g. Maslow, Herzberg, Fiedler, McClelland, Vroom) only have relevance in North America, not in Asia and only unevenly in Europe. Theories of management are therefore relative and mainly only relevant to North America. Even there Canadian–American differences might be important.

It may be observed that IBM possesses a strong corporate culture. Therefore Hofstede's findings paradoxically emphasise the role of cross-cultural differences while not necessarily revealing the specific cultural patterns of the forty nations included in the study. The reasoning is that IBM is unlikely to be a typical employer in these nations. Moreover, there is no indication that the cultural profile of actors from different nations constitutes a systematically consequential causal power.

This point of view is taken up by Sorge (1995). Because the structuration theory of Giddens (1984) combines the level of the actor and of the system then structuration theory provides the reasoning for defining the approach of Hofstede at the actor level rather than at the level of organisational and national institutions. Organisations are characterised by shifting coalitions, conflicting elements and different, often competing, interests. Moreover, as Layder's (1997) domain theory suggests, organisations, systems and actors have to be differentiated as distinct categories with their own dimensions and characteristics. Structuration theory theorises that contradiction, conflict and unintended outcomes between distinct levels are compatible with cross-referencing between actor and system levels. Yet the cross-referencing does not preclude the actors gaining substantial partial autonomy for the mindsets from the systemic features. For example, Guild's

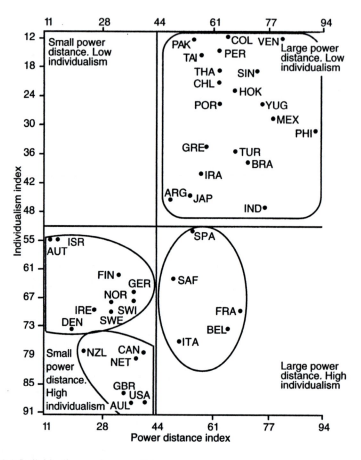

Figure 8.1 Individualism and power-distance
Source: Hofstede (1980).

(1999) study of Californian ski-lift operators concludes that even while performing their expected tasks they adopt an ironic detachment. Likewise, system character-istics may possess different features to those contained in the mindsets of the actors. Systems and actors are partially autonomous and are also involved in cross-referencing. There are therefore contradictory elements between the actor and system levels. However, the distinctive character of each element – actor and system – means that they produce their own outcomes.

The co-existing contradictions between the actor and system levels are illu-strated by the structuralist interpretations (cf. actor culture) of the limited extent to which the actor-culture dimensions of Japanese and German workers explain the performance of firms. Actors, however programmed, encounter specific systemic features including the corporate rules of the game (Crozier and Friedberg 1980). Sorge (1995: 111) reasons that 'the main point is that there are different

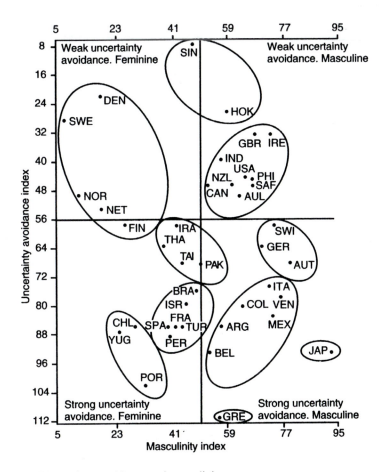

Figure 8.2 Uncertainty avoidance and masculinity
Source: Hofstede (1980).

Key to Figures 8.1 and 8.2:

ARG	Argentina	HOK	Hong Kong	POR	Portugal
AUL	Australia	IND	India	SAF	South Africa
AUT	Austria	IRA	Iran	SIN	Singapore
BEL	Belgium	IRE	Ireland	SPA	Spain
BRA	Brazil	ISR	Israel	SWE	Sweden
CAN	Canada	ITA	Italy	SWI	Switzerland
CHL	Chile	JAP	Japan	TAI	Taiwan
COL	Columbia	MEX	Mexico	THA	Thailand
DEN	Denmark	NET	Netherlands	TUR	Turkey
FIN	Finland	NOR	Norway	USA	United States
FRA	France	NZL	New Zealand	VEN	Venezuela
GBR	Great Britain	PAK	Pakistan	YUG	Yugoslavia
GER	Germany	PER	Peru		
GRE	Greece	PHI	Philippines		

rules of the game making individuals move in different directions, even if their mental programming is the same'. Therefore, even if European and American actors were transplanted into a Japanese firm those rules of the game would generate the same organisational outcomes and the outcomes. This line of reasoning can be used to explore why when Japanese and German workers are 'not necessarily more committed to working hard, their employing firms are economically successful. Sorge states that Germans work comparatively fewer hours than other Europeans and they hate work and 'yet comply with the ground rules of the workplace because they appear legitimate' (Sorge 1995: 117). Lincoln and Kalleberg (1990) conclude that the work commitment of Japanese workers is not greater than that of American workers in similar work situations.

NEW INSTITUTIONAL SCHOOL

The new synthesis

The orthodox, rational contingency approach to organisation design significantly defocalised the firm from its societal and international contexts. The aim of the new institutional theory is to refocalise the firm and to extend earlier institutional approaches (e.g. Selznick) from the national into the comparative, international dimension (DiMaggio and Powell 1991). Scott's (1995) synthesis provides an incisive and penetrating review which, while emphasising a degree of continuity with the earlier approach of Blau and Scott (1963), sets out many of the features of the basic road map now considered to be central. The problem is how to handle the societal features and inter-nation political economy. Scott deals with the former, but only acknowledges the latter.

The new institutionalists focus upon the intermediate, meso area between societal level analysis and organisational analysis and claim that all organisations are institutionalised organisations. Institutions are the infrastructures that constrain and support organisations and so organisations have to embody institutional and cultural logics. Organisation theory has defocalised institutions, thereby creating controversy and confusion about how to analyse institutions.

Scott (1995) provides an overview of the essential requirements and issues through the framework of three pillars and multiple levels. The approach developed by Scott also seeks to address the interface between essentially historical and comparative sociological perspectives and the assumptions of economists about rationality in order to bridge the social and behavioural sciences. The new institutional school (NIS) is highly involved in:

- extending attention beyond the normative pillar that was the centre of Parsons's (1951) systems: the three-pillar approach incorporates Bourdieu's organisation field as a key level of analysis;
- exploring the role of the historical dimension and highlighting the controversy

between social constructionists, universalists and rational-instrumental perspectives;
- highlighting the role of the state and of the professional associations in shaping the culture and structure of organisations;
- reformulating the top-down and bottom-up debate as multiple levels of analysis.

In formulating a societal approach there is much to discard from the normative systems thinking associated with earlier approaches (e.g. Parsons). The contemporary institutional approach draws from the approaches to structuration associated with Giddens and Bourdieu in an eclectic manner where the rules of borrowing are implicit rather than explicit. Giddens's approach emphasises the mutual interpenetrating of structure and action in all social behaviour. Structures represent the persisting features which are the outcomes of past actions and which in turn are both the context and the medium through which ongoing action unfolds. Thus action may reproduce or alter the pre-existing structure. Scott, in common with other contemporary institutionalists (e.g. DiMaggio and Powell 1991), draws from Giddens's theory of structuration by examining the place and interrelation of three pillars of analysis: regulative, normative and cognitive. The purpose of this section is to draw upon Scott's approach.

Three pillars framework

Scott seeks to provide a tightly reasoned approach that unpacks and deals separately with the three main pillars of analysis and avoids treating them as over-integrated or over-determined. These three pillars present the analytic potential of the contemporary institutional theory and reveal the important areas of controversy. The pillars are set out in Figure 8.3.

First, the regulative pillar focuses upon the institutional and societal capacity to establish rules, to inspect and review the extent to which those rules are accepted/rejected and the mix of sanctions and rewards devised to influence action. For example, as early as 1823 the Ordnance Department of the American government in Washington established and distributed regulations for the proof and inspection of small arms made under contract which cover the detail from the gun lock to the wrapping of the boxes in which the guns were supplied. Those regulations were legally sanctioned and compliance presumed both a motive of expedience and a logic of instrumentality. Failure to conform meant the non-acceptance from the supplier. The social logic is instrumental and asks the actors to reflect upon their interests (e.g. material interests) in specific situations. The economic historian North (1990) highlights the transaction costs dimension of the rules. There is an enforcement issue which is part of the essential costs. The state typically plays a role in enforcement. Clark (1987, 1997a, b) contends that the capacity to develop rules and to enforce them was more evident in the American armoury sector than in its British counterpart. Given the centrality of arms making for the insertion of

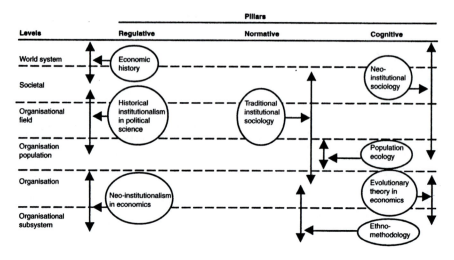

Figure 8.3 Institutional pillars and varying levels: illustrative schools
Source: Scott (1995).

standardisation into the heritage of work organisation, then this analytic pillar has considerable consequences.

Second, the normative pillar is the basis of compliance and involves the feeling of social obligation. There is an issue of the logic of appropriateness in a social situation rather than instrumental benefits. The basis of legitimacy is the morality as defined in particular locales. Normative systems:

- connect values to preferences: to what should be done in a situation;
- define goals (e.g. play to win) and the socially improved means;
- are strongly implicated in the roles.

Nations are likely to be characterised (even stereotyped) as possessing particular normative frameworks.

Third, the cognitive pillar is one which has been a major focus. Cognitive refers to the rules that constitute the nature of reality and the frames of meaning (e.g. classification systems) through which reality is constituted. For example, there were sharp differences of cognitive framework between the early European settlers who entered New England and the indigenous Indian tribes occupying the same terrain. The cognitive frameworks of the settlers defined the terrain in terms of its munificent supplies of edible fish and animals as well as the potential of the climate, soils and slopes for permanent agriculture (Cronon 1983). The indigenous Indians' cognitions led them to migrate through the seasons as they followed the sources of food. They did not consider the potential of the furs for the urban gentry of growing European cities. The rules define the categories and the construction of the typifications. The cognition of the external context emphasises the importance of symbols and meanings as in the notion of the enacted environment (Weick 1969). Sports like American Football require constitutive rules (Searle 1995) which construct the game and identify its differences from Rugby Union and Association Football. Cognitive theorists emphasise that sports do contain rules and their enforcement is in the regulative pillar. In addition there are socially constructed players with different parts (e.g. tight-end) and roles to play (e.g. offence). These cognitive rules are often overlooked and they occupy an uneasy position in orthodox organisational behaviour. Yet, firms can be characterised in terms of their scripts (Clark and Staunton 1989: Chapter 9). Also, for example, visitors to the USA might anticipate encountering cognitive frameworks emphasising individual competitiveness as the basis for occupational advancement and then observe some of these features in sports such as basketball. Cognitive approaches draw attention to the common frameworks of meaning in organisations and how their constitutive rules define the differences between firms, for example, between hospitals and sugar beet factories.

Each of the three pillars elicits different but related sources of legitimacy. The regulative basis is conformity to rules and therefore firms have to conform to a context of rules (e.g. probity of public information about profits). The normative basis stresses moral issues and issues of ethics. The cognitive basis draws legitimacy from correctness in relation to conceptual frameworks. There may be tensions between the sources. So a firm may undertake actions which according to the regulations are legally sanctioned while meeting with normative disapproval. For example, firms supplying a consumption good might design the good (e.g. automobile) so that an unsafe potential is legally correct (e.g. location of petrol tank), yet meets with disapproval from interest groups (e.g. consumer associations).

The three pillars are embedded in different ways in terms of culture, social structure and routines. The regulative pillar is embedded in rules and laws, systems of domination and power and routines such as protocols and standard procedures. The normative framework of values and expectations is embedded in the authority systems and the routines of conformity. The cognitive systems are embedded in scripts and the social structure emphasises structural compliance through isomorphism (DiMaggio and Powell 1983).

The linkage between each of the three forms and their shaping of organisational features within particular societies is an important and also problematic issue. Recent research has given heightened attention to the cognitive basis: for example, in how the forms of knowledge institutionalised in the firm might affect its ability to attend to innovations which might improve the internal capacities for co-ordination (Swan and Clark 1992).

Longitudinal comparative

The NIS seems to advance a processual-longitudinal and comparative perspective. The longitudinal is in two elements: the historical and change of the institution. Scott (1995: 143–150) contends that the NIS provides categories of concepts which capture action as a developmental sequence of events. The techniques for assessing the extent to which there is a path dependency in organisation action has become important in evolutionary economics and in organisation research (Miller and Friesen 1984; Clark and Starkey 1988: Chapter 2).

Because the organisation field is such an important analytic focus there is a requirement for case studies which examine the life course of institutions and the relationship to organisations situated in a field within a co-evolution format (Cochrane 1988; Clark and Probert 1989). There are important issues about how fields which have become stabilised might be transformed. For example, the seminal reconstruction by Abernathy (1978) of the position of Ford from 1906 to the 1970s emphasised the institutional texture which embedded the majestic, firm-driven management of innovation coupled to choreographing of taste in an incremental pattern. Two decades later the organisation field had been heavily penetrated by Japanese firms (not European), yet Ford has massively transformed itself and its array of networks in the field. By contrast, British firms in the automobile sector succumbed to overseas entrants that currently own the industry and are domestically located (Ford, GM, BMW, Honda, Nissan and Toyota). Indeed the British sector is a base for the European supply. To what extent was the zone of manoeuvre and transformative potential of American and British 'field-firm' different and similar. An equally and ongoing British/American dynamic can be found in sectors as diverse as electricity utility supply, the bereavement sector and hospitals.

State and professions

The roles of the state include defence, the monopoly of violence through legitimate coercion and the enforcement of property rights by setting the conditions of private ownership. The state is a collective actor acting semi-autonomously through regulative processes and is a distinctive configuration of institutions. The state can provide different arenas within which conflicts between organisations can be adjudicated (Scott 1995: 95). It regulates the role of the professional associations that have control over the application of certain types of knowledge (e.g. medical knowledge). The professional associations occupy a crucial role in both the control of segments of societal action (e.g. being away from work) and also in shaping action within firms. The accountancy professions significantly control the audit of corporate performance and have utilised that role to gain a strategic position in advising firms on how to use the new information technologies. The major accountancy firms are leading proponents of the claim that knowledge is capital. Also their capabilities in auditing performance have been utilised by states in varying ways. Power (1994) argues that Britain has become an audit society with the influence of the system of audit dispersed through the whole public sector, thereby creating a transparency in performance. In Britain users of the educational and medical systems can now consult extensive league tables which even detail the performance of local specific schools and of hospital departments.

DiMaggio and Powell (1991) contend that the professions are the major players in the field of organisational innovations.

Bottom-up and top-down: multi-level analysis

Figure 8.4 depicts a layered model of institutional forms and flows (Scott 1995: 141–143) showing how societal institutions provide a context through their models and menus to the organisational fields. The models and menus are diffused downward through imposition and upward through negotiation.

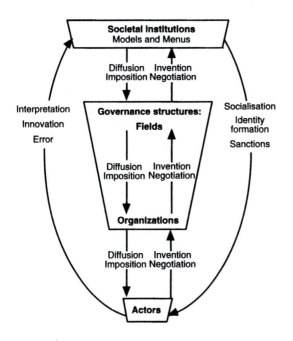

Figure 8.4 Top-down and bottom-up processes in institutional creation and diffusion
Source: Scott (1995).

INTER-SECTORAL DYNAMICS: SORGE

Elective affinities?

The next two sections examine the major revisions to our understanding of strategy, national predispositions and inter-sectoral performance arising from the omission of institutional features in Porter's (1990) account of competition between contexts. In effect Porter's move from the national level to inter-sectoral clusters provides an important causal and explanatory potential to Sorge's (1991) shift from the sectoral level into inter-sectoral clusters. Are there elective affinities between national predispositions of culture and structure with the capacities of some sectoral clusters to survive and prosper?

There are three main steps in the argument. The first two steps arise from Sorge's reasoning and the third (see later) is introduced to articulate the connection with Porter's attention to location and the competitive advantage of certain contexts. The first two steps are:

1   To align the approach known as societal effects developed by Maurice *et al.* (1986) with the neo-contingency approach in organisation studies. Sorge (1989) replaced unidirectional causal approaches (Donaldson 1985; Aldrich 1979) with the multi-directional analysis of elective affinities (Sorge 1991: 23). That led him to explore the elective affinities between the societal tendencies of a nation (e.g. Germany) and a profile of the ideal task-contingency variables of a sector (e.g. automobiles) matched to national predispositions. Initially this appears to be successful. Sorge tests the framework against existing studies to reveal problems with the level of analysis.

2   To demonstrate that it is the relationship between national predispositions and the *complex dynamics and contradictions of inter-sectoral linkages* which may be one of the most important areas for understanding competitive success. The explanation situates analysis above the firm and the sector in the dynamics and tensions between sectors which are coupled through economic exchanges. For example, in Germany and France the dynamics between the sectors supplying machine tools and their users are between sectors which differ in their contingency factors. The French users are large-volume firms seeking machine tools to fit their distinct requirements while the German situation is more or less the opposite. Hence the problem is how those interfaces are handled within the national context. The key question becomes: does the national system of organising provide a regime for absorbing and orchestrating the relationships? The role of national social structure is in being able to absorb and/or inhibit the development of capacities to reconcile differences between economically related sectors (Sorge 1991). Elective affinities contend that national predispositions reciprocally interact with particular configurations of sectors. Similarly Clark (1987) argues that in the British case there are stronger capacities to resolve uncertainties between sectors within science-based sectors than between sectors in engineering.

Neo-contingency, ideal sectoral profiles and national predispositions

Sorge (1989) commences by outlining an approach which connects the societal effects perspective (Maurice *et al.* 1986) to neo-contingency theorising. Sorge starts by considering the neo-contingency approach to the production of ideal sectoral profiles in their elective affinity with national predispositions in human resource management. Neo-contingency approaches can 'be formulated in the language of population ecology' (Sorge 1991: 161) to reason that nations will tend to be populated by ways of organising which most closely correspond to contingency-task environments of the niches within that nation. There is an interaction between the mechanisms of environmental selection posited in the theory with attempts within the firm to arrange organisational design in particular ways. For example, Canada, especially the provinces of Ontario and Quebec, provides certain niches for the indigenous textile industry and these are entered by firms with particular characteristics (Clark 1998). In a rational contingency approach the assumption is that the designers locate the key parameters and devise the ideal architecture of the firm accordingly.

Close attention is given to how within nations there are institutionalised human resources flowing through the educational *filière* into work careers and how these intertwine with societal stratification and with industrial relations. Maurice *et al.* (1986) report that although a sample of firms in France and Germany were similar in respect of their contingencies, they were dissimilar in patterns of organising and these differences could be traced into the different national *filières*. Similar findings had been reported by Gallie (1983) in his detailed comparison of similarities and differences between French and British oil firms. This research contends that there are societal effects on firms and sectors arising from the interdependencies between human resources, the forms of organising and industrial structure. Societal effects impact upon the niches within which organisational forms are constituted and selected in/out. The hypothesis is that societal differences and the pursuit of different business strategies are reciprocally related and that certain elective affinities will unfold over time. The comparative advantage of a nation might reside in the fit between the demands from particular niches and the institutionalised predisposition for human resource management in that nation.

Developing the neo-contingency approach requires an examination of the relationship between institutionalised cross-national differences (e.g. Anglo-American differences) and the organisational forms to explore the societal effects. If these effects are as powerful as is suggested, then orthodox organisation theory and design of the rational contingency variety would require extensive revision.

The reasoning relates the non-specific, task-institutionalised societal patterns to task-specific organisational forms. The analytic issue is to hypothesise elective affinities between societal patterns and the forms of organisation in sectors and firms. For example, the British societal predisposition is towards plurality of centres and functional segmentation (e.g. production/maintenance; management/engineering; supervision/technicians) within hierarchies characterised by financial controls rather than technical expertise with enclaves of specialists who are only slightly integrated. There is more stress on autonomy than bureaucracy (cf. Germany).

The working hypothesis is illustrated in Figure 8.5 (Sorge 1991: 169). On the horizontal dimension output is dichotomised between low differentiation (i.e. standard price, competitive products) and high differentiation (i.e. customised, quality, competitive products). The vertical is dichotomised on volume of output from low volume to high volume. The four quadrants are labelled on Figure 8.5.

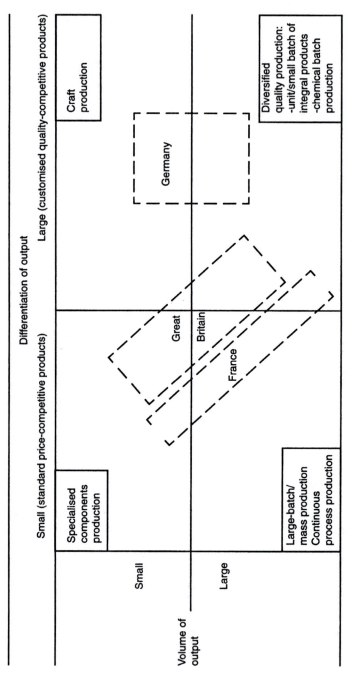

Figure 8.5 Neo-contingency and societal effects
Source: Sorge (1991).

The broken-line boxes schematically display the societally significant types in terms of task contingency and type of strategy. The German box on the right-hand side emphasises highly differentiated products from small to high volume. The British box is for medium differentiation in small and medium volume. The French box shadows the British box in closer proximity to high volume production. The American position is not shown, but would have a strong presence in small differentiation, large batch (e.g. cornflakes to B movies) and with a presence in medium volume customised (e.g. aircraft production).

When viewing Figure 8.5 it is useful to recall the French notion of *filière* (Clark 1987) because this refers to a network of channels through which action flows. For example, there is extensive French data on both the flows of students from primary education through all stages into training at work and also French industrial policy addresses these flows. Thus the approach of Maurice and colleagues is able to draw upon the flows and depict their consequences. The French notion of *filière* requires modification in application to, say, Anglo-American comparisons (Clark 1987), but the sense of cohorts passing along a time-space trajectory which is socially constructed is useful to our analysis (see Giddens 1984).

The neo-contingency view holds that the key units of analyses are the ideal contingency profile for the firm/sector and its reciprocal interaction with the characteristics of the society as illustrated in Figure 8.5. The analytic strength of the framework set out in Figure 8.5 was underlined for Sorge through his decision to test the framework against a small set of recent Anglo-German comparisons. It is worth considering these before revealing some of the problems (Sorge 1991: 173f):

1   The national sets of firms compared from different areas of engineering seemed similar in the requirements of work competence and organisation. In mechanical engineering the German profile seemed to combine societal effects and chosen direction in the most favourable manner.

2   The link between the competence requirements and national human resource strategies was looser than that between the competence requirements and the product strategies being pursued by firms. The two countries seemed to be similar in their competence requirements.

3   Cross-cultural differences in sectoral strengths (e.g. application of micro-electronics, product strategies, recruitment and training policies) were in harmony. Why? In the British case the sectors were larger than in Germany with strong differences between the core, pivotal firms (e.g. electronics, tele-communications, military technology) and those firms whose product architecture involves less integration of the embodied technology. The British core/pivotal firms (Clark and Staunton 1989) handled the recruitment and training issues through their channel from the universities plus the 'poaching' of experienced personnel. The German situation was quite a contrast. Germany had stronger sectors with firms focusing their product strategies on differentiation (customisation) with a constant tendency to upgrade (Porter 1990) their medium-sized firms (cf. Sorge 1991: 174). In Germany there was

a smoother linkage over gaps in status and gaps between areas of expertise. Sorge (1991) observes that these German tendencies had 'implications for the habitus of the groups involved' and 'for the product strategy and personnel in companies' (1991: 174). The human resource policies of the German firms involved craft groups more centrally. The German firms constantly upgraded everyday, well-known products through their redesign to incorporate developments in raw materials and in capacities from micro-electronics (cf. Sorge 1991: 175). In contrast the British firms faced exit because of international competition in their chosen sector.

The neo-contingency approach is an hypothesis. Initially the examination of relevant cross-national comparisons supports the proposition embedded in Figure 8.5. In particular, the Anglo-German comparison of mechanical engineering supported the proposition. However, one of the most striking differences between Britain and Germany evident by the 1980s was in the relative performance of the automobile industries. That gap in performance has been accentuated by the takeover of the British firms of Rover and Rolls-Royce by BMW. The position of the automobile industries suggests a development beyond the neo-contingency approach just discussed.

Sorge's analysis of Anglo-German performance reveals the difficulties of excluding the USA and Japan from the discussion because that market was where high volume coupled to customisation was being developed.

Societal capacities to absorb inter-sectoral contradictions and conflicts

The societal effects and ideal sectoral profiles just discussed contends that national propensities should be matched to ideal profiles of firms and sectors based on the neo-contingency approach. There should be an elective affinity between the societal tendencies in human resource formation and task-contingency characteristics of the sector. In this section Sorge (1991) shows that the elective affinity is flawed and requires revision. Sorge still contends that societal characteristics are a major, neglected ingredient in explaining competition between contexts. However, the crucial elective affinity is not with the ideal profile of firms and sector based on neo-contingency theorising. Instead the elective affinities should attend to the organisational capacities of nations and regions to resolve conflicting contingency profiles. Sorge now suggests that there is 'no such thing as a societal approximation of conditions supposedly ideal for a particular industry' (1991: 178).

The problem for the ideal framework arose from the re-analysis of two pieces of empirical work. First, in the Franco-German comparison of the sectors involved in the manufacture of machine tools the question arose of why the French sector did not perform well in an era of flexible specialisation. The French industry seemed to be typified by firms that were small, made customised products and were less specialised and less industrialised than German firms which were larger and intensive employers of engineers. For example, with respect to the Franco-German differences in their machine tool industries Maurice and Sorge (1989) show that the German firms were rather artisanal and complemented the potential weakness through relationships with centres of advanced research (e.g. technical universities). The German firms were thus able to tap relevant, user-oriented research. The key point is the 'reciprocal intertwining of the craft and technological elements' (Sorge 1991: 180) while the French firms had less interpenetration of these elements which was a significant limitation. The German industry seemed to counter the task-related contingency requirement by combining industrialised machine tools with craft-infused engineering to supply the German users of the machine tools with more standardised equipment than their French counterparts. The French industry which did possess craft elements was located in product markets demanding machine tools customised to particular, powerful, large-scale French firms. The French sector was therefore remote from its societal strengths in human resource production.

These considerations of the intertwining of sectors and their interpenetration plus the presence of success in the absence of sectoral ideal profiles led Sorge to explore another ontological level: the relationships between sectors and their position in the national economy. This level has been tentatively explored in a critique of the limitations of the variant of the firm in sector perspective. The critique contends that the sector is an important level (Spender 1989; Whipp and Clark 1986), but that inter-sectoral relationships are equally significant (Pavitt 1984) because of the role of societally structured systems of knowledge (Clark 1987; cf. Lundvall 1992).

Sorge's contribution is to reason that:

> The strength of the German industry, relative to that of the French, has been that it is closer to the societal regime which allowed forward integration into control system development through cross-fertilisation with research institutes and the electronics industry. It avoided passive dependency . . . and did not waste effort in searching for new customers and markets.
>
> (Sorge 1991: 181)

Thus the significant elective affinity is between the societal capacities and the interface between sectors and their relationships to the making, preservation and dissemination of relevant new knowledge from advanced research institutes. 'The success of an industry appears to depend, therefore, on its characteristic infusion with elements that deviate from the supposed ideal' (1991: 182) of a task contingency profile. Successful performance seems to be an innovative combination of supposedly conflicting task contingencies with societal capabilities. Sorge's postulated explanation draws on the notion of a typical national variety (Clark 1987), but does not incorporate the case of the USA where the same societal system contains Boeing, Ford and entrepreneurial information technology sectors (Clark 1987; Best 1990; Porter 1990). The exceptional case of the USA is also relevant to Figure 8.1 because the British profile is competing directly with the societal capabilities that support US firms in large-scale production of goods and services (e.g. leisure and entertainment).

Second, why did the German automobile industry perform so much more successfully than the British industry when that industry seemed to Sorge to approximate more to the ideal profile as illustrated in Figure 8.5? The small rump of British-owned car production (e.g. Rover and Rolls-Royce) has now passed into German ownership. Sorge would have to reason that German capabilities in general and in the specific case of the two firms – BMW and VW – are believed by their own managements to be better able to attain the relevant elective affinity.

Analytic scope: Sorge and Porter

Combining the frameworks proposed by Sorge (1991) and Porter (1990) increases the analytic scope because although the frameworks are different they are complementary (Clark and Mueller 1995).

One of the major differences between the frameworks is in Porter's attention to the role of the national market and to the specialist firms that interface the manufacturing and service sectors. The Porter framework explicitly highlights how the market context may be societally specific (e.g. USA cf. Japan) and varies along a series of key dimensions. In the case of Germany and France, unlike Great Britain, there is access to the high disposable incomes of central Europe and the ability of consumers to buy customised goods. This attention to the shaping role of the market – both competitive and governmental (Mowery and Rosenberg 1993; Noble 1984) – considerably affects what is relevant and useful knowledge inside firms because there is entrainment for firms to national tastes (Clark 1987). The national market has reciprocal consequences for firms and hence for shaping the human resource *filière*. For example, if as in the British case national firms are taken over by overseas parents as in the automobile industry, then (to some degree) key occupations will be lost and positioned in the country of origin. Likewise, if British textile firms move away from design-led innovation in the upmarket segments into medium-cost goods, then this alters the occupational structure and the discretionary incomes. So, the chosen market contexts are significant. It follows that political leaders like Tony Blair who claim that the national solution is 'education, education, education' are probably underestimating the problems. Likewise the role of the market for theories such as the learning city requires attention (cf. Ranson 1998).

Both Porter and Sorge suffer from lack of attention to the international political economy. Porter gives insufficient recognition to the well-documented role of American foreign policy and the influence which that has had on the Japan–USA relationship before, during and since the Cold War. Nor does Porter sufficiently unpack the requirement of strategic leaders in one nation to analyse the detail of competing contexts, but there are useful guidelines (1990: Chapter 11). Sorge ignores the influence of American corporations and expertise in Europe. In the case of British firms in electronics and engineering they face a very strong American presence. Also, there is a great analytic danger in ignoring the extent to which any British discourse on production knowledge is impacted by the presence of American discourse (Clark 1987; Clark and Newell 1993; Clark 1997a, b).

Both frameworks highlight the knowledge dimension, yet each lacks a concept of societal knowledge making. Sorge builds on the research constructing the time-space (*filières*) along which cohorts in each society journey from school into higher education and then into the educational processes of the workplace. The analysis of *filières* extends the notions of cultural programming suggested by Hofstede and also introduces dynamic elements into the analysis. Moreover, there is also a plausible case for the claim that this early cultural programming of the young adult is an important input to work organisation. However, the initial construction of this *filière* by Maurice *et al.* (1986) and its more recent restatement by Lane (1996) gives slight attention to advanced research centres (Porter 1990). Yet Sorge is led to include the role of German advanced research centres in his explanation and this illustrates the importance of societal knowledge. Sorge will not be able to explain why the British are good at producing, conserving and using scientific knowledge but are less successful with engineering knowledge, while the Germans are strong in each area. Porter gives wider consideration to knowledge than Sorge, but does not sufficiently explore how the knowledge *filières* interface with the corporate sector. Nor does Porter unravel the distinctive knowledge-making capacities found in the USA (see Chapter 9).

NATIONAL TYPICAL VARIETY

An obvious problem with the characterisations of nations by Crozier (1964) and by Hofstede (1980) is that variations within national cultures are over-compressed (Zeldin 1984). Characterising the nation requires theorising from a multi-dimensional viewpoint in which there is room for both a spread of values and non-typical elements (Clark 1987) and also contending, alternative value systems (Lodge and Vogel, 1987). The realist turn draws attention to the stratified nature of social reality and theorising of social objects through detailed consideration (Sayer 1992). Institutional formations are contingently durable and within the nation there may be considerable institutional variation. A prudent analyst might commence by exploring the typical variety of institutional formations in any societal context and note significant variations over time.

First, the notion that there is a typical variety of institutional forms within a society is proposed in Anglo-American comparisons by Clark (1987: 24–25, 294–296). The comparison can be made by using the stylised contrast between managerial systems based on direct control from those permitting loose coupling and responsible autonomy (Friedman 1977). These are shown as a continuum in Figure 8.6. The postulate is that for much of the twentieth century British firms and sectoral institutions possessed a high proportion of forms of work organisation based on loose coupling with responsible autonomy being evident in craft-based areas and industrial districts (Marshall 1919; Arrighi 1994). However, some sectoral contexts were typified by the use of direct control, albeit within paternalistic benevolence as in the sectors of food, drink and tobacco (Clark 1987). The chemical sector was typified by direct control. The skewed distribution of British sectors is stylised in Figure 8.6 to represent the profile in the mid-1980s before the full impacts of market legitimated shifts and the third way (Giddens 1998) were fully developed. Clark (1987) contends that overseas firms replacing British firms through more effective parenting tend to remove responsible autonomy, for example, American and Japanese owned plants. The profile of the American distribution, also stylised for the purpose of comparison, is spread and with different tendencies to those in Britain. It is tempting to introduce the notion of leading and lagging forms of work organisation, but our earlier discussion of temporality and grand narratives cautions against that step.

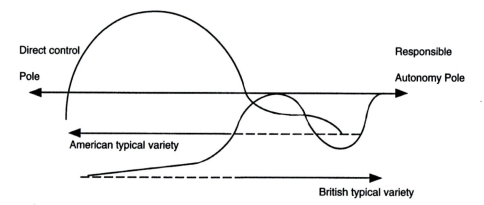

Figure 8.6 Direct control and responsible autonomy in relation to the typical variety in the USA and Britain
Source: Clark (1987).

Second, awareness of the variety of institutional forms within a nation over periods of generations and centuries arises from studies revealing that variety. With respect to American society, Lodge and Vogel (1987) construct two sharply differing political ideologies whose salience varies across the society and through different eras. The five features are summarised in Table 8.1 to contrast between the two different tendencies:

- dependence;
- independence.

Dependency involves hierarchy and consensus as the preferred social relationship based around institutional roles expressing rights and duties. The economic dimension stresses co-operation and harmony coupled to strong state intervention and control. Knowledge is defined as contextual.

Table 8.1 Typical American variety

Dimension	Dependency	Independency
1 Preferred social relationship	Hierarchy consensus	Loose, networks contract (solitude; narcissistic?)
2 Institutional roles	Rights and duties of membership	Property rights; adversarial
3 Economic life	Co-operation and harmony (needs)	External competition plus internal managers and rules for the managed
4 Role of state	Intervention and control	Limited
5 Knowledge	Contextual	Piecemeal and analytic: lists

Independence as a tendency prefers social relationships that are loose, in the form of networks and contractual with institutional roles expressed through property rights in an adversarial form. Economic life couples external competition with internal managers using rules to control those who are managed. The role of the state is limited and knowledge is both piecemeal and arranged in lists and analytic frameworks.

The degree to which variety within a nation is given salience depends in part upon the objective of the analysis, but generally variety has been suppressed, especially when considering the 'typical' variety within a nation.

9 American exceptionalism

INTRODUCTION

For most of the twentieth century American corporate practices and theories about organising have been regarded by everyone as best practice at the leading edge of capitalism (Chandler 1962; Locke 1996). The discourse of 'how to organise' has preoccupied the business schools and social science communities. In the modern period that discourse seemed to be neutral with respect to the singularities of any nation. So, when Crozier (1964, 1973), a great admirer of American life, identified the problems of transferring these practices outside the USA his analysis was marginalised and subsumed within abstract general frameworks (e.g. Perrow 1987; Clark 1979). The French have been active in drawing attention to the kinds of problem which might arise in the misapplication of US practices. Awareness of American exceptionalism in the business school was stimulated by Hofstede's (1980) research and his interpretations. However, as Locke (1996) observed, rather pessimistically and perhaps prematurely, the best-known American practices were being overtaken by new ways of organising from Japan. Paradoxically, it is the performance of Japanese firms that has so impressed the faculty of the American business school rather than that of German business and management.

Why choose American exceptionalism as the title of the chapter? As indicated in the previous three chapters the depth of this exceptionalism makes the USA a very special player in the 'competition between contexts'. Some Americans tend to think of themselves as being markedly different from their European cousins (Lipset 1996), especially those from backgrounds in the arts, humanities and cultural studies. Yet in business schools there is a strong tendency to construct universalistic models and frameworks. Likewise, American corporations often assume that their movement from the domestic market into the global market can readily subsume Canada and the UK in an 'Anglo-American' world view. In the case of the UK there has been a very considerable market for American consultancies and for embodied knowledge in hardware (e.g. computing equipment) and in software for co-ordinating and auditing the firm (Clark 1987; Clark and Newell 1993). American firms in the UK manufacturing sector are reported to be the most productive (McKinsey 1998).

In this short chapter I shall explore selected facets of American exceptionalism. This exploration is equally useful to Americans and for those from other nations. Exceptionalism as a proposition will be explored through six cameos:

- knowledge-based capitalism;
- New World and Europe;
- instrumental rationality: choreographed overlayers;
- constituting large-scale systems;
- American Football as a cultural manifestation;
- UK–USA and J–USA.

KNOWLEDGE-BASED CAPITALISM

In 1848, when composing the Communist Party Manifesto, Marx pointed to the USA as that location where capitalism would unfold very rapidly. A century later Gramsci observed that hegemony was born in the factory and by that he meant the American factory. As Porter (1998) observes, there are many contexts in the USA that favour different sectoral clusters. Therefore understanding American exceptionalism is significant for Americans and non-Americans for five reasons:

1   The political economy and huge capacities of the American context have been obscured and unintentionally suppressed in both organisation theory and strategy. These limitations of the academy are not necessarily reproduced in the retention systems of the leading American corporations. Their retention systems have often been the laboratories where reflexive monitoring has been given an additional edge and where the performativity of heterogeneous corporate knowledge is the subject of continuous experimentation (Clark 1987).
2   The individualistic actor approaches to cross-cultural differences (Hofstede 1980; cf. Sorge 1995) have unwittingly suppressed concern with the societal-institutional features. This suppression was unwittingly reinforced by the failure of the new institutional school to engage in significant cross-cultural comparisons until more recently or to engage with European societal-institutional analyses.
3   Hofstede's claim that there are Anglo-American similarities in individualism, uncertainty avoidance and power distance has created a myth of similarities diffused through the former establishment of organisation theory (Hickson and Pugh 1995; cf. Lammers and Hickson 1979).
4   The absence of a longitudinal perspective in Americanised organisation theory makes it very difficult to weigh structure and agency when attempting to assess the length of time that different degrees of transformation in the structural repertoire require. So, the field of organisational change has a foreshortened sense of temporality. Thus, leading exponents of organisation analysis applied the dichotomies to show that old GM, unlike new GM, was

mechanistic while new GM was virtually organic by 1984 (Kanter 1984). There was an over-reading of the potential for discursive penetration leading to the actioning of blue-sky visions of the future by tomorrow.

5   America as a political-economic configuration of structural powers embedded in hegemonic controls of other nations' contexts is highly consequential. The North American Free Trade Area (NAFTA) has altered Canada's position way beyond anything envisaged by Canadian business school academics. Outside NAFTA, the USA has been the twentieth century's major economic actor and has been able to influence the international position of other major economic actors including Germany and more recently of Japan. In the international political economy America is the major economic actor whose projects and trajectories are as consequential for the national social structures of less influential nations as was British market-based hegemony for dependent regions in India and Pakistan during the nineteenth century. It may be reasoned that the fractured visage of British management is partly (only partly) explained by the presence of American multinationals and their templates of management and best practice (Clark 1987; Clark and Newell 1993).

The theme of American exceptionalism illustrates the claims made in Chapter 6 on the centrality of the political economy of national markets, dependence and hegemony in knowledge-based capitalism. The geopolitical situation of the USA enabled the capacity to organise and manage at a distance by designing forms of control that anticipated system disruption (Beniger 1986; Clark 1997). The portfolio of significant, value-adding sectoral clusters in the USA has had consequences for the rest of the world and has introduced a significant debate across the North Atlantic with European constructions of their markets. Indeed the European Directorate has initiated major research programmes with themes such as the European Innovation Monitoring Systems (EIMS) with the intention of learning about and from the presence of foreign multinational businesses (mainly American) operating in Europe.

American exceptionalism has been a strong stimulus to knowledge-based capitalism in both the regulation of internal competition and in the periodic deregulation of areas. There is a robust regulation of internal competition (Fligstein 1990) and also a significant shaping of the hegemonic rules in the regimes of international trade regulation (cf. Kennedy 1987). Knowledge-based capitalism has been immensely stimulated by American laws and legislation on intellectual property rights (Mowery *et al.* 1998). Knowledge-based capitalism is about coupling innovation to design through developing new knowledge (Clark 1987: Figure 1.4, 215–222). Noble's (1978) thesis of America by design understates the extent of design thought and its potential for recognition through the entry of new occupational groups espousing jurisdictional claims to high fees. The American higher education system is well organised to cope with massification through the application of design thinking to the chunking and reconfiguration of knowledge. The university system is tightly articulated with the publishing industry which owns some of the knowledge and produces the containers (e.g. books, videos) in which the performativity of knowledge is evident. Few universities possess the capacity opportunistically to manage the interdependencies with business, thereby creating a complex diversity, yet possess a strong centre (B. R. Clark 1998).

Knowledge-based capitalism based on a design rhetoric (Clark 1987) uses education very deliberately as in the definition of the syllabus and its chunking coupled to measurement and feedback on performance. The centrality of the examination to rehearsal was sedimented in the military academy (Clark 1987; Hoskins and Macve 1988) and embedded into the development of the distinctly American sports of baseball and American Football. The playing of those games provides – and their subsequent extensive analysis invokes – the notion of the performativity of a form of knowledge that is both explicit and tacit (see Chapter 14). That process of knowledge review anticipates the early twentieth-century process of studying management and the staff. Thus, the death of a salesman in the 1950s, as noted by the playwright Arthur Miller and the sociologist Wright Mills, was set in motion by the Foucauldian elements in American knowledge-based capitalism. The knowledge-based capitalism articulates with the sectoral clusters (Porter 1998) and creates overlayers of instrumental rationality. Elias's attention to emotionality suggests that the overlayers of control need the seeing eye of post-modernism.

In American capitalism the role of government is, relative to continental European nations, limited and adversarial with low income tax and little development of industrial policy except in the regulation of sectors. The welfare system is much less extensive and more subject testing and more reliant on private initiatives. There is slight use of tax transfers from the well off to the more impoverished. The dominant form of production is capital coupled to a strong reliance upon price-mediated markets. The stock market is centrally important and there are strong normative and regulative pressures towards rewarding stockholders continuously and at high levels. Corporate relationships are price driven and tend to rely on power relationships. In the labour market there is low security of employment, high differentials in wages with high labour mobility between firms and also geographically. The unions are relatively powerless and their influence is confined to specific sectors.

NEW WORLD AND EUROPE

Revolutionary war, religion and politics

The USA diverged from the mainstream of democratic nations within the North Atlantic economies (Lipset 1996). Three interlinked factors conjoin to shape America. First, there are the origins of the nation and particularly the revolutionary war against the British. Unlike European nations the founding of the USA was associated with the absence and breakaway from the aristocratic values and post-feudal structures which characterised Europe. The American elites lacked any commitment to a sense of noblesse oblige or to the paternalistic sense of responsibility for those who were poor and unsuccessful. Unlike the English, the American elites were deeply interested in notions of social Darwinism (e.g. Spencer). Significant segments of the American elites were largely agnostic and sceptical about social intervention. Consequently, the cradle-to-grave form of twentieth-century welfarism found in Britain and France was discouraged.

Second, the position of religion was unique. There was and is a strong sensibility about religion and a high proportion of the population are members of groups such as Methodists and Baptists rather than the state-sponsored, hierarchical churches which emphasise the sinfulness of man and the role of collective action in personal life (e.g. Catholic Church). In the USA the religious communities possessed a strong local orientation and were substantially self-governing. These sect-like communities espoused a fervent individualism combined with notions about the perfectibility of human nature. They developed and diffused a strong moral sense of struggling against evil. Arguably, today that leads Americans to depict opponents as evil.

Third, the political philosophy of the founding elites constructed the 'American creed' in terms of classical liberalism with a strong sense of individual agency coupled with a strong sense of optimism about the future. The American creed – in its ideal form – is suspicious of authority (e.g. central state) and promotes a form of egalitarianism (e.g. the level playing field) which exposes everyone (potentially) to competitive forces.

These three factors explain some of the contemporary themes. Thus leading contenders from the right regularly espouse an agenda which tables the abolition of government, including areas of education which European politicians would more often omit. These factors create a contest between positions so that there is a rich collection of what to European senses seems to be extreme viewpoints. America, with its low level of taxes, possesses wide variations in wealth between the richest and poorest. There is a minimal safety net of medical and welfare benefits.

The governing ideology of the American creed is both a real object and also a double-edged sword (Lipset 1996). On the one hand the creed sustains an institutional matrix which cognitises, regulates and defines as appropriate a strong sense of individualism and responsibility, while encouraging behaviour which is self-serving and with a low regard for the communal good. The sense of individualism can weaken social control mechanisms and yet facilitates a rich diversity of forms of behaviour including deviant behaviours.

Founding context

The founding period of the USA is relatively recent and still has some influences into the contemporary period. In Chapter 7 the distinctive features of the American system of manufacture were outlined as an example of a societally institutionalised structure and discourse combining the three pillars of the new institutionalism. Those features developed in the nineteenth century. This section provides a selection of concrete features arising in the founding period up to the early nineteenth century before the emergence of large-scale enterprises. Figure 7.1 provides an abstract framework within which that form of societal learning might have been constituted.

The incoming Europeans found a remarkable context (Cronon 1983). The possibilities inhering in the geophysical location and land surface of America have been and are distinctive. Its location well away from Europe provides certain geopolitical advantages. The coastal areas contained inlets appropriate to the sea-based world economy and interfaced with inland rivers that provided ample, cheap means of transportation and the opportunity to apply steam power to shipping. The inland lakes also modified the potential extremes of climate. Wood of varying kinds was in abundance and could be used to make equipment, to provide the balloon frame of houses (hardwood) and the soft cladding as well as for burning. The sawmill machine became a decisive piece of technology and articulated with related innovations (Rosenberg 1976). There were plentiful supplies of fish, game and meat. The land and climate provided areas suitable for the mass production of cereals. Yet the indigenous population lived quite differently from the incoming Europeans (Cronon 1983). They tended to be in dispersed communities, yet were much less nomadic in their agriculture. There were multiple founding cultures of which the southern plantations and the northern corridor between New York and Philadelphia provided major arenas for the English-speaking colonists.

The Europeans arrived with a highly developed sense of commodities and with societal techniques for the commodification of natural resources (e.g. coal, ore). The incomers enrolled the physical context, but did so in ways which were different from in Europe. Habakkuk (1962) in a speculative essay put forward the argument that economic factors such as the costs of labour provided the major inducement to the development of technology as a rational choice. However, as outlined earlier in Chapter 5, the inducement explanation requires a reconstruction of the specific culture and structure (Clark 1987). For example, the hierarchical systems of privilege associated with European courts and towns were largely absent in the composition of the settlers and in the roles they undertook. The incoming Europeans developed certain characteristics:

1   They began to cognitise their context in ways that differed from Europeans.
2   Despite the variety of nations represented, there was a strong overlayer of discourse derived from those British political values emphasising rights (e.g. Locke) and the politics of local communities.
3   There was strong input of legal regulation embedded in property rights. Contesting and arbitrating these rights involved complex processes of inscribing ownership rules in conjunction with metering their performance to control opportunism. The legal profession originated in these arenas and, in due course, influenced the whole process of commercial transactions.

4   Certain general rules such as the North West Ordnance provided scripts for the expansion of territories (North 1990).

5   There was a very strong sense of the importance of expertise and of the role that documenting and experimenting with practices might reveal. This feature was applied to agricultural activities and resulted in the selling of advice.

6   Distinctive cognitions of space and time were quickly institutionalised.

Despite strong European inputs, the character of servitude in the USA had been transformed by 1783 and a distinctly American language emerged. Also, there were zones of 'Englishness' such as Philadelphia which was a major cultural centre with paved streets, cricket pitches and some street lighting.

The new American state had huge debts and was bankrupt. There was no national government because the states preserved considerable powers of independence until 1866. Yet, in the late eighteenth century the new nation required an army to roll back the English, the French and the Spanish. These problems framed the societal knowledge (see Figure 7.1) shaping the emergent American systems of design and manufactures.

The role of law and of lawyers is of great importance and the latter were often able to persuade the rest of American society that they were best able to cope with the strategic contingencies of internal commence and governance. The form and division of powers in the USA provides for a much more subtle infrastructure to capitalism than is acknowledged by those business school analysts seeking to reduce the powers of government.

INSTRUMENTAL RATIONALITY: CHOREOGRAPHED OVERLAYERS

The USA and Germany possess strong capacities for professional ownership of knowledge and of strong bureaucracy inside firms, but their fusion emerges differently. One of the American modern tendencies has been to use design as a process of drawing the future into the present via a detailed time-space analysis. Thus, American corporate timetabling of activities in all kinds of space (e.g. factory, office, home, outer space) constitutes a hegemonic overlayer on top of activities that enable the co-existence of instrumental rationality with more emotionality and autonomy than might be imagined (Clark 1997a, b; Holmer Nadeesan 1997). The overlayers emerge from the conjunction between the American service class who are associated in university-based professions with the American corporation, its owners and capital. The service class, as savants and organic intellectuals, constructs the lexicon for hegemony.

The modern perspective provided the instrumental rationality of design rules and their limited consumer appeal was clearly signalled and manifest in millions of sales for the new face of organisation theory presented by Peters and Waterman

(1982). The first hundred pages of *In Search of Excellence* are why you should all read Karl Weick and understand social rationality. Those pages are rarely cited and cannot be remembered. The reader – that is the consumer – including many in the academy, do remember, perhaps unwillingly those eight traits signalling a different, more post-modern presentation of a theory of organising. Peters and Waterman (1982) are examples of the performativity of knowledge. Their eight traits are devised to compact generative codes requiring the interpretative expertise and explacit knowledge of an interpreter rather than the design rules of the expert legislator. The eight codes expressly include paradoxes and ambiguity. Their application certainly requires bricolage. Their intention is to accommodate diversity and flexibility with the recognition of surprise. Beneath their friendly surface lurks the instrumental rationality of commodified, compressed time and space (Gregory 1994: 112, 399, 401, 412).

The overlayer of instrumental rationality in the workplace receives impetus from the control cybernetics invested in corporate culture, yet faces the consumer on two fronts. First, from the consumer situation Jameson (1991) opines that post-modernism is the cultural code of the new capitalism (Anderson 1998). So, the consumer is encouraged to invest in a diversity of life styles signified by how one's body is clothed, transported (e.g. BMW or Toyota Starlet), shaped and coloured. For the consumer individualism is encouraged, albeit within peer codes that are the normative frameworks to everyday life. To face the consumer, the corporations supplying goods and services engage in extensive choreographing of the corporation. Contrary to the instrumental notions of efficiency influencing the new institutional school, the post-modern world is one in which survival depends on a great deal of symbolic capital (Lash and Urry 1995; Thrift 1996; Leyshon and Thrift 1997; cf. Harvey 1989). The consumer at work is increasingly the exponent of an ironic detachment while also being subject to the panoptic sort of the specialist firms in intelligence about the consumer (Gandy 1993). Second, the consumer with potential engages the corporation with ironic detachment and increasing skills in emotional labour.

American exceptionalism in knowledge-based capitalism consists in part of being the location in which new organisational forms of control over large-scale projects are noticed, investigated and transformed into actionable understanding. Templates of organisational design are stored, become dormant and, because of the diversity of knowledge-making locations, can sometimes be reactivated. Equally, there are strong capacities – certainly equal to those of the Japanese (Clark 1987; Clark and Staunton 1989: 153–155), for noticing, recording and unbundling alternative forms of work organisation and then chunking these in ways that promise future performance. Thus the American context consists of many zones of manoeuvre with important degrees of freedom and contains potential corporations which experiment with alternatives. Few survive, but because American legislation on bankruptcy is more generous than many nations and the noticing capabilities of trade journalism are so excellent, these elements from the experiments are available for recycling.

These American capacities for doing well in the contemporary phase of knowledge-based capitalism do not preclude significant creative destruction, nor do they preclude management experiencing the iron cage of instrumental and emotional performativity. Nor do they anticipate the emergent possibilities in the European context. However, for the moment the capacities are more robust than the pessimists suggested, at least for the next decade.

CONSTITUTING LARGE-SCALE CORPORATE SYSTEMS

The American system of manufacture (Hounshell 1984), briefly summarised in Chapter 7, was an unintended outcome from multiple conjunctions. An important part of American exceptionalism is the capacity to create large-scale corporate systems (Chandler 1962, 1977; Williamson 1975; Noble 1978; Hughes 1990) in which time-space is compressed and commodified and extensive networks of control are established (Beninger 1986). The American multinational corporation is the highly visible example of this contextual and corporate capacity. Two strands of analysis may be noted: large-scale systems and American corporate timetabling. Chandler (1977) has already illustrated the case for the visible hand hypothesis.

American large-scale systems – power networks – are distinctive social constructions made durable by their embodiment in hardware and software technologies (Hughes 1990). The language of system flows and pace was already evident in the clustering of firms at Pawtucket near the mouth of the Connecticut Valley by the end of the eighteenth century. The whole valley, including the development of precision tooling, represents multiple examples of flowline theory and application (Best 1990). Nearby, Oliver Evans constructed a model and then applications of flowline and waterpower to the grain mill to produce a discourse that anticipated the flowline thinking applied to grain transportation in Chicago in the mid-nineteenth century (Schoenberger 1996). Hughes shows how problem framing was embedded in a distinctive language replete with the possibilities of making money from the removal of blockages to flows. The aim of the inventors was pragmatic, not theoretical or abstract. This context of application (Gibbons *et al.* 1994) was remarkably different from that found by the British inventor of the ship's chronometer, Harrison (Sobel 1995). In the USA inventors were incentivised by the protection of intellectual property to extend their notions of design beyond European confines (Pulos 1983) in a systematic activity that grew from the household into the experimental laboratory of Sperry and others (Hughes 1990). These inventors created a demand for models that could be used to simulate possibilities for future commercial exploitation. Sperry simulated the movements of ships in oceans in order to develop the gyroscope. Part of the metaphorical language used by these inventors included the notion that artefacts have behaviours. Hughes (1990) contends that the military enrolled these capabilities for the development of the navy and army, then later the air force. They created the 'military brain mill' and incorporated higher education (Noble 1984). Soon, the experience of thinking about large-scale projects and then undertaking them became part of

American exceptionalism and provided a co-ordinating mechanism stretching across multiple networks.

Within corporations Chandler (1962, 1977) has analysed and narrated the organisational innovations enabling the increased pace of activity – the economies of speed – and the capacity to design multiple artefacts from trains to the ticketing system that permitted separate payment to different companies. Control systems and communication systems reinforced these capacities (Yates 1989). American firms developed and created a market for genres of systems of corporate co-ordination and timetabling (Clark 1996a, b, 1997a, b).

AMERICAN FOOTBALL

American Football is a significant social analogy for different forms of organising (Clark 1987; Nonaka and Takeuchi 1995). My contention is that notions of organisational cybernetics can be understood more clearly by examining American Football (Clark 1987: Chapter 6). The game is a metaphor for American approaches to knowledge as doing (Clark 1987, 1997a, b). The game occupies a special position in the everyday imagery of the American male and is implicated in certain gender constructions. American Football is one societal template which played/plays a central role in American knowledge creation and retention. The use of American Football as an analogy by academics should be distinguished from its usage in everyday American corporate and social life.

American Football[1] was an unintended, emergent outcome – perhaps an historical accident – from the intentions by the American college strata (future knowledge workers) in the 1860s and 1870s to play soccer (eleven players kicking) and another game possessing inherent interpretative flexibility – Rugby Union (fifteen players carrying). American Football is an example of interpretative flexibility and of the appropriation of an innovation (Clark and Staunton 1989). College boys from key American universities such as Harvard found themselves unable to believe in some of the legal fictions inherent in Rugby Union such as the ball exiting unintentionally from a maul. Other colleges were more sympathetic to Rugby Union and to soccer, but were less influential in the inter-college negotiations over which sets of rules should apply. The Harvard group was relatively powerful and its preferences enabled the hybrid game and inserted some of its key design features. Had they not managed to enrol other key colleges, then a different trajectory would have developed. However, they did so and their social construction of the male game gendered both American sport and also the workplace with a very instrumental view of emotionality (as Elias).

The pre-existing context from which American Football emerged was of similar significance to understanding American service class habitus as the French court was in generating key elements in the habitus of the modernising elites in Europe (Elias 1994). The proposition is that the contextual shaping of American Football should be examined in the same lineage of societal knowledge making as the American system of manufactures, the role of West Point in creating a professional strata and training civil engineers in developing the administrative structure of the railways and the American armouries, especially Springfield (Clark 1987; Hoskins and Macve 1988). American civil engineers became the key knowledge makers and have been characterised as the American samurai.

Corporate and sporting approaches to time and space as an arena for control and mastery are highly significant in American exceptionalism. The twenty key differences between Rugby Union and American Football can be noted to emphasise the differences in time-space mastery (Clark 1987): These include:

- the definitions of time played and the delineation of the pitch;
- constitution of knowledge so that each player receives a 1,200-page handbook plus videos of the team knowledge in diagrammatic and written form – he is a knowledge worker;
- the knowledge is owned by the club which fines players for losing the handbook while coaches control strategy and much of tactics;
- massive, extensive pre-planning and review of past performance so that teams may discuss the previous game via video recording with the public: the game is a vehicle for developing the notion of programmed decisions (as Beniger 1986);
- the game is designed around recurrent action patterns incorporating unarticulated knowledge and habitus;
- aesthetic considerations and choreographing are central (e.g. Hollywood, Disney).

American Football as a choreographed time-space arena possesses some of the features also found in the journeys taken by swimming pool robots. Similar approaches to time-space mastery informed the ways in which the McDonald brothers designed and choreographed the first outlet in San Bernadino in 1940. Those features also lie at the basis of cloning (see Quinn 1993). Anderson (1998) observes that these elements are integral to post-modernism and yet are also evident in the origins of the post-modern in much earlier decades.

Nonaka and Takeuchi (1995) also make extensive usage of the analogy of American Football in their theory of knowledge creation. They give particular attention to the combining of the three elements of bureaucracy and special task forces with databases in the hypertext organisation. Their interpretation is set in the context of American–Japanese comparisons. They observe that American Football is driven by a grand project – the game plan shaping the strategy and tactics – plus a mid-range concept. These are clarified by a collection of project leaders known as coaches. There is a strong use of metaphor and sporting analogies (e.g. relays, Rugby Union and American Football). American Football capitalises on the relay and on Rugby Union. They seek to reformulate the structural emphasis in organisation theory which they contend centres on the 'bureaucracy and/or task-force' prescription. In American Football there is the determination of concepts at an early stage with a clear-cut division of labour and special teams (e.g. offence, defence, specials). The task force dimension is carried by the project leaders (coaches) who are normally involved dialogically in the game plan through the role of the head coach. The key is the early comprehensive plan and having the tactics decided by a few project leaders who confer intensively among themselves (departments focus). Within the game plan the coaches are usually involved in testing of the prototype[2] at rehearsals.

FROM UK–USA TO J–USA

The notion of the long twentieth century (Arrighi 1994) intentionally parallels Braudel's (1972) claim about the long sixteenth century of Spanish influence in the South Atlantic. Arrighi[3], and many others (e.g. Landes 1998) observe that American global influence commenced in the nineteenth century and is likely to persist through the decades of the third millennium (cf. Kennedy 1987). The long twentieth century possibly starts soon after the American navy prised open the Japanese economy (1853–4) and, like the proverbial butterfly in chaos theory, triggered an internal period of liminality (Wilson 1992). From then on the USA progressively replaced the influence of the European nations in the Pacific Region (Gordon 1993) and by World War II (1939–45) had replaced the UK as the home base with the most effective strategies and structure for capital accumulation. Much earlier the Dutch regime (sixteenth century) had established a global logic of capital accumulation by internalising the costs of policing trade. Next, the British acquired those capabilities, displaced the Dutch and added the new capability of internalising production costs (Arrighi 1984: 239). Then, in the long twentieth century the American regimes of capital accumulation internalised transaction costs (Coase 1937; Williamson 1975; Chandler 1977). This section notes a few selected features of the neo-modern political economy in action. Its details can be confirmed by observing the content of courses on American foreign policy.

The British position relative to America in this long century was initially obscured by the glitter and clatter of its empire, including the subordination of the Indian economy as the market for Lancashire textiles (Schoenberger 1996). By World War I (1914–18) the massive British investments in America were being exchanged for the raw materials of warfare. Soon those long-accumulated assets were turned into huge war credits. Even so, 'US capabilities to manage the world monetary system remained distinctly inferior to Britain's own residual capabilities . . . Organisationally, US financial institutions were simply not up to the task . . . New York remained subordinate to London' (Arrighi 1994: 272). But not for long. The final days of the UK-centred world economy drew to a conclusion. World liquidity became centralised in the USA by World War II and US political isolation reached the point of decreasing returns (Arrighi 1994: 276). The differences between the regimes of capital accumulation in the USA and UK are significant. The American system was typified by the vertical integration of processes of production and distribution while the British system was typified by vertical fission and organisational separation. These decentralised and differentiated structures created burdens of interrelatedness (Landes 1969). So, the British world system of flexible specialisation was both functional and also inhibited a technological rationality from developing as in the case of German and American firms. The US corporate capitalism was a powerful agency in the destruction of British market capitalism.

The Cold War and American foreign policy rested upon the immense economic and political capacities of the USA (Kennedy 1987) in surrounding the Soviet bloc and positioning the frontier of the Pacific in the Korea–Japan axis (McMillan 1985; Gordon 1993). The rise of the Japanese capitalist phoenix originated in a relationship of political exchange between the US government and ruling groups in Japan whereby the Japanese ruling strata had been in a position to externalise protection costs. American patronage was – initially – the source of profits for the Japanese enterprise. The Cold War coupled with the hot war in Korea solved the American problem of logistical material for warfare. Japan was the efficient servant of the American warfare-welfare state through development by invitation (Wallerstein 1979: Chapter 4). Japan complied with American foreign policy, for example, throughout the Reagan era.

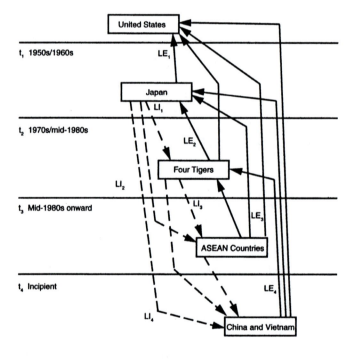

Key: ———— LE: Labour-intensive exports
      — — LI: Labour-seeking investments

Figure 9.1 Late twentieth-century accumulation regimes in East Asia
Source: Ozawa (1993: 143), cited in Arrighi (1994: Figure 24).

There was an explosive growth of Japanese exports to the USA from the enlarged reproduction of the Japanese multi-layered subcontracting system. The Japanese system possessed a decentralised structure, highly stratified in multiple layers of primary subcontractors that were stable and effective mechanisms for vertical and horizontal co-ordination. The Japanese multi-layered subcontracting system provided the co-ordination mechanism with a supply of competent labour. These Japanese firms were able to establish networks into the wider regional complex (e.g. Korea) as illustrated in Figure 9.1. The detailed relationships depicted refer to the late 1980s and mid-1990s. This regime of accumulation and political economy has now come under pressure.

SUMMARY

This chapter has sketched the exceptionalism of America's role in the political economy of knowledge-based capitalism, but has not detailed how its competitive context has enabled and to a marked degree still enables remarkable adaptation to new sectoral clusters. The next chapter examines the competitive context of Britain which, like Japan, occupies a special position in the American political economy, but unlike Japan is offshore to the thriving variants of political economy in Europe.

NOTES

1 I am indebted to David Reisman for his discussion of these points and to his earlier, highly insightful analysis undertaken with Denney. The University of Birmingham has an excellent sub-library on sport science and their facilities are also acknowledged.
2 See role of prototypes and their testing in the knowledge creation cycle for product development. See also the research by Angela Dumas on totem building.
3 This section draws from Arrighi (1994).

10 Sectoral clusters and competition between contexts

INTRODUCTION

The aim of this chapter is to couple the theme of competition between contexts with the analytic category of the sectoral cluster of firms. The exceptionalism of Britain is taken as a case in point. There are four sections:

- a cameo of the sectoral cluster created by Marks & Spencer in Britain;
- examination of the key elements in the sectoral cluster;
- examination of why Henry Ford would probably have failed had he started out from the competitive context of the Birmingham–Coventry corridor in England;
- the entraining features of sectoral clusters and the consequences for facing incoming multinational businesses and for becoming a multinational business.

This chapter bridges from Part II into 'organisations in action' (Part III).

The previous four chapters have set out the case for re-examining and re-theorising the context of firms with particular attention to national capabilities (e.g. institutions) and their cumulative, sticky features. The argument is that there is competition between contexts. Also, that pre-existing forms of structure and their inherent mechanisms impact variously and unpredictably on unfolding events. Therefore, starting points matter for firms both in respect of their location in a particular local-national milieu and their historical moments (Stinchcombe 1965). The role of location has been re-established in the Dunning–Porter perspective (see *Chapter 7*) with full attention to the role of the state, to foreign multinationals, national institutions and the professions.

There is also the issue of the sectoral cluster level of analysis. The notion of taking the perspective of 'firm-in-sector' preoccupied analysis in the 1980s after Pavitt (1980) proposed that the UK contained both successful and unsuccessful sectors as well as having absent sectors. This chapter is on the 'firm-in-sector' in relation to the theme of competition between contexts. There is a short account of the firm-in-sector perspective drawing distinctions between two main variants and linking these to the theme of competition between contexts. Then attention is given to outlining the particular issue of national lock-ins. These arise when the firms within a national sector do manage to survive for some period – possibly several generations – yet fail to achieve significant international transfer and/or find their global forays problematic.

It is therefore useful to examine a pair of cameos that illustrate the problem of lock-in to national contexts and the problem of getting established abroad. They also exemplify quite different kinds of flows of power and dependence (Pfeffer and Salencik 1978) within the cluster. Dicken (1998) contends that many clusters contain pivotal firms that do play a significant role in orchestrating activity along the whole cluster. There are two main variations:

1   Those sectors pulled from firms in the sector interacting with the final customer: these are clusters where the end retailers (e.g. supermarkets) tend to be dominant. The experience of these two sectors and their leading firms from the British context connects the themes of sectoral clusters of firms to competition between contexts.
2   Those sectors driven from pivotal firms early in the work flow: automobile manufacturer tends to drive the dependencies in that cluster.

The first cameo takes an apparently successful British firm with an excellent international reputation: Marks & Spencer. Although enjoying an enviable international reputation, the international presence is more modest and includes periods of less satisfactory performance. There is the possibility that Marks & Spencer's very success in the British market and its stratified distinctions of taste (cf. Bourdieu) coupled to their close alignment with domestically based procurement chains actually leaves them locked into that context. The procurement chains created in the UK by Marks & Spencer deserve close analysis. The example given is of the textile chain and the changing role of key suppliers of merchandise. Moreover, Cochrane (1988) contends that the British retailer has been an unintended, significant shaper of the domestic context, particularly for the former shoe industry. Given the structure of the context it seems unlikely that Benetton – who succeeded from their location in northern Italy – could have succeeded in the same way had they set out from the centre of the British knitwear industry in Leicester and Nottingham.

The second cameo sets out the case for claiming that Henry Ford would have failed had he started out from the West Midland region of England. Henry Ford could succeed in Detroit, USA and then penetrate the British market via Manchester in 1912. British car firms managed to survive the entry of Ford and later of General Motors, but found from the 1960s onward that their competitive position was eroded even in their home base. British car firms never successfully penetrated the European or American markets except with small numbers of specialised products (e.g. Jaguar, Range Rover four-wheel-drive). British car firms were firmly locked into their domestic market and its extension among the former members of the British Empire. Eventually the original domestic British firms were eliminated or taken over by overseas entrants. When the German specialist automobile manufacturer BMW bought Rover in 1995 its domestic market share was down to approximately 12 per cent. So, if Ford enters the third millennium as the leading UK producer, Henry Ford needed to start from the USA to gain the benefits from that context.

The cameo of Marks & Spencer is very different to that of the former British-owned automobile industry, yet there is an element of lock-in that is worth exploring. The transition from being a national player to a global player is more than awkward. Facing experienced foreign entrants can be a daunting experience, as the case of the British funeral industry demonstrates.

CREATING A SECTORAL CLUSTER BY MARKS & SPENCER

This section examines episodes in the creation, development and transformation of a sectoral cluster by Marks & Spencer over a period of many decades commencing in the 1920s (Clark and Starkey 1988: Chapter 6). Marks & Spencer began as a low-cost supplier of cheap clothes, but then faced the incoming multinational business from America known as Woolworths at the time of World War I. The owning family believed that they would have to move into a different market segment and they commenced a lengthy process of creating both a supply chain and also constituting the market. Figure 10.1 illustrates the sectoral cluster for the knitted goods production-distribution chain in the early 1960s. The cluster consists of the interface to the end consumer by Marks & Spencer and preceding sectors of textile manufacturers, the support sectors supplying equipment and raw materials. There are four episodes:

- moving upmarket and establishing the end network in the 1920s;
- extending and enrolling the backward linkages into commercial science in · 1930s;
- sensing problems with the knitwear producing sector in the 1960s;
- facing key issues of cost and sourcing abroad after the 1990s.

This clustering of sectors enabled the continuity of a British-owned knitwear industry well into the late twentieth century, yet also had consequences for the potential zones of manoeuvre available for firms which did not fit with the network values and actions.

First, in the 1920s Marks & Spencer's leaders foresaw a major problem from having to compete head to head with the incoming American retail chains, especially Woolworths. They also anticipated a major opportunity to open up if they could combine American approaches to time-space compression in retail with a move upmarket into a new customer base. Since they neither manufactured nor intended to manufacture, Marks & Spencer sought to procure their upmarket supplies from the leading brand knitwear firms that were members of the Textile Warehouse Association such as Wolsey and N. Corah (St Margaret). However, the Textile Warehouse Association preferred to distribute its quality branded products through the independent retailer and the upmarket department stores situated in

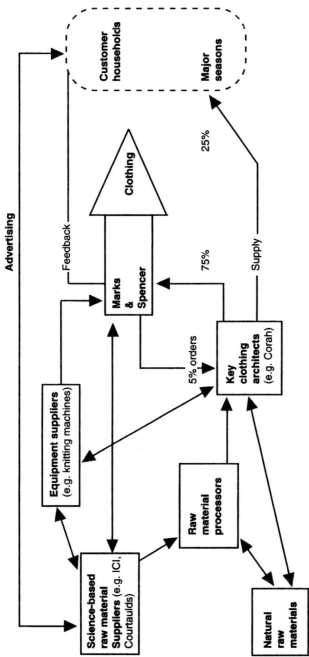

Figure 10.1 Inter-organisational networks: Marks & Spencer
Source: Clark and Stanley (1988).

London and the provincial cities. Marks & Spencer was therefore faced by a blockage and skilfully outflanked the opposition through a special relationship with N. Corah (St Margaret) that tied the two firms in a bilateral relationship. Corah was crucially important for several reasons:

1   Corah provided a well-known branded product (St Margaret) for sale in the stores of Marks & Spencer, which commenced to brand its products from other suppliers under the name 'St Michael'.
2   Corah provided a source of knowledge about the problems of production and innovation that became available for Marks & Spencer to learn and use in its dealings with other suppliers.
3   The relationship provided a platform for further developments in which Marks & Spencer specialised in distribution and the design of goods.

The relationship between the two firms parallels other pairings, for example, between Volvo and Olofstrom in Sweden (Clark and Staunton 1989: 170–172).

Second, in the 1930s Marks & Spencer established a series of special relationships that extended their knowledge base and understanding of future design problems by engaging with the downstream producers of the manmade yarns. This relationship was soon extended into relationships with equipment suppliers and dyers of yarns. During each decade these relationships were deepened and extended. By the 1960s Marks & Spencer technocracy was able to distribute explicit and tacit knowledge within its own sectoral cluster. Moreover, its approach to distribution was complemented by the stress on reflective approaches to production of the downstream firm, Imperial Chemical Industries, a leader in the diffusion of work analysis (Clark 1991). Even so, very little of this knowledge base adhered in the universities.

Third, in the 1960s major shifts occurred in the domestic market as consumers searched for more colourful styles produced in complex stitch geometry. Many of the stylistic developments in Europe unfolded in Italy where Benetton emerged. Marks & Spencer sourced more than 90 per cent of the knitwear supplies in the UK and clearly played a significant role in sustaining the textile sector as a source of employment. However, within the tightly bonded sectoral cluster shown in Figure 10.1 the key firm of Corah (St Margaret), then Europe's largest and regarded in Britain as a leading innovator, did not possess the organisational design for survival (Clark and Starkey 1988).[1] The competitive capability of Corah was the capacity to produce a wide variety of goods in relatively small batches to high quality standards now attributed to the reputation of Marks & Spencer. The weakness faced – unknowingly – by Corah was in not recognising changes of scale, cost and profit. Increasingly, Marks & Spencer sourced new lines with other firms. By the late 1980s Corah was in deep decline and its co-ordinating role was replaced by Dewhirst.

Fourth, by the 1990s the supply of knitwear was being orchestrated through the key firms of Dewhirst, Courtaulds and Baird. However, the policy of sourcing only in the UK now faced quality goods from contexts with much lower levels of labour and location costs (Ostrovsky 1998). The current episode involves dramatic reconfiguration of the domestic supply chain coupled to the trio of problems of being a multinational business: learning; efficiency and flexibility (Bartlett and Ghoshall 1989).

SECTORAL CLUSTERS OF FIRMS

The sector, the sector-cluster-network and the firm-in-sector perspectives have all become much more significant because they qualify attention to the isolated firm. Likewise, the identification of pivotal firms that orchestrate and shape clusters is of central analytic concern.

Figure 10.1 sets out a specific example of an inter-firm network whose structure can be used as a general template (Clark and Staunton 1989: Chapter 8). In this specific case the pivotal firm is at the end of the cluster on the right-hand side. This is the case in retail-driven clusters (e.g. Ikea). There are clusters which are driven from earlier as in the case of the automobile cluster in the USA, Japan and Germany. Intriguingly, the British automobile cluster was more fragmented, with cleavages as well as connections between the major producers, their key suppliers and the distributors. The definition is of sectors in the plural and this includes those in the production chain as well as the supporting firms supplying equipment and raw materials plus the customers. The sectors constitute a clustering of inter-firm networks.

Returning to Figure 10.1 we can identify several sectors each containing domains of activity that are similar involving firms in parallel, possibly inter-connected activities and resulting in the output of rather similar products (e.g. automobiles, dresses). These clusters constitute a pre-existing structure and conditions for future events. So, pre-existing processes may start to unfold in recognisable configurations whereby the past dominates the present and future for several decades until a transitional period leading to a new configuration.

The perspective of 'sectoral clusters of firms' is a synthesis of analytic categories with a very strong emphasis upon the intention to uncover the pre-existing organisational role sets (Blau and Scott 1961), structures, processes, conditions and mechanisms of their reproduction or transformation. The sectoral cluster of firms is a network and provides an important analytic contribution to examining the action of firms. The sector as an analytic unit as proposed by Pavitt (1980) was subsequently located within a inter-sectoral framework (Pavitt 1984). The firm-in-sector perspective was initially used within the five-year work organisation programme[2] examining the longitudinal and comparative dimensions of innova-tion in technology and organisation in Britain. The early thinking set out the domain (Clark and Whipp 1984; Whipp and Clark 1986: Chapter 2) and was applied to a longitudinal case study of the problem of strategic innovation-design at Rover (Whipp and Clark 1986). The review of the Rover case study revealed that sectoral clusters and chains were the more significant structural features (Clark 1987; Clark and Starkey 1988; Clark and Staunton 1989). The analysis of inter-firm clusters and networks by Clark and Staunton (1989: Chapter 9) also draws upon the extensive network studies of Hakansson (1987). The firm-in-sector perspective was also central in the study of Cadbury (Child and Smith 1987; Smith *et al.* 1991).

Examining the sectoral cluster of inter-firm networks includes the power balances between the different sets of actors in the inter-organisational network. The analyst assumes sufficient detachment and analytic grasp to understand the social construction of reality by those firms within particular sectors and to locate the inter-firm dynamics within a realist ontology (see Chapter 4).

Sectors and sectoral clusters tend to possess certain common features:

1   Sectors contain populations of similar types of firm sharing common features of market regulation in relation to governmental action. Firms in the same sector may face similar barriers to entry arising from capital intensity and expenditures on research and development.
2   Clusters vary in their era of founding (Stinchcombe 1965) and life-time profile (Abernathy 1978) and tend to acquire distinctive occupational profiles. There are similar types of corporate structure and hierarchy because of shared templates of best practice.
3   Sectors face similar market conditions and patterns of customer demand in timing (e.g. seasonality) and in taste (e.g. disposable income and heterogeneity). There are common selection environments.
4   Sectors face many common regulations from the central and local state.
5   Sectors tend to share institutionalised cognitive frameworks (DiMaggio and Powell 1991) and types of knowledge. There may be sector recipes (Spender 1989) whereby the firms use similar constructs and rules to cognitise their internal and external contexts and to frame action. There may be deeply sector-sedimented rules and sagas setting out solutions. For example, Corah (in the above example), shared the rule that mass production solutions did not fit and so was unprepared for the eventual emergence of specialisation in the knitwear sector.
6   There is dependence on similar external resources such as finance, customers and technology suppliers.
7   There are similar institutionalised relations to labour and the trade unions.
8   Firms in a sectors may share similar levels of productivity and approaches to innovation. There may be common exemplars of best practice locally and a tendency to import similar exemplars from other national contexts, perhaps because of the influence of consultancies (Swan *et al.* 1998). The sector tends to be a major arena for the establishment and transformation of technologies.
9   Sectors tend to have similar experiences with regard to overseas ventures, both in the incoming competitors and in moving overseas.
10 Firms in the sector share a common design hierarchy (Abernathy 1978) whereby the products and services being offered contain a similar architecture of systems and performance features (e.g. insurance packages).
11 The life course of the sector (Clark and DeBresson 1990) tends to have similar

moments, eras and pressure points affecting all firms, albeit to different degrees. The university sector in most nations has faced similar opportunities and restrictions over the past five decades B. R. Clark 1998).

12 The long-term unfolding of innovation may possess common elements, especially in the emergence and eventual routinisation of occupational structures.

Sectoral clusters tend to be the outcome of actions by firms that eventually become pivotal in establishing a cluster configuration which they then attempt to retain. This often involves complex processes of political enrolment leading to the establishment of shared agendas. Contrary to the actor network theory, it seems likely that the direction of enrolment in a cluster arises through complex bilateral power plays and alliances. Once established, clusters can seem to possess a durability.

The notion of a firm-in-sector-cluster interfaces with the arguments concerning the role of national predispositions in human resources to enable or disable clusters from emerging and surviving. The ensemble of sectors is a key analytic linkage from the inherited past into the future (Schoenberger 1996). The analytic framework builds on the new institutional perspectives, but needs attention not only to the role of the state and of the professions (Scott 1995), but also to the characteristics of the national, domestic market, to the institutions of labour, to management and to the frontier of control between labour and the knowledge professionals.

There is a double interest in the societal effects type of analysis examined in the previous chapters. First, the cluster of sectors and intra-sectoral dynamics is an example of strategic co-ordination of activities largely outside the market mechanisms and inside organised networks. Second, strategic co-ordination is, in effect, just the area of organisation which is most susceptible to the influence of the national habitus (see Chapter 8). However, the analytic category of national typical variety emphasises the range of variation within a nation. This point is emphasised in some of the differences between the cameos that follow.

The next section examines how the institutional and regional context of the English West Midlands shaped its domestic automobile firms and their capacity to construct sectoral clusters comparable to those of Marks & Spencer.

WHY HENRY FORD WOULD HAVE FAILED IF HE HAD STARTED FROM THE BIRMINGHAM–COVENTRY CORRIDOR, ENGLAND

The situation: 1912, 1906, 1908

In 1912 Henry Ford entered the British automobile market from Detroit, USA by exporting knock-down kits to Trafford Park, Manchester, England where they were assembled. Ford gained one-quarter of the British market in that year while

Rover, at that time the world's largest producer of cars, bicycles and saloon cars, was third with sales of 1,200 cars. Could Henry Ford have started out from the Birmingham–Coventry corridor in which much of the British-owned saloon car industry surfaced? Unlikely. Why?

If in 1912 Ford was able to enter the British market and gain one-quarter of the 12,000 sales, why did no British car firms supply that segment earlier and why did they continue to produce saloon cars in relatively small volume until the closure of the domestic industry in the 1980s? We shall compare the contexts of Rover and of Ford. The case of Henry Ford's launching of the Ford T from Detroit, Michigan, USA in 1908 provides a useful instance for exploring, testing and clarifying the debate over competition between contexts (i.e. zones of manoeuvre and strategic choice). This section contends that the contextual intra-dependencies in the British and American contexts provided zones of manoeuvre to the domestic car firms which were very different. The specifics of those zones of manoeuvre were consequential. There was competition between contexts. Detroit was the more enabling context for low cost, standardised products like the Ford T.

If in 1906, the year Ford advertised the forthcoming Model T, we had applied the analytic frameworks from contemporary resource-based strategic analysis (see Chapter 11) to the automobile industry, to the British situation and to the historic role of the industrial district, then we might well have concluded that there were very favourable circumstances (see Figure 10.2). There would seem to have been few impediments. However, the theory of competition between contexts emphasises both the hidden configurations of elements and the specificities of regional contexts. The possibility for high volume technology and mass production became evident in the cigarette industry where the Imperial Group became and remained a leader in technology development and the application of time-space compression (Clark 1972, 1979). By contrast much of the automobile industry experienced a looser time-space regulation.

Could Ford have successfully launched the Model T in Birmingham and gained such a world position? We shall argue that Ford would have found the Birmingham site and the British context contained restricted zones of manoeuvre to develop the organisational capabilities and to dominate the context. In Detroit and in the USA it was possible for an entrepreneur to create capabilities and to draw upon societal capacities as well as regional opportunities which were distinctive.

The Model T (1908)

Henry Ford was an excellent example of entrepreneurship and the building of a vertically integrated network with extensive pillars of power (Clegg 1989; Law 1994). Ford's Model T, when introduced in 1908 for less than $1,000, was a spectacular success. The Model T became the world's best-selling model and totally dominated North American markets, before being replaced in 1926. It sold in cities, but more importantly it sold to the majority in rural and small town America where the roads were often rudimentary. Prior to the appearance of the

Model T, most American automobiles were open top, mainly wooden, very shaky for the passengers, unreliable and difficult to service.

The Model T established the essentials of the future design hierarchy around the chassis and to include the frame, engine, transmission, brakes, wheels, radiator and all other mechanical components except the outer body (Abernathy 1978: 13; Abernathy and Clark 1985). Ford's entrepreneurship provided a synthesis of the existing practices and introduced key innovations such as three-point suspension that separated the engine and the frame, thereby reducing shake and potential disassembly. The Model T incorporated features appropriate to the rough roads and rural market (e.g. high ground clearance) of the USA and not found in the contemporary European markets. In the years before the launch the competition between alternative power sources had been decided in favour of the internal combustion gasoline engine. Before 1908, Ford had redesigned the engine and the power train for greater reliability and ease of maintenance. The design hierarchy embodied in the Model T of 1908 remained stable with incremental extensions for the next eighteen years. The car was light, open, single colour with wooden bodywork and suspended on a chassis.

The Model T was designed to be manufactured from standardised components in-sourced from suppliers and assembled by skilled workers building up sub-assemblies into the final product. At the stage of connecting innovation to design, Ford and his inner network of collaborators articulated the process of assembly with the product. It was some years after the successful launch that innovations in the assembly were introduced. Most famously these introduced the template of the modern assembly line, initially for magneto assembly (1913) and then for the final assembly (Abernathy 1978). There was a dramatic transformation in the organi-sation of work by reducing the work cycle from more than nine minutes to less than two minutes. Ford managed to apply the principles of manufacture imagined for gun making in the late eighteenth century, but not achieved until the mid-nineteenth century to a product with much, much more complexity. The simpli-fication of work reduced the training time, removed the more powerful craft groups and in the American context enabled the increase of managerial influence on the shopfloor.

The template of continuous production had emerged earlier and become established in several industries ranging from the process industries (e.g. sugar, petroleum), the meat industry and cigarette making. After 1885 the bicycle industry increasingly utilised flowline methods. The basic principles of continuous flow had fascinated and preoccupied American business men from the late eight-eenth century onward.

Prior to the launch of the Model T the servicing of the car was done through the local garage and by the driver undertaking irregular, running repairs. The Model T was designed to replace the continuous and irregular servicing by regular preventative servicing by trained agents working to the formalised instructions from Ford. Consequently, Ford set out to control the distributors and to have them inside his network.

Ford announced the car in 1906 through an extensive advertising campaign which invited future owners to start making down payments. Advertising and financial services were already established in a standardised format. Part of the inflow of prepayment was utilised to fund some activities.

The Model T differed from automobiles regarded as the leading edge of European designs in several key respects. The engine was technically coarser, but was more robust and therefore did not require such fine machine tolerances. This led Europeans to look down on the engine.

USA and Detroit

Much attention has been given to Ford's design of the Model T and to the production process within which it was assembled, but this is only one part of the story. Throughout the early period a very high proportion – sometimes 90 per cent – had been sold before the Ford T had been built. Henry Ford had established this practice of advertising and forward selling in 1906, two years before the launch of the Ford T.

The American marketplace for all kinds of goods was, by 1900, serviced by highly competitive firms in both distribution and manufacture. Distribution, marketing and advertising were exceptional American developments in the nineteenth century through both direct selling in urban centres (e.g. Chicago) and indirect selling through mail order. These methods of distribution were accompanied by well-developed systems of financial repayment through standardised means, including advanced and delayed payment. Ford was therefore able to activate a capacity absent in Europe to skilfully advertise his forthcoming car in 1906 and commence receiving payment before delivery. These inflows of revenue came directly to Ford and meant that a major source of uncertainty faced by European manufacturers was removed and that significant onward planning was possible. In contrast British manufacturers tended to wait for orders or to stock a small number of chassis-wheel assemblies (e.g. Austin). The British manufacturers were always in a dependent relationship to the powerful distributors which gave quite limited feedback of information.

The American market differed from Europe in that there was a large potential segment beyond the middle-class urban population. In the USA the low cost of housing and of primary consumption products increased the disposable income available for major products like sewing machines, household furniture and, later, automobiles. The market was prepared for standardised, function goods which could be customised in the home. The public was experienced in learning of possible purchases through catalogues, exhibitions, public trials and newspapers.

The factor conditions were favourable and Ford was able to develop advanced created factors. It may be argued that America was the first nation to take industrial knowledge seriously. Just as in the example of medical monitoring equipment, the position of supporting and related sectors in the American context which formed the pre-existing potentials for Ford were highly favourable. Henry Ford was able to draw upon the world's most highly developed blend of capacities in functional design and the standardisation of components. This was a system of knowledge, forms of organisation and artefacts which had already delivered standardised military equipment, sewing machines, bicycles, wood frame houses and so on (Hounshell 1984; Clark 1987). The production process had mastered the notion of flow (Chandler 1977) at high speed (Rosenberg 1976) and created systems for handling agriculture (e.g. meat) and fluids (e.g. oil) by 1900. The career of Duke and American Tobacco in the cigarette industry provided the template of world markets through rationalisation and vertical integration.

Henry Ford was able to engage with suppliers and to receive robust standardised components at an early stage and know that these would fit into sub-assemblies which could then by assembled into the Ford T. Detroit, Motor City to be, contained many of the necessary ingredients. The machine tool industries occupied a virtuous relationship in respect of their capacities to supply and to diffuse new learning (Rosenberg, 1982).

Ford created one of the most frequently cited templates of corporate organisation and at the launch of the Ford T there was considerable rivalry among the scores of small firms and the few medium-sized firms. That soon changed and by the 1920s the USA had become a three-firm nation.

Ford in Britain

Ford was able to appropriate existing templates of corporate extension by developing large-scale assembly of the American domestic product overseas (Hughes 1990). At an early stage, Ford planned entry into Britain in 1911 and became the leading distributor in 1912. However, the conditions necessary for Ford to develop his network resided in the USA generally and in Detroit specifically. These essential features were absent in England for each of the clusters of features and for the overall configuration. Consequently, when British manufacturers like Lanchester sought to engage in standardised production in Coventry this was undermined by the poor quality of components and the requirement for skilled workers to finish their preparation. It was more than a decade before the British automobile firms developed a competitive small car to Ford and it was the McKenna Duty in the 1930s that provided an umbrella for the cumulative pathway through the zones of manoeuvre for British firms.

British Motor Industry, 1900–12

In 1995 with the sale of Rover,[3] then owned by British Aerospace, to BMW the last of the major firms in the British-owned automobile industry was transferred into overseas ownership. So, although the UK balances its exports and imports, the production of cars is by American, Japanese, French and German firms. Only the motor sport sector remains in domestic ownership. The sectoral cluster of connected sectors in transportation has been hollowed out and even the leading designer and supplier of electrical and electronic systems, Lucas, is now Lucas-Varity and is substantially owned in the USA.

The realist perspective emphasises the importance of the pre-existing structure of necessary and contingent relationships (Sayer 1992). These pre-existing patterns are both enabling and also contain forms of lock-in that make transitions outward a challenging experience of learning (Bartlett and Ghoshall 1989). Figure 10.2 provides a useful way of considering the context of the British automobile industry. The figure was partly derived from economic and technological histories (e.g. Landes 1969) and also from the reconstruction of the corporate history of Rover (Whipp and Clark 1986; Clark and DeBresson 1990). The aim here is to synthesise from the many excellent studies already published.

Birmingham was known in the nineteenth century and early twentieth century as an industrial district (1) and cited by Marshall as an excellent example. Birmingham was a core region in relation to the metropolitan core of London in the development of Britain and its empire. The region had once been the centre of the arms industry for the British Empire and was close to and part of the industrial revolution (Rosenberg 1969). Gun making was an industry of great innovation, especially in reduction in the weight of guns that had enabled their transfer into shipping and then their mobility on land. As an industrial district there were both large firms and many small firms based in streets and even homes which combined and recombined as the product itself altered and as demand fluctuated. Metalwork related to domestic and mercantile trade had blossomed, creating many small firms run by entrepreneurs. Firms were flexible in their response to demand because the craft skills were located with the workforce rather than owned by the employer. The putting-out system and tendencies to quasi-autonomous group working were endemic. Within the industrial district complexity was handled between firms which were proximate and could establish working relationships. The canal system, said to be more extensive than Venice, linked the industrial district and connected it to the export ports of Bristol, London and Liverpool. So extensive was the generation of local wealth that banks (e.g. Midland) later became major players. Birmingham was also a centre for Chartists and for strong associations among the workforce. It has been argued that these labour associations were so embedded and extensive that the days of the week possessed their local distinctiveness. St Monday was for recovering from the weekend exertions and ebullience.

The seeming flexibility of firms in the Birmingham industrial district was deceptive. Although enabling the early phase of the automobile industry, the district lacked the capacity to transform. So, even though the European industry faced a different market structure to that of the USA and therefore moved down a different social trajectory, Birmingham was slow to transform its sectoral clustering. In the crucial decades between 1890 and 1920 when the bicycle sector was displaced by the incoming automobile sector, Birmingham possessed a distinctive, pre-existing structure of social and economic relationships which contained specific powers and liabilities. The pre-existing *filière* and structure enabled small firms to start up and small entrepreneurially led firms (e.g. Jaguar) to enter and survive. Also, car firms that combined the price range with medium volume cheap cars (e.g. Austin) were able to survive in the face of Ford and GM until the 1960s because the advantages to US incomers were slight as long as they also faced the

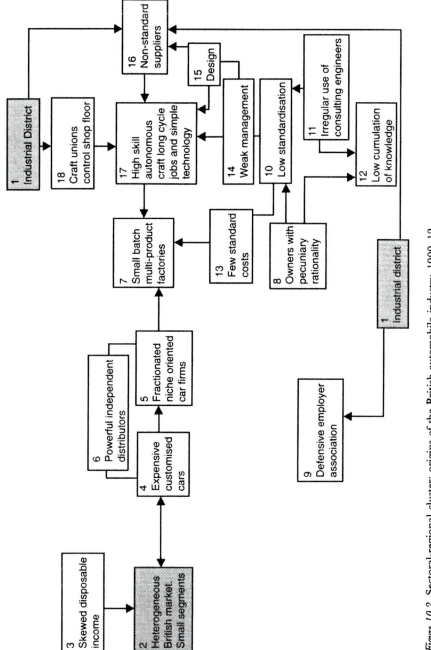

Figure 10.2 Sectoral-regional cluster: origins of the British automobile industry, 1900–12

British market. However, the knowledge communities (11) such as the Motor Industry Research Association that were implicated in the automobile industry became problematic from the 1960s onward.

Demand conditions (2) in the British market were quite different from those in the American market inherited and created by Henry Ford after 1908. British demand was heavily located in the urban, London-dominated middle class at a time when the residual financial benefits of British mercantile capitalism based on world shipping were being heavily eroded. The different, variegated, stratified, middle class competed and displayed themselves through small distinctions in taste. Also, net disposable income of British consumers (3) was distributed so that the middle classes could afford cars, but the large working-class segments were less well off than their American cousins. Consequently the consumers demanded expensive, customised automobiles (4) supplied by niche oriented car firms (5). These niche firms created a segmented market articulating distinctions of taste, and their large number cannot be equated with the notion of high rivalry (as Porter 1990). The barriers to entry were quite low. The British automobile industry was typified by many entrants at its founding, by a higher rate of survival than the USA and by more new entrants in the late 1920s (e.g. Jaguar, Hillman, Jowett). There was high market segmentation and a degree of rivalry.

The consumer-producer nexus was controlled by the increasingly powerful distributors (6) which remained independent from the production firms and tended to retain their detailed knowledge of the consumer. The niche car firms focused upon small volume production runs (7).

The owners of car firms (8) were driven by pecuniary rationality rather than the technical rationality more characteristic of their French and German rivals. The car firms were often founded by entrepreneurs who dominated the board level. There was often low representation of engineering competencies at the top levels and the technostructure was weakly developed relative to other leading international nations (e.g. Germany and France). Because of the 'frontier of control' between employers and employees in the industrial district (1) the employers formed defensive alliances (9) in order to promote their interests and to co-align the actions of their rivals.

Car firm owners tended to rely on market-like mechanisms without and within the firm. There was no equivalent habitus to the American system of manufacture and consequently the potentials for standardisation (10) established in the different sectoral clusters of food, drink and tobacco was absent (Clark 1987). Yet the car was an enormously complex configuration of hundreds and hundreds of components. There was low standardisation (10) coupled to the irregular use of external consultants (11) to supply designs for the cars and to itemise the components to be sought from external suppliers. Consequently, there was a low cumulation of knowledge within the firm and the associations of the work community (12). Within the firms and within the industry there was only slight development of advanced knowledge. There was nothing remotely comparable to the American pattern whereby General Motors sponsored Flint University in Detroit. In England the major civic universities in industrial cities were alleged to be wary of connections. Nockolds's (1976) history of Lucas cites the post-1945 unwillingness of the prestigious University of Birmingham to become connected with the development of industrial engineering. The knowledge community has considerable significance.

Low standardisation slowed the development of costing procedures (13) and reduced the opportunities for reflective monitoring by management (14). Management played a partial role in assembling practices. Management, as an occupational strata, was poorly developed in business knowledge or engineering knowledge. There was little systematic recording and compilation of data to provide standardised costs (cf. the cigarette industry). The incipient techno-structure was slow to develop. Hence reflective learning was inhibited. A large part of shopfloor management was effectively delegated to the relatively autonomous skilled craft groups (17).

Low standardisation also impacted on design (15) of the car and of the production process. This was reinforced by the tendency to co-ordinate the firm by buying in expertise for car design in the founding period. Consequently, the specifications to suppliers and the monitoring of contracts was considerably less developed than in American, French and German competitors.

As indicated, the dominant work practices of the industrial district (1) provided a pre-existing structure in which skilled craft groups offered their expertise in a market relationship with employers that was mediated by the role of Birmingham associations of trade and labour (18). The shopfloor (17) was populated by craft groups whose expertise was learnt through 'legitimate peripheral participation' in the everyday experience controlled by the trade association. Consequently, skilled machinists were needed for the constant adjustment of both outsourced and internally manufactured components. The high levels of uncertainty were handled by recruiting a skilled workforce which was heavily involved in self-organised training and cognitive apprenticeship. The expertise of these workers was required to correct the low standardisation of the components and to respond to the seasonal variability of demand (Turner *et al.* 1967). There was an ample supply of skilled and semi-skilled workers (13) willing to engage in the apprenticeship system, but this was largely a tacit rather than an explicit form of learning. Because the workforces from the Birmingham and Coventry area were required to undertake such complex work in the production process the firms were unable to contemplate the struggle over the appropriation of expertise and learning. This contrasts with British firms in food, drink and tobacco which successfully appropriated major elements in the Taylorist approaches (Clark 1987: 282–286). Indeed, standard work study in the automobile industry was still in its infancy in the 1950s and 1960s (Clark 1991).

The supporting sectors did develop (16). In electronics Lucas became a designer-supplier to the British-owned firms, developing from headlights into the full panoply.

If we look again at Figure 10.2 and introduce the Dunning–Porter framework (Figure 7.3) then we can readily imagine that entering in the lower left-hand space is a hungry, growing multinational business developed in the American context and known as Ford.

NOTES

1 The original case study was written in 1965–6 and revised on a Fellowship at the Ivey School of Business, Western Ontario University, 1977.
2 A firm-in-sector perspective was developed within the five-year programme for the Economic and Social Research Council (1982–7) at the University of Aston (Child, Clark, Loveridge, Tann, Smith, Whipp, Grieco, Starkey, McKinley, Rowlinson) for examining the longitudinal and comparative dimensions of innovation in technology and organisation in Britain. The doctoral theses of Robyn Cochrane, John Hassard and Alan Pilkington also contributed.
3 It is essential to distinguish between the original Rover firm and the application of the name of Rover to the rump of the saloon car industry which was in a strategic alliance with Honda and then purchased by BMW in 1995. The former produced saloon cars in small batches and was the creator of the Land/Range Rover marquee.

Part III

Firms

Capabilities and transformative potential

11 Resource-based strategic analysis

INTRODUCTION

This chapter returns to the purposive, rational model of corporate strategy and the firm introduced in Chapters 3 and 5. The purposive view of firms possesses an image of the strategy analyst as the architect of the firm (e.g. Kay 1993). The contemporary approach in strategy is based on the analytic revolution which focuses heavily inside the firm because the external context is presented as hyper-competition (D'Aveni 1994). This is the Resource Based Strategic Analysis (RBSA) approach, which is associated with three broad strands of theorising the firm from an organisational economics perspective:

- resources-into-capabilities;
- Penrosian learning;
- organisational knowledge.

These three strands have been central to recent debates in the *Strategic Management Journal*.

Over the past four decades the pendulum has swung back and forth between attention to the external environment and to the internal environment (e.g. distinctive competencies). Currently there is considerable attention to the internal environment, but the position of this book is that it is the co-evolution of context and firm which should grip the attention of analysts and practitioners. Therefore, the emphasis upon the Resource Based Strategic approach needs to be thoroughly contextualised. This means that competition between contexts should drive the interpretation given to organisational learning and to the dynamic resource models (Grant 1998).

Situating Resource Based Strategic Analysis (RBSA) within our approach occupies the central sections of the chapter and leads into the following chapters. The interpretation of strategy by Grant (1990, 1998) provides an insightful account and mobilises the recent attention to organisational knowledge as one of the major sources of value adding (Grant 1996a, b). Grant highlights the internal capabilities of the firm as a major starting point for the strategic choice of competitive context.

This chapter will examine those areas from RBSA which most closely relate to the theme of *Organisations in Action*. Then, having established the main position, a series of revisions is proposed and developed further in the following chapters. For example, the review and re-orientation of strategic theory initiated by Rumelt *et al.* (1991) contains a rich variety of shifts in emphasis from the earlier paradigm presented by Hofer and Schendel (1978). My contention is that although this rich variant overlaps with that of Grant there are significantly different implications. Porter (1991), for example, tackles the competencies of the firm and its learning processes in a different manner to that of mainstream RBSA. Also, the difference between the neo-rational purposive approaches to action and competition and the second variant is expressed in Levinthal and March's (1993) account of the myopia of learning.

RESOURCE-BASED STRATEGIC ANALYSIS (RBSA)

The development of organisational economics shows that economic reasoning has prised open the black box of the firm. Now an impressive cluster of frameworks is available, including the resource based approach, organisational routines, dynamic capabilities and Penrosian learning. Moreover, the contribution to tacit and explicit knowledge making by Spender and Grant (1996) adds to the impression that the inside-out view of strategic management is now much more influential than the outside-in view.

The aim is to synthesise the elements of the inside-out approach into a coherent framework as illustrated in Figure 11.1. This framework contends that resources are translated by Penrosian learning into managerial services. Those services are then combined with knowledge and organisational routines to bind together the resources into the capabilities of the firm. The primary aim of RBSA is to determine what the firm can do in different contexts. The 'can do' emphasis is meant to counter the strategic fantasies of formal, written mission statements. The example often given is how Disney mobilised its considerable resource base of land, the corporate library and brand value of Disney characters. Once mobilised the resources become capabilities and provide rich opportunities to earn Ricardian rents because rivals are impeded from direct imitation.

Figure 11.1 sets out the RBSA and our purpose is to identify its elements prior to scrutinising the claims implied. There are five connected and interactive steps in the analysis to be examined in our treatment of RBSA.

First, the analysis of *resources* addresses the gap between the stock market valuation of a firm and the sell-off value of so-called tangible assets such as finance, land, buildings, estimated value of patents and equipment. For large, successful firms there is a massive gap between a simple accounting estimate of tangibles and the stock market valuation. The gap identifies the intangibles. Intangibles are of two major types: reputation and capabilities. Reputation refers to the brands (e.g. Roger the Rabbit) and to the firm (e.g. Microsoft). Capabilities

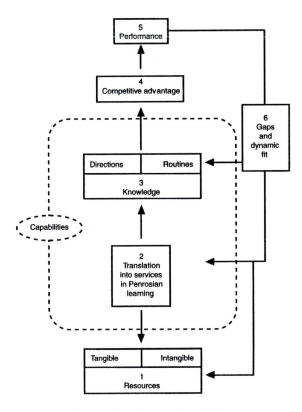

Figure 11.1 Resource-based strategic analysis
Source: Grant (1990, 1995).

refers to what can be done through the design of the organisation and the human resources which cannot be readily traded (Kay 1993).

Intangible resources are by definition of the economic reasoning which informs the RBSA initially residuals that conventional 'factual' analysis could not identify. The role of residuals (e.g. technology, knowledge) in economic reasoning is fascinating. Intangible resources underpin any capabilities (Hall 1992). Some of the intangibles include those assets which enjoy legal protection (e.g. contracts, patents, intellectual property rights, copyrights, registered designs) and the balance sheet valuation of brand names. Their calculation usually leaves a hefty gap which includes the internal skills and culture of the firm (Barney 1995) and the relational inter-firm network within which particular firms are nested (Hakansson 1987).

Grant (1990/1998) links the analysis to the concept of the value chain (Porter 1985) in which the objective is to disaggregate the firm's activities. The aim is to delineate as precisely as possible which clusters of activities most contribute to the firm's financial performance. Often the firms' competitive strengths and weaknesses are hidden from those at the top as, for example, in the experience of American franchisees with the owners of the Body Shop in the late 1990s. Disaggregation of clusters of activities commences by locating the firm in a chain of economic actions preceding the firm and those occurring subsequently so that the input activities (e.g. strategic purchasing) and the output activities (e.g. marketing) can be distinguished from short-term operational activities and the longer term activities of innovation-design. The analysts aim to locate the strengths of the firm relative to other firms through a variety of indicators and through benchmarking. The outcome of the analysis is intended to give top decision makers a better understanding of their firm's relative strengths and weaknesses. This analysis may well be part of a so-called business process redesign. The value chain can be connected to elements in Figure 11.1, particularly the resources and capabilities.

Second, the definition of *capabilities* is vital, yet tends to be rudely descriptive. Often the reader is presented with the name of a well-known firm (e.g. Honda) accompanied by a variety of figures depicting types of engine and the design activities. The implication is that these constitute capabilities. This sketchiness in academic analysis parallels the simple frameworks and descriptions often presented at international seminars by practitioners and consultants. In the context of application (Gibbons *et al.* 1994) it is quite likely that the analytic approaches of the major consultancies are more effective in characterising the combination of explicit and tacit knowledges in firms than approaches such as benchmarking (e.g. 'the Andersen way').

Resources can be traded upon the open market, but the existence of intangible resources provides the opportunity to link resources with what the firm 'can do': its capabilities. Of course, the concern with capabilities and with dynamic capabilities (Metcalfe 1998) in economic reasoning is intentional, purposive and an attempt to characterise the 'firm in action'. So, how within the firm are resources translated into capabilities? Grant boldly suggests two lines of analysis and although not detailing their resolution does follow those recommended by many others. One line is to equate capabilities with organisational routines. The other line of reasoning is to invoke the concept of Penrosian learning. Subsequently, Grant (1996a, b) highlights knowledge as the key element. The contributors discussed in this section tend to imply that there are few mobility barriers in the 'translation' of resources/assets into capabilities, but they rarely provide a realist analysis of the causal mechanisms through which the translation might be occurring.

Since Wrigley's (1972) Harvard doctorate on the hidden competencies of firms and the consulting of work of Krone (1972), the aim of examining what the firm 'can do' has been on the agenda, yet was not given great attention until the limitations of the rational, unitarist contingency and purposive vision of future strategic activity were revealed. Among the earlier contributors to capabilities, mention should be made of Ansoff, Chandler and Itami.

Ansoff, in a series of publications and in his consulting advice over several decades (Ansoff and McDonnell 1990) developed his account of corporate capabilities. He reasoned that firms were frequently unable to anticipate discontinuities in their competitive contexts. Later, this was explained in terms of the politics of managerial control of the firm in respect of alternative elite coalitions. The theme of unrecognised discontinuities and of surprise time (e.g. Gurvitch 1964) became stronger after the mass production tendency was displaced by increasing customisation (see Chapter 6). Ansoff applies organisation theory on the contingency relationship between increasingly uncertain, turbulent environments and the requirement for organisational forms which can detect weak signals foretelling strategic shifts and possessing flexible capabilities. The emphasis upon capabilities rather than structure as the key design choice is vital even if the detailing of the capabilities provides a fairly minimal set of guidelines. Although the perspective of organisational routines is mentioned their problematics are only partly included in the analysis.

Chandler (1990) replaces his earlier use of structure in a rich, historicised perspective (Chandler 1962) with the notion of capabilities. Itami and Roehl (1987), apparently drawing from Penrose (1959) on the fit between resources and capabilities, emphasise the significance of making information, symbols and actions transparent so that they can be leveraged. Itami's notion of being able to leverage capabilities (whatever they may be) has proved attractive to western thinkers, especially because leveraging seems to be explaining the ways in which some Japanese firms outflanked their American rivals. Itami's advice on leveraging and stretching into the future implicitly rejects the static view of the 'strategic fit' literature. Leveraging means going further than anticipating to actively imposing a new strategic logic in the marketplace.

Among the later contributors to analysing capabilities, probably Hamel and Prahalad (1989; Prahalad and Hamel 1990, 1994) are the most heavily cited. Prahalad and Bettis (1986) addressed the differences between firms (Nelson 1991) and argued that there is an explained connection between corporate diversity and performance which labelled the dominant general management logic (Prahalad and Bettis 1986: 485). Their analysis addressed managerial cognitions (cf. Stubbart 1988) and how managers enact their contexts (Weick 1969, 1979) with respect to the problems faced by top management when handling a portfolio of businesses which are unrelated. Prahalad and Hamel (1989, 1990) proposed the concept of strategic intent as a future-oriented concept later refined (1994). Their approach very definitely sought to characterise the firm 'in action'. Strategic intent as an active management process elaborates and validates what Weick (1969) referred to as a consensual grammar within which there are heuristics for allocating resources (Hamel and Prahalad 1989: 64). Strategic intent creates a misfit between resources and ambitions. Japanese firms (e.g. Honda) are often presented as embodying a validated consensual grammar which leverages resources into capabilities (Hamel and Prahalad 1989: 69) in ways that American firms were not doing. Hamel (1991: Table 1) examines what can happen to existing capabilities and learning when international firms from different nations (e.g. British, French, Japanese) engage in a strategic alliance.

Within capabilities there is a strong tendency to invoke *Penrosian learning*

(Penrose 1959) as the mechanism through which resources are transformed into managerial services. Penrosian learning is dealt with more fully in the next section.

There is the attempt to add clarity to the loose notion of capabilities by examining the role of *organisation knowledge* (Grant 1998: 122–128; 433–437). Organisation knowledge contains two elements: routines and directions. Through the literature on organisational routines and reasoning it is now possible to appraise the Ricardian rents which might be generated from resources and capabilities (Grant 1995: 111–117). Organisation knowledge is examined later in the chapter. My position on organisational routines was introduced earlier in Chapter 5 where preference was given to the notion of recurrent action patterns over the quasi-genetic traits (Nelson and Winter 1982; Winter 1995; Cohen *et al.* 1996). Recurrent action patterns may be translated with attention to background assumptions (e.g. Searle 1995) and to habitus (Bourdieu 1977).

The resource-based approach sought resources possessing the features of being valuable, rare, idiosyncratic to the firm, difficult to imitate and having few strategic equivalents to substitute. Resources possessing these attributes would – in an ideal world – create a continuing stream of profits to the firm. So, the resource based strategic analyst locates the *gaps* between the resource base and the strategic choice of the firm.

The RBSA concentrated upon the top management of the firm and tended to be optimistic about its capacities to locate and deploy profitable rescues. This optimism continued even when certain inertial limits contained in some resources were acknowledged (e.g. Grant 1990). The resource based approach was neither systematically longitudinal, nor did it sufficiently address the dynamics of competition between firms. The approach was to concentrate upon the ideal firm rather than the gap between the ideal and actual (Montgomery 1995). These and other problems are evident when the evolutionary approaches are introduced. The evolutionary theories depict a spectrum of rescues and the obdurate presence of organisational routines which are inertial (Rumelt 1995). Moreover, the gap between the ideal and the realist is highlighted when the whole firm rather than simply top management is considered in its historicised long-term trajectory. RBSA has given too little attention to the capacities of the competitive context to deselect firms. Too much attention has been given to the ideal and to the capacities of top management to deliver that ideal when there may be a gap from the real which is unbridgable. Montgomery (1995) outlines the implications of synthesising an evolutionary and dynamic theory with RBA. The definition of the evolutionary contribution is a spectrum from Nelson and Winter (1982) to Penrose (1959) even though these possess rather different theories of organisations in action. Our previous discussions have already identified the difficulties likely to be faced by RBSA and have drawn attention to critique of organisational economics by our perspective. For example, it may be noted that the RBSA framework omits attention to the capabilities of the context, both the indigenous domestic context of a home-based firm and the different competitive context of rivals.

PENROSIAN LEARNING

Introduction

The focus of attention in organisation theory for understanding the firm has shifted from straddling the structure/process dichotomy to the knowledge dimension, learning and capabilities. The problem is to unpack and clarify knowledge, learning and capabilities. The core difficulties are in understanding the differences and complementarities between codified and tacit knowledge and their role in creating dynamic capabilities (e.g. Metcalfe 1998). An awareness of this problem has led to an increasing citation of Penrose's (1959) almost forgotten critique of codified knowledge in economics and its irrelevance to understanding processes inside the firm. Today this is referred to as Penrosian learning. However, much of the re-citation of Penrose does not sufficiently explain how her work might provide the theoretical glue; nor have the developments since Penrose been sufficiently incorporated.

Penrose is reckoned to have made a seminal contribution to the resource-based view of the firm by showing that the explacit knowledge through which managerial expertise actions the resources within the firm limits the choice of markets for the firm. Internal management services limit growth of the firm and define the direction of the firm's capabilities. Firms are political entities locked into struggles, disequilibrium and the uncertainty arising from the dynamics of competition. The firm's resources are unique to the firm (1959: 199) and their significance may change because of the context (1959: 79). The firms distinctive competence includes making better use of its resources (1959: 54). Penrose suggests that the unused productive services arising from resources can sharpen the direction and scope of the search for new knowledge by the top managerial team. Their actions will create the dominant logics.

Receding limits of entrepreneurial expertise

Penrose (1959: 13) is 'primarily concerned with a theoretical analysis . . . of the limits to growth'. She asked the question: what does the team of top decision makers do which enables the firm to grow? Her approach was quite distinctive in prioritising a new theory of the firm and in redefining growth in terms of expertise.

Penrose did not set out to describe managerial tasks and interactions as in studies of Mintzberg (1973), nor did she seek the kinds of material which Chandler (1962) utilised to develop his analysis of the role of organisational innovation in technical change and the growth of American firms. A comment should be added on the empirical materials about management and entrepreneurship and their contribution to the theorising. Penrose was particularly impressed by the published history of Unilever and also makes reference to the various published materials on diversification and acquisition by General Motors. However, it does not seem that she had everyday access to top decisions or that she was aware of the trickle of published studies examining the activities of decision makers. She did have discussions with corporate leaders, but these are not given in specific form. Instead, she launched her approach in terms of a theory of the firm which differed from the theory of firm in economics.

Penrose focused on the growth of entrepreneurial and managerial knowledge, more precisely, the tacit propositional knowledge which a 'team' of top managers must have constituted from their experiences in order for the firm to enter the next iteration of events in its context. This might seem close to the Carnegie School which also built a new paradigm of decision making based upon the new cognitive psychology and the analogy with computing. Yet, her focus was not upon the decision maker, but upon the top decision processes. She sought to characterise and theorise collective thinking and how top-level expertise provided the significant element about the firm which orthodox economic theory ignored. We shall examine her ideas about how the growth of entrepreneurial expertise lies behind the more taken for granted notions of growth used in strategy and in the economics of the firm.

Critique of objective knowledge in economics

Penrose tackles the character of knowledge in economics. She contends that economics has been erected on an objective conception of knowledge which has been mistakenly modelled upon the immutable law-like relationships with which Renaissance science was preoccupied in mechanics and biology. The borrowing from physics is erroneous because human behaviour is surrounded by and immersed in reflexiveness and ambiguity. Penrose is radical in her rejection of orthodoxy in economics about the firm and bold in the proclamation of an alternative set of postulates. At an early stage she rejected the use of biological analogies in evolutionary economics (Penrose 1952), together with equilibrium models and the attention in economics to allocative efficiency (Penrose 1952, 1959). She formulates an extensive critique of the orthodox economic theory of the firm, especially the theoretical treatment of resources, factor prices mechanisms and production functions. Her subject matter of managerial expertise and learning connects to contemporary interest in corporate paradigms, firm-specific problem solving, sector recipes, corporate knowledge and much more.

In 1959 the British economist, Joan Robinson, said that the book belonged to a movement in economics which aims to develop a theory that informs us about the role of management in the growth of the firm. Since then only a small number of revisionists have seriously used her theory (e.g. Best 1990) though many more have proclaimed its relevance (e.g. Itami and Roehl 1987) and the pace of citation has increased (e.g. Porter 1991; Nelson 1991; Kay 1993). In 1995 her original book was reprinted.

Penrose draws a sharp contrast between the economist's conception of an objective knowledge as independent, codified and readily transmitted from experiential knowledge. In order to open the black box of the events inside the firm she chooses to highlight the role of tacit, experiential knowledge. Experiential knowledge is essential. The key is to understand learning from experience. This type of expertise is embodied in individuals (as Grant 1995), but also embedded in the interlocked actions and networks that distribute and organise knowledge communities, including their relationships with other individuals and in their collective interpretation of events.[1] Experiential knowledge can only be learnt in specific contexts and is not teachable as codified knowledge in the classroom. Her formulation is not the same as the 'linguistic and cognitive turn' in organisation studies (e.g. March and Simon 1958), yet does share some elements with the Austrian critique of objective knowledge.

Redefining growth and critiquing size

Penrose rejected conventional, taken for granted definitions of growth in terms of increases in assets, sales, numbers employed and similar. She contends that these common-sense definitions of growth are a by-product, the outcome of some internal processes within the firm. Growth defined in those terms leaves the key problem of their generation unexplored. Yet the orthodox economic theory of the firm relied upon those definitions and so there 'is no notion of an internal development leading to cumulative movements in one direction' (1959: 1) and the expansion of the innovating, multi-product firm cannot be explained (1959: 13). According to Penrose, existing definitions of growth looked at the outcome and neglected the processes occurring within the firm.

Her view of size is comparable to Weick (1969: 23–25) who observed that size as measured in numbers, sales and similar is a 'confounded variable' in organisation theory. This point requires some underlining, because a significant collection of organisation studies has used size as a key dimension. The most useful example is the Aston Programme (Pugh and Hickson 1976), but care is needed here. One interpretation of the Aston Programme which is parallel and also different to that of Penrose can be derived from Mindlin (1974) who places increases in size as the outcome from within the framework of the agglomerated impact of structural variables. Mindlin's list of structural variables illustrates the full roster of variables most used in structure studies, yet shows that the role of managerial expertise is not taken as an explanatory framework (Clark 1998). Penrose would have to argue that expertise drives the other variables. In the language of the seminal analysis by Child (1972, 1997), strategic choice is open and is significantly shaped by the actor's frame of reference within the dominant coalition. Penrose would concur, yet develops a theory of actionable knowledge which is quite distinct from the actor's frame of reference of school (e.g. Silverman 1970).

Managerial expertise and receding limits

Penrose develops her own very distinct theory of growth of the firm by defining growth in terms of reducing the limits upon managerial expertise. This theory provides both a surprising definition of growth and also gives the central element to the role of knowledge and experience among entrepreneurs and managers in the growth of the firm. All learning is bound by its immediacy and to the cognitions of the entrepreneurs/managers, so the central problem is to push back the limits. This refers to the extent to which knowledge in the firm has grown and the degree to which the limits on expertise recede for various reasons. She introduces the notion of the receding managerial limit. This means that the growth in expertise causes the limit to recede and the firm extends its domain of influence.

The postulate of receding limits is exciting, yet awkward to apply and to investigate. There are problems. For example, we must presume that if mergers and acquisitions do work then this is because they were within the managerial limit of the firm undertaking the actions. Conversely, failures, and there are many of them, can be partly explained in terms of a lack of required managerial knowledge. Penrose acknowledges that this perspective faces great dangers of tautology. The problem of defining growth in knowledge and the pushing back of limits must be explained. Growth, if it occurs at all, refers to the capabilities of entrepreneurs and managers to extract a collective understanding from their varied experiences in dealing with the internal and external economic situation of the firm.[2] Therefore what is absolutely central is the growth of knowledge and expertise about strategic co-ordination to complement the allocative actions of the market. Penrose maintains that the knowledge which is most relevant to growth can only be acquired through immersion in experiences whose interpretation is tacit and thus not readily codified. The most relevant knowledge is about planning and administration. The knowledge can only be acquired, she argues, by sharing those experiences. It is now clear that 'growth' is being used in a highly specific and novel manner which differs from the definitions which are common in strategy. Penrose does not equate growth with increases in size as measured by numbers of employees or total sales. Those commonly examined features are treated as being problematic and requiring explanation. Neither does growth involve the use of biological analogies such as the life cycle. Those analogies are explicitly rejected (Penrose 1959: 155).

The growth in expertise pushes back the limits and therefore enables several qualitatively different kinds of growth (cf. Child and Kieser 1981).

Services and resources

Penrose separates the resources available to the firm in the form of land, capital and labour from the uses to which that resource may be put. This distinction between resources and their role in providing services is crucial. Her theorising confronts the practice of economics in treating the outcomes of the use of resources as homogeneous across firms. In Penrose, the resources create services and the services are unique. It follows that firms are heterogeneous (Nelson 1991). For Penrose the forces inside the firm which constitute expertise are productive services which define and shape the internal resources of the firm. The key productive services are those 'available from management with experience within the firm' (1959: 5).

Her approach differs from Hofer and Schendel (1978) who adopt a quasi-accounting approach. They follow orthodox quasi-objective views of the value of resources and apply these equally to their distinction between conventional assets such as buildings and equipment and – so-called – invisible assets. They then apply the same principles of value to the so-called invisible assets of reputation, human resources and knowledge. But this is problematic for Penrose because resources are only given value in their role as productive services and then as part of the managerial expertise in a specific firm.

Managerial 'team'

At the apex of the Penrosian firm is a relatively autonomous planning unit with interconnected activities guided by policies established in the court of last resort (1959: 16) which resolves the problems of fine tuning and of adaptation to new circumstances. The autonomous planning unit handles co-ordination and the creation of authoritative communication. Here there is a crucial, only partly explained relationship between the accumulation of expertise and the emergence of a managerial 'team' (her quotation marks) as a set of players who act collectively. So, it is possible for management to acquire significant knowledge and not be able to constitute itself as a team. It is the organising of this collective understanding about planning and administration which creates a managerial team. The boundaries of teamwork among management set the limits to the growth of the firm. The notion of team is placed between quotation marks and is defined tentatively, yet the notion of team is central to the theorising. We are told that the knowledge accumulated by the managerial team is unteachable in the sense meant when listening to or reading orthodox economists (Penrose 1959: 44–49). Consequently, the rate at which new members can gain the requisite experience is limited. Penrose argues it is impossible to achieve a growth in knowledge through writing formal blueprints. From this distinction between the external prices for resources and their unique formation into services, it follows that the external price of managerial resources cannot be equated with their value in the team because they collectively create a unique knowledge within the firm. In effect it is the firm's culture, broadly and heterogeneously defined (Martin 1992), which shapes the productivity of the assets and resources.

External environment: networks and interstices

An important feature of managerial expertise is the image held of the external environment. Here Penrose's theorising anticipates the sociopsychological concepts of subjectively defined environments in the much cited notion of environmental enactment proposed by Weick (1969). She observes that there is likely to be a significant difference between the images of the environment embedded in the firm's specific knowledge and the definition of that environment by economists and other outsiders. Penrose refers to the economist's interpretation as 'objective', but does so in quotation marks. Her meaning can be ascertained from this citation:

> The environment is treated . . . as an 'image' in the entrepreneur's mind of the possibilities and restrictions with which he is confronted; whether experience confirms expectations is another story . . . the 'direction of expansion' . . . can be analysed with reference to the relationship between its resources and its own view of the competitive position.
>
> (Penrose 1959: 5)

The environment is treated as an image in the mind of the entrepreneur because this is the environment which is relevant to the entrepreneur's decisions (1959: 215). This reinterpretation of the economist's objective environment is reflected in the comments about the relationship between the firm-specific knowledge and demand levels. Penrose (1959: 80) observes that we shall find that 'demand' is no more important, and is possibly less important, than the existing resources because the really enterprising entrepreneur often takes the demand not as a 'given' but rather as something he ought to do something about.

Penrose highlights the difference between her conception of the relationship between the growth in the firm's knowledge and growth in size through mergers and acquisitions. As indicated earlier, she is well aware of the dangers of tautology and this problem does arise in her examination of General Motors. It follows from her theory of the firm that the existence of a large complex firm like General Motors with a record of diversification and acquisition can only be explained by arguing that the receding managerial limit has been pushed further and further into the distance. With respect to acquisitions and mergers she observes:

> Techniques for decentralising administrative organisation have been developed to a fine point, and the task of central management is apparently not one of attempting to comprehend and run the entire organisation, but rather to intervene in a few crucial areas and to set the 'tone' of the organisation. Operating control is affected largely through accounting devices which, to be sure, are highly centralised, but which place the task of co-ordination in an entirely different framework, and incidentally permit the use of extensively mechanised techniques in carrying it out.
>
> (Penrose 1959: 18–19)

This interpretation would surely be contested by Johnson and Kaplan (1987) in the review of twentieth-century American usage of accounting methods.

Penrose examines the paradox of competition, noting the existence then of inter-firm alliances and knowledge pooling. The relationship between large firms defined in terms of size and smaller firms is shaped by the spaces which the larger firms leave around their areas of agency. Small firms, in her analyses, typically occupy the spaces left by and to some degree shaped by the larger firms. Smaller firms inhabit the interstices rather than some open terrain.

Services as capabilities

Penrose's use of experiential knowledge suggests various areas in which it may be cumulated. Five may be noted:

1   Through understanding of the environment, experiential knowledge has to identify and define market niches which are viable and sustainable to provide the firm with revenue.
2   The firm must develop services and products which are appropriate to the chosen niches in the market.
3   The firm has to develop managerial services for handling the basic operating cycle of the firm. This may be a weekly pattern, as in retail, or much longer in the provision of specialist goods.
4   In order to survive beyond the founding period and the immediate, local context the firm has to develop managerial services which cope with the longer term and which apprehend changes in all areas. This is the area of innovation-design.
5   The firm has to develop services which underpin internal authoritative communication and also articulate with interests and values in the relevant external environment.

Cumulated experiential knowledge is extensive and neglected in most analyses.

Achievements and limits

The main achievements of Penrose are in setting the agenda and providing a benchmark against which subsequent theorising can be compared.

First, with respect to tacit knowledge and expertise Penrose was a forerunner of those who placed the content of expertise and corporate paradigms as a core feature in explaining strategic directions and tracks. The dichotomy between tacit and codified is less significant in the long run than the theory of growth and of receding limits. There is now a considerable literature on organisational knowledge in terms of recipe knowledge, paradigms, frames, sector recipes, learning spirals, C-space, modes of rationality and rules of practice. Some of these developments show how complex is the agenda and the many branches developed to refine it: especially, for example, studies of the degree to which managerial expertise can be translated into procedures, raw materials, buildings/equipment and into products (Thevenot 1984). However, many of the developments lack an explicit concern with how the content of the knowledge can be related to corporate action. It is here that the notion of receding limits directs attention towards the dynamics of their use and towards comparing expertise between firms. As yet, this is relatively underdeveloped.

Second, the role of intra-firm networks in strategic co-ordination has been neglected because of the focus upon structure/process and the debates about hierarchy. Penrose was insufficiently political in her analysis of teams. Her analysis of teamwork hints at the problems arising from intra-managerial politics, but requires considerable amplification. The politics of organisational decision making has been established since the studies of intra-managerial struggles reported by Dalton (1959); the seminal analysis of managerial concerns for status and careers by Burns and Stalker (1961) and Pettigrew's (1973) politics of decision making. Each of these early studies adopted a view of the organisation as potentially divided and as precariously integrated.

Third, the external analyst who wishes to assess the strategic capabilities of any firm requires the discovery of analytic procedures which either model the firm's expertise or are relevant proxies for the knowledge in action. The implications to Penrosian learning of Schumpeter's theory of creative destruction are undeveloped. In her determination to show biological models of growth are limited she misses the opportunity to examine how the former reduction of limits can be reversed. Also, Penrose does not take into account the institutional influences upon managerial expertises (Powell and DiMaggio 1991) or the likelihood that managerial expertise is nationally shaped. Nor is attention given to the borrowing of learning or the development of expert systems (Giddens 1991).

RESOURCE-BASED STRATEGIC THEORY

Key problems

Grant states that organisational routines, especially their analytic development by Nelson and Winter (1982), provide the key linkages. The problematic nature of this proposition has already been introduced in Chapter 5. Grant comes close to adopting a constructivist, computer analogy which is unsuited to analysing organisational processes. This problem will be examined more fully in the next chapter with attention to the concept of recurrent action patterns. Which are the major problems with the resource based solution? Four related problems may be noted.

The first problem concerns the weight given to the internal factors compared to external factors in strategic theory. Strategy as a discipline has experienced a number of shifts in emphasis since Andrews's (1971) influential recipe. Two major shifts can be detected. First, and very much in the management science tradition, Hofer and Schendel (1978) used special conferences and edited collections to reformulate the orthodox architecture of the discipline from the late 1970s into the late 1980s. Their model contained six areas of analyses each connected through feedback loops. Hofer and Schendel depicted the ideal, linear, rational, multi-stage decision process, yet included a key footnote which emphasised that real strategic decision making was iterative, convoluted and boundedly rational. This provided the platform for a series of further developments, especially in the Porterian contribution. However, the growth of influence from economic reasoning (e.g. resource based approach) and the quite different impacts of explaining the success of non-American firms introduced new issues on the agenda.

Second, a new series of conferences at the close of the 1980s provided a strong sketch with radically different implications to the earlier Hofer–Schendel framework. This thinking was initially edited by Rumelt *et al.* (1991) and known as RST. Rumelt and colleagues articulated and stimulated major new thinking that when connected to parallel developments in organisational theory suggests a different analytic route to that of the bold hypothesis.

The second problem concerns organisational learning in general and the incomplete analysis of formative, contextual learning. Levinthal and March (1993) note that there is a 'rediscovery of organisational learning as a major issue'. In fact, organisational learning was central to the very early work of the Carnegie School (e.g. Dill 1962). In the rediscovery that early perspective was overpowered in strategic management by the search for organisational intelligence as a competence of calculative rationality. This led into an overoptimistic account of the plasticity of corporate capabilities (Clark and Staunton 1989; Rumelt 1995) and into an assumption that strategic analysts possessed discursive penetration: that is, their analysis is sufficient to design both the architecture of the firm and its actions. Levinthal and March state that this new literature on organisational learning is very limited because in the real world experiences are ambiguous and situated in a conflicting and competing agenda while also being embedded in the political struggle between historicised knowledge and any search for new knowledge. Given that the actions of an actor are embedded in an ecology of actions spanning the firm and its contexts, then it is difficult to understand what is happening and what might unfold. There are so many sources of limitations to discursive penetration that it is more prudent to commence from the myopia of learning. This contends that the interpretation of experience mainly proceeds through the two mechanisms of simplification and specialisation. The consequence of these mechanisms varies according to the tightness/looseness of the organisation, but in general terms learning tends to inhibit long-term actions and mainly searches for the ingredients of alternative actions in a limited number of locations. Moreover, future learning tends to be embraced – positively and negatively – by the cumulated learning (Levinthal and Cohen 1989). Organisational learning constantly faces the problems of ambiguity, ignorance and conflictual situations.

The notion of a formative context which shapes corporate learning was central to the examination of 'Competition Between Contexts' (Part II) and is implicit in Porter's (1990) account of the influence of the home base and the possible role of the formative context in placing institutional demands on the firm. Penrosian learning rightly seeks to express social processes through appropriate analogies. Her notion of the receding limits to managerial expertise and her account of expertise about the context are major contributions. However, their fit with the bold hypothesis is loose and somewhat contradictory.

The third with organisational routines.

The fourth problem concerns difficulties in the use of Penrosian learning and with the view of knowledge.

This section addresses the problems and indicates how they are addressed in the next four chapters. Figure 11.2 sets out the relationship between this chapter

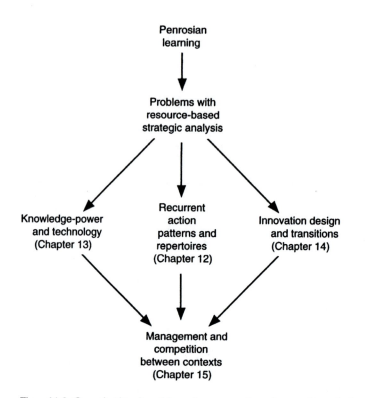

Figure 11.2 Organisational problems in resource-based strategic analysis

and the next three and then how the final chapter draws the analysis together. Chapter 12 examines recursiveness in organisations and the revisions which it introduces into the static resource based view. Chapter 13 restates the incomplete aspects of Penrosian knowledge with respect to the central feature of design and innovation in firms. Chapter 14 theorises the role of management in assembling practices. Chapter 15 draws together the competition between contexts and the dynamics of organisations in action.

SUMMARY

The resource based theory of strategy as proposed and developed by Grant (1990, 1998) is fruitful in defining the analytic problems and has illustrated the power of economic reasoning within the purposive, analytic notion of strategy. Equally, some important limitations are now evident.[3]

NOTES

1 I have inserted this stress upon knowledge communities (see Chapter 4).
2 Penrose is obscure about the politics of decision-making and of the struggles of governance within the firm. Her analysis is limited on the politics of decision-making (cf. Burns and Stalker 1961). It is necessary to note that she expressly implies that management is able politically to utilise the expertise.
3 Scarborough (1998) provides a critical view of the resource based approach.

12 Contingent recurrent action patterns and repertoires

INTRODUCTION

We start from the position explained in Part II that firms are embedded and shaped by their national contexts and that the contexts vary in the capabilities which inhere. The typical variety of sectoral clusters in a national context is part of the stratified reality within which firms exist. Moreover, the context contains those multinational businesses and sectoral clusters that affect the action of any focal firms in our analysis. Contexts imply zones of manoeuvre. Likewise firms have zones of manoeuvre within those contexts. The zones of manoeuvre for the firm also depend upon the capabilities in its repertoire and the political capacity of the firm's constitution to action those capabilities.

The previous chapter expressed scepticism about those approaches to strategy that ignore the stratified reality of the context and the finite, actual capabilities of the firm. The analytic problem is therefore one of developing a processual perspective and its key concepts with appropriate analogies and exemplars. The task is to unravel the process perspective on 'in action' by going beyond the familiar injunctions to be longitudinal, historical and in 'real-time'. My argument is that the open system perspectives in organisation analysis have so far provided a limited roster of guidelines and illustrative materials because the issue of temporality and the production of space in which permanencies agglomerate has been neglected. In this chapter the main sections are:

- event cycles and temporality;
- structural pose or recurrent action patterns;
- distributed activity systems;
- repertoires and their activation.

This chapter starts by considering the extent to which the social anthropological approach of reconstructing the recursiveness of action will reveal patterns within organisational flux and process which can be the basis for an analytic approach (cf. Pugh and Hickson 1976). This line of enquiry has potential connections to the earlier discussion by organisational economists of the usefulness of recurrent action patterns. To illustrate the theme of recurrent action patterns in a sociological approach, the key exhibit will be from my studies of the operation of sugar beet factories and the persistence of a particular repertoire of recurrent action patterns over a period of more than a generation. The chapter will close by outlining a theory of repertoires and their activation and point to its implication for the organic/mechanistic debate. The theory of repertoire activation incorporates elements previously highlighted for their relevance to organisations in action: organisational routines, recurrent action patterns and procedural memory; the habitus and organisational field from Bourdieu; the role of conversation as mechanism in the activation of the repertoire.

For analytic purposes this chapter addresses the requirements of reproduction rather than transformation. The emphasis is upon the tension between tendencies towards inertia and dissolution. The purpose is to confront the implicit claim noted in the bold hypothesis of the previous chapter about the inherent rationality of organisation design. Hence the emphasis given to organisational routines and recurrent action patterns. Reproduction will involve considerable variety and oscillations as well as facing the potential of dislocation. A distinction is drawn between:

- action in/of organisations which is the outcome of ongoing struggles yet retains pre-existing mechanisms, repertoires;
- the transformation of those features.

The capacity of an organisation to deploy a variety of recurrent action patterns and structural forms is expressed in the notion of its repertoire (Clark 1985; Clark and Staunton 1989: 183–189) and these are the firm-specific knowledges. The metaphor of repertoire will be central. No repertoire of structural poses and recurrent action patterns = no organisation = no organising.

The problem of the scope and richness of the repertoire is illustrated by Burton Clark's (1998) analysis of the major problems facing the modern university and his observation that pre-existing repertoires provide powerful internal challenges to the capacities of the required repertoire. The challenges include the increasing number of students combined with a falling unit of resource to provision the educational process. At the same time external stakeholders (e.g. future employers) are creating labour markets of specialised knowledge at the interface with the universities. University departments face an apparent explosion in the production of new knowledge and its supply. Universities face complexity and uncertainty. They appear to respond by becoming over-extended and under-focused. Burton Clark suggests that universities should become more entrepreneurial by simultaneously strengthening the steering mechanism at the centre with the selection of academics and administrators while also developing a periphery of boundary spanning units drawing upon diverse sources of funding. Schools within the university will need to combine teaching and research with the integration and application of knowledge.

This chapter addresses the array of issues originally raised by Burns and Stalker (1961) but not fully developed since, despite many significant contributions. Burns and Stalker raised the issues of contextual shaping, especially national influences on competitiveness and of how to handle history and temporality (see 1966: Preface) when acknowledging the influence of pre-existing forms of structuring on future action. Chapter 13 will examine the conditions under which transformations unfold irrespective of whether they are favourable to the future of the organisation.

EVENT CYCLES AND TEMPORALITY: WEICK OR KATZ AND KAHN?

Pugh and Hickson (1976: 1) claim that processes are too varied to provide a systematic basis for understanding organisations. This section will seek to qualify and refute that claim. The notions of event cycles, recursiveness and temporality are integral to process (Clark 1985). The view of process developed in this chapter has certainly been influenced by Elias's contention that the analyses of social processes require the choice of analogies and metaphors based on social processes and certainly not the imposition of analogies from the natural and biological sciences. Following that injunction requires the development of exemplars and a specific lexicon of concepts related to the exemplars. This section mainly examines the approach suggested by Weick (1969, 1979).

David Harvey (1989, 1996) explains the process perspective as flows and their agglomeration into permanencies like cities and firms that depend for their continuity upon the reproduction of the flows and upon some self-organising features. Perhaps the most cited notion is that of event cycles as characterised by Katz and Kahn (1966). However, there are few examples of the application of their approach even in their own extensive material. One might imagine that the kibbutz and its future was an ideal topic (e.g. Golomb and Katz 1974) for event cycles, but even that study lacks a rigorous application, thereby illustrating the extent of the problem.

Understanding organisational processes requires a more thorough development of temporality in the firm (Moore 1963; Thompson 1967; Clark 1975, 1985; Hassard 1996). Developing an exquisite sense of temporality requires a minimum set of analytical tools (Weick 1969). Although the temporality of the clock and the calendar are each central to modern time calculation and practice they are insufficient to account for temporality (Moore 1963; Clark 1985; Thrift 1996; Clark 1998).

In 1969 Weick launched a cool attack on the theorising and observational competencies of the disciplinary community of organisation behaviour and simultaneously outlined an alternative direction. Since then, in a succession of articles, books (e.g. Weick 1979) and extended essays (e.g. Weick 1995), the Weickian programme has been elaborated. It is fashionable to claim that the Weickian challenge on how to analyse organisational processes has been taken up even though his thinking is not the mainstream (Czarniawska 1998) and occupies such a quiet place in organisation theory and design (e.g. Daft 1997). Weick claims that an exquisite sensitivity to time is essential to processual analysis (1969: 64f).

Weick's approach is about organising from a mainly sociopsychological perspective and starts with the critique of existing studies followed by the revised theory. Weick's (1969, 1979) critique of organisation theory argued that organisation theory was too heavily based in anecdotal case studies which were situation specific, ahistorical, tacitly prescriptive and one-sidedly favouring managerial short-term interests (1969: 18). Weick, like Pugh (1966: 243), argued that the usefulness of a theory is not defined in terms of pragmatics (1969: 20) because there is insufficient analytic description of organisational action (1969: 103). However, in a crucial few pages, Weick reasoned that 'size is a confounded variable' (1969: 23–25) because it is a misleading starting point for understanding the relationship between process and structure (cf. Pugh and Hickson 1976: 1). More passionately Weick argued that the term 'organisational behaviour' does not sensitise the investigator and directs attention away from the key mechanisms associated with organisational repertoires, their content and the conditions under which they control attention (1969: 26) and added that 'too little attention has been paid to actions and too much to cognitions, plans and beliefs' (1969: 30).

Weick introduced the notion of the enacted environment in order to develop the study of action: organisations define and respond to their own collectively and self-constructed environment. The environment requires careful specification to acknowledge that the human actors create the environment to which they then adapt (1969: 64). The enacted environment is a crucial concept and its analysis requires an exquisite understanding of time (1969: 64f), in part because future perfect time (Schutz 1967) is so poorly understood. Enactment is only loosely structured (1969: 71). The enacted environment was linked to the evolutionary theory from Campbell (1965) and Weick's own interpretation of systems theory. Underlying this critique of established organisational theory was the implication that even the highly regarded statement of open systems theory by Katz and Kahn (1966: 20f) as the structure of events (Allport 1962) remained substantially undeveloped. Weick's intention is to deliver a theoretically significant perspective on organising based on socio-evolutionary theory (Campbell 1965) and open, loosely coupled, systems thinking. Weick implicitly sought to move the analogy of system up from the middle to the top of Boulding's nine-level scale.

Weick (1969, 1979) set out the analytic features of the proposed approach in which an 'organisation is the way it runs through the process of organising' (1969: 90). It is useful to think of Weick's bridging between his own vision of systems thinking and Garfinkel's analysis of rule making. This leads into a demanding list of eight analytic elements:

1   Processes recur and unfold only if repetitiveness is continually accomplished. Processes do not just happen, they have to be accomplished by relationships in which control is prominent.
2   Organising is accomplished through many recurrent processes within a collective structure of interlocked actions (1969: 43). A collective structure

consists of interstructured behaviours and individuals are partially, not wholly, included. There are families of interlocked behaviours.

3   It is the perceptual sets – the ready-made explanations – which constitute the attentional processes and are the crucial determinant of organising. An organisation can reconcile flexibility and stability through either alternation and/or their simultaneous expression in different parts of the organisation.

4   Organisation operates with informational inputs which are ambiguous, uncertain and equivocal. This view of indexicality is drawn from Garfinkel (1967) and is blended with the Law of Requisite Variety (Ashby 1956) which states that equivocality varies and that systems must (in order to survive) match their capacity to handle equivocality with the level of equivocality in the context.

5   Weick amends Campbell's theory of evolution to state that there are choice points and that haphazard variation is less likely to be prominent in socio-cultural evolution (1969: 61). Three processes are responsible for evolution: variation, selection and retention (1969: 54–58). Variations occur and various mechanisms operate either to select or reject the variations. Retention refers to the process of storing behaviours. Retention may select inconsistent behaviours. The retention system is subject to editing.

6   The constitution of the control system is a pattern of conditionalities within any pattern of relationships. Organisations do possess order and continuity without consensus on goals because rationality is about making sense of what has been, not what will be (1969: 38).

7   Weick postulates the existence of rules by which processes are constructed (1969: 73). These rules can be invoked and once invoked they assemble elements from the relevant pool of interlocked behaviours. Therefore the rules are implicitly labelled. All information coming into an organisation encounters an internal array of rules representing the organisation's capacity to encode and interpret the equivocality (1969: 77, Figure 2). The information is enacted and rules are used to assemble a process containing a number of interlocked rules.

8   Given that there are many processes, the issue arises of how they are connected (1969: Chapter 7). Weick makes a clear use of causal mapping and connected flow charts to produce causal networks for situations which are recurring. Richardson (1991) notes that there are technical problems with the balance of negatives and positives in the models shown, but the analytic intention is praised. Finally, Weick considers situations in which external ecological change might disrupt (or not) established recursiveness. The full model (1969: 93) provides a clear attempt to model processes in an evolutionary framework.

This Weickian model is very different to that proposed by Katz and Kahn (1966) and in drawing the implications of the proposed model Weick exposes the problems in the pro-participation theories then dominating organisational psychology. Weick proposed an approach to process and action rather than to structure and behaviour. His theory of organising highlights considerable self-reproducing and self-regulating and there is an implicit anticipation of autopoetic theories. Organising is based on a consensually validated grammar containing a set of negotiated recipes and rules for building organisational processes. Weickian approaches require a systematic account of the rules and the shared sense of appropriate procedures. The consensually validated grammar is used to reduce the equivocality in puzzling situations and events and to activate interlocked behaviour so that organisational practices are assembled (Weick 1979; Giddens 1984; Reed 1992).

STRUCTURAL POSE AND RECURRENT ACTION PATTERNS

Structural pose format

Three social anthropological studies provide the ingredients for exploring the persistence of processes and relevance of the concept of structural pose to describing and analysing recursiveness:

- Mauss (1904) on the Eskimo;
- Evans-Pritchard (1940) on the Nuer's year;
- Gearing (1958) on the structural poses of the Cherokee Indian village in the seventeenth century.

My purpose here is to use one social example rather than a non-social analogy as the analogy for the notion of a configuration of relationships, positions and roles in another setting: the organisation. So, although there are well-known dangers in transferring concepts from different settings, these provide a more analytically secure base than abstract analogies such as the swimming pool robot. Intriguingly this section depicts a time-space trajectory as a pattern of events.

Mauss (1904)

Mauss (1904) reconstructed the annual migrations of the Eskimo from various accounts in order to demonstrate that they possess at least two quite different forms of social organisation and that each form possesses a distinctive temporality. His purpose was to explain their social morphology – their recurrent distribution of activities and actions through time and space. In winter the objects of food were the seals and these were concentrated. The Eskimo lived in stone-walled and snow houses that were connected by tunnels so everyone was close-by and there was very slight dispersal. The habitat was occupied by a number of families spread through the generations. It was used for assembly and for all the social functions which were part of a very intense collective social life. By contrast, in summer the objects of food were dispersed and the Eskimo dispersed themselves over wide areas which they traversed. Their habitat was the cone-shaped tent made from poles and skins held in place by stones. The tent was occupied by a single family who used the habitat for eating and sleeping. There was a strong feeling of social isolation with a sense of danger, despite their knowledge of the environment.

Mauss was not a geographical determinist. The Eskimo do synchronise their social organisation with the changing configuration of the physical environment and the available sources of food. There is co-evolution between the Eskimo problem solving and the capabilities of the frequently frozen context. The social technology mediates that synchronising. There are two distinct social rhythms. In the winter the social life is heightened. Mauss suggests that the Eskimo have developed collective rules and temporal signs for organising and synchronising their activities. Mauss claimed (1904: 127f) that these (seasonal) variations could be found in early twentieth-century Europe, yet they were not recognised. The contribution of Mauss influenced Durkheim's account of time and also Braudel's (1972) claims about the hidden, deep mentalities which structure civilisations. Mauss (not surprisingly) tended to emphasise the continuity and gave rather minimal attention to disruption and the mechanisms of reproduction (Clark 1975a: 19). However, he did provide a sketch of persisting patterns of activities and actions.

Evans-Pritchard (1940)

The reconstruction of the Nuer annual migrations by Evans-Pritchard (1940) provides a much more informed and extensive illustration of continuity. Evans-Pritchard makes explicit reference to the time dimension by showing how everyday events at different stages of the cycle provide the markers used in chronological codes. The analysis of the Nuer annual migrations reveals contrasts between the wet (March/September) and dry (September/March) periods. In the rainy period the rivers become flooded and the food source is from horticulture. The Nuer live in villages and their life has a high eventness with frequent feasts, ceremonies and dances. The sequence and timing of daily tasks is very similar and stable so there are few problems of tribal co-ordination. Daily timekeeping is less uniform, less precise and makes greater use of the lunar movements to calculate the passing of time. By contrast, in the drought and dry period they live in camps and the main food sources are fish and cattle. Although the sequence of daily tasks is stable, their timing is varied and there are more problems of co-ordination. The social life is much less eventful. Daily timekeeping is more uniform and precise and there is a decline in the use of the moon for time reckoning. Evans-Pritchard concludes that the Nuer use moving configurations of regular events in the environment (e.g. clouds, appearance of plants) and the movement of animals and birds to calculate the ending of one season and the starting of the next. The Nuer scan for signs. He hints at a transitional period from one season to the next. Most importantly he begins to explain and describe some of temporal mechanisms, social frameworks and Nuer frames of reference. Evans-Pritchard explores how the Nuer experience different durations within the annual cycle. Nuer conceptions of the past are anchored in events within the development of kin networks.

Gearing (1958)

Gearing's (1958) reconstruction of the annual round of time for the eighteenth-century Cherokee Indian village utilises and demonstrates the structural pose as an analytic device. Changes in the structural pose provide insight into the key transitional periods within the annual round of life for the Cherokee and manage to illustrate some of the individual tensions which were likely to have occurred. Given that human communities of all kinds do rearrange themselves through time and space to accomplish various distributed activities, then how does the concept of the structural pose provide analytic leverage? The social structure of any organisation or grouping typically is a plural set of positional, interstructured relationships and role sets (Nadel 1957; Clark 1975b, 1985). Social structures shift according to the tasks, which are often stable and recursive when examined over the period of a decade or a generation. There are various combinations of organised groups that come into being and then dissolve while undertaking various activities. Within the Cherokee there was positional and role differentiation based upon gender and age. In addition there were positions based on membership of specific, matrilocal kinship groups. Men moved from being boys, to young man and then beloved man with parallel female positions. These biographical features penetrated everywhere and were taken for granted dispositional systems. Men of certain ages hunted and warred while women cooked, raised infants and undertook local horticulture. Both sexes were involved in ceremonies, although men undertook the major responsibilities. These gender- and age-based positions did not seem to conflict.

The four basic structural poses shown in Figure 12.1 provided the normative, regulative and cognitive pillars of Cherokee life throughout the year. Figure 12.1 sets out the sequence of structural poses assumed by males in the annual rhythm of Cherokee social structure. There are four major structural poses:

- for ceremonials and councils as well as for agriculture: these events occur at more or less fixed points during the year;
- for war, for negotiations and for ball games: these events are variable within the fixed seasons;
- for the regulation of marriage and for revenge against another clan within the Cherokee: these events occur at unpredictable times;
- for hunting and for general household matters: these events are variable, but within fixed seasons.

As shown in Figure 12.1 there is a trajectory involving periods when particular structural poses are activated and used, followed by transitional periods. This trajectory reveals a man's typical year and even hints at the life course associated with changes in age.

These three examples each illustrate recursive processes that were stable over longish periods of time: decades, generations and possibly centuries. Figure 12.1 might seem like the time-space trajectory of the robot cleaner in the modern

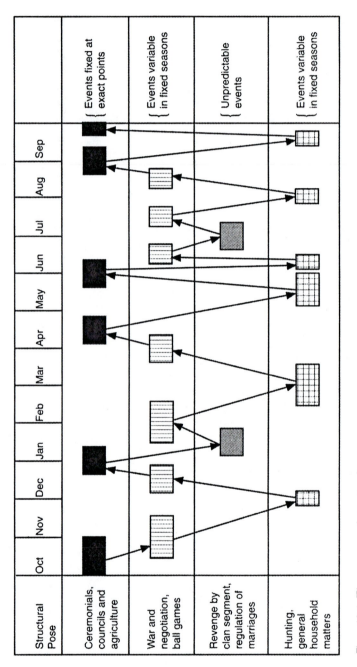

Figure 12.1 Time-space and structural poses
Source: Gearing (1958).

swimming pool, but there are crucial differences. Although these social phenomena – according to our perspective – possess stable relationships with seemingly law-like patterns with regularities and sequences we need to reconstruct the mechanisms and causal structures that constitute the patterns (Harre 1979; Miles and Huberman 1984; Sayer 1992: Figure 12).

Two further questions arise. First, to what extent might analogous configurations be found in modern firms? Can the claim of Mauss (1904) and the spirited speculation of Etzioni (1961) on the successive division of compliance be applied in an organisational setting? The claim here is that recursiveness and the temporal, sequential division of work organisation is ubiquitous and consequential. Second, the structural pose obviously contains agglomerations of the shared routines mentioned in Chapter 5. The issue here is whether structural poses, routines or recurrent action patterns (see next section) provide the best analytic leverage. The next section notes that there is a preference among some evolutionary economists to replace the concept of organisational routines with that of recurrent action patterns.

Recurrent action patterns

The concept of routines has been used widely in the behavioural theory of the firm and in evolutionary economics as discussed in Chapter 5. Organisation routines are exclusively about organisational routines, not individual routines. The basic features of individual routines were outlined in March and Simon (1958) and then given a distinctly organisational format by Cyert and March (1963). Organisational routines involve the interlocked actions which are constituted from the partial involvement of individuals as proposed by Weick (1969). The basic features of organisational routines compatible with recurrent action patterns as a concept include:

- patterned sequences of actions that are repeated;
- co-ordinated by communication and authority;
- distributed among several actors;
- in interlocked role sets;
- knowledge is tacit and unarticulated;
- routines are situated and emergent.

These are more than standard operating procedures because the latter are explicit rules. They are the fundamental building blocks without which organisations would not exist.

Recently the wide variety of usages of the concept of routines has been reviewed and refined in a revised formulation has been by Cohen *et al.* (1996). Organisational economists contend that there has been very little advance in basic theory since Cyert and March (1963). The conclusion is that routines are still a useful concept, but that the notion of recurring action patterns provides much more analytic leverage on the recursive features of organisations in action.

March and Simon (1958) stated that individual routines are easy to research, but Cohen *et al.* (1996) report that organisational routines are awkward to research (Cohen *et al.* 1996). Organisational routines have proved to be less easy to investigate in actual firms than implied by March and Simon because the analytic unit does not readily sit in either the micro-level economic studies nor yet into the anthropological studies of organisations. Because organisational routines are hard to grasp, the design of organisations based on routines is rarely reported by academics and the academic theories of design rarely start with routines as a fundamental building block (Clark 1972). However, the building of recurrent action patterns into organisational life is undertaken in many organisational settings ranging from the military to the early cloning of the McDonald's outlet (Clark and Staunton 1989: 96–102).

There has been only slight advance in the basic theory because the concept of routine has often been used to mop up the residuals of rationality as a post hoc explanation of the non-rational aspects (Cohen and Bacdayan 1994: 556). Examining routines and recurrent action patterns means understanding action which is distributed across space, involves a multiplicity of actors of whom some may be absent-present within a context (e.g. aircraft landing) involving an episode of time for which starts and finishes have to be established. Because recurrent action patterns unfold as patterned sequences of action learned in specific settings, there is an emergent character and a range of variability in their specific content at any one episode. Moreover, describing recurrent action patterns requires the access to and understanding of several actors whose activities will involve considerable tacit, non-verbal knowledge gained from cognitive apprenticeships (Lave and Wenger 1991). Recurrent action patterns contain the history-specific and firm-specific idiosyncratic elements – as frequently repeated action sequences – representing both the pace and efficiency of the firm. Equally, they contain the inertial elements and habitus that sets the zone of manoeuvre for future changes in the repertoire and in the performance of the firm. That is why their description and analysis is so awkward and yet they seem to represent a keystone in the architecture of the firm.

Cohen and Bacdayan (1994) suggest that routines and recurrent action patterns are not associated with the storage of facts, propositions and events as in declarative memory, but are associated with the procedural memory that stores the cognitive and motor elements of skilled actions (1994: 557; Figure 1). Procedural memory is where people can learn and demonstrate improved performance. It is more durable and less subject to decay while also being less accessible to explicit learning or to transfer between settings. So memory lasts of how to solve problems of a particular type. People forget rules of grammar, yet can distinguish grammatical sentences. The link from procedural memory to organisational routines was established through experiments which involved many actions within which a sequence occurred on about one-fourth of the occasions. That sequence was done with increasing reliability and speed in joint behaviour. However, if the procedural memory confronts novelties then switching of skills requires the much slower activation of propositions from declarative memory and this is dramatically slower (1994: 566). The procedural character of information-processing routines limits the ability of organisational members to remember because firms are not frictionless reflections of their momentary environments, but are frequently highly inertial repertoires. In cases of organisational change the procedural memory slows the pace of change, but if those involved are made 'more conscious of their current practices then this may facilitate change' (1994: 566).

The preference of economists studying dynamic capabilities[1] is to define routines as 'an executable capability for repeated performance in some context that has been learned in response to selective pressure'. A capability may be characterised as the capacity to generate action, to guide an unfolding action sequence that has been 'stored' in some distributed form. Context is a significant part of the process of remembering and is therefore a source of shaping to the unfolding action and hence the non-social context (e.g. artefacts) can play an important role. There is a variety of 'forces' which operate to make a sequence of action more likely. These are the selective pressures. This definition lays stress upon the replicators and agrees with the claim of Nelson (1991) that firms will find it easier to transfer their routines abroad than other firms will find it to copy them. The concept of recurring action patterns seems to be wider than most evolutionary economists prefer.

Units of analysis

The choice as unit of analysis between structural pose and recurrent action patterns needs to be considered in relation to the necessity to explicate organisations in action while also connecting to a variety of purposes in analysis. The structural pose obviously contains many collections of recurrent action patterns. The latter taken alone may be of contingent value to organisational designers, yet requires anchoring in communities of practice (see Chapter 14).

DISTRIBUTED ACTIVITY SYSTEMS: SUGAR BEET

This section provides an example of a contemporary work situation characterised by recursiveness among its activity systems that are distributed through the annual calendar. The example has been chosen because it illustrates temporal differentiation and distribution of activities. The specific instance refers to the operating level of the British sugar beet industry. The original research was undertaken in the 1960s over three years and followed through with periodic visits over the next three decades. The original patterning largely remained in place for a generation and was only radically transformed recently. Thus, contrary to the claims of Pugh and Hickson (1976: 1) about flux and process it is possible to detect and research durable, sequential and durational patterns (Clark 1975a, 1985). The analytically structured narrative shows the possibilities for applying the notion of structural poses containing recurrent actions and patterns.

Sugar – since its discovery – has been and is a key ingredient in the diet of western societies. The seventeenth-century development of cane sugar in the West Indies was part of the triangle of wealth creation which linked North West Europe to North Africa and the sugar plantations (Wallerstein 1979). The sugar trade was an integral part of struggles between European nations. In the nineteenth century various nations experimented with the domestic growth of sugar beet as an alternative source. In the 1870s the British firm, Tate & Lyle, imported beet sugar from the Austro-Hungarian Empire. It was then discovered that the British soils and climate provided ideal conditions. A processing factory was opened at Norwich in 1912, but the nascent industry struggled even though the farmers' lobby (National Farmers' Union) was very active in pushing out Tate & Lyle. In 1925 the government provided guaranteed price protection for ten years and there was a burst of growth in factories. From 1936 until Britain's entry into the European Economic Union the domestic industry was handled through the state-owned British Sugar Corporation. Then the setting of European quotas and requirements led to the privatisation of the industry.

One of the defining features of sugar beet processing is that factories operate for less than one-third of the year (October until January) after which the factory is closed down and refurbished. There is a durable recursive pattern alternating between 100–120 days of sugar processing and 265–245 days of refurbishment. The length of time for processing the sugar beet depends upon the state of the crop, but the variations from 100–120 days can be largely anticipated through quotas and satellite monitoring of the crop. Sugar beet factories are one of the clearest examples of the variability of activity which characterises most work organisations. The same workforce operates and refurbishes the factories. Their forms of organisation move regularly between mechanistic in the operating period to organic management systems for refurbishment within the annual cycle (Clark 1974a, b, 1985). The processes, like those already referred to in non-industrial societies, remained relatively stable with some oscillations for more than a generation.

Figure 12.2 overviews the key chunks of recurrent action patterns and events within the annual cycle. The period when the factory is processing sugar beet – known as the campaign – is one in which the workforce is distributed across the shifts and factories are running 24 hours per day continuously. The campaign is handled by the introduction of a structural pose containing many recurrent action patterns.

Factories start processing on a given, deadline data. Before the start there is a strong sense of excitement for most of the employees. Several key events occur in the same period. One of the politically significant events is the unilateral allocation by senior management of the workforce to positions in the factory which are in the form of job ladders. The gaining of a higher position is based on management's interpretation of the contributions made by the employee during the refurbishment as well as performance in the previous campaign. The position on the job ladder precisely indicates advancement and defines the pay level. In this period before the start-up there is a sense of anticipation because of changes in relationships among the workforce as well as between them and their families.

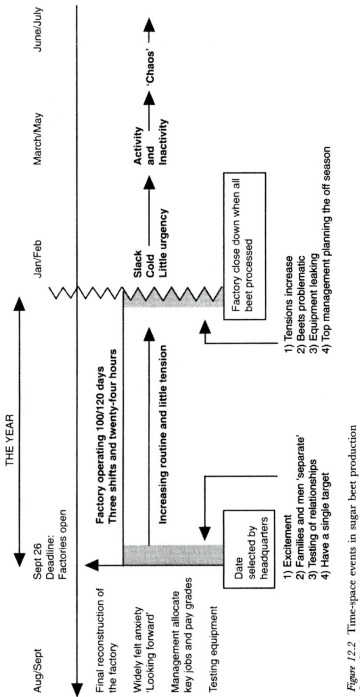

Figure 12.2 Time-space events in sugar beet production
Source: Clark (1985).

Shift working interacts with family life. The management and engineering staff are also very focused and watching for all kinds of small signs indicating that the factory will function perfectly without leaks – very sticky – and shows a robustness. The management have to reorient themselves and everyone else into the interface with the farmers and the logistics of collecting and delivering beet into the reception areas. Rules have to be re-established, especially those governing the measurement and quality of deliveries because these determine payments to the farmers.

Once the campaign is underway there is an increasing sense of routine and a degree of boredom for operators which is mingled with a strong sense of control by management. This continues into the Christmas period and the New Year. By then the factory is being tested and the quality of the beet might have fallen. Even though tensions increase, the senior management tend to leave everyday running to the younger management while they focus upon the details of what has to be accomplished in the period of refurbishment. For senior management and engineers this planning not only relates to incremental innovation, but also has to accommodate any major innovations in technology and/or work organisation. The experienced management are anticipating that the end of the campaign will bring about a significant shift in relationships. The notion of a transitional period which has to be managed is everyday for experienced managements though not always seen in a similar way by the less experienced management.

Once the factory stops production there is a tendency for a period of indulgency to unfold. The workforce is relatively stable and so is familiar with both this indulgency and its limits. There is a gradual and definite shift in roles which for some individuals brings reversals in power and authority and for most individuals involves working in small groups which are both self-organising and also involved in migrations from one set of tasks to another. The initial tasks are dismantling and checking the state of the equipment. This involves complex, often verbally transmitted assessments which are then formalised by the engineering staff. In this period the engineers provide a flexible framework.

The main differences between the campaign and the refurbishment can be expressed by applying the mechanistic-organic management systems framework.

In the campaign there is high continuity and similarity of tasks day after day. The workforce is relatively concentrated in fixed locations and deployed across the shift systems for more than 2,500 continuous hours. The composition of the groups is large (i.e. the factory shift) and loosely connected. For example, the senior operator is the sugar boiler who might also be a trade union representative yet is absorbed in a complex set of control activities. Group stability is steady, but there are low interaction opportunities within and between shifts. Management meets twice daily and the information about the factory is checked in a reporting framework which is largely hierarchical and centralised. The foremen become more influential and the engineers' influence decreases. Engineers can be away on training during this period. The superintendent is a key figure and overall management have high felt control. The workforce reports that supervision is more lenient than in the period of refurbishment.

In the refurbishment period everyone is on day working and more normal weeks. The continuity is broken up and so there is more variety of tasks. Work is organised into sub-projects within the major chunks (e.g. dismantling, refurbishing, assembling). The workforce is dispersed with more open spatial mobility and working in quite small groupings. Management meetings occur once per day and are less centralised. The engineers' influence increases since they are both co-ordinating activities and also estimating progress through the overall cycle of activities and actions to be completed before the next campaign. Superintendents have less influence and overall the felt authority of management is less while the workforce report that supervisors are more often pushing them.

This example illustrates the character of distributed activity systems and shows parallels with the case of the eighteenth-century Cherokee. The next section suggests that the concept of organisational repertoire can be fruitfully applied to describe and explain these patterns.

REPERTOIRES: ACTIVATION AND ASSEMBLING

The cameo of the sugar beet industry illustrates similar structural and temporal features to those noted in the studies of seasonal variations among the Eskimo, the Nuer and the Cherokee Indians. The activities and actions of the firm are unevenly spread through time so that there is temporal differentiation. The firm possesses a repertoire of recurrent action patterns which are brought into play in anticipation of some future events.[2] Management occupies a central role in that process by anticipating and assembling recurrent action patterns. Temporal differentiation has been largely neglected, possibly suppressed in organisation studies. The view of process as temporal differentiation introduces a new requirement in theories of organisational change and of programmed change. The problem is how to theorise the temporal heterogeneity and the notion of a repertoire.

Social and cultural structures are unequally active when temporality is considered. The theory of structural activation contends that structures are multiple and that any organisation has a repertoire of structures in the form of linked recurrent action patterns. These are sequences with durational attributes as illustrated earlier in Table 7.1. Elements from the repertoire are connected with defined situations within and external to the organisation. The occurrence of these situations is anticipated in the strategic and tactical time reckoning systems found in every organisation and without which there would be no organising. The recurrent action sequences in the repertoire are triggered and activated in anticipation of enacted events as defined by strategically located timekeepers (e.g. market intelligence). These timekeepers often occupy boundary roles. The repertoire of recurrent action patterns is the retention system (as Weick) and represents the selected variations (as Weick). The repertoire occupies a central position in any socio-evolutionary process (Clark 1996: Figure 2). An appropriate theory of structural repertoires and activation should when fully formulated satisfy certain basic requirements:

1   It should conceptualise the sequential and durational aspects of recurrent
    action patterns. Also theory must connect the spatio-temporal dynamics of
    interlocked actions to the social mechanisms through which they are con-
    stituted and actors develop models which drive everyday action.
2   The notion of a repertoire requires specification with respect to the scope and
    richness of the repertoire.
3   Repertoires contain active and dormant patterns. How are these activated?
    In the case of patterns which are dormant for long periods how are they
    retained in the repertoire?
4   Recurrent action patterns in the repertoire provide the basis for the re-
    production of ongoing action. What are the conditions in which these
    patterns collapse, are disrupted and might be the objects of change?

Organisations have to cope with three major forms of temporality in the
structures. These distinctions arise from disaggregating the firm into the two
major levels of analysis: the operating unit level (e.g. offices, retail outlets,
branches of a firm, departments, schools); the technostructure and adaptive
sub-systems. First, there is the basic round of time at the operating level of the
factory, office, supermarket, hospital theatre. The specific length will vary when
measured in calendar time from days to the week (e.g. supermarkets), the season
(fashion goods), to the year (e.g. universities). Second, as organisations increase in
size they develop technostructures whose periods of adaptation through innovation and design tend to be in months and years. It is reported that Benetton
utilises a twenty-four month cycle, that car designing is a thirty-forty month cycle
and that in the pharmaceutical industry the cycles are more than a decade. Third,
most organisations contain special capabilities used to handle contingencies and
these cut across all levels.

The examples already noted from the Eskimo, the Nuer and the Cherokee are
largely concerned with the basic round of time in the year. By coincidence, the
sugar beet example is also from the year and there are many annual examples, but
not all examples are annual. The basic round of time depends on the specifics. For
example, in retail, especially in surpermarketing, the basic round is more likely to
be a weekly pattern with its variations in trading by days of the week. Firms which
grow in size face the problem of having to adapt their offerings of goods/services
to changing circumstances. This introduces the problems of designing new outputs
and associated aspects of innovation, research and development. Chapter 14
examines the example of developing a new saloon car.

The notion of a repertoire is used routinely in the professional accounts of sport
and the performing arts, but not in relation to work organisations. Yet, one of the
most useful ways of developing an understanding of fuzzy notions such as
capabilities is to specify them in terms of doing activities comparable to those
analysed in sports, especially exemplars such as American Football (see Chapter 9).
The absence of a notion of repertoire permits an impractical, unrealisable view of
strategic futures while the notion that organisations possess finite repertoires
anchors strategy in a quite different and more exacting reality.

CONVERSATIONS AND AGENDAS AS MECHANISMS: BODEN

Boden (1994) shows how corporate conversations and agendas are integral to the mechanisms involved in structural activation. The issue is how processes and action shape structure and how the causal mechanisms implicated in what we call structure shape future action. Incorporating the dynamics of action into organisational analysis requires the re-specification of an analytic language and the choice of key exemplars for the proposed language. There is a long history of attempts to respecify action with key contributions from Silverman's (1970) action frame of reference and in various approaches to time and structuration with information processing in the ways suggested by March, Weick and Stinchcombe. For example, March's emphasis upon information stresses ambiguity and temporality. According to this perspective firms understand their past and present in terms of the interface between the conditions for and of action with the spectrum of uncertainty. As in Giddens (1984) actors are knowledgeable and competent, yet are also confused, tend to focus upon outcomes and get distracted. Consequently there are frequent episodes of tension between the organisation processes and the situational conditions and that flexible tension affects the ways in which meanings unfold into structural forms. Many autonomous actions are involved in the unfolding of the processes which make up the sequences and durations found in episodes (cf. Giddens, 1984: 374). March contends that in this unfolding into sequences the actors allow problems to seek solutions and that it often appears as though both actors and solutions are seeking problems. Actors interact as though time and space were simultaneous rather than causal. Also, meaning is given through 'reasons' that are attributed from retrospection when actors reflexively sift through the locally relevant possibilities (Boden 1994: 41).

Boden (1994) provides an important account of organisational agendas and conversations as a major mechanism through which future action is constructed. Her account emphasises the structuration perspective and implicates a future orientation which complements Weick's (1995) account of sensemaking. Boden does not directly link into the activation of structures or to the notion of procedural memory because of the emphasis upon fuzzy, ambiguous elements. The problem of developing an 'in action' perspective is to re-specify action as an active component driving structure showing how people 'do' rules, covering the incompleteness of rules and illustrating their elasticity in situated actions. Stinchcombe's (1990) theory of information flows and their shaping of action implies that conversation both generates and potentially orders many parallel processes. Boden (1994) places conversations at the centre of her account of organisations in action because the analysis of structure requires 'a powerful notion of human agency' (1994: 13) in order to avoid treating structure as big and the discrete actions of actors as effects. Boden uses the analysis of language and conversation to track the accomplishing of organisational agendas in which time and space are bracketed. Organisational agendas are where actors' conversations provide a sense of temporal co-ordination and of what comes next (1994: 193). The attendees discuss the recipes and rules to be worked in the situation and they define which rules are to be relevant. Having done so they tend to gloss the decisions and make them look acceptable. Thus, those conversations which are agenda setting are the practical structure of action and the local logic of the pre-existing rules (in an ethnomethodological sense) is untangled. In the organisational agendas the key element is the production of recurrent, sequential action patterns or episodes. Through the processes in the organisational agenda the inter-penetrating of agency and structure is dialectical and simultaneously contingent and contradictory (1994: 198, cf. Archer 1995). Arrays of organisational agendas in different locations and involving different layers of the firm produce sequencing and collectively intertwine to produce structuring: 'adjacently organised units of action are at the core of the temporal and sequential organisation of action' (1994: 110).

NOTES

1 Cohen *et al.* (1996) *Industrial and Corporate Change* 5 (3): 653f.
2 This section draws from articles on time and structure (Clark 1985) and from Clark and Staunton (1989: Chapter 9) on the 'Structural repertoire and corporate expertise'.

13 Knowledges

Contested, distributed and explacit

INTRODUCTION

Our analysis so far has emphasised the degree to which knowledge and learning are socially and contextually constructed so that American Football (Chapter 9) and the British automobile sectors (Chapter 10) are contingently and dynamically specific outcomes. By contrast the intra-firm, resource based strategic approach (Chapter 11) has situated knowledge and Penrosian learning as key ingredients of successful corporate performance very largely within the firm. There are some problems to be examined. These centre around the notions of control, situatedness and dynamics: the problems of knowledge in action. This chapter[1] presumes the dynamic, contingent recursivness of organisational repertoires and their activation (Chapter 12) and leads into organisation transitions and innovation-design (Chapter 14).

The chapter commences by noting how the notion of knowledge capital and the claims to be doing knowledge management have become salient. In the last decade there has been a strong reaction to the constructivist tendency to focus tightly upon explicit knowledge by emphasising tacit knowledge (Suchman 1988). The attention to tacit knowledge is mainly supported by reference to Polyani's seminal essays on the role of tacit knowledge, but there has been some neglect of the detail of his reasoning. Combining explicit and tacit knowledge in the same framework – explacit knowledge – is implied in the analytic frameworks of Boisot (1987, 1998) and Nonaka and Takeuchi (1995)

The problem of knowledge in action is not resolved by the resource-based strategic approach and there is too much neglect of the constitution of knowledge through competition between contexts. Also, the assumptions about the mechanisms for knowledge retention and direction implicate metaphors drawn from the arsenal of the modern period more often than from the new political economy. In the resource-based approach there is too much reference to idealised sequences without attention to how such sequences of action are to be theorised with attention to organisations in action. Considerable metaphorical re-description is required before the metaphor mechanisms bears sufficient analytic weight to inform practice. However, although these proposed revisions are weighty and test the absorptive capacity (Cohen and Levintal 1990) of the resource-based strategic theorists, the cross-cutting connections can and should be made.

NEW PRODUCTION OF KNOWLEDGE CAPITAL

Marx proposed that knowledge is a factor of production alongside land and capital and the same theme is central to the notion of knowledge capitalism examined in Part II (e.g. Dunning 1997). Increasingly, analysts refer to differences of knowledge between firms and nations as the key factors explaining differences in the economic performance of firms, regions and nations. In the field of strategy the analytic approaches of Porter (1990) and of Grant (1990, 1995, 1998) have placed knowledge in a central role. Knowledge as capital is closely associated with the internal focus of the resource based approach to the firm.

The attention to knowledge and attempts to commodify knowledge through ownership have been stimulated by the various ways in which the information and communication technologies permit the precise recording, aggregation and processing of vast amounts of data. Lyotard referred to data sets as the new nature (see Chapter 2). Now, there are many new occupations in which knowledge is part of the title. There are advertisements for knowledge architects (Demarest 1997) and knowledge officers (Nonaka and Takeuchi 1995). Arthur Andersen has appointed a 'keeper of knowledge capital' (Carter 1998). The major accountancy firms are key players with respect to their own knowledge and to the knowledge of their clients. Accountancy firms are usually among the leading contributors to the conferences on knowledge management. Calculating the value of the knowledge capital tends to be primitive. The calculation sometimes consists of the previously unexplained gap between the sale value of tangible assets such as land and equipment and the value of the firm as expressed on the stock market. Frequently the gap is enormous. Part of the gap may be attributed – through complex reasoning – to the reputation of the firm. The remainder is then attributed to the knowledge possessed by the firm. That will include proprietary knowledge as well as firm-specific knowledge that is not covered by intellectual property rights.

The new production of knowledge is a very broad theme based on the observation that the universities in general have lost their monopoly position in the creation and diffusion of knowledge (Gibbons *et al.* 1994). Only a small number of universities occupy key positions in knowledge production for particular sectors. Examples include carpet making (Georgia Tech), wine making (University of California at Davis, Sacramento) and medical technology (Johns Hopkins). For the greater proportion of universities their specialist departments (e.g. science) are faced by the enormous growth of highly cited research done inside corporations (Darbishire and Katz 1997). In Europe there is a clear recognition that universities are – at the moment – in competition with multiple alternative sources of knowledge. These alternative sources include not only the corporate training centres with highly qualified staff, especially in North American firms, but more significantly the plethora of specialist research agencies. In Britain, for example, the retail sector is served by a variety of agencies among which Verdict is frequently mentioned. Few universities could compete even though many possess some relevant elements. Burton Clark (1998) suggests that most universities lack the capacity to cope with the degree of differentiation and integration necessary to enable significant knowledge-making institutes within the campus location. The context of application for knowledge tends to define what is relevant and what the state will pay for (Gibbons *et al.* 1994). The audit of knowledge value is lengthy and extensive (Power 1994) and in Britain is leading to systematic criticism of the usefulness of research by universities on school education.

The theme of the new production of knowledge implicitly and explicitly acknowledges much of the post-modern critique of modern knowledge. But what is meant by knowledge and why so much attention to tacit knowledge? In the age of the smart machine (Zuboff 1988) it is not easy to define informating as knowledge assets (Boisot 1998) without locating knowledge in a community of knowledge workers (Grint and Woolgar 1998).

KNOWLEDGE MANAGEMENT

Knowledge management is heavily, although not totally influenced by explicit knowledge. The section draws from the approach of Demarest (1997) who has aimed to draw from social theories.[2] Knowledge management as a discipline:

- defines the relationship between knowledge and the performance of the firm with reference to market place innovation, internal efficiency and profitability;
- describes the basic models for understanding how knowledge is created, embodied and distributed;
- traces the relationship between knowledge management and the infrastructure of the firm.

First, the plurality of corporate knowledges are defined as 'an explicitly developed and managed network of imperative patterns, rules, scripts embodied in some aspect of the firm and distributed throughout the firm to create marketplace performance' (Demarest 1997). There are multiple, plural forms of knowledge distributed around networks with varying degrees of connectedness. The four categories of knowledge are as follows:

1   *Strategic imperatives* are based in the corporate dogma of behavioural directives: these exist, yet may be wrong for the firm's success. There are behavioural directives that are unchallenged and taken for granted imperatives to action derived from the analysis of strategy as a pattern, both ongoing and with attention to emergent elements.

2   *Patterns* describe stylised models of the internal and external contexts based upon the regularly expected scenes requiring particular forms of knowledge

(e.g. the Cherokee year; sugar beet cycle): there are sequences and patterns of events known from within the firm and also available for reconstruction (as Senge 1990: Chapter 6). Patterns are revealed by their use and are in the form of stylised models embracing contexts and actions, for example, how particular suppliers should be handled.

3 *Rules and heuristics* define a basic set of guidelines for performing in specific situations: they can be fuzzy, detached and are often in conflict with each other. The extensive collections of rules and heuristics are based on the truces and outcomes of previous actions (Nelson and Winter 1982).

4 *Scripts* are prescriptions, recipes and stories about performance, yet differ from rules. Scripts are co-ordinated sets of rules focused on particular patterns and are the raw material of cognitive apprenticeships. Scripts are situational configurations and prescriptions for performance based upon the raw experience of the structuring of behaviour. In practice they are impacted by the rules and heuristics. In the application of knowledge management these scripts are edited and re-authored by the knowledge architect.

However, in the typical firm before the arrival of the knowledge architect there is no commonly held model for knowledge creation, embodiment and dissemination. Neither are there processes or systems focused upon supporting or creating knowledge. Also, the problem of distributed knowledge and its disconnectedness is hardly recognised. There are prescriptions for performance.

Knowledge management advocates a conscious approach informed by the metaphor of the knowledge architect (Demarest 1997: 377) as an expert who can compress knowledge to achieve time-space mastery. Although only slight attention is given to the importation of external knowledge or external organisational innovations, there are clear implications that when the firm's knowledge is managed these processes are more effective. Therefore, firms only manage knowledge if they do so explicitly as an objective of the architecture of the firm. The goal of knowledge management is effective performance. The commercial knowledge that creates market performance is defined by its performativity (Lyotard 1984) as a managed network 'of imperatives, patterns, rules and scripts' which are embodied in the managed culture as well as the artefacts (e.g. procedures, equipment, buildings) and distributed throughout the firm. All commercial knowledge is social, provisional, partial and muddled.

Second, all firms have knowledge production economies. The process of knowledge management possess four major activities: construction, embodiment, dissemination and use. Construction involves the discovering and structuring of knowledge in the firm. Embodiment is the deliberate choosing of a container such as rituals, procedures, choice of equipment and the design of layouts. Dissemination refers to the networks through which knowledge is distributed. Use refers to the creation of commercial value with the firm's customers. There are additional vectors arising from the construction of knowledge to three other areas:

- where knowledge is being put into practice while being developed;
- where knowledge in a fully operating system is disseminated at the testing stage (cf. Nonaka and Takeuchi 1995);
- where processes are not undertaken until there is a network of users.

These are all in the knowledge economy of the firm.

Third, knowledge management has to develop the infrastructures of cultural, operational and technical knowledges of the firm. All of these are hidden and subterranean, yet require observation, selective measurement and instrumentation. The knowledge architect asks: How does your knowledge work/relative to others/how do we create knowledge?/how do we create robust bodies of knowledge? Once accomplished there has to be the systematic exnovation of outdated knowledge.

In summary this view of knowledge management by Demarest incorporates the explicit knowledge associated with constructivist notions of knowledge while making a sharp incursion into socially constructed, tacit knowledge. This view of knowledge management seeks to make the firm's hidden, unwritten rules of the game transparent in every knowledge community within the firm and to edit those knowledges according to the principle of performativity in the marketplace.

RESOURCE-BASED THEORY OF KNOWLEDGE: PROBLEMS

Hegemonic despotism and consent

Kamoche (1996: 226) in an exploratory examination of the interface between the resource-based view and that of strategic human resource management adopts a two-level approach – from the firm and from the individual – to face the problems inherent in the resource based approach to knowledge and routines. Kamoche argues that the 'firm acts opportunistically through its retention activities, resource barriers, rent appropriation and through integrative mechanisms' that are reminiscent of 'hegemonic despotism' (Burawoy 1985) to achieve control through consent rather than force. Meanwhile the individual seeks autonomy and wishes to retain control over expertise. This neat formulation introduces the problems of knowledge for organisations in action. The resource based strategic theory illustrated earlier in Figure 11.1 locates knowledge as a key organisational asset determining the performance of the firm. Moreover, some disembodied actor is implied to manipulate and direct the knowledge. This same social group is assumed to have the power to garner knowledge and manage its architecture and utilisation. No doubt there are events taking place which give anecdotal credence to this narrative and its metaphor of design rules. However, the theorising tends to objectify and extract knowledge from its varied, distributed contexts of production.

Three problems are introduced in this section and these lead into the examination of situated action:

- power-knowledge;
- distributed knowledge and contexts of application;
- problem ownership and control metaphors.

Knowledge is power

The knowledge-is-power perspective is awkward to embrace and continuously to implicate in analysis. There are two steps in the argument: synthesis between macro-institutional and micro-processual perspectives that also incorporates the three dimensions of power proposed by Lukes (1974); the contention that knowledge is power.

First, there is a tendency towards the use of frameworks that highlight an enduring structural and institutional containment, but the temporality of the long-term flows into the future through the present (Gurvitch 1964). The aim should be to treat all action as a temporary patterning from which the dislocation of the pre-existing structural constraints may unfold. Even so, there is an important tension between the macro-institutional (DiMaggio and Powell 1991) and the more meso-processual (e.g. Foucault). The institutional and structural approach at the macro-societal level emphasises that power is a differentially distributed capacity inherent in structural forms. These structural forms provide strategic resources, yet confine the capacities of agents to mobilise those forms. For example, the constraints inhere in the structure of markets as they are socially constituted. In the meso-political approach attributed to Foucault, power is pervasive and located widely, yet possesses strong local and contingent elements. Emphasis is concentrated upon how the power embodied and embedded in disciplinary practices of all kinds, ranging from the loosely articulated forms reported for the Birmingham engineering trades engaged in the founding of the British automobile industry (see Chapter 10) to the more exacting forms found at West Point (Hoskin and Macve 1988). The meso-level practices in particular settings generate forms of disciplinary regimes and distinct forms of discourse, for example, in the professions (Larson 1979; Abbott 1988). At the meso-level these forms of discourse mediate between the level of sectoral clusters (see Chapter 10) and the societal level involving the role of state strategies (see Chapters 6, 7, 8) while also mediating at the level of particular firms in their local contexts.

In certain respects the three dimensions of power proposed by Lukes (1974) create a dialogue between the institutional and processual through: episodic, manipulative and hegemonic. The episodic dimension highlights opposing interests and overt conflicts between various social actors in a setting as they encounter various opportunities to insert choices of direction. In contrast the manipulative view highlights those often hidden, back-stage activities through which powerful groups manipulate situations to screen off actions which may disturb their power. The hegemonic dimension (see Chapter 6) is strategic in level, yet so embedded in the ideological and social structural formations that it 'silently' sets the selection criteria for the possible ranges of action in particular settings. Domination is not only hidden, domination is collusively (albeit unwillingly) inserted into the everyday, material practices that continue to unfold. Hegemonic domination is a more precise explication of the notion of truces in the behavioural theory of the firm (e.g. Cyert and March 1963).

Second, the intention with the knowledge-is-power perspective is to explain contemporary forms of organisational and governmental control in terms of ongoing negotiations between a variety of social actors as being at least potentially emergent and transformational (Clegg 1987). So alliances between firms, strata and groupings as well as between key individuals could contain potentials for instability and dislocation. Contingency is rampant. So, for example, the diffusion of innovations across national boundaries might consist of co-ordination systems as a dynamic configuration in contingent specificity (Clark and Staunton 1989: 51–77). Layder (1997) highlights the four domains (see Chapter 4) in which locally embedded stocks of knowledge are used by agents to assemble the activities and interactional order that actually constitute the permanence we refer to as an organisation.

Knowledge as applied to organisational events can be described as a hetero-geneous actor network containing a 'scenario for the future replete with a stage, roles and directions governing the interactions between actors who supposed to assume those roles' (Akrich 1992: 174). Organisation knowledge also typically involves an attempt to maintain control at a distance through establishing networks and – by implication – by the rehearsed recurrent action patterns sometimes referred to as cloning activity. Extensive cloning of recurrent action patterns underpins the operation of franchised firms like Benetton and McDonald's. Moreover that degree of cloning can be combined with high levels of flexibility, especially through subtracting modules of action. Exnovation and ablation are sometimes more obvious as mechanisms of transformation.

The difference in contingency and the sense of temporariness between knowledge-is-power and the earlier discussion of power in this section is proble-matic. Here the analytic dualism (Archer 1995) of analysing both the pre-existing and the emergent independently and in depth with attention to mechanisms and structures is useful and will be developed in the Chapter 14.

Distributed knowledge

Knowledge is distributed and this can be illustrated by the everyday problem in hospitals of suppressing legionella disease and preventing the hospital staff from being infected by needle-stick injuries from hypodermic needles (Robinson and Clark 1997). The front line might seem to be the nurses on the wards and their position is shown in the left-hand corner of Figure 13.1. The nurses have been through the socialisation, education and training of their association. They are expected to apply evidence-based approaches drawn from research studies previously published (Hicks 1998). The nurses are not alone. There is a whole panoply of actors involved from the locality of the hospital (e.g. Civic University Medical School), the regional associations plus the local Public Health Laboratory and its network. Everywhere there are licensed medical practitioners. At the

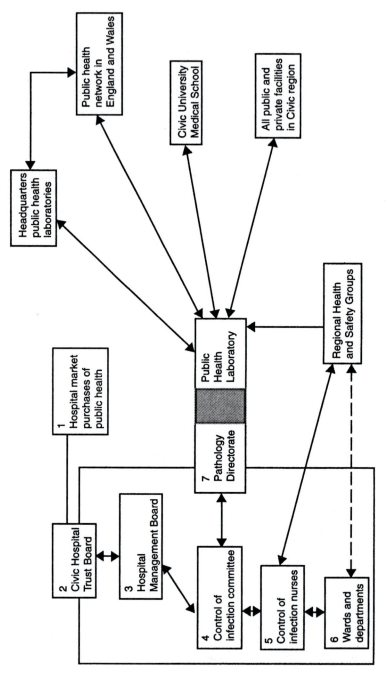

Figure 13.1 Distributed activities: hospital infection control in Civic City
Source: Robinson and Clark (1997).

hospital board and trust level are the lay managers and the medical directorate. Tackling these everyday problems implicates a distributed, extensive, varied network of knowledge communities on differing levels.

The new production of knowledge hypothesis contends that large sections of the production of knowledge in universities and similar locations are so disconnected from the contexts in which application might occur that the performativity of knowledge is undermined. The commodification of research and knowledge is well underway. However, those contexts are typified by distributed knowledge and by knowledge that is implicated in the politics and power of specific groups and communities.

Awareness of the possible disjuncture between the context of application and the generation of knowledge which the academic community considers relevant is an old theme. In the modern period there was a strong tendency among academics in organisation theory towards knowledge that provided design rules. In that period there was a vigorous debate between academics promoting organisation theory and design and those who preferred the banner of action research and organisation development (Clark 1972). The latter claimed that the utilisation of knowledge only occurred when those in the context of application translated academic knowledge into operable knowledge. The debate is best noted. Coming back to present and future we can observe that the debate between explicit and tacit knowledge possesses some parallels with the earlier debate.

Problem ownership and control metaphors

According to the resource-based view shown earlier in Figure 11.1 one of the attributes of knowledge is control and direction (Grant 1998; Spender 1996; Grant 1996b). However, the metaphors and analogies underpinning the notions of control and direction in Grant (1996: Figure 1) appear to be close to the swimming pool robot. Boisot (1998) suggests that there are extensive problems of controlling knowledge even under relatively favourable conditions. Also, the literature on problem ownership and on the capacity of particular coalitions to establish closure around integer-power networks suggests that in social organisations there is a huge problem with the appropriation of knowledge.

The status of control notions derived from the modern perspective is still pervasive, possibly because their application to many non-social systems is so impressive and awesome. However, the revolution in some areas of system control (Beniger 1986) requires metaphorical redescription when applied to social entities. As noted earlier there is a shared tendency in the managerial literature and some of the critical literature in the de-skilling perspective to collude in their claims about corporate control capacities (Burawoy 1979). Likewise, the iron-cage perspective invoked by some of the new institutionalists provides a heightened account of social control without sufficiently distinguishing the areas of increasing tightness from those of increasing looseness.

In part the debate is about which social groups are able impose their social constructions on other groups. The example of the conflicting groups involved in the origins of the British automobile sectoral cluster (see Chapter 10) illustrates the degree to which overt potentials for conflict can challenge the capacity of management hegemonically to define the situation of 'efficiency' in their interests and impose that definition. Likewise, Bijker's analysis of the evolution of the bicycle shows that many different social groups, each with different agendas, are implicated and that the outcome is a variant on unplanned order. Problem ownership is contested and involves extensive power struggles.

The issue is one of which metaphors most fruitfully inform the understanding of the dynamics and struggles around the appropriation of knowledge in organisations.

SITUATED ACTION

Tacit knowledge: Polyani

Polyani's (1958) action oriented theorising of knowing may be seen as having intriguing parallels and differences from Penrose (1959). Polyani (1957) is mis-leadingly known for tacit knowledge when his view of knowledge is more embracing and significant. It is also complex because of the position of routines and recurrent action patterns (Chapter 12). There are seven main features:

1   Polanyi began with the proposition that knowledge in the form of scientific discoveries cannot be accounted for by a simple set of rules (cf. Boisot) because knowledge is both public and personal, possibly passionately personal, yet is social and rooted in the tacit experiences. The act of knowing in science – and other areas – is based on many years of study within a community. Although some of the knowing may be codified in ways that the community understands, that community may be quite small and so the range of diffusion for codified, abstract knowledge may be very small because utilisation requires tacit experience.

2   In the act of knowing there are two mutually exclusive and complementary dimensions. There is focal knowledge about the phenomena in focus and there is tacit knowledge utilised to improve the focus. Conversely, loss of focus through attention to the tacit in the wrong moments can disrupt as for example in playing the piano. Therefore prepositional knowing of nurses about infection control (see Figure 13.1) is merely the 'tip of the iceberg' and is unusable without tacit background.

3   The tacit knowledge is the background (also Searle 1995) and is situationally specific, therefore varying between contexts. Knowledge is the activity and process of knowing. Integrating knowledge between these two dimensions is a personal skill.

4   Knowledge might be imagined as articulating an object in words, film, pictures[3] and languages can be used to make knowledge explicit and available to reflection. Articulation – based on the actors' symbolic definitions – reconstructs the elements of situations in a different scale and plane that

may be open to the manipulation of the elements. In this way individual and collective knowledge can be distributed.

5   Knowledge may be regarded as a tool to gather further knowledge. There is an implicit investment in categories even though that may not be explicit (cf. Nonaka and Takeuchi 1995). The degree to which knowledge is a tool depends upon particular actors. Because the tool possesses rules their application and improvised alteration is influenced by the normative community. So, some language communities may possess very static tools (e.g. organisation theory) and others may possess dynamic tools (e.g. organisation in actionalists).

6   Knowing is the capacity to do something: for example, as with the medical practitioners and nurses handling infectious diseases. Within, there is a distinction between those who do and those who reflect upon the doing that is especially significant in contemporary symbolic manipulation.

7   Knowledge of all kinds is transferred very largely through the community of practice by the acquisition of the patterns of action and their constitutive rules, values and normative frameworks.

Polyani's theory embraces explacit knowledge (see shortly).

Legitimate peripheral participation

The anti-constructivist school maintains that the explicit, codified knowledge found in documented instructions that often accompany new equipment cannot alone provide the basis for activity and action (Suchman 1988). This claim can explain why in the late eighteenth century when American textile entrepreneurs purchased British textile equipment they were unable to make it operable until the appearance of men like Samual Slater who had been trained in the British textile community (Jeremy 1980). It seems likely that Slater had acquired the focal and tacit knowledge. There is the learning of activity areas within distributed knowledge as shown earlier in Figure 13.1 from a practitioner community. There are numerous studies of activity areas in this perspective (e.g. Chaiklin and Lave 1993). Hutchins (1993) investigated the flight cockpit and the role of the master navigator in bringing ships on the final leg from the ocean into the port. Weick examined the flight-deck of an aircraft carrier. Di Bello *et al.* (1992) used observation and carefully constructed games to observe how within the community of production controllers using software to co-ordinate factories there was a division of activities. These and many other everyday situations such as repairing equipment and going shopping seem to point to forms of knowledge quite similar to the theorising of Polyani already noted. It is concluded that knowledge is situated, provisional and pragmatic, but especially that knowledge is distributed.

One way in which newcomers acquire the focal and tacit knowledge is through participation in the occupational community. Such participation may commence with the new member being peripheral and needing to establish legitimacy within the normative and regulative framework of the occupational community. This is referred to as legitimate peripheral participation (Lave and Wenger 1991). These studies reveal interpersonal tensions within the activity-based communities. Structural tensions and conflicts are more readily observed in multi-activity studies. The studies of professional groups in the perspective of Larson (1979) and Abbott (1988) exemplify the extent to which occupational groups may seek to impose closure around their knowledge and to engage in jurisdictional struggles with other groups. Conflicts may also be in the open where some occupational groups have the specialist task of acquiring the focal and tacit knowledge of other groups.

A realist perspective applied to these activity groups and the discussion of legitimate peripheral participation introduces the structural context that pre-exists. Shopping, flying onto aircraft carriers and sailing across the Pacific all occur within structural contexts that have a 'history', and contested knowledge. Hutchins (1993) reveals how the history of the master navigator enters the analysis, but many studies in this perspective tend towards the 'here and now'.

EXPLACIT KNOWLEDGE FRAMEWORKS[4]

Explicit and tacit

The previous sections illustrate the scope for debate between those who concentrate upon knowledge that is already organised, codified, abstracted and explicit in the approaches of knowledge capital from those who highlight knowledge as tacit, embedded in activities, fragile, contested, distributed and in knowledge communities. Also, it is clear that knowledge management is seeking to expand its earlier focus upon explicit knowledge into tacit knowledge (e.g. Demarest 1997). These discussions draw attention to the potential for revision and amplification to the position of knowledge in the resource-based strategic approach as shown earlier in Figure 11.1. The approaches of Boisot (1987, 1995, 1998) and Nonaka and Takeuchi (1995) are developing frameworks combining[5] tacit and explicit knowledge as dimensions. This section overviews both frameworks and uses the example of distributed knowledge displayed in Figure 13.1.

Nonaka and Takeuchi

Their approach has been presented as an insight into distinctly Japanese methods of managing knowledge, yet key analogies are drawn from knowledge management in American Football and in the American military during its Pacific campaign against Japan. We should therefore be cautious of assuming either that their account represents all Japan or that Americans firms and sectoral clusters are incapable of successfully managing the interacting dynamics of both dimensions (cf. Nonaka and Takeuchi 1995). However, it may be that the Japanese are especially adept with 'dynamic metaphors' and that the use of metaphors is not sufficiently understood within western firms.[6] The contributions of Polyani and Penrose are acknowledged and embedded in the two basic steps.

1   Knowledge is examined through two dimensions: tacit and explicit. Tacit knowledge is defined as a personal quality that is hard to formalise and is rooted in action in a specific context. Cognitive, normative and regulative elements are continuously involved in the process of knowing. Experience constitutes knowing and the sharing of experiences creates tacit knowledge. Explicit knowledge is formal, systematic and located in records, figures, databases and archives. This definition of the two dimensions is similar to Polyani's account;

2   The two dimensions are used to construct a typology of knowledge conversion.

Knowledge creation takes the form of successive spirals through four possible quadrants. For example, when tacit–tacit is examined reflectively then the potential fragile outcomes of a local level become available for externalisation into a wider community. The externalisation provides for the translation of tacit–tacit into explicit and the next step in the spiral is when multiple instances of explicit are combined. The explicit–explicit in its combined form provides forms of knowing that can then be transposed back to the original arena through internalisation and the spiral continues. This knowledge creating spiral can be scrutinised more closely in the five steps:

- the sharing of tacit knowledge to
- create concepts that
- are put through a process of justification to
- constructing an archetype or template leading to
- the use of the archetype of leverage knowledge.

Returning to the example of infection control at Civic Hospital (Figure 13.1) then the sharing of tacit knowledge can occur in the teams handling an outbreak. That involves several teams including those in the laboratory and the specialist infection control team. The concepts are articulated in the committee that hosts the infection control team where any justification and construction of future templates for action occurs. In this committee there is a process of cross-functional justification using criteria from several different arenas and bridging between the medical and administrative rationalities. The whole process is distributed across a number of activity groups.

Nonaka and Takeuchi provide a rich array of illustrations to show where this spiral works and they set out some of the requirements for successful knowledge creation. The requirements include the combining of some uncertainty with autonomy. It is likely that the control of infectious diseases such as legionella introduces the uncertainty and that the structure of relationships in the health sector contains areas of autonomy. However, it is not clear that these can be sufficiently diagnosed within the framework proposed. Rather, it is necessary to introduce more forcefully the national-institutional and sectoral-institutional levels and the small narratives of national, regional and local specificities.

The references to American Football are intriguing. On the one hand American

Football is a very American cultural form and icon. Nonaka and Takeuchi (1995) contend, in their conclusions, that the analogy provided by that sport comes close to their ideal of the hypertext firm. The hypertext firm combines three elements: specialist task groups; the bureaucracy of the game plan and rehearsals as a form of innovation-and-design; extensive utilisation of highly sophisticated databases showing trajectories of action. American Football contains these feature to such an extent that the actual playing of the game is a very small part of the total action required to deliver the games for the consumer. On the other hand, Nonaka and Takeuchi state, very clearly, that western firms have a predisposition towards mainly explicit knowledge and give insufficient credence to tacit knowledge. My analysis suggests that we should examine American Football as an instantiation of explacit knowledge; likewise, the origins of the British automobile sectoral cluster. These two examples are from the examination of competition between contexts although they also illustrate organisations in action. The point is that explacit knowledge cannot be detached from its contexts of application.

Codification-diffusion framework: Boisot

The codification-diffusion framework aims to provide an analytic space that is clearly calibrated so that specifics can be located and their space-time trajectories can be tracked. Boisot (1998) has added a third dimension of abstractness in the account of knowledge assets from the earlier framework:

1   The vertical dimension expresses codification of knowledge from uncodified to codified. Uncodified knowledge is tacit and consists of 'fields of forces' between various discrete items of codified knowledge in the form of patterns (see Polyani). Doing activities create actual learning irrespective of the desirability and outcomes from the use of that learning (see Penrose) and that is continuously interacting with new events and experiences in locally specific forms of interaction. Codified knowledge involves the sacrifice of discrete bits by their relocation inside categories and codes. At a simple level the codification can be represented by any timetables for public transport by air, train and buses. At more complex levels the theory of DNA provides a highly abstract code. This dimension can be used to locate an enormous variety of events and forms.
2   The horizontal dimension refers to the extent to which knowledge is diffused. This ranges from slight to very extensive and the whole of the analytic space is available. Price systems are codified and may be highly diffused and if so would be located in the top right-hand corner.

The codification-diffusion framework can also be applied to the case of infections in hospitals. The uncodified and undiffused knowledge is continuously being involved with the other three quadrants and it is not obvious that there is a single routing in a clockwise direction from the lower, left quadrant (Robinson and Clark 1997).

Explacit knowledge

Knowledge is potentially fragile, may not be captured or retained, is distributed among activities and knowledge communities within which there are interactions between elements of knowledge that highly situated, embedded and local with elements that are more abstract, codified and explicit. The latter may only be operable as knowledge to small communities of practitioners and these may be located within a large-scale system of the kind analysed by Hughes (1990). The various analytic frameworks briefly overviewed represent attempts to construct categories of analysis that extend the earlier contributions of Penrose and Polyani. These may be referred to as explacit knowledge and the notion of explacit knowledge can be reapplied to knowledge capital (e.g. Boisot 1998) and to knowledge management. It is important in explanations and practice not to impose metaphors of control that mislead about the degree to which explacit knowledge can be controlled. The notion of learning audits tests that requirement.

DISCIPLINES

Townley (1998) applies a Foucauldian analysis to replace the modernist tendency to dichotomies with a perspective of depth. Thus the dichotomous treatment of powerful/powerless is replaced by a plethora of divisions in order to capture the diversity and complexity of structured reality. In application to power this entails a revision to the notion of negative power. Now power is positive and negative, repressive and creative. These are applied to domains of governmentality (e.g. workplace relations) and before any domain can be governed the domain must be rendered knowable. Rendering a domain knowable requires a detailed, minute knowledge of the chosen domain. To achieve governmentality requires the construction and exercise of discipline. This applies to any local setting and also to governing a distant locale (Latour 1987, 1988). The detailed knowledge is achieved through investment in categories (Thevenot 1984). Their application requires disciplinary practices for the analysts, their clients and the subjects/ objects of the categories that constitute the knowledge. Disciplines are a way of knowing that can be translated into a system of power. So, scientific management is a way of knowing that can be used to construct detailed activities and the workforce may be inducted into particular practices that govern their bodies. Foucauldian analysis focuses on the practices that structure social relationships.

In the organisation of a workplace there are three principal areas of knowledge (Townley 1998: 194):

- of the workforce and their bodies (e.g. speaking with a smile);
- of the activities to be undertaken (e.g. landing an aircraft on a carrier);
- of the individual (e.g. the biopsychological profile).

Disciplines are required to achieve ordering through these three domains.

The disciplines implicate categories, forms of classification and measurements through recording and analysis. The disciplines are social technologies (as Perrow 1967; Clark 1972) that provide analytic grids capable of being used to overview the domain being targeted. The social technology attempts to delimit the discretion of individuals and in the actor network perspective. So, individuals in the workplace become fixed in time and space within the knowledge and its disciplinary gaze such that it is possible that the flow of individuals is perceived as being similar to that of the swimming pool robot. The gaze of the disciplinary knowledge renders actions knowledgeable within the social construction of that gaze. So, the gaze of an industrial engineer from Toyota travelling back in time to the British car plant of Rover in Solihull would have a different gaze from that of the local industrial engineers.

The discipline and knowledge becomes embodied in a discourse which is independent of individuals, more enduring and pervasive. The metaphor of depth (Marsden 1993) is to show that the binary oppositions between scientific management and human relations can be dissolved in the sense that the disciplinary gaze from human relations adds to the disciplinary gaze from scientific management and the combined knowledge provides management with a deeper potential for control. Each new fad in management can therefore be seen as potentially offering additional depth to the disciplinary gaze being applied (reflexively) to the workforce. Additions may alter the original architecture of knowledge. Clark (1997a, b) suggests that Japanese categories of time-space analysis are being inserted into American forms of corporate timetabling. So, the rise and fall of total quality control and business process engineering should not be seen as isolated fads, but rather as carriers of distinct knowledge-power disciplines that might increase the depth of control. There are also increases in scope as with the extension of the gaze from hourly paid employees into monthly paid employees and the whole of the service class.

Western nations have, according to the account in Chapter 6 based on Landes (1998), possessed strata that – based on their social construction of reality – specialised in the creation of a very detailed account of the activities they sought to govern. By extension the social technologies associated with human resource management (HRM) provide knowledge-power disciplines that address some of the same domains as the resource based strategic analysis. However, their application probably resides away from the operational workplace (e.g. the supermarket) and is centralised among the strata of the service class known as symbolic analysts. These players are located offstage in the script writers' quarters and frequently detail the space-time trajectories to the point where aesthetic considerations are choreographed in a manner similar to that used in film making (e.g. Busby Babes). It seems likely that corporate universities in the fast food business and in themed mid-price eating chains are where these activities are constructed into sequences. However, it also seems likely that there are differences between sectoral clusters and nations in the constitution and utilisation of these social technologies.

Because the individual is such an item for disciplines like human resource management then it may be presumed that the social construction of identity (see Layder 1997) is intimately involved (see Thompson and McHugh 1995).

CORPORATE KNOWLEDGE AND PARENTING

Organisation theory gained an important impetus from the design rules anchored in the theory of social technology formulated by Perrow (1967). As an ideological-cum-intellectual approach (Alexander 1995) it has powerful implications for design. The social technology grids of knowledge are based on dichotomised pairs of dimensions used to construct quadrants locating the key dimensions. There are four layers of quadrants and the design rules define the blueprint. The design rules are based on the degree to which activities can be categorised and measured to provide a measure of routineness along a scale from routine to non-routine.

By using the framework it is possible for an analyst believing in the disciplinary framework of Perrow (1967) to designate some organisations and firms as being essentially routine (and vice versa) in the type of knowledge required. This has the implication that the parenting of the firm will approximate to the mechanistic management system. Conversely, firms whose stock of knowledge can be characterised as non-routine should possess management systems approximating to the template of organic. Perrow theorises on the likelihood that new sectoral clusters and established firms experiencing the onset of long waves of new technologies should adopt forms of knowledge that are highly non-routine, yet may become routinised over several decades.

Goold and Campbell (1987) refer to the role of the strategic elites in the organisation through the metaphor of parenting and – for this moment – the metaphor is convenient. The cycle of events just described implies a shift in the knowledge and disciplines required to parent the organisation. Now suppose that a firm emerges at the interstices of several sectors (as Penrose 1959) with the belief that they are better at parenting firms with simple, routine knowledge and their associated disciplinary practices. Suppose also in terms of the social technology theory that there are routine-knowledge firms noted for their performance. Then, speculation suggests that firms with capabilities at managing routine-knowledge firms could build up a portfolio starting with small firms and progressing towards larger firms. Moreover, it is more than likely that the incumbent parents and their local sub-set of the service class will believe that their high performance arises from some superior qualities.

The sketch in the previous paragraph can now be applied to the emergence four decades ago in the North East of England of a firm specialising in parenting and today – many iterations on – known as Hanson. If we follow their trajectory of extending the family being parented then one of the defining characteristics is that the firms brought into the portfolio possessed both routine knowledge and successful disciplinary practices. At the same time these firms continued to engage in expensive activities of research and development whose value added was limited. Hanson took over a stream of firms until it encountered and bid for the dominant firm in the tobacco industry known as the Imperial Group. The bid of Hanson was successful and it rationalised some of the very expensive accoutrements to work life in the major subsidiaries including Players. An earlier study of Players had shown that its social technology was becoming increasingly routinised as it shifted to system forms of organisation (Touraine 1955; Clark 1972, 1979). From that base Hanson examined the firm considered then to be at the pinnacle of British manufacturing performance: Imperial Chemical Industry (ICI). The bid was rejected, but soon ICI demerged to separate the different knowledge construction characteristics required for pharmaceuticals (now Zenecca) from the more routine areas of paint and bulk chemicals.

The theory of social technology can be transformed into a more explanatory and practically useful theory by being incorporated into the examination of explacit knowledge and knowledge-power and knowledge-discipline within the neo-modern political economy.

NOTES

1 I am indebted to discussion with Frank Blackler at Lancaster University and to his review article (Blackler 1995).
2 Marc Demarest has made extensive use of an earlier book on innovation in technology and organisation (see Clark and Staunton 1989), thus confirming the way in which knowledge is commodified from the cognitive, regulative and normative pillars of social action.
3 The position in articulation of systematic recording through film and video of performances and their reflective analysis is reconstructed here.
4 This section draws upon exploratory research in the health sector to explore how these frameworks operate with Lenore Robinson (Robinson and Clark 1997) and Natterly van der Linder (1998).
5 The usage is evident in Nonaka and Takeuchi (1995) and operates differently in Boisot (1987) and more so with the approach to knowledge assets (Boisot 1998).
6 I am indebted to Angela Dumas for emphasising this aspect. See Clark *et al.* (1995).

14 Morphogenesis/stasis

INTRODUCTION

The aim of this chapter is to develop a collection of ideas that has explanatory possibilities to resolve the problems inherent in the orthodox approaches to change and innovation in organisations.

The resource based theory of strategy (see Chapter 11) assumes that the organisation can change almost without friction. Hence there are notions such as the ambidextrous organisation. However, those assumptions ignore the finite capabilities of the repertoire of recurrent action programmes possessed by the organisation (see Chapter 12). Finite capabilities mean that there are limited zones of manoeuvre for the organisation. Therefore it is necessary to distinguish between whether an organisation remains the same through many completed cycles of its activities (stasis) or whether there is transformation (morphogenesis). This distinction suggests some basic problems and the limits of existing solutions. One of the alternative possibilities to be explored is to examine the theories of stasis and morphogenesis sketched by Buckley (1967) and explored further by Archer (1995). This approach to stasis and morphogenesis provides certain basic questions to put to claims about organisational innovation and change. There are six sections:

- the limitations of existing solutions;
- reproduction or transformation;
- temporality of stasis and morphogenesis;
- innovation-and-design;
- retro-organisational change and innovation;
- differences and alternatives.

This chapter leads into the final part where the two themes of organisations in action and competition between contexts are more explicitly drawn together.

LIMITED SOLUTIONS

There are major problems inherent in existing approaches to organisational change and innovation, especially to the enormous literature on organisational change.

First, it is necessary in the new political economy to account for the *design intensity* of organisational activities (Pine 1993; Lash and Urry 1994). The position of design as a central element in corporate life arises in all areas from intensive care in hospitals for newborn babies with defects to the end of life where the bereavement and burial sector is redesigning the ritual and eventual location of our bodies/ashes. In the cases of American Football and the production of automobiles there are vast investments of working capital that precede the playing of the game and the distribution of an automobile. Design intensity should be an integral part of strategic thinking, yet few case studies of organisations match the analytic exemplar of design by Abernathy (1978). Design is not acknowledged inside organisation studies and the treatment of design in contemporary attempts to 'redirect' organisation theory is unacceptably brief. Firms that lack capacities in innovation-design do not survive. Design capacities represent the alignment of the firm with one of its major constituencies: the customers and consumers (Clark and Starkey 1988; Clark and Staunton 1989).

Second, both the positivist and mainstream approaches to organisation theory and design have adopted the view that any pre-existing organisational knowledge and repertoires of recurrent action patterns can be transformed rather quickly in *frictionless change* (Clark 1975a, b; Clark and Starkey 1988: 19–47; Thompson and McHugh 1995). Exponents of organisation design frequently conclude that the preferred design blueprint is achievable, while in strategy its implementation is often handed over to the social scientist as an 'implementation problem'. Programmed change strategies presume success, yet offer tenuous research bases for that conclusion (Wilson 1992: Chapter 7). Contemporary approaches to organisational change are involved in rhetorical closure (Bijker *et al.* 1987). There are, however, signs of recognition of the problems of pre-existing structures with the introduction of concepts such as receptivity to change (Pettigrew *et al.* 1992: 267–299) and these provide a welcome extension to earlier theorising (Pettigrew and Whipp 1991).

Third, attention to the *processual dynamics* in organisation studies has developed considerably (Clegg 1989; Clegg *et al.* 1996). This development has been tortuous and difficult with many empty promises. The analytic grip provided by the intellectual brilliance of organisation theorists like J. D. Thompson (1967) directed attention to the generic problems of the vertically integrated corporation largely choreographing its customers' desires. Abernathy's (1978) analytically structured narrative of Ford from 1896 to the 1970s exemplifies that situation and adds in a whole lot more analytic weight. Yet, Abernathy broke the frame in that analysis and turned to the more institutional issues suggested by Burns and Stalker (1961) in his very suggestive scrutiny of American theory and practice. It has been much easier to attack positivism than to develop the alternative neo-modern and political economy approaches. The development of alternatives has been central to Whittington (1989, 1992a, b, 1994) and a long series of essays by Reed reveal a rapid movement from managerial realism in a structuration-like framework (Reed 1992) to process as a series of events over time rather than a set of relations among variables (Mohr 1982; Langlois 1995; Reed 1997). However, the competition between contexts and the international political economy largely remains at the margins even though knowledge has moved to centre stage. Also, the handling of temporality requires development.

Fourth, the development of theory and research on the diffusion and adoption of a wide range of organisational and technological innovations indicates that the pre-existing situation and its causal dynamics is central to the possibility of transformation.

Fifth, one stream of theorising strongly suggests that some organisations lack the capacities to undertake any new round of *innovation-design* requiring a trans-formation of the existing knowledge and repertoire. Much of this reasoning has relied upon some variant of the post-positivist theorising on structure and agency as structuration (e.g. Giddens 1979, 1981, 1984). The structuration solution was given some degree of impetus by the earlier attempts to reformulate systemic elements into the action frame of reference (Silverman 1970) and enactment (Weick 1969). Structuration theory is simply a suggestive collage of analytic problems and possible solutions in which Giddens certainly gives consideration to the international political economy. Also, some attention is given to commend-ing the historical dimension. However, as Archer (1988, 1995) robustly demon-strates, there is the issue of whether Giddens's variant of structuration theory forces agency to elide too easily from pre-existing structure. Is temporality breached?

REPRODUCTION OR TRANSFORMATION[1]

The earlier discussion of recursiveness and repertoires of recurrent action patterns can now be connected to knowledge-power-discipline and to the distinction between the reproduction of the pre-existing structure or its transition into a different structure. In Chapter 4 the approach of Buckley was introduced. We have emphasised the centrality of sequences of recurrent action patterns as implicated in the pre-existing structure. Therefore in relation to the examination of societal technique in Figure 7.1 and to that of structuration in Figure 5.1 it is argued that chronic recursiveness is prevalent, contingent and varies in durability through successive cycles. This view of structure seems similar to that of structura-tion and certainly structuration theory is associated with chronic recursiveness. However, the theorising and research on structural activation (see Chapter 12) was a revision to the different notions of structure as a mosaic of performance programmes (March and Simon 1958) and the more structurational notion of Burns and Stalker (1961) to incorporate the theory of morphogenesis/stasis proposed by Buckley (1967). Six points may be emphasised:

1   Organisations are theorised as possessing structural repertoires that are real and whose contents embrace dynamic sequences in various degrees of dormancy, yet often capable of activation and recomposition. This inter-pretation of structure is quite consistent, as such, with the realist turn and

with revisions to structuration theory to enhance temporality. The focus upon the activation of structural repertoires theorises that they pre-exist their activation and that the activation possesses emergent potentials (Buckley 1967).

2   It follows that dynamics has two distinct and related meanings: first, as the sequences of recurrent action patterns and their durational dimensions; second, as the theory of structural activation dynamics refers to the difference between reproduction of the existing structural form or its transformation.

3   Any alteration to the structural form is a case of non-reproduction and morphogenesis (Buckley 1967).

4   Morphogenesis is equivalent to the rampant literature on organisation change and should, according to theory of structural activation, be anchored in the notions of repertoires, recursiveness, recurrent actions patterns, strategic time reckoning and repertoire activation (Clark 1975a, b, 1985). Consequently, any claim to have recorded change must precede claims to have caused and explained change. Additionally, all change statements have to show that the pre-existing repertoire and the strategic time reckoning systems have been altered. These requirements are rarely met in concurrent research on change because the time scale is inadequate (Clark and Ford 1970).

5   The measure of event-time is process and not linear, calendrical time. Thus the claim to have discovered long waves in the performance of the economy operating in fifty-year cycles should be reformulated so that the pattern of the data constituting the process is taken as the metre of event-time. Then the unfolding of processes could be quite varied in respect of linear time.

6   The problem of measuring and confirming that change has taken place can now be formulated in terms of a recognisable alteration within either the organisation or the context or the interaction between organisation and context. This definition goes beyond the pragmatic schema of Miller and Friesen (1984). Moreover, if the presence of an alteration is assessed quite simply in terms of yes/no in the organisation, the context and the interaction, then we have a more expanded frame of reference than the dubious measurement of only the configuration within the organisation.

The six points cover both planned organisation change as well as emergent and evolved changes and reformulate the tentative approach to the new historicism by Reed (1997).

There are therefore some basic requirements in distinguishing between stasis and morphogenesis:

1   Analysis must specify the antecedent, pre-existing cycles of structuring in both the context and organisation. This unpacking goes much further than a static notion of starting points.

2   Organisations and contexts have finite and emergent capacities that constitute zones of manoeuvre which are more limited than voluntaristic

approaches have suggested. The strawman of determinism is barely resolved by introducing a strawman of voluntarism.

3   The analysis of the pre-existing structural cycles in the organisation and context also provides a frame of reference against which to assess where change or change/transformation has occurred and how extensive the changes have been or are likely to be in the future. This examination distinguishes stasis from morphogenesis. Distinctions should be made between the innovation by introducing new capabilities and the exnovation of existing capabilities.

4   The time span of stasis and morphogenesis should be sketched with respect to both linear and event time frames. Also, attention should be given to the durational tendencies as suggested by Gurvitch (1964) and summarised in Table 7.1. These sketches can then inform an examination of the pace of transformation necessary in future situations.

5   Analysis should anticipate emergence and unplanned change as well as being aware that unplanned order can arise and falsely seem like chaos to analysts with very narrow time frames and somewhat closed system minds.

The realist perspective known as analytic dualism is open to a wide range of perspectives including the neo-modern political economy proposed here. The next section sets out the reasoning and format which is then applied to the area of innovation-design.

MORPHOGENESIS/STASIS: ANALYTIC DUALITY

Structuration again: Archer-1

While escaping the deterministic and reification tendencies of the modern perspective, the leading edge in social theory (e.g. Giddens) and in organisation studies (e.g. Child 1972) moved into the equally awkward extreme of voluntarism. Structuration theory, in avoiding reification, conflates structure into agency when the realist turn argues that they should be separated sequentially in the strategy of analytic dualism. The formulation and resolution of the structure-agency issue through the duality of structuration (Giddens 1984) is problematic because the recognition of pre-existing structure in one part of the theorising is undermined by the temporal compacting of structure and agency. Giddens effectively fuses structure and agency, thereby denying an ontological status to structure. The notion of a virtual structure being instanciated by agential actions denies the pre-existence of structure and suspends temporality. The notion of instanciation renders the notion of reproduction meaningless. Archer (1996) contends that structure and agency are sequential in different tracts of time.

Giddens's contribution to the structure-agency debate has preoccupied theoretical developments in the past two decades. Generally the solution known as structuration and developed especially by Giddens has been the most salient text on the stage. Giddens's solution to the structure-agency problem – structuration – is sharply criticised for conflating structure and agency and failing to recognise that each possesses its own emergent powers (Thompson 1989; Layder 1997; Archer 1995). In structuration theory it seems that structure elides into agency and the features of emergence, autonomy, pre-existing and causal influence can be defined. Consequently agency and structure presuppose each other in a vicious circle (Smith and Turner 1986). The problem arises because the structuration perspective does not sufficiently disaggregate the stratified nature of social reality. Giddens does acknowledge the strata of the natural, biological and social, but neglects the personal (see Layder 1997) and how the socio-cultural structures are emergent from social relations (Archer 1995: 102). Giddens is criticised for an overactive view of the agent and an understratified view of the actor which strips them of inner reasons and tends to be one-dimensional. Giddens's view of structure has to be replaced by defining structure as composed of resources which are actual and of schemas which are virtual (Sewell 1992). Structures are not virtual. Resources have real effects which are independent (Archer 1995: 112–114). Given that Giddens has explicitly highlighted the time dimension it is perhaps surprising to discover that his critics find that structuration suffers from the conflation of the temporal dimensions. This criticism is made in an important and relevant claim for the approach to process known as the analytic duality (Archer 1988, 1995).

According to the realist ontology humans find that they are often located – albeit unknowingly – in positions and roles which are part of structures holding positions in defined relationships (Sayer 1992) Even so, these structures permit individual interpretation and individual capacity to alter the structure. The realist approach makes clear distinctions between events and conditions which are synchronous from those happening over extended periods of time. Equally, the realist approach searches for a language and metaphors appropriate to explaining the distinctions between:

- stasis (the reproduction of existing configurations);
- morphogenisis, or transformation of existing configurations.

There is no doubt about the realist interest in the diachronic as in qualitative studies of innovation (Miles and Huberman 1984) and in the sequential actions with stable processes (Harre 1979) .

Structure is always dependent upon agency but is emergent from structure. Agential directions to action are differentially conditioned from the causal powers and liabilities inhering in structure. Structure therefore precedes agency in a sequence whereby structure sets degrees of freedom or zones of manoeuvre that place limits upon what those occupying positions in the structure should and can do. Structures possess internal relationality between positions that are relatively enduring and ontologically distinguished from agency. There are therefore contextual limits to the transition of structures, yet transitions are possible. The theorising of transitions owes a considerable debt to Buckley's (1967) introduction of the notion of morphogenesis in open systems to replace self-regulation (cf. Weick 1969). Buckley separated the causes acting on phenomena from the possible consequences and possible mutual interactions. He also referred to how emergent processes could be outcomes of feedback processes, negative and positive. Buckley conceptualised agency in terms of degrees of freedom providing for the possibility of selecting courses of action. Here the feedback loops are contained in those relational properties within and between organisations that actually constitute the system. Archer (1995) tightens the analytic specification introduced by Buckley with the threefold sequence of structural conditioning → social interaction → structural elaboration.

Archer-2

How does the analytic duality proposed by Archer cope with social process and temporal ordering? Archer contends that much of orthodox theory on process tends towards hyperactivity because of the prevalence of micro-level 'here-and-now approaches' in sociology (e.g. Friedland and Boden 1994). Realist approaches are able to theorise open systems as 'flows, cycles and movements' and not be floored by the flux (Archer 1995: 156).

Archer's contribution unfolds in two main steps. Archer-1 has strong concern to theorise the comparative and longitudinal while enabling significant cross-national studies of central institutions such as educational systems. In her comparative, longitudinal analysis of four national educational systems there is a strong sense of how far pre-existing structural conditions and international differences have persistent, durable shaping consequences (Archer 1979). Archer-1 (1988) unpacks the temporal ordering, though without reference to the realist position of Bhaskar (1975).

Archer-2 (1995) provides a strong incorporation of Bhaskar's (1989) realist position in which the temporal ordering is vitally important, especially the sequence from 'structural pre-conditions' onward. Bhaskar (1989) provides a sixfold statement:

1   There are social forms consisting of the connections between people – the social structure – that are separate from people. So, societies are reducible to social structure, not to people.
2   Social forms have a pre-existence which establishes their autonomy as possible objects of enquiry.
3   Social forms have a causal power which establishes their reality.
4   Social forms are a necessary condition for any intentional act.
5   Because social forms pre-exist social activity they entail a transformational model of that social activity.
6   Human agency mediates the causal power of social forms.

The first three points define the social structure as always pre-existing, and as both autonomous and possessing its own emergent properties.

Archer-2 proposes two basic propositions about the temporal flow of social and organisational life:

- that pre-existing structures and their causal mechanisms pre-date action;
- that action sequences pre-date the elaboration and transformation of existing structures and the emergence of new structures.

This sequence occurs in processual time, not with simultaneity, but with temporality. Therefore, structure and agency have to be viewed separately in their interplay because each possesses emergent properties and must be analysed in parallel as an analytic dualism. The outcome may be the reproduction of the pre-existing structure or its transformation. The issue of transformation and the form that transformation takes leads Archer-2 to scrutinise Bhaskar's position and to propose a model based on realist social theory.

Given analytic dualism and a realist ontology, how is emergence theorised? Analytic dualism requires the practical analyst to know what reality is and to be able to explain reality in respect of any problem. Methodology is therefore an explanatory programme with the necessary linkage between social ontology and practical theory (Archer 1995: 5). Archer proposes a temporal sequence in which the pre-existing structural conditioning interplays with the emergent socio-cultural interaction. Her theorising is presented in an extensive set of diagrams (Archer 1995: 82) including Figure 14.1. The figure aims to show the difference between structuration theory and morphogenesis. The three horizontal elements from T^1 to T^4 are from Archer and their full scope embraces temporality. The details will be explained shortly. In contrast to morphogenesis there are three unfortunate tendencies to conflate temporality: downwards, upwards and central. The conflationary theories, including and especially structuration theory, occupy a limited time span. Returning to the morphogenetic three steps, the first two phases of T^1 and T^2/T^3 are separable and cannot be analysed by conflating them and/or eliding between them. There is a threefold sequence: structural conditions → social interaction → structural elaboration (transformation/emergence). The emergent property of the pre-existing structure and the actual experiences of the agents involved in activities shown as T^2/T^3 are separable, not synchronised. Yet, there is interplay between them and T^1, the structural conditions that pre-exist. The interplay possesses an intrinsic influence of the past. Actors are frequently unaware of the prior events which have constituted the pre-existing structure. These social structures possess a flow which can be located in phases (Archer 1995: 156). Social agency mediates the causal power of the social forms and this mediatory process is implicated in the first phase of any transformation cycle. People can exercise their powers and liabilities relative to the pre-existing socio-cultural powers. How can this mediation be conceptualised to avoid conflation? The pre-existing structural and cultural emergence shapes the social arenas that people inhabit. There is structural conditioning which in effect gives directional guidance, yet presents degrees of interpretative freedom.

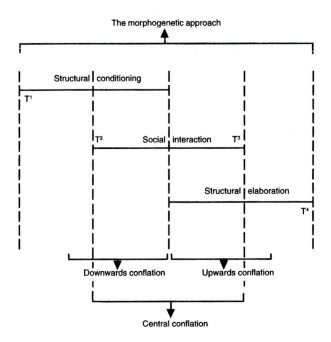

Figure 14.1 The limited time span of conflationary theories compared with the morphogenetic approach
Source: Archer (1995).

Archer next seeks to overlay the core elements of Bhaskar's model with her own as in Figure 14.2. Archer (1995: 157–161) reasons that the dualism is a theoretical requirement of explaining the processes involved in any structuring and in any restructuring as that unfolds in time. Figure 14.2 shows the tri-element cycles of structuring that are previous and subsequent to the focus of the analysis between T^1 and T^4. The pre-existing structures are generative mechanisms that interplay with other objects in a stratified world leading to non-predictable outcomes. There is no period that is unstructured. After T^2/T^3 of social interaction in the cycle which is the subject of analysis then the outcome at T^4 can be reproduction or transformation. This variant of social realism is compatible with a range of social theories. There are parallels here between this figure and the earlier accounts of the longitudinal (e.g. Figure 7.1). There is a long-term flow through the three steps so they must be split into episodes. The realist analysis aims to make statements about structuring without reference to the agent (Archer 1995: 169). Social structures (T^1) and agency (T^2/T^3) are separable. Agency only reproduces or transforms structure in any succession of processes in configurations. The distinction between structure and the agents rests upon the distinction between system integration and social integration introduced by Lockwood (1964). This permits various combinations of the two dimensions (Archer 1995: Figures 17 and 18). There is a crucial distinction between the emergent properties

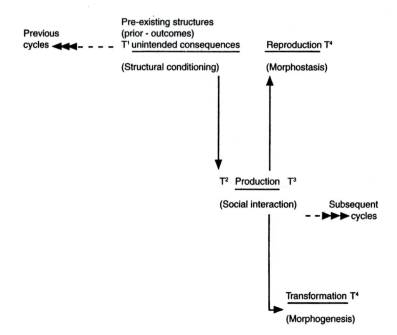

Figure 14.2 Superimposing the transformational model of social action and the
        morphogenetic/static cycle
Source: Archer (1995).

and the relatively enduring pattern of social life. Structurally emergent properties
are differentiated by a primary dependence upon material resources such as land,
food and weapons. The structurally emergent properties are not reducible to
people (cf. Elias).

The analytic dualism has considerable consequences for organisational change
theory and practice. As indicated earlier, theories of organisation change have a
fragile basis. Theories of organisation change tend to presume that pre-existing
structural conditions in the firm-context configuration are so thoroughly understood and so open to transformation that steered transformation can occur without generating unforeseeable emergent properties.

Analysts[2] of organisation change should adopt the three steps already identified. First they should examine the pre-existing structure and culture as an object
which conditions action patterns and supplies agents with strategic directional
guidance (Archer 1995: 196). This point articulates with my notion of structure
and activation by agents (Clark 1985). Pre-existing cultural systems already
contain specific doctrines and knowledge such as that of Toyota about just-in-
time and Honda of time-to-market. The pre-existing doctrines and knowledge
shape the social environment to be inhabited so that the outcomes of previous
actions are deposited in the unfolding situation. This is real, not virtual (cf.
Giddens 1984). Past scripts set the stage (Clark and Staunton 1989). People are

distributed through the structure with limited and contingent degrees of freedom (i.e. limited choice) and they are endowed with different vested interests. Moreover, resource distribution at T2 of material, symbolic and cultural resources is relatively durable. The degrees of interpretative freedom are somewhat finite. Even so the strongest constraints never fundamentally determine the agent. Whatever unfolds is, as in the case of habitus, a directional guidance (see Archer 1995: 196, 205, 209–210, 218, 246).

Second, agents interpret the pre-existing in terms of their projects and the conditions. It may be that new cycle of actions or some part of the cycle introduces new external conditions as postulated by Weick (1969) in his theory of environmentally triggered disturbances. However, the Weickian schema requires modification according to the theory of morphogenesis developed from Buckley (1967). Archer suggests that transformation arises in the third phase when certain elements are present in the second phase. Transformation is more likely – subsequently – in the differences between situational logics and vested interests. Stasis is most likely to occur when there is high social integration combined with both high and low system integration. Morphogenesis (transformation) is, according to Archer, more likely when low social integration is combined with either high or low system integration. It is the interface between the structures of resource distribution and vested interest groups which mediates the shift from stasis to transformation and that is illustrated in her account of educational change in England.

Third, the final phase is social elaboration and this arises from the previous sociocultural interaction that was conditioned in an earlier context. The aim here is not to predict (Sayer 1992), but instead to pinpoint the processes guiding action in a particular direction and to explain the specific configuration that arises. This is an analytic history of emergence: an analytically structured narrative (see Chapter 6). Archer's explanatory format consists of providing analytic histories of emergence (Archer 1995: 327). In the final phase there may be reproduction of the pre-existing structural conditions and habitus. However, transformation may occur.

The analytic dualism has considerable consequences for the many putative histories of work organisation and related domains such as trade union history and corporate histories. Even so, there is much more thinking and exploration necessary to the conceptualisation of structural conditioning and on how structural conditions are transmitted to particular agents. We know little about the strategic combinations that lead to reproduction rather than transformation.

INNOVATION-AND-DESIGN

The interface between organisation theory and strategy has been prised open by the resource-based theory discussed in Chapter 11. Exponents of the resource-based theory have constituted a language by which resources, routines and knowledge seem readily to slip into theory of organisations in action. It is claimed that the resource-based theory is dynamic because of the role of routines and because of the direction given to knowledge making (Grant 1995). Moreover, from organisation theory it has been argued that the strategic human resource perspective can contribute to the learning and appropriability of capabilities (Kamoche and Mueller 1997). However, the previous chapters and the sections of this chapter have noted key problems and suggested alternative directions.

This section addresses another aspect of the temporal conflation of action by organisation theory and the resource-based theory when the role of innovation and design is presumed rather than articulated. As indicated in Chapter 6, knowledge-based capitalism involves considerable intensity in design and design is the structural carrier for innovation (Clark and Staunton 1989; Clark *et al.* 1992). A large section of those known as knowledge professionals and members of the service strata are involved in design. Organisations, especially multinational businesses, spend high proportions of total costs in design, both within the firm and through outsourcing and shared relationships in the inter-firm network. Organisations need to develop a whole stream of recurrent action patterns in their repertoire to anticipate the direction of design and to deliver design from the strategic levels to the operating levels. These require a capacity to edit knowledge in the firm. Giddens (1984, 1990) contends that organisations are crucial sites whereby novel forms of social thought can be considered and even realised through reflexive self-regulation based on the monitoring of action. Reflexive self-regulation involves action which is continuous whereby knowledge of the mechanisms of the reproduction of the system is employed in self-control:

> The modern capitalist enterprise is in some respects both typical of modern organisations and one of the main sources of innovation generating the circumstances in which they have arisen. As analysed by Marx, capitalism is a mode of production in which reflexive self-regulation within the enterprise – a phenomenon clarified by Weber's account and demonstration of the significance of double-entry book-keeping to the capitalist firm – is not matched by reflexive control over economic life as a whole.
>
> (Giddens 1984: 205)

Established firms engage with knowledge communities specialising in auditing existing practices with the aim of experimenting with novel arrangements in the future (Lash and Urry 1987, 1995). Those knowledge communities will be both inside the firm and also in specialist agencies and consultancies. Their actions may be referred to as reflexive monitoring. Their activities frequently address the issue of time-space competition and compression (Schoenberger 1996). Members of the knowledge community were known as the technostructure (Galbraith 1963) and more recently are referred to as symbolic analysts (Reich 1991) and knowledge architects (Nonaka and Takeuchi 1995). Their roles are central to handling the problems of design intensity and hence of innovation-design.

Sectoral clusters frequently possess locations in towns and regions where inter-firm networking and collective learning occur in untraded interdependencies between firms (Storper 1995; Camagni 1991). Innovation and design are about continuous learning and that is generally agglomerated in particular socio-cultural networks because the complex geo-technical problems require specialised, dynamic milieus where learning is fast, is retained and can be transmitted. This is a double process that sustains the autonomy of multinational businesses from control by national governments and alters the locus of governance to quasi-regional clusters. Storper (1995) emphasises the role of localised clusters as a nexus of untraded interdependencies that facilitate effective co-ordination locally.

The significance of innovation-design to firms has been grossly neglected in the depthless ontologies that dominate understanding about organisations (Abernathy 1978; Clark and Staunton 1989). Firms without a capability to undertake reflexive self-regulation in the relaunch of their products and services in ever renewed cycles simply disappear (Clark and Starkey 1988; Clark and Fujimoto 1991) and even those that do undertake innovation-design regularly fail (Whipp and Clark 1986). Abernathy (1978) cogently described and explained the centrality of innovation-design. His analytic influence has inspired and shaped a genre of studies of innovation-design, especially the studies of Clark and Henderson.

Miles and Snow (1986) disaggregated the vertically integrated firm and also identified the role of design. The role of design in mass customisation (Pine 1993) was discussed in Chapter 6 and comparisons drawn between the USA and Japan in Chapter 9. Also, the case studies in Chapter 10 gave design and innovation a central role in the growth of sectoral clusters. In Abernathy's (1978) analysis, the process of innovation-design envelops the whole firm over a period of time covering the work organisation, the product/service, the process through which an output is constructed and distributed. Firms acquire a capability for innovation-design in their repertoire and periodically activate that capability to engage in a new cycle (Clark and Starkey 1988; Clark and Staunton 1989). Typically that repertoire for innovation-design contains a firm-specific language and a specialised community of practitioners that undertakes special roles over many months and years. There is extensive interaction from the firm to outside sources. Although Abernathy's analysis has established the field of enquiry, that feature has been largely excluded from the 'here-and-now' mindset of organisation studies.

The process of innovation-design requires considerable analytic development. Two simple analytic devices may assist exploratory research. First, the episodes and steps in the designing process can be depicted as in Figure 14.3. Along the lower part of the figure the existing constellations of production are shown as ongoing along calendar time until they are interfaced with the new innovation-design requirements for a new operating system. Too much attention has been given to this level and to the narrow time window shown in the shaded circle. Too little attention has been given the events shown on the diagonal from the activation and mobilisation of the design group onwards. This is depicted in four stylised episodes that are overlapping and iterative. The four stylised episodes are based on the study of major factory redesigns (Clark 1972; Clark and Whipp 1984). They are simply illustrative of situations in which the firm is activating a

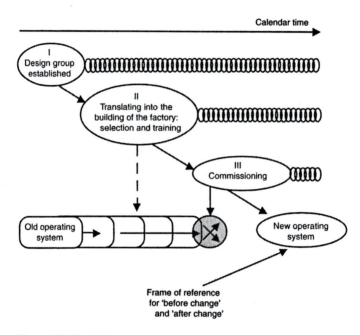

Figure 14.3 Designing processes

pre-existing repertoire. The Harvard case studies of Benetton have been particularly good at reconstructing this feature. The stylised format would be even more
fragmentary in a firm still developing its repertoire and/or altering the existing
repertoire. Second, Figure 14.4 proposes an analytic grid for matching the four
episodes to three of the core capabilities of the firm (Abernathy 1978):

- the work organisation being introduced;
- the new output being devised;
- the production and distribution processes including new technologies, new
  raw materials and new facilities.

Design capability can now be theorised as the means by which the firm
approaches the dilemma of whether to pursue efficiency or innovation.

The role of innovation-design in reflexive monitoring directly implicates the
perspective of competition between contexts. The contextual dimension constitutes the selection environment for firms and their sectoral clusters. In the case of
individual firms their position can be explored by examining how far innovation-
design connects the flow of revenue into the firm with the flow of outputs from the
firm. Figure 14.4 is devised to show the configuration between work organisation
and the characteristics of the output in terms of the degree to which the product is
medium volume, high value (e.g. executive saloon cars) or high volume, low value

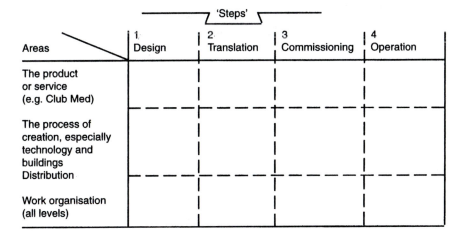

Figure 14.4 Total design grid

(e.g. cigarettes). High added-value items such as executive cars (e.g. Jaguar and Ford Lincoln) potentially create a revenue flow depending upon the market characteristics (see Chapter 7) and the capabilities of the supplier in terms of production and distribution.

The processes of reflexive self-regulation and of innovation-design are clarified in the perspective of analytic dualism discussed in the previous section. The next section seeks to illustrate how one study of innovation-design might be considered from this perspective. The cameo which follows is an instance when morphogensis takes place, yet the new organisational capability is unsuccessful in transforming its context. Consequently, the cameo is also an example of where the theme of competition between contexts was only very partially understood.

RETRO-ORGANISATION THEORY?

The purpose of this section is to explore the potentials and problems of applying the perspective of analytic dualism (Archer 1955) by reviewing a lengthy, published case study involving the intention massively to transform the pre-existing product, factories, technology and work organisation of a major firm. The review of the case study concentrates upon the organisation and sketches the 'competition between contexts' dimension. The case for review is by Whipp and Clark (1986) who examined a major project in the British automobile industry to produce an executive car from the Birmingham–Coventry corridor of England to capture a major slice of the European market. The new factory, work organisation and car barely achieved one-fourth of the target figures and closed after six years. The case study refers to a similar context to that examined in Chapter 10 with respect to the issue of whether Henry Ford could have succeeded had he started off from

Birmingham, England. Therefore, it may be theorised that the context possesses its own capabilities and that these impinge very directly on that part of the sectoral cluster in which the transformation was being attempted. There were limited zones of manoeuvre in the context and rival contexts in continental Europe provided more competitive contexts. Equally, the firm possessed finite capabilities. Whipp and Clark concluded that in this instance the firm's pre-existing repertoire of recurrent actions patterns, structural poses and its communities of practice possessed such strong tendencies to reproduction that they overpowered the mission and vision proposed by the task forces involved in innovation-design. So, the new socially constructed technology, factories and product operated according to a script and roles that the top level task forces, senior management and the state considered were outdated.

Applying the analytic dualism means treating the pre-existing situation fully and separately from the new cycle of events that is unfolding. Archer's theory of transformation provides a useful test of the many claims being advanced in contemporary longitudinal theories of strategy implementation and of organisational change to have identified a universal checklist of key elements. The reconstruction of events was undertaken in two major parts and a minor part. The two major parts were:

- the most recent events over a period of approximately ten years that includes the whole innovation-design cycle;
- the reconstruction of the firm's capacities to undertake innovation-design over the preceding period of more than six decades.

The minor part was to reconstruct the preceding short eight-year cycle of innovation-design. That was an initial, traumatic attempt to alter the structural repertoire.

The original analytic approach of structure-event-structure was adapted to explore and scrutinise the contention that history shapes the future (Clark and Whipp 1984). Although the analytically structured narrative was presented as sequential, the two major parts were theorised separately and the two authors reversed the analytic roles with which they were most familiar. To sharpen the contrast required by the analytic dualism, the more recent cycle can be considered before the earlier cycle. A brief retro-history of events then would run as shown in Box 14.1 (cf. Burrell 1997).

This retro-calendar of events is analytically driven by the location and performance of the design capability (Clark and De Bresson 1990). When the firm entered the automobile industry in 1906 the design of the cars and the factory was contracted out to consulting engineers. That solution has limited parallels with the contemporary sourcing by car firms. In contrast the penultimate cycle of innovation-design for P6 was undertaken within the firm and mythologised as a successful executive saloon car. The reality was that the annual sales of 30,000 cars were very small relative to European competitors in the executive market. There was considerable failure in the work organisation. In order to position this

BOX 14.1 FINAL CYCLE: SD1

- Closure of the factory and end of production of the SD1 car (1982)
- Sales achieve only 20 per cent of target (1976–82)
- Commissioning and launching the SD1 executive saloon car (1976)
- Commissioning and opening of the new factory and work organisation (1976)
- Concept design and translation for SD1 (1972–4)
- Concept design and translation for P8–P10 (1968–71)

Preceding cycle: P6

- Design, concept, commissioning and production (1963–71)

Cumulative pre-existing repertoire

- Possess internal capacity in innovation-design in P-series (1934–1960s)
- Severe financial losses and facing exit (1928–32)
- Attempt to create internal capacity; search for differentiated focus (1918–28)
- Hire in design capacity: from cycles into the automobile industry (1896–1918)

retro-history in the framework of the analytic dualism, it is necessary to imagine that the most recent period was driven by the attempts of one strata, top management, to transform the firm from a small batch to a volume producer in the design conscious, profitable, executive market.

The next sections run the analytically driven narrative in reverse.

Most recent cycle of innovation-design: Rover SD1

The most recent cycle is summarised on the design process and grid shown in Figures 14.3 and 14.4. In this study the Rover management possessed four episodes in the innovation-design repertoire. The four episodes are overlapping, iterative, convoluted and contested (Whipp and Clark 1986: Chapter 4). Closer examination of the innovation-design grid shows the interweaving of attempts to transform the pre-existing structure and culture at the factory while reproducing the procedural and declarative knowledge embedded in the separate activity of innovation-design. The problems for innovation-design were not only of the distributed nature of the design activity, but especially of the knowledge bases that could be included. Whipp and Clark (1986) list a series of design choices reflecting a very firm specific knowledge about paint plants, about Swedish innovations and about the problems of transition.

Immediately preceding cycle: Rover P6

When, in the mid-1960s the P6 executive car was built, it was generally considered to be a successful design with the potential to compete in continental Europe. Very quickly the Rover factory became the site for some of the most famous industrial strife in the British car industry (Whipp and Clark 1986: 75: 83). This was partly because the P6 was intended to be Rover's first medium volume car. Rover's management intended that the new work organisation and new production facilities should embody the principles of assembly line, standard production rather than the hand-build of Land Rover[3] and of the P5.

Pre-existing structural repertoire (1968 → 1906)

The analytically structured narrative winds backward. More recently, but prior to the P6, the previous P1–P5 (1963→1934) had been designed and built for three decades according to a basic recipe. In order to create sufficient revenue from the British market, the P-car attained volume over several years from its target consumers who preferred a conservative style of wood and leather interiors different to that of Jaguar. The tastes of Rover's customers changed slowly. So, from the 1930s into the 1950s it was possible to continue with a craft-based (as Perrow 1967) work organisation for small batch production, thereby preserving long-established forms. Relative to the shop floor levels, those involved with the innovation-design cycle were more modern in their organisation. These designers were central to the discovery and successful launching of the four-wheel-drive (4WD) after 1947 so the traditional form of work organisation was replicated. The 4WD became the major source of revenue to finance the next costly design cycle.

Between 1928 and 1932 Rover faced exit from the automobile industry at the very moment that new entrants were appearing (e.g. Hillman, Jaguar, Volvo). It was the external influence of two major customers that rescued the firm. Rover's supplier of electrical goods and major designer of electrical systems in Britain was Lucas whose top management insisted on the appointment of people with engineering expertise at the board level. The bankers, Lloyds, insisted on a senior appointment in financial management control.

In the ten years after World War I the top management struggled. Initially they sought to retain the diversified product range by buying up a nearby firm producing small cars as a means of building in some design capacity. In addition there were a small number of appointments of automobile experts at the level below the board, but their influence was constrained. Increasingly innovation-design was undertaken in-house for the car, but excluded the design of its production to economise on new dies and castings. The work organisation in that period was craft based and much control was implicitly delegated to the local institutions, including the unions. Serious attempts to appropriate explicit knowledge into the technostructure were absent. There was a flirtation with Bedeaux systems which focused upon time-study, incentives and the workbench, but minimised major alterations to the layout of the factory and its workflow.

From 1906 when designs for the first car were purchased by the already successful bicycle firm of Rover, a strategy of diversification was immediately undertaken. By 1912 Rover was able to boast that it was the world's largest firm manufacturing bicycles, motor cycles and saloon cars. The boast was hollow. In the same year Ford entered the British market and gained one-quarter (see Chapter 10). Rover produced about twenty-five cars each week with skilled craft workers assembling non-standardised components around a traditional box-like car design.

Analytic dualism

The Rover case establishes the role of pre-existing structural repertoire and illustrates how its problem-solving communities imposed corrigable closure on interpretative flexibility (cf. Bijker *et al.* 1987). The social was made durable, but the time-space commodification and compression was not competitive with executive saloons developed in other contexts by Mercedes and BMW or by Volvo and Saab. The difficulties faced by the configuration of problem-solving communities in Rover for 'building and sustaining a receptive context' (Pettigrew *et al.* 1992: 272–273, Figures 9.1, 9.2) were enormous. The British context for executive saloon cars was not an innovation pole (Clark and De Bresson 1990) even though the continental European market boomed.

DIFFERENCES AND ALTERNATIVES

This cameo is about organisational design for a totally new factory complex and new forms of work organisation at John Players new factory in Nottingham (Clark 1972, 1979).[4] Chandler (1977) reports that cigarette-making technology was at the frontier of technological developments in the nineteenth century and this tendency continued well into the late twentieth century when a new systems technology became available. John Players was a major national player with a strong domestic market position within a group that possessed a special international relationship with former American competitors. The technology for the product being manufactured was highly complex, among the most advanced of any sector, but the consumer product was relatively uncomplex compared to an automobile. Moreover, the problem-solving community of top management who were promoting the massive transformation of their technology, layouts and work organisation were in a powerful position relative to other rival groupings. The original case study covered a five-year period in real time with exceptionally good, continuous concurrent access to the innovation and design process for a new factory intended to be 'the most advanced technologically in the world'.

The Horizon Group design team intended to create a massive two-floor modernist building in which the total work flow time from start to finish would be four hours rather than the one hundred hours in the existing three sites containing small workplaces. In almost every respect this case was an example of business process redesign. The existing forms of work organisation were to be transformed and new occupational groups inserted by management. After five years the new factory was successfully commissioned. From the start of the design for the new factory and work organisation the Horizon Group sought and considered a variety of forms of external advice including advice from social scientists. In that respect they were similar to other leading firms in the British cluster of food, drink and tobacco. The second cameo is a sharp contrast to the Rover SD1 example just discussed.

How does this case differ from the standard study of organisational change and what can analytic dualism contribute? The Horizon Group within John Players was the project team responsible for the total design process in all areas of the grid shown in Figure 14.3 and Figure 14.4. Indeed the notion of the design grid was based on that study. The Horizon Group set out from day one to discover external social science advice.[5] The social science input concentrated upon two basic issues. First, to construct accounts of the differences between:

(a) the existing, ongoing social structure and culture in the time-space framework of the factories;
(b) the intended future social structure and culture in the proposed time-space framework for the new factory.

Second, the social scientists drew attention to how the gaps between (a) and (b) presented a variety of alternative possibilities. The social scientists reported that theirs was the Alternatives and Differences Approach (ADA).

The centrepiece of differences and alternatives was to ensure that social structural analysis of the pre-existing and the proposed was graspable by those centrally involved. This included an understanding inter-departmental relationships based on the theory of interdependence (Thompson 1967), the changes in social technology (Perrow 1967) and Touraine's (1955) theory of the evolution of tasks and relationships. Over a period of five years many extended pieces of observation, studies of documents and more than 250 interviews were undertaken. Detailed comparisons were made of the semi-autonomous groups in cigarette packing (Clark 1972: Chapter 5) and the impact of changes on the role sets of packers, supervisors and mechanics. The comparisons involved those to be in working at the future factory. The aim was to bring the implied future into the discussion and also to develop alternative futures.

This approach was grounded in the theory of structural activation with its contention that organisations possess finite repertoires of recurrent action programmes and that these are both the objects and subjects for organisational change. These features are barely mentioned in the largely socio-psychological literature on group process.

The theory of social science utilisation was developed from the suggestions by Miller and Rice (1967) and the claims by members of the Tavistock Institute about creating a 'knowledge utilisation network' at the commencement of the research. In the John Players study and two others the creation of the utilisation network was relatively successful when assessed against several criteria, but three other cases had much less impact (Clark 1972). Comparing the cases suggests that pre-existing power distributions coupled to antecedent capacities of the knowledge communities inside the host firms were key factors (Clark 1975a). This observation corresponds with the analysis of knowledge absorptive capacity by Cohen and Levinthal (1990) and confirms the impression that capabilities are finite with limited degrees of freedom.

SUMMARY

Unravelling 'transformation' from 'stasis' poses considerable problems, especially for theorists of programmed and planned organisational change (Wilson 1992). Too little attention has been given (so far) to balancing between the recent recognition that there are powerful emergent properties in contexts and to some degree inside organisations while undertaking a nuanced appraisal of the degree to which pre-existing structural conditions constrain. The latter is variable.

It is essential to develop better temporal units of analysis and to apply them to the context and to the organisation. The analytic dualism requires attention to the pre-existing forms of temporality and to the emerging forms. Moreover, this requires that the temporal conflation of the organisation is addressed. Unless these requirements are met then many statements about existing situations being researched are weightless and perhaps worthless.

This chapter completes the proposed revisions to the resource-based theory of the firm in strategy by exploring a collection of ideas with explanatory possibilities for organisation change. Ideally, much more of the theme of competition between contexts should have been drawn into the exploration. The context and the organisation possess finite capacities, powers and liabilities.

NOTES

1 This section draws heavily from my paper presented to the British Academy of Management, Aston University, September 1996. I am indebted to David Wilson (now Warwick University) and especially to Chris Carter (now North London University) for their generous encouragement and observations.
2 This section follows Archer (1995: 196f), but does so within my theoretically laden selection.
3 To be compared with the hand-got methods of coalmining in the sociotechnical tradition.
4 The Social Science Research Council five-year programme on 'The Utilisation of the Social Sciences' (1967–72). My contributions involved research and consultancy in major redesigns of factories and similar (e.g. Clark 1972).
5 The case study was supported by the Social Science Research Council's five-year programme of research on 'The Utilisation of the Social Sciences' to A. B. Cherns and P. A. Clark.

PART IV

Zones of manoeuvre

15 Organisational management and zones of manoeuvre

INTRODUCTION

In this final chapter I shall review the two themes and direct attention to the interesting problems. Figure 15.1 summarises the examination of the five perspectives in the preceding chapters to establish that organisations and contexts should be analysed within a neo-modern political economy (NMPE) perspective. NMPE shares the critique of the positivist and modern architecture of organisation theory and strategy with the major developments through post-modernism, social construction of reality and the realist turn. Those three analytic positions have moved beyond critique into the establishment of their own distinctive positions. My concern has been to contribute to a synthesis by showing that NMPE offers a major theoretical position complete with robust implications for policy and practice.

This final chapter looks backward and forward. My purpose in looking back and scrutinising organisation theory, international business and strategy is to highlight the problems which are still only partly resolved. At the present time the interface between organisation theory and strategy has been prised open, but the cross-cutting analytic linkages tend to be passive rather than active. So, accounts of organisation theorising rarely do more than offer discussions of strategy (e.g. Daft 1997; Clegg et al. 1996; Hatch 1997). Meanwhile, in strategy there has been the significant development of organisation economics and Grant's (1990, 1995, 1996a, b, 1998) use of the resource-based theory provides a major opening to organisation theory. However, each of these developments neglects the recent theory and comparative research on national systems of business, innovation, knowledge and organisation. Hence my choice of the theme of competition between contexts and the examination of a selection of key contributions to that theme. The logic of my reasoning is that this theme is so significant that its persistent bracketing and location at the end of texts is impractical and implausible. That situation is beginning to alter. Temporality, however, has yet to be properly acknowledged. Many claims have been made about the importance of an exquisite sense of time (e.g. Weick 1969) in order to really theorise organisations in action (e.g. Clegg 1989). Much still needs to be done. Equally, the competition between contexts has to accommodate the temporal dynamics. Therefore, the two

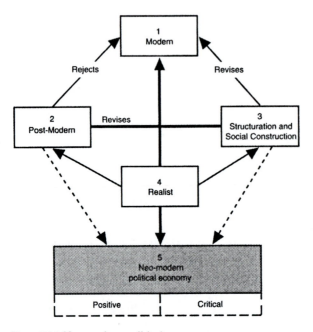

Figure 15.1 Neo-modern political economy

themes of organisations and contexts should acknowledge the dynamics of competition.

The neo-modern political economy perspective selectively embraces the orga-nisational, strategic and comparative study of international business systems. NMPE rejects the positivist-modern perspective and selectively draws elements from post-modern and social constructions perspectives while taking the realist turn as a major influence. NMPE ranges from the critical variant (e.g. Bailey *et al.* 1994; Gregory 1994; Thompson and McHugh 1995; Hobsbawm 1998) to the positive variant in which the continuity of capitalism is presumed, yet not neces-sarily taken for granted (e.g. Dicken 1998).

Figure 15.1 restates the position introduced in Chapter 2. The aim is to redirect organisational analysis towards a more robust understanding of the futures of organisations. Too much previous thinking has neglected the pre-existing stratified social reality and has presumed that discursive penetration is sufficient to trans-form existing organisations. Equally seriously too much thinking about the future ignores the degrees of freedom and zones of manoeuvre. Robust analysis acknow-ledges the pre-existing, the unfolding and the future configurations of events.

According to the realist and neo-modern political economy perspectives orga-nisational management occurs in a stratified context in which the zones of manoeuvre available to the firm tend to be impacted by competition with the causal effects upon organisations occurring in other contexts. Consequently, the issue in strategic choice is less one of overturning positivism (Thompson and

McHugh 1995; cf. Child 1972) and more a matter of understanding a variety of contexts by undertaking and being able to utilise rich, comparative analytic description (Scott 1995; Clegg *et al.* 1996). The aim is to create actionable understanding. Moreover, because organisations in action are repertoires of generative recursive systems requiring activation and self-regulated revision then the zones of manoeuvre for strategic choice are practically constrained in the short-run. Penrosian leaning is likely to be impregnated with the domestic declarative knowledge and imprinted with domestic experiences (Chapter 11). Even so, American exceptionalism still provides a significantly enabling context for certain types of organisation (Chapter 9). Hence the proposition that Henry Ford would have failed had he set out from the West Midlands of England (Chapter 10).

It has not been easy to formulate and answer the question of what is management and managing. There is considerable acceptance of the claim that managerial hierarchies exist and have causal effects. These managerial hierarchies are the targets of the time-space commodification and compression arising from the contemporary state of capitalism and of the global economy. There has been massive transformation of the cadres employed in managerial activities (Scarborough and Burrell 1996). Also, there is widespread acceptance that management and managing are implicated in the two themes of 'organisations in action' and 'competition between contexts'. Hence the title of this chapter. Even so, there is considerable disagreement about what managers do and what management designates. Therefore the position of management will be explored through the realist perspective introduced by Tsoukas (1994) in which managers are important as part of a causal structure and as a mechanism.

RESTATING THEMES AND PERSPECTIVES

The two themes of organisations in action and competition between contexts cross-cut the three disciplinary fields of organisation theory, strategy and international business. The two themes couple firms and contexts into a dynamic theorising of capabilities with attention to dislocation and unplanned order. The co-analysis of context-and-firm has been given impetus from several directions, both in the everyday world and in the academy of the business schools. The purpose of examining the two themes is to provide focus to issues arising from shifts of analytic perspective to a neo-modern political economy after the ravaging of the modern-positivist perspectives by the trio of post-modernism, structuration theory and the realist turn. Figure 15.1 restates the position introduced in *Chapter 1*. The new ideological-cum-intellectual configuration that is surfacing is neo-modern with strong elements of political economy. This configuration is removing the barriers between organisation, strategy and national systems. The perspective of neo-modern political economy selectively embraces the organisational, strategic and comparative study of international business systems. NMPE rejects the positivist-modern perspective and selectively draws elements from post-modern and structuration and symbolic perspectives while taking the realist turn as a major influence. NMPE ranges from the critical variant (e.g. Thompson and McHugh 1995) to the positive variant in which the continuity of capitalism is presumed, yet not necessarily taken for granted. The aim is to redirect organisational analysis (Scott 1995; Clegg *et al.* 1996) towards a more robust understanding of the futures of organisations. Too much previous thinking has neglected the pre-existing stratified social reality and has presumed that simplistic collections of headings can be used to transform existing organisations. Robust analysis acknowledges the tri-ality of the pre-existing, the unfolding and the future configurations of events. The structure of the book (as Figure 1.1) commenced with a discussion of the five perspectives and three disciplines in Part I leading into two parallel parts each devoted to one of the two themes. Part II dealt with competition between contexts and Part III with competition between contexts. Part IV brings these together to discuss the zones of manoeuvre available to organisations.

Chapter 2 examined the five intellectual-cum-theoretical perspectives shown in Figure 15.1. So far most attention has been given to attacking the positivist-modern point of view and to proclaiming a single alternative drawn from either the post-modern and/or the structuration and symbolic realist perspectives. Post-modernism provides many elements in its own perspective that are relevant to the perspective of neo-modern political economy. Putting post-modernism and structuration with the modern into the same arena was achieved by Hatch (1997) and she also sought to cross-connect organisation theory with strategy. In strategy the leading edge of theorising has, since the seminal conferences organised by Rumelt, *et al.* (1991) sought to shift away from positivist, deterministic theorising. Porter's (1991) essay neatly illustrates the direction being taken. However, at the same moment strategic theory moved from an external preoccupation towards the resource-based theory and the organisation economics of the firm as illustrated by Grant (1990) compared with Grant (1998). This has meant that the theme of competition between contexts has only slowly been incorporated (e.g. Foss and Erikson 1995). There is quite a gap between recent accounts of new organisation theory (e.g. Reed 1996) and the developments in organisation economics and strategy. Rowlinson (1997) is exceptional in addressing significant sections of that gap.

Chapter 2 also introduced the realist turn and its claims to reposition political economy as the analytic cutting edge of the move from significant critique towards neo-modern political economy as the contemporary intellectual-cum-theoretical movement. The realist turn gives sustenance to some of the dynamic elements linking the future with the present and past, thereby escaping the temporal conflation and extended present that besets so much of organisational analysis. The realist turn has been partially recognised in organisation theorising, but its citation tends to lack substance and critical scrutiny of the variety on offer or the problems arising. This chapter parallels and extends the conversation between perspective that is ongoing (e.g. Clegg *et al.* 1996).

Chapter 3 argued that the modern-positivist perspective has shaped the cluster of research programmes within organisation theory and that these have supplied design rules. They ensured that design rules. The seminal organisation theory by

J. D. Thompson (1967) of 'organisations in action' is a theory of contextual containment in the just-in-case format and a brilliant example of design rules through the analogy of computer program design by defining a sequence of activities leading to a defined end output (Clark and Staunton 1989). The protective belt of strategic choice introduced ambivalence and confused the early critics. However, the critiques of organisation from the post-modern and labour process perspectives did not so much remove the protective belt as they stimulated significant alternative clusters (e.g. critical theory). Organisation theory has been and is robustly protected against the implications of the structuration perspective typified by Giddens even though there are increasing citations of structuration. Organisation theory now covers a clutch of variants and their position is likely to continue. However, the two themes of organisations in action and competition between contexts provide a fruitful crystallisation to the existing debates and conversations, especially when more sociological perspectives are acknowledged.

Chapter 4 focused upon sociological variants of structuration theories and the realist turn. Structuration as conceived by Giddens was the major cutting edge in replacing the positivist perspectives. Structuration claimed to resolve a number of problems and to spearhead a post-positivist social science capable of handling temporality and the structure/agency issue. Revising structuration involves briefly examining the theory of habitus and social fields (Bourdieu), social configurations (Elias) and domains (Layder). Also, the realist turn (Harre, Bhaskar, Sayer, Archer) is of major interest (e.g. Layder, Reed).

The new political economy takes the market seriously and seeks to provide a sociological analysis of economic action (*Chapter 5*). However, it becomes evident that organisational economics has made a considerable impact, especially through notions of rational expectations and incentivising.

Competition between contexts as a theme commences in *Chapter 6* by examining the temporality and the historical with reference to explaining the relative economic performance of nations over decades, generations and centuries. How far do geographical elements still influence political economy? *Chapter 6* introduces the international political economy in a neo-modern perspective through a long-term exploration of the North Atlantic economies and their use of markets to create hegemonic dependence between nations. The notion of the analytically structured narrative is coupled with the new geography (Gregory, Harvey, Dicken) to unpack Figure 5.1 and the periodisation of major episodes in the economies of nations. The long-term structuration changes slowly as an ensemble, yet is subject to dislocation from external and internal factors. Geography and history interact (Landes) through various features, including the role of the state in property rights and their enforcement in regions that become core. The twentieth century is one in which knowledge-based capitalism is now central (Dunning) with its attention to innovation-design in mass customisation. Design intensity has increased with shorter design cycles. The differences between Japan and the USA exemplify innovation-design as competition between contexts.

Comparing international business systems has been greatly stimulated by the debate between Dunning and Porter as well as by the many theories of national business systems (e.g. Lundvall, Whitley). The Porter/Dunning debate highlights markets, the role of multinationals, sectoral clusters of firms, governmental action and national capacities to constitute explicit and situated knowledge. *Chapter 7* examines three frameworks for analysing the knowledge-making propensities of the nation with respect to design and innovation First, Clark expands on the structuration dimension with a focus upon societal problem solving and possibility that there are societal techniques of social technologies. The American system of innovation-and-design rather than manufacture and the role of the American service class provide a useful illustration. Second, the Porter/Dunning eclectic diamond combines the five intra-nation factors (endowed, market, rivalry, state, sectoral clusters) with the overseas diamonds and the mediating role of multi-national businesses (see Figure 7.3). Third, the national business systems perspective (Whitley) reveals the need to develop the societal-institutional dimension further.

Chapter 8 weaves in the societal-sectoral cluster dimension (Sorge). The issue is to confine the actor perspective (Hofstede) and to insert the societal-institutional pillars of normative, regulative and cognitive (Scott) to the interface with sectoral dimension. The proposition that national institutions 'select-in/out' certain sectoral clusters is explored (Sorge). Within nations there is likely to be a typical variety of sectoral clusters (Clark).

Chapter 9 applies the competition between contexts theme to American exceptionalism. The centrality of the USA in the international political economy has been re-articulated by the transition from the Cold War. There is American exceptionalism and American firms are major players in addressing the problems of time-space commodification, compression and competition. Moreover, the typical variety of US firms is wide and there are openings for new forms of organisation. The American situation is central to the neo-modern political economy perspective.

Sectoral clusters are a key context within the nation and sectoral clusters are that nation's base for international competition. *Chapter 10* explores the typical variety between two sectoral clusters in Britain and the USA focusing upon how the former handles multinational businesses from the latter. The sectoral cluster created over three generations by Marks & Spencer drove out foreign entrants through its inter-organisational network of innovation-design. However, this sectoral cluster also entrained its pivotal firm in specific zones of manoeuvre. This example is generalised and then applied to the sectoral cluster of the automobile sector at its origins in the early twentieth century at the moment when Ford entered. These two examples are nationally specific and varied. It is argued that Marks & Spencer would have faced considerable difficulties to be successful in the USA: neither could Henry Ford have succeeded by starting with the Ford T from the English Midlands; nor could Benetton have succeeded so much in starting from the English Midlands sectoral cluster of textiles.

The perspective of neo-modern political economy and economic sociology have been established and exemplified. Competition between contexts is now established as a theme across the three disciplinary fields of organisation studies and international business and has considerable implications for strategy. However, the theme of competition between contexts has not penetrated the resource-based strategic theory sufficiently. The resource-based theory of internal capabilities has so far ignored the formative influences of context on the firm's knowledge, routines and capabilities. The theme of organisations in action can now be introduced.

Chapter 11 sets out the resource-based view of strategy proposed from organisational economics and scrutinises the linkages in the theory, especially the claims of dynamic capabilities as a proxy for organisations in action. The resource-based theory claims that resources are transformed by Penrosian learning and organisational routines into knowledge that gives direction and dynamic capabilities. It might be anticipated that Resource Based Strategic Theory (RBST) provides the ideal statement of this theme and there is an interesting case to be examined. Three major problems are discovered. These are of structure, culture and agency. RBST is:

- largely static and fails to theorise organisations in action;
- the treatment of knowledge and Penrosian learning is bold, yet limited;
- transitions cannot be explained.

RBST also fails to engage adequately with competition between contexts. These problems are addressed starting with the role of Penrosian learning.

Chapter 12 notes the recent critique of organisational routines by organisational economists proposing the notion of recurrent action patterns as the foundational concept. The issue is recursiveness as a concept in correcting for the suppression of process and for temporal conflation. Recurrent action patterns are introduced into the theory of repertoires and of structural activation in anticipation of future situations (Clark).

Chapter 13 notes that knowledge in the resource-based theory of strategy tends to be objectified and static using hegemonic despotism to create the appearance of organisations in action. Penrosian learning and Polanyi's distinction between focal and tacit knowledge lead into the theory of knowing and of typologies of explacit knowledge.

Chapter 14 unpacks recursiveness to introduce organisations' transformation in the analytic separation of the pre-existing structural conditions from the agential action of agents activating the structure of recurrent action patterns.

Part IV examines the role of organisational management for organisations in action and competition between contexts. Firms, contexts and organisational management face finite degrees of freedom and have to discover actionable zones of manoeuvre that are considerably less pliable than presumed in resource-based strategic theory. *Chapter 15* connects organisational management to organisations in action and competition between contexts. Organisation theory needs to take strategy and organisation economics seriously, especially the resource-based strategic theory. Yet that is insufficient. Contexts contain constraints as well as zones of manoeuvre. Strategic choice ought not to ignore those zones of manoeuvre and strategic choice never needed to be simply a proclamation that agency is possible. Strategic choice does matter. What managers do cannot be confined to a simple account of activities. Managerial work faces zones of manoeuvre and constraints and issues of critical political economy, yet also potentially provides a major source of do-able action to address the problem of competition between contexts.

NEO-MODERN POLITICAL ECONOMY

Why formulate the neo-modern political economy perspective?

First, because there are widespread, continuous and varying levels of corporate failure and failures in the launches of new products and services. Exit is the normal experience. Only a small proportion of the organisations that are founded survive the founding period and few open additional locations. Few firms experience periods of dramatic growth, but these tend to be short-lived. A recent list of the annual hundred fastest growing small firms in Britain shows considerable fluctuation with many new entrants and therefore exits (*Sunday Times*, 1998). Surviving is difficult. Many surviving firms and some failing firms are taken over and subject to different parenting. All theories of the firm emphasise differences in parenting competencies. Open system theorising reveals that the parenting of firms is frequently self-referential (autopoeisis). This is known as single-loop learning. Self-referentiality is also coupled to inertial qualities where the past repertoire is reproduced even when those external events to which it was originally connected have altered. Therefore the version of Penrosian learning as defined in the resource-based theory is beyond most managerial teams and they are unaware of the principles.

Second, because the search for the dynamic capabilities of the firm has developed organisation theorising. Boulding's (1956) taxonomy of system complexity requires revision to show how the more complex levels from seven to nine are being analysed. In the new organisation theorising major contributions arise from complexity theory and from developments in organisation economics. The intellectual defeat of rationality and its replacement by bounded rationality led to notions such as the garbage can models. These models challenge management theorists to develop new schools of thought. Among the new thinking it may be observed that Peters and Waterman (1982) give pride of place to Weick and March before succinctly outlining a new set of eight principles based on the social open systems. In the search for new principles of organising, Jameson's comment that 'post modernism is the new cultural logic of capitalism' is worth a thousand smiles.

Third, the claim that strategic choice overturns determinism is of limited value in the post-positivist era. We have ample support for the proposition that ideal designs cannot be implemented and will be ignored (see self-referential autopoeisis and inertia). The problem is how strategic choice copes with degrees of freedom, action determinism and zones of manoeuvre. The modern firm is minutely monitored through auditing and there is increasing attention to bringing research and development in knowledge into the context of application. In the British health sector the intention is to develop evidence-based medicine. Knowledge is capital. There are learning audits. The firm's financial capital and future revenue are subjected to risk analysis and other future-oriented devices such as futures and derivatives.

Fourth, because theories of capitalism are revised to accommodate new phases, new crises and the problems of regimes of international regulation of debt. In knowledge-based capitalism corporate viability, survival and success can be deeply influenced by its context and whether that context enables forms of Penrosian learning that steer the firm to surplus producing activities. There is competition between contexts. In knowledge-based capitalism design and innovation are both connected and also basic to survival. Contexts are shaped by indigenous forces that are inherently local plus the impacts of both multinational businesses that enter and those operating over the horizon in other contexts against which there is latent competition. The Porter–Dunning framework is central to understanding the performance of sectoral clusters. The USA and Great Britain possess considerable differences as contexts for competition The societal-institutional milieu of the region and nation is a major shaper of the performance of sectoral clusters.

Fifth, because the new economic theories of organisational design place dynamic capabilities at the centre and incorporate earlier attention to culture. The resource based theory of strategy is an excellent example. These are implicated in the new cultural logics of capitalism through their commodification of time and space in human activities. Their logics of the hypertext firm are a powerful input to instrumental rationality. The resource based theories of strategy possess problems in handling 'organisation in action' and they neglect the consequences of the political economy of 'competition between contexts'. Also, there are specific problems with the temporal conflation of knowledge, innovation-design and organisation transitions. The steering systems of the RBTS require enlightenment.

This is the agenda for the neo-modern political economy. There are zones of manoeuvre arising from the finite capabilities inhering separately in firms and their contexts as well as in the interaction between firms and contexts. We need a neo-modern political economy of contexts and organisations.

ACTIONABLE UNDERSTANDING

Neo-modern political economy contains considerable potential for a selective synthesis from the many frameworks and certainly demonstrates that existing approaches should give the theme of competition between contexts much greater priority. Indeed, many multinational businesses routinely undertake and subcontract studies designed to provide this form of understanding.

Organisation theory and strategy did not find any great interest in the specificities of the nation with regard to performance until the 1980s. Since then the task of incorporating a comparative national systems perspective has been awkward. Positivist perspectives encouraged the search for universal patterns, thereby weakening the cross-national position until – ironically – Hofstede's massive study did reveal national differences within IBM among actors though not necessarily in structures (Sorge 1995). This apparent lack of interest in the consequences of contexts was most evident in American theorising and remained in place until the unbalancing of international trade after the mid-1970s, especially between the USA and Japan. Porter's (1990, 1991) account of the specificities of context and location galvanised attention. *The Competitive Advantage of Nations* (Porter 1990) symbolised the emergent position with a very readable narrative whose plot revealed that the performance of sectoral clusters was partly explained by national specificities. Nelson (1991) underlined the similarities between Porter's framework of the diamond and other parallel studies such as those of Chandler (1990) and the earlier framing of the problem by Abernathy and colleagues (Abernathy *et al.* 1983). The significance of consequences of competition between contexts are better understood and that understanding is being developed.

National specificities introduce a number of major analytic requirements:

1   There are national systems of knowledge, formative learning, innovation, organising and business. The national systems should not be treated as an all-embracing stereotype because there are significant and consequential differences that ride above the similarities. Within nations there is likely to be a typical variety.

2   There are considerable limitations in the equating of the American and the British forms of organising. Equally, German and American differences are worthy of equal treatment to the Japanese–American comparisons.

3   Examining national systems requires frameworks drawing from Dunning, Porter and various contingency perspectives coupled with a thorough analysis of the institutional milieu and of local, regional features. The sectoral cluster provides a useful area for focusing analysis provided that the long-term dynamics and emergent possibilities are considered.

4   The formative learning by firms within national sectoral clusters is likely to constitute the specific, firm-based explacit knowledge referred to as Penrosian organisational learning.

5   The markets in which the firm chooses to operate constitute one of significant learning contexts. For many firms the domestic market is a major source of key experiences. However, the development of some Swedish firms (e.g. Volvo) illustrates the significance of an industrial sub-culture which encourages new firms to market and learn in different national contexts.

6   The national context contains sectoral clusters with varying exposure to international competition. Durable products like cars and cameras can be designed in a few contexts from which their production can be cloned. In contrast many services are consumed in specific domestic markets, thereby providing local firms with a potential advantage.

There are three major customers in addition to students for the analysis of competition between contexts: governments, multinational corporations (MNCs) and consultancies specialising in advising governments and MNCs.

1   Governments generally believe that they have some influence upon events within their national context. Multinational firms face the need to customise their outputs and so are interested in understanding national specificities.
2   Multinational firms compare and benchmark the performance of their subsidiaries across national contexts. These firms often use their own interpretation of their own intra-firm comparisons to obtain financial support for major projects from national governments.
3   Consultants provide a range of support services and are major suppliers of public knowledge. McKinsey (1998) provided a detailed comparison and explanation of British performance in weak and strong sectors.

Delivering actionable understanding to these constituencies means also taking the theme of organisations in action very seriously, both with respect to the dynamics of inertia and transformation and also with respect to using and developing the finite capabilities of the organisation.

Zones of manoeuvre exist in contexts, for organisations and in their interaction. In these complex systems, zones of manoeuvre can be altered – expanded or contracted – by unforeseen emergent effects. Zones of manoeuvre are finite and their extension and alteration require actionable understanding. Consequently, the voluntarism and agency that pervade organisation theory, strategic analysis and the business schools in general are considerably more actionable than is claimed. The legacy from the modern perspective of instrumental rationality requires replacement by the neo-modern perspective.

From legislators to interpreters

The debate about the ontological and epistemological base to the knowledge produced from organisation theory, strategy and comparative international business systems is expressed in the shift from the metaphor of the legislator to the analyst as interpreter (Bauman, 1988).

Legislator viewpoint

The legislator viewpoint is grounded in positivism and the modern period. The legislator makes the following presumptions:

1   There is a reality and theories can align themselves with that reality through correspondence, thereby providing truth. The theories are abstract and universal, free from the specifics of time and place. Time and space are theorised through the application of uniform, abstract scales with a heavy emphasis upon linearity and a tendency to give that linearity a direction. The functionalist tendency to work backwards from outcomes into 'design' is combined with the view that history is efficient. This tendency to conflate time and space leads to the assumption that transitions occur almost frictionlessly

so that inefficient organisations disappear and those organisations applying 'the knowledge' will achieve successful transformations. These are depthless ontologies: organisations without action.

2   Knowledge about organisations should largely attend to structures and static social constructionism within the organisation and can deal with the context by calibrating scales for uncertainty, variability, complexity, simplicity, speed of change and similar. Attention is intra-organisational and these organisations are virtually organisations without contexts. Consequently key features of the domestic and international contexts are omitted from the analyses. Even though the existence of international differences has been widely acknowledged, the analytic treatment of competition between contexts has hardly commenced.

3   The knowledge is defined as objective and scientific and the legislator is presented as a politically neutral expert.

Interpreter viewpoint

The interpreter viewpoint draws from the critique of positivism by the various anti-modern strands depicted in Figure 15.1 leading to the neo-modern political economy perspective (NMPE).

1   Knowledge can now be addressed from multiple and tensioned perspectives. First, the realist turn draws attention to the hidden underlying causal structures and their mechanisms so that patterns of events must now be regarded as the problematic starting point for an open systems analysis. Pre-existing conditions are absolutely central and the excesses of that version of strategic choice espousing Silverman's (1970) action frame of reference have to be interactively situated in the co-evolution of contexts and organisations. Strategic choice is rife with a voluntarism that is casual about the causes of success and failure (Thompson and McHugh 1995). Pre-existing conditions in the realist turn amount to much more than starting points (Clark 1972, 1985; Sayer 1992; Archer 1995). Additionally, attention to unintended outcomes and emergence is espoused and to some degree implicated in ongoing analyses. The unintended outcomes are central to explaining the existence of such enduring social artefacts as the English House of Commons and American Football. Also, the future may defy reproduction of the earlier patterns. Now unintended outcomes are brought to centre stage and the notion of design in the interpreter viewpoint requires careful specification (Clark 1975a; cf. Mintzberg 1990). The future can be emergent and different.

Second, post-modern perspectives challenge the possibility of design based on theory and totally problematise claims about linearity – even about reverse linearity (e.g. Amiss 1990) and pose challenges to the notion of a retro-organisation theory (e.g. Burrell 1997). Holmer Nadeesan (1997) essays the dislocation of instrumental time and disorder. This means replacing the metaphor of the clock by the snake-pit.

Third, within NMPE the explorations by historians of events which did not/might not have happened, as Schama's (1991) 'Dead Certainties' and Ferguson's (1997) over-serious, but certainly interesting, virtual history plus Hawthorn's (1994) notion of possibilities, all stretch conventional ways of explanation and theory. The comedic elements do not need to be confined to post-modernism and NMPE requires notions of contradiction, paradox and irony in the analytic structured narratives. In NMPE knowledge is causal and indeterminate, situated, mediated and contested. There are many frameworks doing local tasks and held together in bricolage. The new production of knowledge (cf. Gibbons *et al.* 1994) is significantly outside the university sector in agencies of various kinds – probably fragmented and requiring interpreters in some roles. In NMPE the intention is to examine organisations and contexts in action. That requires considerable bridging with the social sciences.

2   The previous split between the organisation and its context is replaced by the co-analysis of the organisation and the context. NMPE replaces the earlier use of a few thin variables by rich analytic description influenced by the considerations raised by the realist turn. Variables are not necessarily dismissed, but the role of configurations is massively heightened and becomes pre-dominant. Configurational perspectives have a great deal to contribute to the analysis of major health issues such as the food chain crises in Europe.

3   Expertise will be recognised to be explacit knowledge – slowly, eventually. Perhaps!

CONTRA VOLUNTARISM AND DETERMINISM

The perspective of strategic choice was formulated by Child (1972, 1997) to provide a robust critique of determinism in positivist organisation theory, yet confused the difference between organisation design and managerial choices. Organisation design was developed as a crypto-functionalist collection of rules for correcting the deficiencies of existing strategic choices by managements (Clark 1972; Galbraith 1977; Starbuck and Nystrom 1981). Therefore, there was little doubt that top managements were able to make choices. That notion was implicit in the earliest statements of strategy as a pattern by Andrews (1971). Whittington (1992a, b) scrutinises the claim that strategy makes a difference. Moreover, as Aldrich (1979) and Thompson and McHugh (1995) observe, strategic choice implies too much agency.

The collection of research programmes within modern-positivistic organisation theory discussed in Chapter 3 was held together by many cross-cutting analytic connections and its protective belt certainly involved the notion of strategic choice (Child 1972, 1997; cf. Aldrich 1979). There has been looseness between Child's intentions as an author and the interpretation given to strategic choice within its knowledge-community of organisation theorists. The latter have ignored the mention of the pre-existing context external to and within the firm. Consequently, the message of voluntarism and strategic choice has been used to romanticise management as the cybernetic mechanisms removing ineffective organisation designs through instrumental rationality. Within that rhetoric the problems of the pre-existing reality have been swept away and attention has been upon implementing the chosen strategy and design (see Figure 3.1) as though implementation was simply the application of programmatic change. Wilson (1992: Chapter 7) incisively reveals the limitations of inserting implementation as the penultimate step in competitiveness and strategy.

There has been too much voluntarism in interpretations of strategic choice. The realist turn has sharpened our understanding of the degrees of freedom and the zones of manoeuvre available to firms. The pre-existing capabilities inherent in contexts and firms enables and limits strategic choice as a form of instrumental rationality intended to contribute to the firm's performance (Clark 1996; Child 1997). The firm in reality is not acting alone, nor is it able to reconfigure its repertoire of capabilities as a design rule except within certain degrees of freedom (Foss and Erikson 1995). Existing design rules based on instrumental rationality cannot (so far) handle the doing capabilities of the firm-context configuration.

Organisational management needs to develop an actionable understanding about competition between contexts. Complexity theory provides a general language for examining contexts and from economic perspectives both the eclectic theory (Dunning 1993) and the competitive advantage of nations (Porter 1990, 1998) provide extensive argument about the 'stickiness' of locations and local clusters. The socio-institutional-political perspectives examined in Part II extend our understanding of the singularities operating in specific contexts of nations and sectoral clusters. All these analyses imply that there are zones of manoeuvre within which firms have certain potentials and outside which there are – other things being similar – problems of performance. Porter's (1998) recent account of clusters provides a wide range of examples of where contexts contain enabling features. Consequently, Penrosian learning and Polyani's accounts of focal knowledge are likely to be shaped by the cognitive, regulative and normative features of a national context.

Therefore, one can anticipate that indigenous British management will – as a stratified social reality – contain particular mechanisms and tendencies. The same will apply to all nations, sectoral-clusters and regions, but the British example is a convenient illustration. Child (1983) scrutinised the claim that 'being professional' in Britain necessarily delivered performance for the employing firms because professionalism was being shaped by pre-existing structural tendencies in the professions (as Perkin 1996). With respect to Britain he observed that management was/is highly segmented and over-specialised along traditional functional lines. Those tendencies are reinforced by the aspirations and identities of the professional and quasi-professional associations which are bearers of these mechanisms and tendencies. If so, then we could enquire whether firms adopting the multidivisional structure would have strong capacities towards divisional autonomy, but might lack the capacities to enable the centre to be informed about the common knowledge pools embedded in new products. If so, then attempts by British firms to use North American forms of organisational development might also encounter the national habitus. The case of Imperial Chemical Industries (ICI) before de-merger provides an intriguing exploration of the proposition (see Pettigrew 1985). Certainly ICI was regarded as a very British firm. An earlier study of 2,000 managers indicated a strong tendency towards social rewards. Likewise, it could be hypothesised that studies of innovations in firm-wide systems of co-ordination such as production and inventory control (Burcher 1991) might also be infused with the typical variety of Britishness. These enquiries point to zones of man-oeuvre inhering in the learning of the managerial teams and impacting on their capacity to remove obstacles to further growth in knowledge (cf. Penrose 1959). The impact of contextual social structures upon corporate learning, expertise and knowledge extends to the crucial area of strategic and tactical time-reckoning systems. In the theory of structural activation these represent the evolutionary code of the organisation (cf. Nelson and Winter 1982). We must expect the categories used in everyday discourse to reflect distinct national characteristics. The understanding of bottlenecks may differ between American and British management (Clark 1987; cf. Rosenberg 1982).

THE REALIST PERSPECTIVE ON ORGANISATIONAL MANAGEMENT

Position of managers and management

The position of managers and managing in the modern-positivist and neo-modern political economy perspectives contains an almost cybernetic capacity to encode complexity and steer the firm through rational control systems. In this view managers are self-perceived as important and powerful. Their dominant coalitions possess strategic choice (Child 1972). Critical perspectives also empha-sise the capacity of management to control (e.g. Marglin) and search for alter-native, more emancipatory forms of managing. The Centre for Alternative Organisation Studies, Warwick University, England, is a research programme for articulating these linkages with critical management. On the other hand managers are depicted as being squeezed by agency theory (Donaldson 1996), reluctant to manage (Scase and Goffee 1989) and dreading being sacked (Scarborough and Burrell 1996). The early pluralist perspectives certainly posi-tioned management as simply one collection of stakeholders among many within and outside the firm. Moreover, contemporary accounts of power and politics contend that the capacity of managers to influence is restricted by power frame-works in which there are multiple, overlapping and intersecting networks (Clegg 1989). In terms of frameworks of power strategic choice is the outcome of a complex, multi-way interaction within the firm and in its contexts. There is unplanned order and unintended, emergent consequence. Also, agency theories seem to suggest that managers shirk and can only be trusted to pursue narrow, vested interests and distort corporate performance. Therefore, it is necessary to insert externally based forms of corporate governance enabling greater transparency. Management's taken for granted role as a generalist is being transformed, but the new formation is unclear except for the reduction in their discretion. Management is under-appreciated according to Ghoshall (1996; Bartlett and Ghoshall 1994) who observes that researchers need a new theory of the managerial role in value creation: a managerial theory of the firm. The realist perspective claims to offer just such a theory.

Realist perspective

Examining managerial work is beset with problems because many perspectives have been identified and are used by analysts. The perspectives differ and are to some degree incomensurable. Tsoukas (1994) suggests that the realist perspective and political economy perspectives can be used to situate the different perspectives in a hierarchy of ontological layers running down from the surface to three layers of management and managing:

- roles set and task characteristics;
- functions;
- causal powers.

These are three ontological layers containing causal capabilities and liabilities that have been sedimented, laid down over the long term and constitute the structure in which, at any one moment, managerial action is situated.

First, there are widely differing accounts of managerial roles. Two examples will illustrate the diversity: agency theory and labour process theory. In agency theory (see Chapter 5) the assumption is that the owners of capital have to delegate functions because of limits on their time. The theory highlights the problems of control for principals over the activities of agents, that is, of salaried managers. By contrast, labour process theory (LPT) acknowledges the notions of roles in agency theory, but the critique focuses upon how presentation of agency theory as a neutral form of discourse might be a form of hegemonic despotism (Burawoy 1985). From the perspective of labour there is a massive asymmetry in the ownership of the knowledge and in drawing rents from knowledge.

The micro-level study of managerial tasks occupied considerable attention. Mintzberg (1974) is one of the most salient studies. In a crypto-work study approach Mintzberg shadowed five very senior executives for one week recording and timing their activities. Mintzberg provided the most widely cited account of how long the executives spent on phone calls, on corridor conversations, in meetings and in reading reports. We know the average length of these activities. Looking at the data it is possible to conclude that the CEOs were spending large chunks of time zapping between phone calls and corridor conversations. Only rarely were they reading lengthy reports or simply reflecting. Mintzberg turns this interpretation into a critique of the rational analytic vision of strategy based theory. For example, the CEOs searched for 'hot news' more than formalised data. Mintzberg (1974) also claimed that managerial work was episodic, but this claim requires revision in the light of the theory of structural activation (Clark 1975a, b; Sharifi 1986). The episodes may be short, but they are often part of a patterned portfolio.

Second, the notion of the functions of management was introduced by Fayol and the classical school who sought to create a fundamental check list of functions based on a mixture of observation and reflection. The frequently revised lists were intended to direct managerial attention to essential features of their activities. Later, the historical perspective on functions was given its impetus by Chandler (1962, 1977, 1990) and sought to relate the functions to the historical evolution of firms and to argue that management had become differentiated into a number of areas. Chandler transformed the lists into structural features and into the actions of management as the visible hand (Chandler 1962, 1977). Then structures were replaced by capabilities and Chandler (1990) used the American profile of capabilities as a framework for interpreting them in European firms. Also from a historical perspective on functions Teulings (1986) proposed four main areas:

- the ownership function which is concerned with the accumulation of capital and the preservation of legitimacy;
- the allocation of investments;
- undertaking innovations in the development of new product markets;
- operational level and the direct labour process.

These operate in four different time scales ranging from the long-term to the short-term. The practical, everyday attempts by managements to align these four different time frames represents a major source of problems and potential sources of competitive strength.

Third, causal powers are illustrated in the industrial structure within which management as a collective institution may be analysed as set out in Figure 15.2. The mode of production is capitalist (1) and there is therefor a division of labour (2) driving the separation of capital owners (3) from non-owners supplying their labour power (4). Through the division of labour (2) there is a distinction between superior (5) and subordinate (6). This industrial structure has pervasive superior/subordinate distinctions. There are particular positions – senior superiors such as managers – that endow the occupants of those positions with certain causal powers.

The set of causal powers held by holders of superior positions in a capitalist system is inherent in the market economy. Three of these causal powers held by superordinate managers are:

- (CP-1) the ability to control the transformation of labour power into actual labour;
- (CP-2) the ability to elicit active co-operation through rewards and sanctions, including material rewards and symbolic rewards;
- (CP-3) managers are 'organisationally compelled' to transform resources into

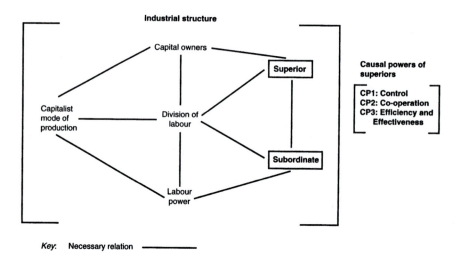

Figure 15.2 Industrial structure and the causal powers of management
Source: Tsoukas (1994).

teamwork (as Penrose 1959) so that output is legitimated in the external context (see Child 1972: Figure 1).

Management therefore possesses degrees of freedom because the causal powers are only tendencies requiring the occupant of positions to construct those mechanisms which create the causal effects and outcomes (Tsoukas 1994: 298). Managers must create the conditions whereby certain activities are controlled – the discretion is limited – to construct closure around material and social objects (Bijker *et al.* 1987).

Managerial realism

Managerial realism is an approach identified by Reed (1992) from his comparison of five different approaches to the study of organisations. Reed concludes by commending managerial realism as a useful perspective on the firm, the context and the roles of management. The category of managerial realism focuses upon the detailed practices through which managers aim to achieve effective organisational assembly and control at the meso level interface between firm in sector and its markets (e.g. Whipp and Clark 1986; Clark and Starkey 1988; Whittington 1989). Managerial realism is recognised through four elements:

1   Managers are unavoidably involved in a struggle for control over the administrative mechanisms and procedures through which the organising of work is realised.

2   Organising is a set of situated practices in which environmental constraints
     and opportunities are inextricably intertwined with administrative power.
3   Managers use ideologies to obscure their interests and to bind in those
     interest groups external and internal to the firm.
4   The notion of organisation design is best understood as a political struggle to
     assemble collective action into viable forms.

Existing organisational designs face problems arising from market and technologies in the sectoral context. Organisational transformations have to be mediated
through new sets of rules and mechanisms in a highly complex political process.
New sets of rules and mechanisms are organised in loose, ambiguous and often
unformalised sets in an attempt to create new structural repertoires. The logic of
effectiveness is pursued through organisational politics in which intra and extra
organisational power networks are central. The design capacities of the firm
require linking and legitimising through status and authority systems to external
networks of power.

In managerial realism the analysis of managerial work is examined in the
context of the longer term transformation in sectors and in societal institutions
and the politics of managerial action is implicated in connecting the firm with
sectoral evolution. Externally located transformations (e.g. new technologies) are
translated into new corporate packages of rules, procedures and mechanisms to
facilitate the reassembly of activities into organisational forms. The perspective of
managerial realism sustains the notion of organisations in action. However, the
context tends to be defined abstractly, somewhat along the lines of firm in sector
rather than in terms of firms being situated in the global 'competition between
contexts'. Also, the influence in and on management of information technology
and audit requires highlighting.

Managerial realism does indicate the restricted degrees of freedom contained in
the theme of organisations in action, but does not sufficiently acknowledge the
theme of competition between contexts and international dynamics.

LOCATION AND THE HOME BASE: ENTRAINMENT AND EXPOSURE

Not only is there competition between contexts – as shown in Part II – but also the
domestic, home base of the firm and its sectoral cluster is highly consequential for
the growth of managerial expertise through Penrosian learning. Porter contends
that having a 'home base in the wrong nation raises fundamental strategic concerns' (Porter 1990: 577). Four potential problems affect the home base:

1   The home base shapes the firm's capability to innovate quickly.[1] The home
     base tends to involve the whole value chain and its sectoral clusters. The
     situation in the home base might be a positive feature because firms should be
     able to learn from their own markets.

2   The home base can entrain the learning of the firm so that there is a limited capacity to move abroad.
3   Firms inside the home base are, to varying degrees, exposed to the actions of firms in other nations.
4   The analysis of the home base might show that it is less than ideal.

The logic of the Porter/Dunning/Sorge thesis has to be that few home bases are ideal because they possess ineffective diamonds perhaps coupled with the disruptive presence of foreign multinational businesses (see Figure 7.3).

These four problems pose management in the firm and industrial policy analysts with a considerable challenge. What can management do about the home base thesis? The full analysis of the home base includes going further than the Porter/Dunning perspective (Figure 7.3) into the institutional-societal fabric (Chapter 8) and the political economy of international markets, dependence and hegemony (Chapter 6). Two of the key features are the societal production of knowledge for innovation-design (Figure 7.1) and the role that the domestic market plays. It is in the home base that the multiple layers of knowledge are implicated in the failure or success of success of clusters. Knowledge and learning are the central themes in knowledge-based capitalism (Dunning 1993; Lundvall 1992) for the firm (Porter 1990) and for the formative context of the nation, the region and the sectoral cluster.

These pointers suggest that there are areas of intervention in the diamond that management and industrial policy can recognise and understand, but that actionable understanding leading to improving the competitiveness of a particular context is quite daunting. Industrial policy and national and regional levels might improve the level of rivalry and invest in the creation of endowed factors, but have to ensure that its firms make the linkages to the endowed factors. Declaring a regional or industrial policy that is not actionable is not the monopoly of the enlightenment and modern movement. It is extremely difficult for any one set of policy actors to develop competitive national sectoral clusters. How, for example, can a nation's consumers be transformed by public policy as distinct from the emergence of conditions in the international political economy?

One track for firms is to elect for a combination of the home base with other locations. This approach was adopted by Volvo from the time of its founding in 1927 when it entered the markets of North America as well as the Dutch and Belgium markets in order to tap selective advantages in several nations (Clark and Staunton 1989). It may be that the most useful consumers from the long-term point of view of the organisation are in other nations. This is especially likely to be the case when organisations in a sector search those customers who indicate future trends. If so, then the logic of the argument suggests that management engages those consumer, but some nations are likely to provide rather favourable contexts for detecting new customer trends. American exceptionalism (Chapter 9) indicated certain potentials in the large North American Free Trade Area.

Most of the world's largest one thousand firms have, for the moment, managed to overcome their exposure to incoming multi-national businesses and to escape entrainment to their home base. However, two-thirds of this population retain strong ties into their home base.

STRATEGIC CHOICE REVISITED

The conversation around John Child's (1972, 1997) account of strategic choice provides a useful means to calibrate the relationship between the two themes of 'organisations in action' and 'competition between contexts' in the three disciplinary areas. The twenty-five years spanned since the original article and its recent representation neatly cover the debates between the five perspectives positioned in Figure 15.1. The earlier article attacks the determinist elements in the positivist-modern perspective of organisation behaviour and proposes voluntarism for the dominant organisational coalition while the latest version opines a crypto realist viewpoint (Child 1997).

Child (1972) adds additional weight to Silverman's (1970) account of the action frame of reference when he enacts organisation research and theory as possessing two key features:

- the assumption of deterministic relationships between a high proportion of key variables;
- as claiming that organisation theory forced the dimension of the environment to determine the choice and design of organisation structure and politics.

Organisation design is situationally determined order (Child 1997: 43). Child (1972: Figure 1) offers a clearly thought out, subtle, multi-factor model of decision choices for the firm and its environment. At the same time Child argues that other theorists have presented an over-detrained account of the actual role of the external environment in affecting the choice of strategic direction by the dominant coalition. He argues that organisations do actually have choice of direction. The same model is reproduced in Child (1997).

Three points may be raised about the original version. First, Child did not distinguish between explanations of actual events in organisations and the construction of a theory of design claiming to provide a model based on design rules (Clark 1972 a, b; Clark and Starkey 1988). The conventional distinctions of 'is', 'ought' and 'can be' are useful and should have been incorporated. Normative theories of organisation design do not express what organisations will actually do, but instead they provide instruction on what organisations should do. Therefore designers would not be surprised that existing organisations and intended organisations are mis-designed (Clark 1972). Members of the socio-technical school seem to take it for granted that the 'ideal' design is frequently not applied (Miller and Rice 1967). Consequently to claim that there is strategic choice is agreed. Second, Child's account of the dominant elite seems to assume an integer-power centre (Hutte 1968) and that is not known to be typical. Third, the attention of organisation designers to the environment is stereotyped and over-determined so that the temporality of the firm and the context is conflated into an extended present with slight anticipation of emergence or surprise or discontinuity. There is little sense of organisations undertaking innovation-design (Aldrich 1979; Clark and Staunton 1989).

The impact of Child's presentation has been considerable as measured in citations (see Starbuck and Nystrom 1981). However, the problem of determinism has been transformed by post-modern critiques and by the social constructionist claim that reality is socially constructed because we all enact our environments and then respond to the stimuli we have designated (Weick 1979). The later version of strategic choice addresses that conversation (Child 1997). Child (1997) offers a robust account of the continuing relevance of strategic choice and introduces some fine-tuning on some small points plus three major points (see below). One area of fine-tuning is in respect of action, process and dynamics. Previous references to dominant collations become 'shifting dominant coalitions'. Another area of revision is in the new attention given to organisation learning.

Most recently the major features of strategic choice have become:

- action determinism;
- the subjective/objective definitions of the environment;
- firm-in-sector framework.

First, there is a notable and problematic extension of the earlier version through the introduction of action determinism as a realist qualification to any overstating of earlier voluntarism (Clark and Staunton 1989; Thompson and McHugh 1995). Action determinism (Elster 1984) refers to the built-in tendencies of organisations to continue with forms of organisation that limit their degrees of freedom to have a totally open choice about future directions and about their capacity to ingest new innovations. Child suggests action determinism enriches organisation analysis (Child 1997: 51), but the discussion does not unpack the degrees of freedom (Clark and Starkey 1988). However, the deployment of action determinism agrees with our earlier critique of the resource-based theory of strategy by revealing limits. As such, action determinism qualifies strategic choice very considerably. Child does not consider either the possible shaping of action determinism as discussed in Part II or the extent to which an existing structure might be transformed through emergence or through programmed change interventions (Wilson 1992: Chapter 7).

Second, Child enrols the notion of the enacted environment from Weick (1969), but differs from a social constructionist position (Layder 1997) by invoking Whittington (1989) as a proponent of realist analysis. Thus Child refers to the subjective (enacted) environment and the objective (realist) environment. The use of these concepts is illustrated from the interpretation by Smith *et al.* (1991) of how one organisation, Cadbury-Schweppes, managed to shift from a diversified to a more focused product strategy in the chocolate sector. There are elements here that resonate with the discussion of Sayer's realist methodology for social science, as examined in Chapter 4, yet the detailed argument could be elaborated.

Third, great analytic weight is given to the firm-in-sector perspective (Child and Smith 1988), but this ignores why the original version was modified.[2] The limitations of a simple firm-in-sector perspective become more evident when international comparisons are undertaken (Clark 1987): hence the theme of competition between contexts, especially the role of home bases in sectoral clusters.

The recent version of strategic choice certainly clarifies earlier tension between the model (Child 1972: Figure 1) and the freewheeling claims for voluntarism. Strategic choice recognises the role of the pre-existing, yet needs a further step to embrace organisations in action and competition between contexts.

IS/CAN

The two themes of organisations in action and competition between contexts highlight the extent to which theorists in organisation and strategy have allowed discursive penetration to be equated with the capacity to alter 'what is' towards their preferred outcomes irrespective of the causal forces involved. The tendency is widespread and is a legacy from modernist theorising. A distinction has to be drawn between knowability (i.e. discursive penetration) achieved in the academy from the actionability of correct knowing. The distinction is an old one. In any temporal horizon there are degrees of freedom and finite capacities. There are also emergent potentials. Transforming the forces implicated in the existing temporal horizon requires much more attention to the zones of manoeuvre in the firm and in the context. Understanding what is actionable relates 'what is' to 'what can be'.

NOTES

1 This section draws upon Porter (1990) Chapter 11.
2 Clark and Whipp (1984) set out the original framework in a comparative, historical format explaining innovation. Different parts of the framework were used in the empirical study of innovation in the British automobile industry (Whipp and Clark 1986) and summarised (Clark and Whipp 1987). By then the analytic scope had widened to sectoral clusters (Clark and Starkey 1988; Clark and Staunton 1989; Cochrane 1988) with national/regional elements forming the competition between contexts.

Bibliography

Abbott, A. (1988) *The System of Professions. An Essay on the Division of Expert Labour.* Chicago: Chicago University Press.

—— (1992) 'From causes to events: notes on narrative positivism', *Sociological Methods and Research* 20: 428–455.

Abernathy, W. J. (1978) *The Productivity Dilemma. Roadblock to Innovation in the Automobile Industry.* Baltimore: Johns Hopkins University.

—— and Clark, K. B. (1985) 'Innovation: mapping the winds of creative destruction', *Research Policy* 14: 3–22.

——, Clark, K. B. and Kantrow, A. M. (1981) 'The new industrial competition', *Harvard Business Review,* September/October: 68–81.

——, Clark, K. B. and Kantrow, A. M. (1983) *Industrial Renaissance: Producing a Positive Future for America.* Boston: MIT Press.

—— and Hayes, R. H. (1980) 'Managing our way to economic decline', *Harvard Business Review,* September/October: 69–77.

Abo, T. (1994) *Hybrid Factory. The Japanese System in the United States.* Oxford: Oxford University Press.

Abrahamson, E. and Fombrum, C. J. (1992) 'Forging the iron cage: interorganisational networks and the production of macro-culture', *Journal of Management Studies* 29: 175–194.

Adam, B. (1990) *Time and Social Theory.* Cambridge: Polity Press.

Aglietta, M. (1987) *A Theory of Capitalist Regulation: The US Experience.* London: Verso.

Akrich, M. (1992) 'Beyond the construction of technology: the shaping of people and things in the innovation process', in M. Dierkes and U. Hoffman *New Technology at the Outset. Social Forces in the Shaping of Technological Innovations.* Frankfurt: Campus Verlag, pp. 173–190.

Albrow, M. (1996) *The Global Age.* Cambridge: Polity Press.

Alchian, A. A. and Demsetz, H. (1986) 'Production, information costs, and economic organization', in L. Putterman (ed.) *The Economic Nature of the Firm: A Reader.* Cambridge: Cambridge University Press.

Aldrich, H. (1979) *Organizations and Environments.* Englewood Cliffs, NJ: Prentice-Hall.

Alexander, J. C. (1995) *Fin de Siècle Social Theory: Relativism, Reduction, and the Problem of Reason.* London: Verso.

Allaire, Y. and Firsirotu, M. E. (1984) 'Theories of organizational culture', *Organization Studies* 5 (3): 193–225.

Allport, F. H. (1962) 'A structuronomic conception of behaviour: individual and collective', *Journal of Abnormal and Social Psychology* 64: 273–300.

Alvesson, M. (1993) *Cultural Perspectives on Organization*. Cambridge: Cambridge University Press.

—— and Willmott, H. (1996) *Making Sense of Management*. Sage: London.

Amit, R. and Schoemaker, P. J. H. (1993) 'Strategic assets and organizational rent', *Strategic Management Journal*, 14: 33–46.

Anderson, E. S. (1996) *Evolutionary Economics. Post Schumpeterlian Contributors*. London: Pinter.

Anderson, P. (1998) *Origins of Postmodernity*. London: Verso.

Andrews, K. R. (1971) *The Concept of Corporate Strategy*. Homewood, IL: Dow Jones-Irwin.

Ansoff, I. and McDonnell, E. (1990) *Implanting Strategic Management*. London: Prentice-Hall International.

Aoki, M. (1988) *Information, Incentives, and Bargaining in the Japanese Economy*. Cambridge: Cambridge University Press.

Appleby, J., Hunt, L. and Jacob, M. (1994) *Telling the Truth About History*. New York: Norton.

Archer, M. (1979) *Social Origins of Educational Systems*. London: Sage.

—— (1982) 'Structuration versus morphogenesis: on combining structure and action', *British Journal of Sociology* 33 (4): 445–483.

—— (1988) *Culture and Agency: The Place of Culture in Social Theory*. Cambridge: Cambridge University Press.

—— (1995) *Realist Social Theory: The Morphogenetic Approach*. Cambridge: Cambridge University Press.

—— (1996) 'Social integration and system integration: developing the distinction', *Sociology* 30 (4): 679–699.

Argyris, C. and Schon, D. (1978) *Organisational Learning: A Theory of Action Perspective*. Reading: Addison-Wesley.

Arrighi, G. (1994) *The Long Twentieth Century. Money, Power and the Origins of our Times*. London: Verso.

Arthur, W. B. (1989) 'Competing technologies, increasing returns, and lock-in by historical events', *Economic Journal* 99 (393): 116–131.

Ashby, W. R. (1952) *Design for a Brain*. London: Wiley.

—— (1956) *Introduction to Cybernetics*. London: Chapman & Hall.

Backhouse, R. (1998) 'Economics the unsociable science?' Inaugural lecture, Department of Economics, the University of Birmingham, England.

Bailey, D., Harte, G. and Sugden, R. (1994) *Making Transnationals Accountable: A Significant Step for Britain*. London: Routledge.

Baker, M. and Barker, M. (1997) 'Leveraging human capital', *Journal of Knowledge Management* 1 (1): 63–74.

Bannister, D. and Fransella, F. (1971) *Inquiring Man. The Theory of Personal Constructs*. Harmondsworth: Penguin.

Barley, S. R. (1986) 'Technology as an occasion for structuring: evidence from observation of CT scanners and the social order of radiology departments', *Administrative Science Quarterly* 31: 78–108.

—— (1990) 'The alignment of technology and structure through roles and networks', *Administrative Science Quarterly* 35: 61–103.

—— and Kunda, G. (1992) 'Design and devotion: surges of rational and rational ideologies of control in managerial discourse, *Administrative Science Quarterly* 37 (3): 363–369.

Barney, J. B. (1986) 'Organisations culture: cannot it be a source of sustained competitive advantage?', *Academy of Management Review* 11: 656–665.

—— (1990) 'The debate between traditional management theory and organizational economics: substansive differences or intergroup conflict?', *Academy of Management Review* 15 (3): 382–393.

—— (1995) *Advanced Strategic Management*. Reading, MA: Addison Wesley.

—— and Ouchi, W. G. (eds) (1986) *Organizational Economics*. San Francisco: Jossey-Bass.

—— and Zajac, E. J. (1994) 'Competitive organizational behaviour. Toward an organizationally-based theory of competitive advantage'. *Strategic Management Journal* 15: 5–9.

Barnhardt, M. A. (1995) *Japan and the World Since 1868*. London: Edward Arnold.

Bartlett, C. and Ghoshall, S. (1989) *Managing Across Borders. The Transnational Solution*. Cambridge, MA: Harvard Business School Press.

—— (1994) 'Changing the role of top management: beyond strategy to purpose', *Harvard Business Review,* November–December: 79–88.

Bateson, G. (1973) *Steps to the Ecology of Mind*. London: Paladin.

Baudrillard, J. (1975) *The Mirror of Production*. St Louis: Telos Press.

—— (1983) *Simulcra and Simulations*. New York: Semiotext.

—— (1988) *America*. London: Verso.

Bauman, Z. (1987) *Legislators and Interpreters.* Cambridge: Polity Press.

—— (1989) *Modernity and the Holocaust*. Cambridge: Polity Press.

—— (1992) *Intimations of Postmodernity.* London: Routledge.

Becker, G. (1965) 'A theory of the allocation of time', *Economic Journal* 75: 493–517.

—— (1976) *The Economic Approach to Human Behavior.* Chicago: University of Chicago Press.

—— (1981) *A Treatise on the Family.* Cambridge, MA: Harvard University Press.

Bendix, R. (1956) *Work and Authority in Industry: Ideologies of Management in the Course of Industrialization*. New York: Wiley.

Beniger, J. R. (1986) *The Control Revolution. Technological and Economic Origins of the Information Society.* Cambridge, MA: Harvard University Press.

Bennis, W. G. (1966) 'Theory and method in applying behavioural science to planned organizational change', in J. R. Lawrence (ed.) *Operational Research and the Social Sciences*. London: Tavistock.

Bernstein, B. (1975) *Class, Codes and Control: Towards a Theory of Educational Transmissions*. London: Routledge & Kegan Paul.

Berg, M. (1984) 'The power of knowledge: comments on Marglin's "Knowledge and Power"', in F. H. Stephen (ed.) *Firms, Organization and Labour: Approaches to the Economics of Work Organization*. London: Macmillan.

Berle, A. A. and Means, G. C. (1967) [1932] *The Modern Corporation and Private Property.* New York: Macmillan.

Best, M. (1990) *The New Competition. Institutions of Industrial Restructuring.* Cambridge: Polity Press.

Best, S. and Kellner, D. (1991) *Postmodern Theory. Critical Interrogations*. London: Macmillan.

Bhaskar, R. (1975) *A Realist Theory of Science*. Leeds: Basic Books.

—— (1989) *The Possibility of Naturalism*. London: Harvester.

Bijker, W. E and Law, J. (1992) *Shaping Technology/Building Society. Studies in Sociotechnical Change*. Cambridge, MA: MIT Press.

——, Hughes, T. P. and Pinch, T. (1987) *The Social Construction of Technology.* Cambridge, MA: MIT Press.

Blackler, F. (1995) 'Knowledge, knowledge work and organizations: an overview and interpretation', *Organization Studies* 16 (6): 1021–1046.

Blau, P. M. and Scott, W. R. (1961) *Formal Organizations; A Comparative Approach*. London: Routledge.

Boden, D. (1994) *The Business of Talk. Organisations in Action*. Cambridge: Polity Press.

Boguslaw, R. (1966) *The New Utopians*. New York: Prentice-Hall.

Boisot, M. H. (1987) *Information and Organizations. The Manager as Anthropologist*. London: Fontana.

—— (1995) *Information Space. A Framework for Learning in Organizations, Institutions and Culture*. London: Routledge.

—— (1998) *Knowledge Assets: Securing Competitive Advantage in the Information Economy*. Oxford: Oxford University Press.

Boltanski, L. (1987) *The Making of a Class: Cadres in French Society*. Cambridge: Cambridge University Press.

—— and Thevenot, L. (1988) *Les économies de grandeur*. Paris: Presses Universitaires de France.

Boulding, K. E. (1956) *The Image*. Ann Arbor: University of Michigan.

Bourdieu, P. (1977) *Outline of a Theory of Practice*, Cambridge: Cambridge University Press.

—— (1984) *Distinction: A Social Critique of the Judgement of Taste*. Cambridge, MA: Harvard University Press.

Bourdieu, P. and Wacquant, L. J. D. (1992) *An Introduction to Reflexive Sociology*. Cambridge: Polity Press.

Bowles, S. and Gintis, H. (1993) 'The revenge of homo economics: contested exchange and the revival of political economy', *Journal of Economic Perspectives* 7 (1): 83–102.

Boyer, R. (1990). *The Regulation School. A Critical Introduction*. New York: Columbia University Press.

Bradford-Landau, S. and Condit, C. W. (1996) *The New York Sky Scraper 1865–1913*. Yale: Yale University Press.

Braudel, F. (1958) *Time, History and the Social Sciences. Varieties of History: From Voltaire to the Present*, F. Stern (ed.). New York: Free Press.

—— (1972) *The Mediterranean and Mediterranean World*. London: Collins.

—— (1977) *Afterthoughts on Material Civilisation and Capitalism*. Baltimore: Johns Hopkins University Press.

—— (1979, 1985) *The Wheels of Commerce. Volume II. Civilization and Capitalism, 15th–18th Century*. London: Fontana Press.

Braverman, H. (1974) *Labour and Monopoly Capital: The Degradation of Work in the Twentieth Century*. New York: Monthly Press.

Brown, J. S. and Duguid, P. (1991) 'Innovation in the workplace: a perspective on organizational learning', *Organization Science* 2 (1): 40–57.

Brown, S., Bell, J. and Carson, D. (1998) *Marketing Apocalypse. Eschatology, Escapology and the Illusion of the End*. London: Routledge.

Bruner, J. S. (1996) *The Culture of Education*. Cambridge, MA: Harvard University Press.

Bryman, A. (1995) *Disney and his Worlds*. London: Routledge.

Buckley, P. J. and Casson, M. (1993) *Multinational Enterprises in the World Economy*. London: Macmillan.

Buckley, W. (1967) *Sociology and Modern Systems Theory*. Englewood Cliffs, NJ: Prentice-Hall.

Burawoy, M. (1979) *Manufacturing Consent: Changes in the Labor Process under Monopoly Capitalism*. London: University of Chicago Press.

—— (1985) *The Politics of Production*. London: Verso.

Burcher, P. (1991) 'The use of capacity requirements planning in manufacturing planning and control systems', unpublished doctoral thesis, Aston University.

Burns, T. (1966) 'On the plurality of social systems', in J. R. Lawrence (ed.) *Operational Research and the Social Sciences*. London: Tavistock.

—— and Stalker, G. M. (1961) *The Management of Innovation*. London: Tavistock.

Burrell, G. (1988) 'Modernism, post modernism and organizational analysis 2: the contribution of Michael Foucault', *Organization Studies* 9 (2): 221–235.

—— (1992) 'Back to the future: time and organization', in M. Reed and M. Hughes (eds) *Rethinking Organization: New Directions in Organization Theory and Analysis*. London: Sage.

—— (1996) 'Normal science, paradigm, metaphors, discourses and genealogies of analysis', in S. R. Clegg, C. Hardy and W. R. Nord, *Handbook of Organizational Studies*. London: Sage.

—— (1997) *Pandemonium: Towards a Retrospective Organization Theory.* London: Sage.

—— and Morgan, G. (1979) *Sociological Paradigms and Organisational Analysis: Elements of the Sociology of Corporate Life.* London: Heinemann.

Burt, R. (1982) *Toward a Structural Theory of Action.* New York: Academic Press.

Cahoone, L. (1996) *From Modernism to Postmodernism.* Oxford: Blackwell.

Callinicos, A. (1985) 'Anthony Giddens: a contemporary critique', *Theory and Society* 14 (2): 133–166.

—— (1989) *Making History.* Cambridge: Polity Press.

—— (1995) *Theories and Narratives. Reflections on the Philosophy of History.* Cambridge: Polity Press.

Callon, M. (1986) 'Some elements of a sociology of translation: domestication of the scallops and the fisherman of St Brieue Bay', in J. Law (ed.) *Power, Action and Belief: A New Sociology of Knowledge? Sociological Review Monograph 32.* London: Routledge.

—— (1997) 'Actor–network theory – the market test', working paper. Paris: Ecole des Mines de Paris.

——, Law, J. and Rip, A. (eds) (1986) *Mapping out the Dynamics of Science and Technology: Sociology of Science in the Real World.* London: Macmillan.

Campbell, D. T. (1965) 'Variation and selective retention in socio-culture evolution', in Barringer, G. I. and Mack, R. (eds) *Social Change in Developing Areas.* Cambridge, MA: Schenkman, pp. 19–49.

Carroll, P. N. and Noble, D. W. (1977) *The Free and the Unfree. A New History of the United States.* London: Penguin.

Carter, C. (1998) 'Keeper of the knowledge capital', paper at British Academy of Management, University of Nottingham.

Chaiklin, S. and Lave, J. (1993) *Understanding Practice: Perspectives on Activity and Context.* Cambridge: Cambridge University Press.

Chandler, A. D. (1962) *Strategy and Structure*, Cambridge, MA: MIT Press.

—— (1977) *The Visible Hand*, Cambridge, MA: Belknap.

—— (1984) 'The emergence of managerial capitalism', *Business History Review* 58 (4): 473–503.

—— (1990) *Scale and Scope. The Dynamics of Industrial Capitalism.* Cambridge, MA: Harvard University Press.

—— and Daems, H. (1980) *Managerial Hierarchies. Comparative Perspectives on the Rise of the Modern Industrial Enterprise.* Cambridge, MA: Harvard University Press.

Child, J. (1972) 'Organizational structure, environment and performance: the role of strategic choice', *Sociology* 6: 1–22.

—— (1997) 'Strategic choice in the analysis of action, structure, organisations and environment: retrospect and prospect', *Organisation Studies* 18 (1): 43–76.

—— and Kieser, A. (1981) 'Development of organizations over time?', in P. C. Nystrom and W. H. Starbuck *Handbook of Organization Design*. Oxford: Oxford University Press, pp. 28–64.

—— and Smith, C. (1987) 'The context and process of organizational transformation: Cadbury Limited in sector', *Journal of Management Studies* 24: 563–593.

Chirot, D. (1985) 'The rise of the west', *American Sociological Review* 50 (2): 181–194.

Church, R. (1994) *The Rise and Decline of the British Motor Industry.* London: Macmillan.

Churchman, C. W. (1986) *Challenge to Reason.* New York: McGraw-Hill.

Clark, B. R. (1998) *Creating Enterpreneurial Universities – Organizational Pathways of Transformation.* Rotterdam: Elsevier.

Clark, K. B. (1985) 'The interaction of design hierarchies and market concepts in technology evolution', *Research Policy* 14: 235–251.

—— and Fujimoto, T. (1991) *Product Development Performance. Strategy, Organization and Management in the World of Auto Industry.* Cambridge, MA: Harvard Business School.

Clark, P. A. (1972) *Organizational Design: Theory and Practice.* London: Tavistock.

—— (1975a) 'Key problems in organization design'. *Administration and Society* 7: 213–256.

—— (1975b) 'Time reckoning systems in organisations', paper given at Invited Workshop, Society for Applied Anthropology, Netherlands.

—— (1978) *Time Reckoning Systems in Large Organizations. Study of Time III.* Berlin: Springer-Verlag.

—— (1979) 'Cultural content as a determinant of organizational rationality: an empirical investigation of the tobacco industries in Britain and France', in C. J. Lammers and D. J. Hickson (eds) *Organizations: Alike and Unlike.* London: Macmillan.

—— (1985) 'A review of theories of time and structures for organization studies', in S. Bachrach and S. Mitchell (eds) *Organizational Sociology: Research and Perspectives*, vol. 4. New Haven. JAI Press, pp. 35–79.

—— (1986a) 'Le capitalisme et la réglement du temps de travail: une critique de la thèse E. P. Thompson', *Temps Libre* 15: 27–32.

—— (1986b) 'The economy of time and the managerial division of labour in large British construction firms', *BISS Proceedings VII.* London: University College.

—— (1987) *Anglo-American Innovation.* New York: De Gruyter.

—— (1990) 'Corporate chronologies and organisational analysis', In J. Hassard and D. Pymm. *The Theory and Philosophy of Organisations.* London: Croome Helm.

—— (1991) 'Organisation failures: work study in Britain (1941–1991)', in G. Lee (ed.) *Owning Corporate Problem Solving.* Birmingham: Centre for the Professions, pp. 5–28.

—— (1996) 'Organizational performance', in M. Warner (ed.) *Encyclopaedia of Business and Management.* London: Thompson. pp. 3943–3954.

—— (1997a) 'American corporate timetabling, its past, present and future', *Time and Society* 6 (2/3): 261–285.

—— (1997b) 'The duality of strategic time reckoning and the influence of national predispositions on Production and Inventory Control Systems', in D. Morello *The Managerial Experience of Time.* Palermo: ISIDA.

—— (1998) 'Aston Programme: describing and explaining the structure of Canadian textile firms', in D. S. Pugh, *The Aston Programme: Volume II.* Aldershot: Dartmouth. pp. 431–509.

—— and De Bresson, C. (1990) 'Innovation-design and innovation policies', in R. J. Loveridge and M. Pitt. *Strategic Management of Technological Innovation.* Chichester: Wiley. pp. 223–250.

—— and Ford, J. R. (1970) 'Theoretical and methodological problems in the study of planned organizational change', *Sociological Review* 18 (2): 29–52.

—— and Mueller, F. (1995) 'National systems of organising: corporate agency and zones of manoeuvre', in R. Whittington, H. Bouchikhi and M. Kilduff, *Action, Structure and Organisations.* Coventry: Warwick Business School Research Bureau.

—— and Mueller, F. (1996) 'Organisations and nations: from universalism to institutionalism?', *British Journal of Management* 7 (2): 125–140.

—— and Newell, S. (1993) 'Societal embedding of production and inventory control systems: American and Japanese influences on adaptive implementation in Britain', *International Journal of Human Factors in Manufacturing* 3: 69–81.

—— and Probert, S. (1989) 'The American tufted carpet revolution and two established British carpet firms – 1950/1985', paper to European Group on Organization Studies, Berlin.

—— and Starkey, K. (1988) *Organisation Transitions and Innovation Design.* London: Frances Pinter.

—— and Staunton, N. (1989) *Innovation in Technology and Organisation.* London: Routledge.

—— and Swan, J. (2000) *Organizational Innovations.* London: Sage.

—— and Whipp, R. (1984) 'Industrial change in Britain: a comparative historical enquiry into innovation design', ESRC, Work Organisation Research Centre, Aston University.

——, Dumas, A. and Hills, P. (1995) 'Design and technology: increasing the output through innovation in organisation', in D. Bennett and F. Steward, *Technology Innovation and Global Challenges.* Birmingham: Aston University.

——, Newell, S., Swan, J., Bennett, D., Burcher, P. and Sharifi, S., (1993) 'The decision episode framework and computer aided production management', *International Studies in Management and Organization* 22 (4): 69–80.

Clegg, S. R. (1987) 'The power of language, the language of power', *Organization Studies* 8 (1): 60–70.

—— (1994) 'Weber and Foucault: social theory for the study of organizations', *Organization* 1: 149–178.

—— (1989) *Frameworks of Power.* London: Sage.

——, Nord, J. and Hardy, C. (1996) *Handbook of Organisation Studies.* London: Sage.

——, Barrett, M., Clarke, T., Dwyer, L., Gray, J., Kemp, S. and Marceau, J. (1996) 'Management knowledge for the future: innovation, embryos and new paradigms', in S. Clegg and G. Palmer (eds) *The Politics of Management Knowledge.* Sage: London.

Coase, R. (1937) 'The nature of the firm', *Economica* 4: 386–405.

Cochrane, R. B. (1988) 'The environmental features which limit organization and industry viability: a study of the UK footwear industry', doctoral thesis, Birmingham: Aston University.

Cohen, M. and Bacdayan, P. (1994) 'Organizational routines are stored as procedural memory: evidence from a laboratory study', *Organization Science* 5 (4): 554–568.

Cohen, W. M. and Levinthal, D. A. (1990) 'Absorptive capacity: a new perspective on organisational learning and innovation', *Administrative Science Quarterly* 55: 28–152.

Coriat, B. (1976) *L'Atelier et le Chronometre.* Paris: Seuil.

—— (1990) *L'atelier et le robot: essai sur le fordisme et la productio de mass à l'âge de l'électronique.* Paris: Bourgois.

Corke, D. (1985) *A Guide to Computer Aided Production Management (CAPM).* London: Institute of Production Engineers.

Crafts, N. F. R. (1985) *British Economic Growth during the Industrial Revolution.* Oxford: Oxford University Press.

Craib, I. (1992) *Anthony Giddens.* London: Routledge.

—— (1997) *Classical Social Theory.* Oxford: Oxford University Press.

Cronon, W. (1983) *Changes in the Land. Indians, Colonists, and the Ecology of New England.* New York: Hill & Wang.

—— (1991) *Natures Metropolis: Chicago and the Great West.* New York: Norton.

Crosby, A. (1998) *Measure of Reality.* Cambridge: Cambridge University Press.

Crozier, M. (1964) *The Bureaucratic Phenomenon.* Chicago: University of Chicago Press.

—— (1973) *The Stalled Society.* New York: Viking Press.

—— and Friedberg, E. (1980) *Actors and Systems.* Chicago: University of Chicago.

Currie, M. (1998) *Postmodern Narrative Theory.* London: Macmillan.

Cusumano, M. A. (1985) *The Japanese Automobile Industry. Technology and Management at Nissan and Toyota.* Cambridge, MA: Harvard University Press.

Cyert, R. M. and March, J. G. (1963) *A Behavioural Theory of the Firm.* Englewood Cliffs, NJ: Prentice-Hall.

Czarniawska, B. (1998) *A Narrative Approach to Organisation Studies.* London: Sage.

Daft, R. (1997) *Organization Theory and Design.* St Paul: West.

Dalton, M. (1959) *Men Who Manage.* New York: Wiley.

Darbishire, D. and Katz, H. C. (1997) 'Converging differences: worldwide changes in employment', Working Paper, NYSSILR, Cornell University.

Das, M. (1997) *Symposium Knowledge Capitalism: Competitiveness Reevaluated.* Boston: American Academy of Management.

D'Aveni, R. A. (1994) *Hypercompetition. Managing the Dynamics of Strategic Manoeuvring.* New York: Free Press.

David P. A. (1975) *Technological Choice, Innovations and Economic Growth. Essays on American British Experience in the 19th Century.* Cambridge: Cambridge University Press.

—— (1986) 'Understanding the economics of QWERTY: the necessity of history', in W. N. Parker (ed.) *Economic History and the Modern Economist.* Oxford: Blackwell, pp. 30–49.

Davis, G. and Stout, S. (1992) 'Organization theory and the market for corporate control', *Administrative Science Quarterly* 37: 660–633.

Demarest, M. (1997) 'Understanding knowledge management', *Journal of Long Range Planning* 30 (3): 374–384.

Denzig, A. (1956) *The History of American Football: Its Great Teams, Players and Coaches.* Englewood Cliffs, NJ: Prentice-Hall.

DeSanctis, G. and Poole, M. S. (1994) 'Capturing the complexity in advanced technology use: adaptive structuration theory', *Organisational Science* 5: 121–147.

Di Bello, L., Kindred, J. and Zazanis, E. (1992) *Third Annual Report. Cognitive Studies of Work. Laboratory for Cognitive Studies of Activity.* New York: City University of New York.

Dicken, P. (1998) *Global Shift. Transforming the World Economy.* London: Paul Chapman.

Dill, W. R. (1958) 'Environment as an influence on managerial autonomy', *Administrative Science Quarterly* 2: 409–443.

—— (1962) 'The impact of environment on managerial autonomy', In S. Mailick and G. H. Van Ness (eds) *Concepts and Issues in Administration Behaviour.* New York: Prentice-Hall.

DiMaggio, P. J. and (1983) 'The iron cage revisited: institutional isomorphism and collective rationality in organisational fields', *American Sociological Review* 48: 147–160.

—— and Powell, W. W. (1991) 'Introduction', in W. Powell and P. DiMaggio (eds) *The New Institutionalism in Organisational Theory.* Chicago: University Chicago Press. pp. 3–45.

Dodgson, M. (1993) 'Organisational learning: a review of some literatures', *Organisational Studies* 14: 375–394.

Donaldson, L. (1985) *In Defence of Organisation Theory: A Reply to the Critics.* Cambridge: Cambridge University Press.

—— (1990) 'A rational basis for criticisms of organizational economics: a reply to Barney', *Academy of Management Review* 15 (3): 394–401.

—— (1995) *American Anti-Management Theories of Organization: A Critique of Paradigm Proliferation.* Cambridge: Cambridge University Press.

—— (1996) 'The normal science of structural contingency theory', in S. Clegg, J. Nord, and C. Hardy. *Handbook of Organisation Studies*. London: Sage, pp. 57–76.

Dosi, G., Egidi, M., Marengo, L., Warglien M. and Winter, S. (1996) 'Routines and other recurring action patterns of organizations: contemporary research issues', *Journal of Industrial and Corporate Change*: 653–686.

Douma, S. and Schreuder, H. (1991). *Economic Approaches to Organizations*. London: Prentice-Hall.

Dubinskas, F. (ed.) (1988) *Making Time*. Memphis: Temple.

Duncan, R. B. (1972) 'Characteristics of organisation environments and perceived environmental uncertainty', *Administrative Science Quarterly* 17: 313–327.

Dunning, J. H. (1993) *The Globalisation of Business*. London: Routledge.

—— (1997) 'Knowledge capitalism: competitiveness reevaluated. a macro-organisational viewpoint', in M. Das *Symposium Knowledge Capitalism: Competitiveness Reevaluated*. Boston: American Academy of Management.

Durkheim, E. (1915) *The Elementary Forms of the Religious Life*. London: Allen & Unwin.

—— (1964) *New Rules of Sociological Method*. New York: Free Press.

Eagleton, T. (1996a) *The Illusions of Postmodernism*. Oxford: Blackwell.

—— (1996b) *Literary Theory: An Introduction*. Oxford: Blackwell.

Eisenstadt, S. N. (1963) *The Political System of Empires*. New York: Free Press.

—— (1966) *Modernisation: Protest and Change*. Englewood Cliffs, NJ: Prentice-Hall.

—— (1985) 'Macro-societal analysis: background development and indications', in S. Eisenstadt and H. Helle (eds) *Macro-Sociological Theory: Perspectives on Sociological Theory*, vol. 1. London: Sage.

—— (ed.) (1986) *The Origins and Diversity of Axial Age Civilizations*. Albany: SUNY Press.

Ekelund, R. B. and Tollison, R. D. (1981) *Mercantilism as a Rent Seeking Society. Economic Regulation in Historical Perspectives*. College Station, TX: Texas A & M University Press.

Elbaum, B. and Lazonick, W. (eds) (1986) *The Decline of the British Economy*. Oxford: Clarendon Press.

Elias, N. (1982) *State Formation and Civilization*. Oxford: Blackwell.

—— (1983) *The Court Society*. Oxford: Blackwell.

—— (1992) *Time: An Essay*. Oxford: Blackwell.

—— (1994) *The Civilising Process: The History of Manners and State Formation and Civilisation*. Oxford: Blackwell.

—— and Dunning, E. (1970). 'Folk football in medieval and early modern Britain', in E. Dunning (ed.) *The Sociology of Sport*. London: Frank Cass, pp. 313–327.

Elster, J. (1984) *Ulysses and the Sirens: Studies in Rationality and Irrationality*. Cambridge: Cambridge University Press.

—— (1989) *The Cement of Society: A Study of Social Order*. New York: Cambridge University Press.

Emery, F. E. (1959) *Characteristics of socio-technical systems: a critical review of theories and facts*. London: Tavistock Institute. Paper 527.

—— and Trist, E. L. (1965) 'The causal textures of organisational environments', *Human Relations* 18 (1): 21–32.

Etzioni, A. (1961) *A Comparative Analysis of Organizations*. New York: Free Press.

—— (1968) *The Active Society: A Theory of Societal and Political Processes*. New York: Free Press.

Evans, P. (1995) *Embedded Autonomy*. Princeton, NJ: Princeton University Press.

Evans, R.J. (1997) *In Defence of History*. London: Granta.

Evans-Pritchard, E. E. (1940) *The Nuer*. Oxford: Oxford University Press.

Featherstone, M. (1991) *Consumer Culture and Postmodernism*. London: Sage.

Ferguson, N. (ed.) (1997) *Virtual History: Alternatives and Counterfactuals.* London: Picador.

Fligstein, N. (1987) 'The intraorganizational power struggle: the rise of finance presidents in large corporations', *American Sociological Review* 52: 44–58.

—— (1990) *The Transformation of Corporate Capital.* Cambridge, MA: Harvard University Press.

—— (1996) 'Markets as politics: a political-cultural approach to market institutions', *American Sociological Review* 61: 656–673.

Fogel, R. W. (1964) *Railroads and American Growth: Essays in Economic History.* Baltimore, MD: Johns Hopkins University Press.

Foss, N. J. and Erikson, B. (1995) 'Competitive advantage and industry capabilities', in C. A. Montgomery *Resource-Based and Evolutionary Theories of the Firm: Towards a Synthesis.* Cambridge, MA: Harvard Business School.

Foucault, M. (1972) *The Archaeology of Knowledge.* London: Tavistock.

—— (1977) *Discipline and Punish: The Birth of the Prison.* Harmondsworth: Penguin.

—— (1984) *The History of Sexuality: An Introduction.* Harmondsworth: Penguin.

Freeman, C. (1974) *The Economics of Industrial Innovation*, 2nd edn. London: Frances Pinter.

—— (1983) *Longwaves in the World Economy.* London: Butterworth.

—— and Soete, L. (eds) (1985) *Technical Change and Full Employment.* Oxford: Blackwell.

Friedland, R. and Boden, D. (1994) *Space, Time and Modernity.* Los Angeles: University of California Press.

Friedman, A.L. (1977) *Industry and Labour: Class Struggle at Work and Monopoly Capitalism.* London: Macmillan.

Fromm, E. (1955) *The Sane Society.* New York: Reinhard.

Galbraith, J. R. (1971) *Organizational Design.* New York: Addison Wesley.

—— (1977) *Organizational Design.* Reading: Addison Wesley.

Gallie, D. (1983) *In Search of the New Working Class.* Cambridge: Cambridge University Press.

Gandy, O. H. (1993) *The Panoptic Sort. A Political Economy of Personal Information.* Boulder, CO: Westview.

Garfinkel, H. (1967) *Studies in Ethnomethodology.* London: Prentice-Hall.

Garland, D. (1990) *Punishment and Modern Society: A Study in Social Theory.* Chicago: University of Chicago Press.

Gearing, E. (1958) 'Structural poses of the eighteenth century Cherokee villages', *American Anthropologist* 60: 1148–1157.

Geertz, C. (1973) 'Ideology as a cultural system', in C. Geertz *The Interpretation of Cultures.* New York: Basic Books. pp. 193–233.

—— (1983) *Local Knowledge.* New York: Basic Books.

Gell, A. (1992) *The Anthropology of Time. Cultural Constructions of Temporal Maps and Images.* London: Berg.

Gell-Mann, M. (1994) *The Quark and the Jaguar. Adventures in the Simple and the Complex.* London: Little, Brown.

Ghirardo, D. (1996) *Architecture After Modernism.* London: Thames & Hudson.

Ghoshal, S. (1996) 'The new agenda on management', seminar, University of Warwick, England.

Ghoshal, S. and Bartlett, C. A. (1994) 'Linking organizational context and managerial action: the dimensions of quality of management', *Strategic Management Journal* 15: 91–112.

Gibbons, M., Nowotony, H., Schwartzman, S., Scott, P. and Trow, M. (1994) *The New Production of Knowledge. The Dynamics of Science and Research in Contemporary Societies.* London: Sage.

Giddens, A. (ed.) (1974) *Positivism and Sociology.* London: Heinemann.

—— (1977) *Studies in Social and Political Theory.* London: Hutchinson.

—— (1979) *Central Problems in Sociological Theory: Action, Structure and Contradiction in Social. Analysis.* London: Macmillan.

—— (1981) *A Contemporary Critique of Historical Materialism.* London: Macmillan.

—— (1984) *The Constitution of Society.* Cambridge: Polity Press.

—— (1985) *The Nation State and Violence.* Cambridge: Polity Press.

—— (1990) *The Consequences of Modernity.* Cambridge: Polity Press.

—— (1991) *Modernity and Self-Identity: Self and Identity in the late Modern Age.* Cambridge: Polity Press.

—— (1994) *Beyond Left and Right.* Cambridge: Polity Press.

—— (1998) *The Third Way.* Cambridge: Polity Press.

Giedion, S. (1967) *Space, Time and Architecture. The Growth of a New Tradition.* Oxford: Oxford University Press.

Gille, B. (1978) *Histoire des Techniques.* Paris: Piriade.

Glennie, P. and Thrift, N. (1996) 'Reworking E.P. Thompson's "Time, Work-Discipline and Industrial Capitalism"', *Time and Society* 5 (3): 275–299.

Goffman, E. (1959) *The Presentation of Self in Everyday Life.* Harmondsworth: Penguin.

Goldthorpe, J., Lockwood, D., Beckhofer, F. and Platt, J. (eds) (1969) *The Affluent Worker and the Class Structure.* Cambridge: Cambridge University Press.

Golomb, N. and Katz, D. (1974). *The Kibbutz as an Open System.* Israel: Ruppin Institute.

Goodey, J. (1977) *The Domestication of the Savage Mind.* Cambridge: Cambridge University Press.

Goodrich, C.L. (1975) *The Frontier of Control.* London: Pluto Press.

Goold, M. and Campbell, A. (1987) *Strategies and Styles. The Role of the Centre in Managing Diversified Corporations.* Oxford: Blackwell.

Gordon, A. (ed.) (1993) *Post-war Japan as History.* Los Angeles: University of California Press.

Grabher, G. (1993) *The Embedded Firm: On the Socioeconomics of Industrial Networks.* London: Routledge.

Gramsci, A. (1971) *Selections from the Prison Notebooks.* London: Lawrence & Wishart.

Granovetter, M. S. (1973) 'The strength of weak ties', *American Sociological Review* 78: 1360–1380.

—— (1985) 'Economic action and social structure: the problem of embeddedness', *American Journal of Sociology* 91: 481–510.

—— (1990) 'The old and the new economic sociology: a history and an agenda', in A. F. Robertson, R. Friedland, (eds) *Beyond the Marketplace: Rethinking Economy and Society.* New York: Aldine, pp. 89–112.

—— and Swedberg, R. (eds) (1992) *The Sociology of Economic Life.* Oxford: Westview Press.

Grant, R. M. (1990/1995/1998) *Contemporary Strategy Analysis. Concepts, Techniques and Applications.* Oxford: Blackwell.

—— (1991) 'Porter's "Competitive Advantage of Nations": as assessment', *Strategic Management Journal* 12: 535–548.

—— (1996a) 'Prospering in dynamically-competitive environments: organizational capability as knowledge integration', *Organization Science* 7 (4): 375–387.

—— (1996b) 'Towards a knowledge-based theory of the firm', *Strategic Management Journal* 17: 109–122.

—— and Spender, J.-C. (1996) 'Knowledge and the firm', *Strategic Management Journal,* special issue, 17.

Gregory, D. (1982) *Regional Transformation and Industrial Revolution. A Geography of the Yorkshire Woollen Industry.* London: Macmillan.

—— (1994) *Geographical Imaginations.* Oxford: Blackwell.

Griener, L. (1967) 'Antecedents of planned organisational change', *Journal of Applied Behavioural Science* 3 (1): 51–85.

—— (1972) 'Evolution and revolution as organisations grow', *Harvard Business Review* 50 (4): 37–46.

Grint, K. and Woolgar, S. (1998) *The Machine at Work. Technology, Work and Organization.* Cambridge: Polity Press.

Guild, W. (1999) 'Using categories to provide customised service: meanings created in ski resort subcultures', in R. A. Goodman (ed.) *Modern Organizations and Emerging Conundrums: Exploring the Postindustrial Subculture of the Third Millennium.* Oxford: Lexington Books.

Guillen, M. (1994) *Models of Management: Work, Authority, and Organization in a Comparative Perspective.* Chicago: University of Chicago Press.

Gurvitch, G. (1964) *The Spectrum of Social Time.* Dordrecht: Reidel.

Habakkuk, H. J. (1962) *American and British Technology in the 19th Century.* Cambridge: Cambridge University Press.

Habermas, J. (1976) *Legitimation Crisis.* London: Heinemann.

—— (1984) *Reason and the Rationalization of Society.* London: Heinemann.

Hage, J. (1998) 'Aston Group', in M. Warner, *The Handbook of Management Thinking.* London: Thompson, pp. 24–31.

Hakansson, H. (ed.) (1987) *Industrial Technology Development. A Network Approach.* London: Croom Helm.

Hales, C. P. (1986) 'What do managers do? a critical review of the evidence', *Journal of Management Studies* 23 (1): 88–115.

—— (1989) 'Management processes, management divisions of labour and managerial work: towards a synthesis', *International Journal of Sociology and Social Policy* 9 (5/6): 9–38.

Hall, J. (1985) *Powers and Liberties: Causes and Consequences of the Rise of the West.* Oxford: Oxford University Press.

Hall, R. A. (1992) 'The strategic analysis of intangible resouces', *Strategic Management Journal* 13: 135–144.

Hall, R.H. (1972) *Organisations: Structure and Process.* Englewood Cliffs, NJ: Prentice-Hall.

Hamel, G. (1991) 'Competition for competence and inter-partner learning within international strategic alliances', *Strategic Management Journal* 12: 83–103.

—— and Prahalad, C. K. (1989) 'Strategic intents', *Harvard Business Review,* May–June: 63–76.

Hammer, M. and Champy, J. (1993) *Re-engineering the Corporation. A Manifesto for Business Revolution.* London: Harper.

Hannan, M. and Freeman, J. (1977) 'The population ecology model of organisations', *American Journal of Sociology* 82: 929–964.

—— and Freeman, J. (1989) *Organisational Ecology.* Cambridge, MA: Harvard University Press.

Harre, R. (1979) *Social Being a Theory for Social Psychology.* Oxford: Blackwell.

—— (1985) *Varieties of Realism.* Oxford: Blackwell.

—— and Madden, E. H. (1975) *Casual Powers.* Oxford: Blackwell.

—— and Secord, P. H. (1972) *The Explanation of Social Behaviour.* Oxford: Blackwell.

Harvey, D. (1989) *The Condition of Postmodernity.* Oxford: Blackwell.

—— (1996) *Justice, Nature and the Geography of Difference.* Oxford: Blackwell.

Hassan, I. (1987) *The Postmodern Turn: Essays in Postmodern Theory and Culture.* Columbus, OH: Columbus.

Hassard, J. (1996) 'Images of time in work and organization', in S. Clegg, J. Nord and C. Hardy, *Handbook of Organisation Studies*. London: Sage. pp. 381–398.

Hatch, M. J. (1997) *Organisation Theory*. Oxford: Oxford University Press.

Hawthorn, G. (1991) *Plausible Worlds: Possibility and Understanding in History and the Social Sciences*. Cambridge: Cambridge University Press.

Heatherington, K. (1997) *The Badlands of Modernity*. London: Routledge.

Hedlund, G. (1994) 'A model of knowledge management and the N-form corporation', *Strategic Management Journal* 15: 73–90.

Heimer, C. A. (1985) *Reactive Rise and Rational Action: Managing Moral Hazard in Insurance Contracts*. Berkley: University of California Press.

Henderson, R. M and Clark, K. B, (1990) 'Architectural innovation: the reconfiguration of existing product technologies and the failure of established firms', *Administrative Science Quarterly*, 35: 9–30.

Henderson, R. and Cockburn, I. (1994) 'Measuring core competence? Evidence from the pharmaceutical industry', *Strategic Management Journal* 15: 63–84.

Hesterley, W. S., Lieberkind, J. and Zenger, T. R. (1990) 'Organisational economics: an impending revolution in organization theory', *Academy of Management Review* 15: 402–420.

Hexter, H. J. (1972) 'Fernand Braudel and Monde Braudellian', *Journal of Modern History* II (3): 1–23.

Hicks, C. (1998) 'Barriers to evidence-based care in nursing: historical legacies and conflicting cultures', *Health Services Management Research* 11: 137–147.

Hickson, D. J. (ed.) (1997) *Exploring Management Across the World*. London: Penguin.

—— and McMillan, C. J. (eds) (1981) *Organisation and Nation: The Aston Programme IV*. Farnborough: Gower.

—— and Pugh, D. S. (1995) *Management Worldwide*. Harmondsworth: Penguin.

——, Hinings, C.R., McMillan, C.J. and Schwitter, J. P. (1974) 'The culture-free context of organisation stucture: a tri-national comparison', *Sociology* 8: 59–80.

Hirsch, P., Michaels, S. and Friedman, R. (1990) 'Clean models vs. dirty hands: why economics is different from sociology', in S. Zukin and P. DiMaggio, *Structures of Capital: The Social Organization of the Economy*. New York: Cambridge University Press.

Hislop, D., Newell, S., Scarborough, H. and Swan, J. (1997) 'Innovation and networks: linking diffusion and implementation', *International Journal of Innovation Management* 1 (4): 427–448.

Hobsbawm, E. (1998) 'The death of neo-liberalism', *Marxism Today*, November–December: 4–8.

Hodgson, G. M. (1988) *Economics and Institutions: A Manifesto for a Modern Institutional Economics*. Cambridge: Polity Press.

Hofer, C. W. and Schendel, D. (1978) *Strategy Formulation: Analytical Concepts*. St Paul, MN: West Publishing.

Hofstadter, R. (1955) *Social Darwinism in American Thought*. Boston: Beacon Press.

Hofstede, G. (1980) *Culture's Consequences: International Differences in Work-related Values*. Beverly Hills, CA: Sage.

Holmer Nadeesan, M. (1997) 'Essai: dissecting (instrumental) organisational time; *Organisation Studies* 18 (3): 481–510.

Holton, R. J. (1986) *Cities, Capitalism and Civilization*. London: Allen & Unwin.

—— (1992) *Economy and Society*. London: Routledge.

Homans, G. C. (1951) *The Human Group*. London: Routledge.

Hopwood, A. G. and Miller, P. (1994) *Accounting as Social and Institutional Practice*. Cambridge: Cambridge University Press.

Hoskin, K. W. and Macve, R. (1988) 'The genesis of accountability: the West Point connections. Accounting', *Organizations and Society* 13: 37–73.

Hounshell, D. A, (1984) *From the American System to Mass Production, 1800–1932*. Baltimore: Johns Hopkins University Press.

Hughes, T. (1983) *Networks of Power: Electrification in Western Society*. Baltimore: Johns Hopkins University Press.

Hughes, T. C. (1990) *American Genesis*. Baltimore: Johns Hopkins University Press.

Hutchins, E. (1993) 'Learning to navigate', in S. Chaiklin and J. Lave (1993) *Understanding Practice. Perspectives on Activity and Context*. Cambridge: Cambridge University Press.

Hutte, H. (1968) *The Sociatry of Work*. Leiden: Van Gorcam.

Inkeles, A. and Smith, D. H. (1974) *Becoming Modern*. Cambridge, MA: Harvard University Press.

Itami, H. and Roehl, T. W. (1987) *Mobilizing Invisible Assets*. Cambridge, MA: Harvard University Press.

Jameson, F. (1980) *The Political Unconcious: Narrative as a Socially Symbolic Act*. Ithaca: Cornell University Press.

—— (1984) 'Postmodernism, or cultural logic of late capitalism', *New Left Review* 146: 53–93.

—— (1988) 'Postmodernism and consumer society', in E. A. Kaplan, (ed.) *Postmodernism and its Discontents*. London: Verso, pp. 13–29.

—— (1991) *Postmodernism, or, The Cultural Logic of Late Capitalism*. London: Verso.

Jay, M. (1973) *The Dialectical Imagination*. Boston: Beacon.

Jenkins, K. (1997) *The Postmodern History Reader*. London: Routledge.

Jeremy, D.J. (1981) *Transatlantic Industrial Revolution*. Oxford: Blackwell.

Johansson, H. J, McHugh, P., Pendlebury. A. J. and Wheeler, W.A. (1993) *Business Process Re-engineering*. New York: Wiley.

Johnson, T. H and Kaplan, R. S (1987) *Relevance Lost. The Rise and Fall of Management Accounting*. Boston: Harvard Business School Press.

Kamoche, K. (1996) 'Strategic human resource management within a resource-capability view of the firm', *Journal of Management Studies* 33 (2): 1–17.

—— and Mueller, F. (1997) 'Human resource management and appropriability', Working Paper, Department of Commerce 97/01, University of Birmingham.

Kanter, R. M. (1984) *The Change Masters. Corporate Entrepreneurs at Work*. London: Allen & Unwin.

Katz, D. and Kahn, R. L. (1966) *The Social Psychology of Organisations*. New York: Wiley.

Kay, J. (1993) *Foundations of Corporate Success. How Business Strategies Add Value*. Oxford: Oxford University Press.

Kennedy, P. (1987) *The Rise and Fall of Great Powers: Economic Change and Military Conflict 1500–2000*. New York: Random House.

Kenney, M. and Florida, R. (1993) *Beyond Mass Production. The Japanese System and its Transfer to the United States*. Oxford: Oxford University Press.

Kern, S. (1983) *The Culture of Time and Space, 1880–1914*. London: Weidenfeld & Nicolson.

Kieser, A. (1998) 'Organizational, institutional, societal evolution: medieval guilds and the genesis of formalization', *Administrative Science Quarterly* 34: 540–564.

Kilduff, M. (1993) 'Deconstructing organisations', *Academy of Management Review* 18 (1): 13–31.

Kogut, B. (1993) 'Country capabilities and the permeability of borders', *Strategic Management Journal* 12: 33–47.

—— (1997) 'Regional networks and markets', in M. Das, *Symposium Knowledge Capitalism: Competitiveness Revisited*. Boston: American Academy of Management.

Krieken van, R. (1995) *Norbert Elias*. London: Routledge.

Krone, G. C. (1972) 'The open system approach to organisational design', organizational development document, Procter & Gamble, Cincinatti.

Ladurie, E. Le Roy (1979) '"The event" and the "long term" in social history: the case of the Chouan Uprising' in E. Le Roy Ladurie, *The Territory of the Historian*. Paris: PUF.

Lammers, C. J. and Hickson, D. J. (eds) (1979) *Organisations Alike and Unlike: International and Inter-institutional Studies in the Sociology of Organisations*. London: Macmillan.

Landes, D. (1969) *The Unbound Prometheus: Technological Change and Industrial Development in Europe from 1750 to the Present*. Cambridge: Cambridge University Press.

—— (1983) *Revolution in Time Clocks and the Making of the Modern World*. Boston: Belknap.

—— (1998) *The Wealth and Poverty of Nations*. London: Little, Brown.

Lane, C. (1996) *Management and Labour in Europe: The Industrial Enterprise in Germany, Britain and France*. London: Edward Elgar.

Langlois, R. N. (1995) 'Capabilities and coherence in firms and markets', in C. A. Montgomery, *Resource-based and Evolutionary Theories of the Firm: Towards a Synthesis*. Cambridge, MA: Harvard Business School.

Larson, M. S. (1977) *The Rise of Professionalism. A Sociological Analysis*. Berkeley, CA: University of California Press.

Lash, S. (1990) *Sociology of Postmodernism*. New York: Routledge.

Lash, S. and Urry, J. (1987) *End of Organized Capitalism*. Cambridge: Polity Press.

—— and Urry, J. (1994) *Economy of Signs and Spaces*. London: Sage.

Laslett, P. (1965) *The World We Have Lost Further Explored*. London: Methuen.

Latour, B. (1987) *Science in Action: How to Follow Scientists and Engineers Through Society*. Milton Keynes: Open University Press.

—— (1988) *The Pasteurization of France*. Cambridge: Cambridge University Press.

Lave, J. and Wenger, E. (1991) *Situated Learning. Legitimate Peripheral Participation*. Cambridge: Cambridge University Press.

Law, J. (1986) 'On the methods of long-distance control: vessels, navigation and the Portuguese route to India', in J. Law (ed.) *Power, Action and Belief: A New Sociology of Knowledge? Sociological Review Monograph 32*. London: Routledge & Paul Kegan, pp. 234–283.

—— (1994) *Organising Modernity*. Oxford: Blackwell.

Layder, D. (1985) 'Power, structure and agency', *Journal for the Theory of Social Behaviour* 15 (2): 131–149.

—— (1997) *Modern Social Theory*. London: UCL Press.

Lazonick, W. (1991) *Business Organization and the Myth of the Market Economy*. New York: Cambridge University Press.

Le Goff, J. (1980) *Time, Work and Culture in the Middle Ages*, Chicago: University of Chicago Press.

Lears, J. (1994) *Fables of Abundance. A Cultural History of Advertising in America*. New York: Basic Books.

Legge, K. (1995) *Human Resource Management: Rhetorics and Realities*. London: Macmillan.

Levinthal, D. A. and March J. G. (1993) 'The myopia of learning', *Strategic Management Journal* 14: 95–112.

Leyshon, A. and Thrift, N. (1997) *Money/Space. Geographies of Monetary Transformation*. London: Routledge.

Lievegoede, B. C. J. (1973) *Organisational Development*. Assern: van Gorcam.

Lincoln, J. R. and Kalleberg, A. (1990) *Culture, Control and Commitment: A Study of Work Organisation and Work Attitudes in the United States and Japan.* Cambridge: Cambridge University Press.

Lipietz, A. (1992) *Towards a New Economic Order: Post Fordism, Ecology and Democracy.* Cambridge: Polity Press.

Lipset, S. M. (1996) *American Exceptionalism. A Double Edged Sword.* New York: Norton.

Locke, R. R. (1996) *The Collapse of the American Management Mystique.* Oxford: Oxford University Press.

Lockwood, D. (1964) 'Social integration and system integration', in G. K. Zollschan and W. Hirsch (eds) *Explorations in Social Change.* London: Routledge & Kegan Paul.

Lodge, G. C. and Vogel, E. F. (1987) *Ideology and National Competitiveness: An Analysis of Nine Countries.* Cambridge, MA: Harvard University Press.

Luhman, N. (1995) *Social Systems.* Stamford, CA: Stamford University Press.

Lukes, S. (1974) *Power: A Radical View.* London: Macmillan.

Lundvall, B. A. (1992) *National Systems of Innovation. Towards a Theory of Innovation and Interactive Learning.* London: Pinter.

Lyotard, J. F. (1984) *The Postmodern Condition: A Report on Knowledge.* Minneapolis: University of Minnesota Press.

Macintosh, N. B. (1994) *Management Accounting and Control Systems. An Organisational and Behavioural Approach.* Chichester: Wiley.

McCloskey, D.N. (1990) *If You're So Smart: The Narrative of Economic Expertise.* London: University of Chicago Press.

McKinsey Global Institute (1998) *Driving Productivity and Growth in the UK Economy.* London: McKinsey.

McLuhan, M. (1967) *The Medium is the Message.* New York: Random House.

McMillan, C. J. (1985) *The Japanese Industrial System.* Berlin: De Gruyter.

Mandel, E. (1978) *Late Capitalism.* London: Verso.

—— (1980) *Longwaves of Capitalist Development: The Marxist Interpretation.* Cambridge: Cambridge University Press.

March, J. (1961) 'The firm as a political coalition', *Administrative Science Quarterly* 2: 23–41.

—— (1981) 'Footnotes to organizational change', *Administrative Science Quarterly.* 26: 563–577.

March, J. G. and Simon, H. A. (1958) *Organizations.* New York: Wiley.

Marcher, J. T., Mowery, D. C. and Hodges, D. A. (1998) 'Reversal of fortune? The recovery of the U.S. semiconductor industry', *California Management Review* 41 (1): 329–43.

Marglin, S. A. (1974) 'What do bosses do? The origins and functions of hierarchy in capitalist production', *Review of Radical Political Economics* 6: 60–112.

—— (1991) 'Understanding capitalism: control versus efficiency', in B. Gustafsson (ed.), *Power and Economic Institutions: Reinterpretations in Economic History.* Aldershot: Edward Elgar.

Marsden, R. (1993) 'The politics of organisational analysis', *Organisation Studies* 14 (1): 93–124.

Marshall, A. (1919) *Industry and Trade.* London: Macmillan.

Martin, J. (1992) *Cultures in Organizations: Three Perspectives.* New York: Oxford University Press.

Maurice, M. (1979) 'For a study of "The societal effect": universality and specificity in organization research', in C. J. Lammers and D. J. Hickson *Organisations Alike and Unlike: International and Inter-institutional Studies in the Sociology of Organisations.* London: Macmillan.

—— and Sorge, A. (1989) 'The societal effect in the strategies of French and German machine tool manufacturers'. In Kogut, B. (1993) *Country Competitiveness*. Oxford: Oxford University Press.

——, Seller, F. and Silvestre, J.-J. (1986) *The Social Basis of Industrial Power*. Cambridge, MA: MIT Press.

Mauss, M. (1904) 'Essai sur les variations saisonniers des sociétés Eskimaux', *L'Annee Sociologique*, 9.

Mayr, O. and Post, R. C. (eds) (1981) *Yankee Enterprise. The Rise of the American System of Manufacture*. Washington, DC: Smithsonian Institute.

Meinig, D. W. (1986) *The Shaping of America. A Geographical Perspective on 500 Years of History*. New Haven: Yale University Press.

Merton, R. K. (1957) *Social Theory and Social Structure*. Toronto: CollierMacmillan.

Metcalfe, J. S. (1998) *Evolutionary Economics and Creative Destruction*. London: Routledge.

Meyer, J. W. and Rowan, B. (1977) 'Institutionalized organizations: formal structure as myth and ceremony', *American Sociological Review* 83: 340–363.

Miles, M. B. and Huberman, A. M. (1994) *Qualitative Data Analysis*. London: Sage.

Miles, R. E. and Snow, C. C. (1986) 'Organizational flexibility: new concepts for new forms', *Californian Management Review* 28 (3): 62–73.

Milgrom, P. and Roberts, J. (1992) *Economics, Organization and Management*. London: Prentice-Hall.

Miller, D. and Friesen, P. H. (1984) *Organizations. A Quantum View*. New Jersey: Prentice-Hall.

Miller, E. J. and Rice, A. K. (1967) *Systems of Organization: The Control of Task and Sentient Boundaries*. London: Tavistock.

Miller, P. (1994) 'Accounting as social and institutional practice: an introduction', in A. G. Hopwood and P. Miller, *Accounting as Social and Institutional Practice*, Cambridge: Cambridge University Press.

Mills, C. W. (1956) *The Power Elite*. New York: Oxford University Press.

Mindlin, S. E. (1974) 'Organisational dependence on environment and organizational structure: a re-examination of the findings of the Aston Group', MS thesis, NYSSILR, Cornell University.

Mintzberg, H. (1973) *The Nature of Managerial Work*. New York: Harper & Row.

—— (1994) *The Rise and Fall of Strategic Planning*. Chichester: Wiley.

——, Raisinghani, D. and Thoret, A. (1976) 'The structure of unstructured decision processes', *Administrative Science Quarterly* 21: 246–275.

Mohr, L. B. (1982) *Explaining Organisational Behaviour: the Limits and Possibilities of Theory and Research*. San Francisco: Jossey-Bass.

Monden, Y. (1981) 'What makes the Toyota production system really tick?', *Industrial Engineering* 13 (1): 36–46.

Montagna, P. (1990) 'Accounting rationality and financial legitimation', in S. Zukin and P. DiMaggio (eds) *Structures of Capital: The Social Organization of the Economy*. New York: Cambridge University Press, pp. 227–260.

Montgomery, C.A. (1995) *Resource-based and Evolutionary Theories of the Firm: Towards a Synthesis*. Cambridge, MA: Harvard Business School.

Montmollin, M. de (1981) *Le Taylorisme a Visage Humain*. Paris: PUF.

Moore, W. E. (1963) *Man, Time and Society*. New York: Wiley.

Mowery, D. C. and Rosenberg, N. (1979) 'The influence of market demand upon innovation: a critical review of some empirical studies', *Research Policy* 8: 103–153.

—— and Rosenberg, N. (1989) *Technology and the Pursuit of Economic Growth*. Cambridge: Cambridge University Press.

—— and Rosenberg, N. (1993) 'The U.S. national innovation system', in R. R. Nelson (ed.) *National Innovation Systems*. Oxford: Oxford University Press.

—— and Rosenberg, N. (1998) *Paths of Innovation: Technological Change in 20th-Century America*. Cambridge: Cambridge University Press.

Nadel, S. F. (1957) *Theory of Social Structure*. London: Cohen & West.

Nelson, R. R. (1991) 'Why do firms differ, and how does it matter', *Strategic Management Journal* 12: 61–74.

—— (1993) *National Innovation Systems*. Oxford: Oxford University Press.

—— and Winter, S. G. (1977) 'In search of useful theory of innovation', *Research Policy* 6 (1): 36–77.

—— and Winter, S. G. (1982) *An Evolutionary Theory of Economic Change*. Cambridge, MA: Harvard University Press.

Newell, S. and Clark, P. A. (1990) 'The importance of extra-organization networks in the diffusion and appropriation of new technologies. The role of professional associations in the United States and Britain', *Knowledge: Creation, Diffusion, Utilization* 12 (2): 199–212.

——, Swan, J. and Clark, P. A. (1993) 'The importance of user design in the adoption of new information technologies. The example of production and inventory control systems', *Journal of Production and Operations Management* 13 (2): 1–22.

Nicolis, G. and Prigogine, I. (1989) *Exploring Complexity*. London: Freeman.

Noble, D. (1978) *American by Design*. New York: Knopf.

—— (1984) *Forces of Production. A Social History of Industrial Automation*. New York: Knopf.

Nockolds, H. (1976) *Lucas. The First Hundred Years,*, 2 vols. Newton Abbott: David and Charles.

Nohria, N. (1992) 'A quasi-market in technology-based enterprise: the case of the 128 venture group', in N. Nohria and R. Eccles (eds) *Networks and Organizations*. Boston: Harvard Business School Press, pp. 240–261.

Nonaka, I. and Takeuchi, H. (1995) *The Knowledge Creating Company. How Japanese Companies Create the Dynamics of Innovation*. Oxford: Oxford University Press.

Noponen, H. G. and Markusen, A. (1993) *Trading Industries, Trading Regions: International Trade, American Industry*. London: Guilford Press.

North, D. (1981) *Structure and Change in Economic History*. New York: Norton.

—— (1990) *Institutions, Institutional Change, and Economic Performance*. New York, Cambridge University Press.

Nowotony, H. (1994) *Time. The Postmodern Experience*. Cambridge: Polity Press.

Oberschall, A. and Leifer, E. M. (1986) 'Efficiency and social institutions: uses and misuses of economic reasoning in sociology', *Annual Review of Sociology* 12: 233–253.

Oliver, C. (1991) 'Strategic responses to institutional processes', *Academy of Management Review* 16: 145–179.

—— (1992) 'The antecedents of deinstitutionalisation', *Organization Studies* 13 (14): 553–588.

O'Malley, M. (1990) *Keeping Watch: A History of American Time*. New York: Viking Penguin.

Orlikowski, W. J. (1992) 'The duality of technology: rethinking the concept of technology in organizations', *Organization Science* 33: 398–427.

—— and Robey, D. (1991) 'Information technology and the structuring of accounting, management and information technology', *Organizations, Information System Research* 2 (2): 143–169.

Ostrovsky, A. (1998) 'Keeping manufacturers alive – at a cost', *Financial Times*, 21 May: 33.

Ozawa, T. (1993) 'Foreign direct investment and structural transformation: Japan as a recycler of market and industry', *Business and the Contemporary World* 5 (2): 129–150.

Parkes, D. N. and Thrift, N. J. (1980) *Times, Spaces and Places. A Chronographic Perspective*. Chichester: Wiley.

Parsons, T. (1951) *The Social System*. New York: Free Press.

—— (1956) 'Suggestions for a sociological approach to the theory of organisations', *Administrative Science Quarterly* 1: 63–85, 225–239.

—— (1979) *Sociological Theory and Modern Society*. New York: Free Press.

—— and Smelser, N. J. (1956) *Economy and Society*. New York: Free Press.

Pavitt, K. (1984) 'Sectoral patterns of technical change: towards a taxonomy and a theory', *Research Policy* 13: 343–373.

—— (1980) *Technical Change and Britain's Economic Performance*. London: Pinter.

Penrose, E. T. (1952) 'Biological analogies in the theory of the firm', *American Economic Review* 42: 804–819.

—— (1959) *The Theory of the Growth of the Firm*. Oxford: Blackwell.

Perkin, H. (1996) *The Third Revolution: Professional Elites in the Modern World*. London: Routledge.

Perrow, C. (1967) 'A framework for the comparative analysis of organizations', *American Sociological Review* 32: 194–208.

—— (1986) *Complex Organizations: A Critical Essay*, 3rd edn. New York: Random House.

Peters, T. J. and Waterman, R. H. (1982) *In Search of Excellence: Lessons from America's Best Run Companies*. New York: Harper & Row.

Pettigrew, A. M. (1973) *The Politics of Organizational Decision Making*. London: Tavistock.

—— (1985) *The Awakening Giant. Continuity and Change in ICI*. Oxford: Blackwell.

—— and Whipp, R. (1991) *Managing Change for Competitive Success*. Oxford: Blackwell.

——, Ferlie, E. and McKee, L. (1992) *Shaping Strategic Change*. London: Sage.

Pfeffer, J. and Salancik, G. (1978) *The External Control of Organizations: A Resource Dependence Perspective*. New York: Harper & Row.

Pine, B. J. (1993) *Mass Customization. The New Frontier in Business Competition*. Cambridge, MA: Harvard Business School.

Piore, M. and Sabel, C. (1984) *The Second Industrial Divide*. New York: Basic Books.

Polanyi, K. (1944, 1957) *The Great Transformation*. Boston: Beacon Press.

—— (1962) *Personal Knowledge: Towards a Post Critical Philosophy*. New York: Harper.

Porter, M. E. (1985) *Competitive Strategy: Techniques for Analysing Industries and Competitors*. New York: Free Press.

—— (1990) *The Competitive Advantage of Nations*. New York: Free Press.

—— (1991) 'Towards a dynamic theory of strategy', *Strategic Management Journal* 12: 95–117.

—— (1997) 'Location, knowledge creation and competitiveness', in M. Das, *Symposium Knowledge Capitalism: Competitiveness Reevaluated*. Boston: American Academy of Management.

—— (1998) 'Clusters and competition: new agendas for companies, governments, and institutions', in M. E. Porter, *On Competition*. Cambridge, MA: Harvard University Press.

Powell, W. W. (1990) 'Neither market nor hierarchy: network forms of organization', in B. Staw and L. L. Cummings (eds) *Research in Organizational Behavior*. Greenwich, CT: JAI Press, pp. 295–336.

—— (1996) 'Weber and Schumpeter: turbulent lives, ideas never at rest', *Industrial and Corporate Change* 5 (3): 917–924.

—— and Brantley, P. (1992) 'Competitive cooperation in biotechnology: learning through networks?', in N. Nohria and R. Eccles (eds) *Networks and Organizations*. Cambridge, MA: Harvard University Business School Press, pp. 366–394.

—— and DiMaggio, P. J. (1991) *The New Institutionalism in Organization Analysis*. Chicago: University of Chicago Press.

——, Koput, K. W. and Smith-Doerr, L. (1996) 'Interorganizational collaboration and the locus of innovation: networks of learning in biotechnology', *Administrative Science Quarterly* 41: 116–145.

Power, M. (1994) *The Audit Explosion*. London: DEMOS.

Power, M. and Laughlin, R. (1992) 'Critical theory and accounting', in M. Alvesson and H. Willmott (eds) *Critical Management Studies*. London: Sage.

Prahalad, C. K. and Bettis, R. A. (1986) 'The dominant logic: a new linkage between diversity and performance', *Strategic Management Journal* 7: 484–502.

—— and Hamel, G. (1990) 'The core competence of the corporation', *Harvard Business Review* 90 (3): 79–91.

—— and Hamel, G. (1994) 'Strategy as a field of study: why search for a new paradigm?', *Strategic Management Journal* 15: 5–16.

Prigogine, I. and Stengers, I. (1984) *Order out of Chaos*. London: Heinemann.

Pugh, D. S. (1966) 'Modern organization theory', *Psychological Bulletin* 66: 235–251.

—— and Hickson, D. J. (1976) *Aston Program,* vol. 1. London: Saxon House.

Pulos, A. J. (1983) *American Design Ethic. A History of Industrial Design to 1940*. Cambridge, MA: MIT Press.

Purcell, M. and Ahlstrand, B. (1994) *Human Resource Management in the Multidivisional Company.* Oxford: Oxford University Press.

Putterman, L. (ed.) (1986) *The Economic Nature of the Firm: A Reader.* Cambridge: Cambridge University Press.

Quinn, J. B. (1993) *Intelligent Enterprise: A Knowledge and Service Based Paradigm for Industry.* New York: Free Press.

Ramsay, H. (1996) 'Managing sceptically: a critique of organisational fashion', in S. Clegg and G. Palmer (eds) *The Politics of Management Knowledge*. London: Sage.

Ranson, S. (1998) *The Richness of Cities. Urban Policy in a New Landscape*. London: Demos.

Reed, M. (1989) *The Sociology of Management*. Brighton: Harvester Wheatsheaf.

—— (1992) *The Sociology of Organizations: Themes, Perspectives and Prospects*. Brighton: Harvester Wheatsheaf.

—— (1997) 'Expert power and control in late modernity', working paper, University of Lancaster Business School.

Reich, R. (1991) *The Work of Nations: Preparing Ourselves for 21st Century Capitalism*. New York: Knopf.

Reich, R. B. and Donahue, J. D. (1986) *New Deals: The Chrysler Revival and the American System*. London: Penguin.

Reve, T. (1990) 'The firm as a nexus of internal and external contracts', in M. Aoki, B. Gustafsson and O. E. Williamson (eds) *The Firm as Nexus of Treaties*. London: Sage.

Rice, A. K. (1963) *The Enterprise and its Environment*. London: Tavistock.

Richardson, G. P. (1991) *Feedback Thought in Social Science and Systems Theory.* Philadephia: University of Pennsylvania Press.

Riesman, D. (1954) *Individualism Reconsidered*. New York: Doubleday.

Riesman, D. R. and Denney, N. R. (1954) 'Football in America: a case study', In D. Reisman (ed.) *Culture Diffusion, Individualism Reconsidered*. New York: Doubleday.

——, Glaser, N. R. and Denney, N. R. (1975) *The Lonely Crown. A Study of Changing American Character.* New York: Doubleday.

Robinson, L. and Clark, P. A. (1997) 'Creating explicit knowledge', paper given at

European Conference on 'Competing Through Knowledge', University of the West of England.

Rogers, E. M. (1995) *Diffusion of Innovations*, 3rd edn. New York: Free Press.

Rosenberg, N. (1969) *The American System of Manufacturing*. Edinburgh: Edinburgh University Press.

—— (1976) *Perspectives on Technology.* Cambridge: Cambridge University Press.

—— (1982) *Inside the Black Box, Technology and Economics*, Cambridge: Cambridge University Press.

—— and Steinmuller, D. (1988) 'Can Americans learn to become better imitators', working paper, San Francisco: Stanford University Working Paper.

Roth, J. A. (1963) *Timetables.* Indianapolis: Bobbs-Merrill.

Rowlinson, M. (1997) *Organizations and Institutions*. London: Macmillan.

Rugman, A. M. (1995). *Research in Global Strategic Management, Vol. 5: Beyond the Diamond.* Hampton Hill: JAI Press.

Rumelt, R. P. (1974) *Strategy, Structure and Economic Performance.* Cambridge, MA: Harvard University Press.

Rumelt, R. P. (1995) 'Inertia and transformation', in C. A. Montgomery *Resource-based and Evolutionary Theories of the Firm*. Cambridge, MA: Harvard Business School.

——, Schendel, D. and Teece, D. J. (eds) (1991) 'Strategic management and economics', *Strategic Management Journal* 12: 5–29.

Sackman, S. A. (1991) *Cultural Knowledge in Organizations: Exploring the Collective Mind.* Newbury Park, CA: Sage.

Sayer, A. (1992) *Method in Social Science.* London: Routledge.

Scarborough, H. (1998) 'Path(ological) dependency? Core competencies from an organizational perspective', *British Journal of Management* 9: 219–232.

—— and Burrell, G. (1996) 'The axeman cometh: the changing roles and knowledges of middle managers', in S. R. Clegg and G. Palmer (eds) *The Politics of Management*. London: Sage, pp. 173–189.

Scase, R. and Goffee, R. (1989) *Reluctant Managers.* London: Unwin Hyman.

Schama, S. (1991) *Dead Certainties. (Unwarranted Speculations).* London: Granta.

Schoenberger, R. J. (1981) *Japanese Manufacturing Techniques. Nine Hidden Lessons in Simplicity.* New York: Free Press.

—— (1996) *The Cultural Crisis of the Corporations.* Oxford: Oxford University Press.

Schumpeter, J. A. (1942, 1975) *Capitalism, Socialism, and Democracy.* New York: Harper Row.

Schutz, A. (1967) *The Phenomenology of the Social World.* Evanston, IL: North Western University Press.

Scott, W. R. (1987) 'The adolescence of institutional theory', *Adminstrative Science Quarterly* 32: 493–511.

—— (1995) *Institutions and Organizations.* London: Sage.

Searle, J. R. (1995) *The Construction of Social Reality.* London: Penguin.

Senge, P. M. (1990) *The Fifth Discipline.* New York: Doubleday.

Sennett, R. (1998) *The Corrosion of Character. Personal Consequences of Work in the New Capitalism.* New York: Norton.

Sewell Jr, W. H. (1992) 'A theory of structure: duality, agency, and transformation', *American Journal of Sociology* 98: 1–29.

Sharifi, S. (1986) 'A critique of the episodic thesis in managerial work', doctoral thesis, Aston University.

Silverman, D. (1970) *The Theory of Organizations.* London: Heinemann.

Simon, H. A. (1991) 'Organizations and markets', *Journal of Economic Perspectives* 5: 24–44.

Smith, C., Child, J. and Rowlinson, M. (1991) *Reshaping Work. Innovation in Work Organisation – The Cadbury Experience*. Cambridge: Cambridge University Press.

Smith, J. C. (1972) *The Native American Ball Games. Sport and the Socio-Cultural Process*, M. Hart, (ed.). New York: Dubeque.

Smith, J. W. and Turner, B. S. (1986) 'Constructing social theory and constituting society', *Theory, Culuture and Society* 3: 125–33.

Sobel, D. (1995) *Longitude.* London: Fourth Estate.

Sorge, A. (1989) 'An essay on technical change: its dimensions and social and strategic context', *Organization Studies* 10 (1): 23–44.

—— (1991) 'Strategic fit and the societal effect: interpreting cross-national comparisons of technology, organization and human resources', *Organization Studies* 12: 161–190.

—— (1995) 'Cross-national differences in personnel and organisation', in A. W. Harzing, and J. V. Ruysseveldt, *International Human Resource Management*. Heerlen: Sage, pp. 99–123.

Spender, J.-C. (1989) *Industry Recipes: The Nature and Sources of Managerial Judgement*. Oxford: Blackwell.

—— (1992) 'Business policy and strategy: a view of the field', working paper. New Jersey: Rutgers University.

—— (1996) 'Making knowledge the basis of a dynamic theory of the firm', *Strategic Management Journal* 17: 45–62.

—— and Grant, R. M. (1996) 'Knowledge and the firm: overview', *Strategic Management Journal* 17: 5–9.

—— and Kessler, J. (1995) 'Managing the uncertainties of innovation: extending Thompson (1967)', *Human Relations* 48 (1): 35–56.

Starbuck, W. and Nystrom, P. C. (1981) *Handbook of Organisational Design*. Oxford: Oxford University Press.

Stark, D. (1992) 'Bending the bars of the iron cage: bureaucratization and informalization in capitalism and socialism', in C. Smith and P. Thompson (eds) *Labour in Transition: The Labour Process in Eastern Europe and China*. London: Routledge.

Stigler, G. (1968) 'Competition', in D. L. Sills (ed.) *International Encyclopedia of the Social Sciences*. New York: Macmillan and Free Press.

Stiglitz, J. E. (1991) 'Symposium on organization and economics', *Journal of Economic Perspectives* 5 (2): 15–24.

Stinchcombe, A. (1965) 'Social structure organization', in J. March (ed.) *The Handbook Organization*. Illinois: Rand McNally, pp. 142–193.

—— (1968) *Constructing Social Theories*. New York: Harcourt, Brace & World.

—— (1983) *Economic Sociology.* London: Academic Press.

—— (1990) *Information and Organizations*. Oxford: University of California Press.

Storper, M. (1995) 'The resurgence of regional economies, ten years later: the region as a nexus of untraded interdependencies', *Journal of European Urban and Regional Studies*.

—— and Walker, R. (1989) *The Capitalist Imperative*. Oxford: Blackwell.

Stubbart, C. I. (1988) 'Managerial cognition: a missing link in strategic management research', *Journal of Management Studies* 26: 325–347.

Suchman, L. (1988) *Plans and Situated Actions. The Problem of Human-Machine Communication*. Cambridge: Cambridge University Press.

Swan, J. and Clark, P. A. (1992) 'Organization decision-making in the appropriation of technological innovation: political and cognitive dimensions', *European Work and Organizational Psychologist* 2 (2): 103–127.

Swedberg, R. and Granovetter, M. (1992) 'Introduction', in M. Granovetter and R. Swedberg *The Sociology of Economic Life*. Oxford: Westview Press.

Swedberg, R., Himmelstrand, U. and Brulin, G. (1987) 'The paradigm of economic sociology: premises and promises', *Theory and Society* 16: 169–214.

——, Himmelstrand, U. and Brulin, G. (1990) 'The paradigm of economic sociology', in S. Zukin and P. DiMaggio, *Structures of Capital: The Social Organization of the Economy.* Cambridge: Cambridge University Press.

Sztompka, P. (1993) *The Sociology of Social Change.* Oxford: Blackwell.

Teulings, A. W. M. (1986) 'Managerial labour processes in organised capitalism: the power of corporate management and the powerlessness of the manager', in D. Knights and H. Willmott (eds) *Managing the Labour Process.* Aldershot: Gower, pp. 142–165.

Thevenot, L. (1984) 'The investment in forms', *Social Science Information* 23 (1): 1–45.

—— and Boltanski, L. (1988) *Economies de Grandeur.* Paris: Presses Universitaires de France.

Thompson, E. P. (1967) 'Time, work-discipline and industrial capitalism', *Past and Present* 35: 56–97.

Thompson, J. B. (1989) 'The theory of structuration', in D. Held and J. B. Thompson (eds) *Social Theory of Modern Societies: Anthony Giddens and his Critics.* Cambridge: Cambridge University Press.

Thompson, J. D. (1967) *Organisations in Action.* New York: Wiley.

Thompson, P. and McHugh, D. (1995). *Work Organisations: A Critical Introduction.* London: Macmillan.

Thrift, N. (1996) *Spatial Formations.* London: Sage.

Tilly, C. (1984) *Big Structures, Large Processes, Huge Comparisons.* New York: Russell Sage Foundation.

—— (1992) *Coercion, Capital and European States, AD 990–1992.* Oxford: Blackwell.

Tiryakian, E. (1991) 'Modernization: exhumetur in pace', *International Sociology* 6 (2): 165–180.

Toulmin, S. (1992) *Cosmopolis. The Hidden Agenda of Modernity.* Chicago: Chicago University Press.

Touraine, A. (1955) *L'evolution du travail ouvrier aux usines Renault.* Paris: CNRS.

—— (1965) *Workers' Attitudes to Technical Change.* Paris: OECD.

Townley, B. (1994) *Reframing Human Resource Management.* London: Sage.

—— (1997) 'Beyond good and evil: depth and division in the management of human resources', in A. McKinley and K. Starkey (eds) *Foucault, Management and Organisation Theory.* London: Sage.

Trist, E. L. and Murray, H. (eds) (1990) *The Social Engagement of Social Science: A Tavistock Anthology, vol. 1: The Social-Psychological Perspective.* Philadelphia, PA: University of Philadelphia Press.

Tsoukas, H. (1989) 'The validity of idiographic research explanations', *Academy of Management Review* 24: 551–561.

—— (1994) 'What is management? An outline of a metatheory'. *British Journal of Management* 5: 289–301.

Tsuru, S. (1993) *Japan's Capitalism. Creative Defeat and Beyond.* Cambridge: Cambridge University Press.

Turner, H. A. (1970) *Is Britain Really Strike Prone?* Cambridge: Cambridge University Press.

Turner, H. A., Clack, G. and Roberts, G. (1967) *Labour Relations in the Motor Industry.* London: Allen & Unwin.

Urry, J. (1991) 'Time and space in Giddens' social theory', in C. Bryant and D. Jary (eds) *Giddens' Theory of Structuration.* London: Routledge, pp. 160–175.

Uzzi, B. (1996) 'The sources and consequences of embeddedness for the economic performance of organisations: the network effect', *American Sociological Review* 61: 675–698.

Vanderlinden, N. (1998) 'An exploratory investigation into the feasibility of the partial application of the knowledge creation by Norika and Takeuchi within the Royal College of Speech and Language Therapists', MBA dissertation, University of Birmingham.

Van Krieken, R. (1998) *Norbert Elias*. London: Routledge.

Van Maanen, J. (1991) 'The smile factory: work at Disneyland', in P. J. Forst, L. F. Moore, M. R. Louis, C. C. Lundberg and J. Martin (eds) *Reframing Organizational Culture*. Newbury Park, CA: Sage.

Von Bertalanffy, L. (1968) *General System Theory: Foundations, Developments, Applications*. New York: Braziller.

Wallerstein, I. (1979) *The Modern World-System II, Mercantilism and the Consolidation of the European World-Economy 1600–1750*. New York: Academic Press.

Waswo, A. (1996) *Modern Japanese Society 1868–1994*. Oxford: Opus.

Weber, M. (1922, 1978) *Economy and Society: An Outline of Interpretive Sociology*. Berkley: University of California Press.

—— (1923, 1982) *General Economic History*, trans. F. H. Knight, New Brunswick: Transaction Books.

—— (1947) *The Theory of Social and Economic Organization*. London: Routledge.

Weick, K. E. (1979) *Social Psychology of Organising* New Haven: Addison-Wesley.

—— (1991) 'The nontraditional quality of organizational learning', *Organization Science* 2 (1): 116–124.

—— (1995) *Sensemaking in Organisations*. London: Sage.

Wenger, E. (1998) *Communitites of Practice: Learning, Meaning and Identity*. Cambridge: Cambridge University Press.

Wernerfelt, B. (1984) 'A resource-based view of the firm', *Strategic Management Journal* 5: 171–180.

—— (1995) 'The resource-based view of the firm: ten years after', *Strategic Management Journal* 17: 171–174.

Whipp, R. and Clark, P. A. (1986) *Innovations and the Auto Industry: Product, Process and Work Organization*. London: Pinter.

White, H. (1987) *The Content of Form: Narrative Discourse and Historical Representation*. Baltimore: Johns Hopkins University Press.

Whitley, R. (1989) 'On the nature of managerial tasks and skills: their distinguishing characteristics and organisation', *Journal of Management Studies* 26: 209–224.

—— (1992a) 'The social construction of organizations and markets: the comparative analysis of business recipes', in M. Reed and M. Hughes (eds) *Rethinking Organization: New Directions in Organization Theory and Analysis*. London: Sage.

—— (ed.) (1992b) *European Business Systems*. London: Sage.

Whitley, R. D. (1994) 'Dominant forms of economic organization in market economies', *Organization Studies* 15 (2): 153–182.

Whittington, R. (1989) *Corporate Strategies in Recession and Recovery: Social Structure and Strategic Choice*. London: Unwin Hyman.

—— (1992a) *What is Strategy and Does it Make a Difference?* London: Sage.

—— (1992b) 'Putting Giddens into action: social systems and managerial agency', *Journal of Management Studies* 29 (6): 694–713.

—— (1994) 'Sociological pluralism, institutions and managerial agency', in J. Hassard and M. Parker, *Towards a New Theory of Organisations*. London: Routledge, pp. 53–74.

——, Bouchikhi, H. and Kilduff, M. (1995) *Action, Structure, and Organisations*. Coventry: Warwick Business School Research Bureau.

Wiener, N. (1948) *Cybernetics: or Control and Communication in the Animal and the Machine.* Cambridge, MA: MIT Press.

Wight, O. (1985) *Manufacturing Resource Planning: MRPII.* Vermont: Oliver Wight.

Williamson, O. E. (1975) *Markets and Hierarchies: Analysis and Antitrust Implications.* New York: Free Press.

—— (1985) *The Economic Institutions of Capitalism: Firms, Markets, Relational Contracting.* London: CollierMacmillan.

Wilson, D. C. (1992) *A Strategy of Change.* London: Routledge.

Wilson, G. E. (1992) *Patriots and Redeemers in Japan. Motives in Meiji Restoration.* Chicago: University of Chicago Press.

Winter, S. G. (1987) 'Knowledge and competence as strategic assets', in D. J. Teece (ed.) *The Competitive Challenge.* New York: Harper & Row.

—— (1990) 'Survival, selection, and inheritance in evolutionary theories of organization', in J. V. Singh (ed.), *Organizational Evolution: New Directions.* London: Sage.

—— (1995) 'Four Rs of profitability: rents, resources, routines and replication', in C. A. Montgomery *Resource-based and Evolutionary Theories of the Firm: Towards a Synthesis.* Cambridge, MA: Harvard Business School.

Woodward, J. (1958) *Management and Technology.* London: HMSO.

—— (1964) 'Industrial behaviour: is there a science?', *New Society* 8 October.

—— (1965) *Industrial Organization: Theory and Practice.* Oxford: Oxford University Press.

—— (ed.) (1970) *Industrial Organization: Behaviour and Control.* Oxford: Oxford University Press.

Woolgar, S. (1981) 'Interests and explanation in the social study of science', *Social Studies of Science* 11: 365–394.

Wrigley, L. (1970) *Divisional Autonomy and Diversification.* Cambridge, MA: Harvard Graduate Business School.

Yates, J. (1989) *Control Through Communication: The Rise of American Management.* Baltimore: Johns Hopkins University Press.

—— and Orlikowski, W. J. (1992) 'Genres of organizational communication: a structural approach to studying communication and the media', *Academy of Management Review* 17 (2): .

Zeldin, M. (1989) *The Large Corporation and Contemporary Classes.* Cambridge: Polity Press.

Zeldin, T. (1984) *The French.* London: Flamingo.

Zerubavel, E (1978) 'Timetables and scheduling on the social organization of time', *Sociological Inquiry* 46 (2): 87–94.

Zuboff, S. (1987) *The Age of the Smart Machine.* New York: Basic Books.

Zukin, S. (1990) 'Socio-spatial prototypes of a new organization of consumption: the role of real culture capital', *Sociology* 24: 37–56.

—— (1991) *Landscapes of Power: From Detroit to Disney World.* Berkely, CA: University of California.

—— and DiMaggio, P. (1990) *Structures of Capital: The Social Organization of the Economy.* New York: Cambridge University Press.

Index

Printed in the United Kingdom
by Lightning Source UK Ltd.
116401UKS00004B/4